My Prior Year:
A 333 Soul Anthology

My Pryor Year:

A 333 Soul Anthology

Phil Doubet

iUniverse, Inc.
New York Lincoln Shanghai

My Pryor Year: A 333 Soul Anthology

iUniverse books may be ordered through booksellers or by contacting:

iUniverse
2021 Pine Lake Road, Suite 100
Lincoln, NE 68512
www.iuniverse.com
1-800-Authors (1-800-288-4677)

ISBN-13: 978-0-595-39157-8 (pbk)
ISBN-13: 978-0-595-83544-7 (cloth)
ISBN-13: 978-0-595-83543-0 (ebk)
ISBN-10: 0-595-39157-5 (pbk)
ISBN-10: 0-595-83544-9 (cloth)
ISBN-10: 0-595-83543-0 (ebk)

Printed in the United States of America

Contents

Editor's Note xv

Acknowledgements xvii

Introduction xix

1 Willie Smith. 1

2 Ernie Harburg 4

3 Sally Stone. 9

4 Michael Arthur Weinstein 10

5 Betty Gerber 13

6 Karen Slate. 14

7 Cory Cooper 18

8 Staff Sergeant Minter 19

9-12 The Margarita Sisters. 20

13 Amber Padillo 22

14 Fred Sturgis. 23

15 Dorothy Berkel 25

16 Harold Quinn 26

17 Kunjali Padahya. 28

18 Earl Flatt 29

19-20 Kailey and Robin Lemons. 32

21 Mary Ann Shea 35

22 Ralph Edmunds. 36

23 Mike Hammes. 39

24 Rhonda Foster 41

25 Dennis Ronk 43

26 Kelly Billington 45

27 Noriko Yasui Fenald 46

28 Gene Muehrig 48

29 Richard Pryor Jr. 51

30 Steve Kiesewetter 55

31 Adam Kessler 56

32 Elaine Lindsey 58

33 George Manias 59

34 Jack Brogan 61

35 Theresa Shane 62

36 Louis Naseem 64

37 Robert Jackson 65

38 Darren Mobry 69

39 Greg Williams 70

40 Sara Zielke 72

41 Latonya McClain 73

42 Megan Davis 75

43 Wendy Blickenstaff 76

44 Joshua Seldeck 79

45 Lane Knouse 80

46 Lorna Smith 82

47 Dan Martino 83

48 Michael Reagan 86

49 Colin Boland 91

50 Marc Zoschke 93

51 Pat Lingon 94

52 Harold Petersen 96

53 Joe Hott 97

54 Richard Greene 100

55 Larry Melaik 101

56 Rhonda Stephens 104

57 Gary Perkins 106

58-59 Rich Waschek and Katy Rose Gabriel 107

60 Jonathon Wells 110

61 Daniel Lane 113

62-63 Marie-Jo Schneider and Lois Becker 115

64 Omar Terrie. 117

65-66 John Wateler and Bill Snyder 119

67 Marilyn Chambers 120

68 Lydia Wraight 125

69 Conrad Stewart 126

70 Heather Carter. 128

71 Raymond Spicer. 129

72 Mary Ann Watkins 132

73-74 Anne Siberling and Christa Stucky 133

75 Ralph Higgs. 135

76 Ken Smith 136

77 Linda Labbee Howell. 137

78 Patty Armstrong. 141

79 Steve Wallace 142

80 M.K. Riddel. 145

81 David Morgan 147

82 Valerie Louck. 149

83 Evelyn Hutcheson 151

84 Han Zhang 153

85 Angela Ashburn 154

86 Natalie Haurberg 157

87 Tom Nauman 159

88 Louie Dalton 160

89 Adonis Porch 163

90 Lynn Niemeier. 165

91 Nicholas Frain 166

92 Ron Stalter. 168

93 Don Zessin 170

94 Randy McCallister 172

95 Don Gonyea 174

96 Frank Pignataro 179

97 Raj Mohan 180

98 Paul McLaughlin 182

99 Fred Dirkse 183

100 W.L. Yarosz 185

101 Pastor Dan 187

102 April Rose Steffeck 190

103 Sebastian Fuksa 192

104 Joe Slyman 194

105 Bill Kellerstrass 195

106 Bob Long 196

107-108 Ryan Graham and Julie Habstritt 197

109 Perry Rice 200

110 Frank Abagnale 202

111 Patty McMullen 206

112 Paul Stevens 207

113 Eric Roland 209

114 Elaine Mendez 211

115 Sophia Salazar 212

116 Bob Hewiit 214

117 Paul Baker 215

118 Ed Kiesewetter 218

119 Anne Morris 219

120 Drew Hastings 221

121 Al Poling 225

122 Mike Hidden 226

123 Father Mike Driscoll 227

124 Steve Bilbrey 232

125 Jay Wright 234

126 Peggy Wilson 236

127 Bill Greene 237

128 Melissa Rives 239

129 Daniel Hartmann 240

130 Carrol Van Velkinburgh 242

131 Wayne F. McDaniels 244

132 Sara Schwarzentraub 246

133 Edgar Winter 247

134 Chris Sollenberger 252

135 Donna Robinson 253

136 M.J. Dunn 254

137 Charles Ash 256

138 Taru Sharma 258

139 Elsie Hallman 260

140 Michael K. Medlen 261

141 Leslie Emery 262

142 Steve Cigolle 264

143 Don Shoemaker 266

144 Sue Parrott 267

145 Teri Huss 269

146 Matt Jones 271

147 Anna Jacobson 272

148 Janette Smith 275

149 Heywood Banks 277

150 David Flites 281

151 Mike White 282

152 Sam Wright 284

153-154 Mallory Williams and Amanda Douglas 285

155 J.T. 287

156 Ken Ferino 288

157-158 Sean and Amanda Fitts 290

159-160 Tom and Shawn Armbruster 293

161 Nancy Richards 294

162 Marlene Allen 296

163-164 Jane and Tim Johnson 297

165 Cecil Brown 299

166 Paul Steffeck 301

167 Fay Opper 303

168 Dan Uphof 305

169-170 Arlo and Annie Guthrie 307

171-172 Tracy Hillyer and Khloe 311

173 Luke Curtis 313

174 Michael White 316

175 Frankie See 318

176 Robert Branan 320

177 Adeletraud Smith 321

178 Kay Price 323

179 Lori Hadley 325

180 Sue Hughes 326

181 Lisa Neal 328

182 Ellen Johnson 329

183 Mary Koonce 332

184 Charlie Kear 335

185 Pat Crouch 337

186 Susan Lawson 338

187 Daniel Bronski 340

188 Sandy French 341

189 Jeremiah Schaub 343

190 Dave Stovall 345

191 Bryan Thomas 346

192 Roxy Whitmore 348

193 Lori Fleming 349

194 Laura Picker 351

195 Bill Staines 352

196 Ruth Mitchell 355

197 Candy Werneburg 356

198-199 Pam and Michael Parks 358

200 Cynthia Bond 360

201 Latisha Jackson 361

202 Amy Sielaff 363

203 Deb Johnston 365

204 Christine Engel 366

205 Tony Johnson 368

206 Pam Witzig 369

207 Ed "Too Tall" Freeman 372

208 Anetta Strawn 375

209 Dawn Stewart 376

210 Rizzo 378

211 Laura Kosko 380

212 Greg Funk 382

213 Jerry Bratcher 384

214 Mary Knobloch 385

215 Matt Coker 386

216 Jill Grube 388

217 Ngoc Minh 392

218 Jay Navin 393

219 Kelly White 395

220 Connie Schwarzentraub 397

221 Jared Brown 398

222-223 Jeannie and Ken Hupp 401

224 Jerry Thomas 404

225 Earl Vittitoe 405

226 Elaine Lucas 407

227 Juana Lucio 409

228 Joe Lowry 410

229 Harriet Sue Glidewell Stiles 413

230 Joyce Mitchell 415

231 Shelly Hines 417

232 Andrew Young 419

233 Stella Cieslinski 422

234 Christina Cherry 423

235-236 Mary and Dick Van Norman 424

237 Jan Stoia 427

238 Ken Baxter 429

239 Melinda Feger 431

240 Juanita Kurtz 433

241 Tim Popp 434

242 Joseph Khouri 437

243 Jim Klaus 439

244 Doug Smith 441

245 Philip Jose Farmer 444

246 Kris Hoak 446

247 John Bennington 447

248 Jim Fyke 449

249 Mildred Snyder 451

250 Taylor Johnston 453

251 Rachael Allen 455

252 Sarah Foster 457

253 Chris Caras 460

254 Ron Davis 461

255 Aldeine Witzig 463

256 James Dillon 464

257 Jerry Martis 466

258 Joyce Mercer 467

259 Whoopi Goldberg 469

260 Jesus Castillo 471

261 Charles Martin 472

262 Jim Rainey 474

263-264 Dan and Kim Philips 477

265 Nancy Roggy 478

266 Jim D'Orazio 479

267 Ian Zelinski 481

268 William Marion 482

269 Theresa Thomason 484

270 Nick Dykstra 487

271 Katherine Miller 488

272 Greg Wessel 491

273 Carol Patton 492

274 Gabriel Johnson 493

275 Ken Hamm 494

276 Perry French 495

277 Sonny Moore 497

278 Bob Bishop 498

279 Bill Henness 501

280 Santa Claus 503

281 Crystal Potter 506

282 K. Morris 507

283 Duane Collins 508

284 Ken Jennings 509

285 Bill Jaynes 512

286 Sue Troxall 513

287 Gary Sandberg 515

288 Jane Smiley 518

289 Simone Morgan 520

290 Tony Nishimura 522

291 Darryl Simmons 523

292 Beth Green 525

293 Paul Eschelman 527

294 Mark Hagen 530

295 Jane Curry 531

296 Chris Carr 532

297 Louis Patterson 534

298 John Simison 535

299 B.J. Ponder 536

300 Pam Putney 539

301 Stan Harris 540

302 Bob Hutchens 542

303 Edward Bailey 543

304 Barb Leslie 546

305 Ray Williams 548

306-307 Barbara McGee Pryor and Sharon Wilson Pryor 551

308 Carla Mellins 553

309 Mike Fitzgerald. 554

310 Monica Poncinie. 555

311 Riley Robinson 556

312 Brian Sagko 559

313 Angela Britmeyer 560

314 Thomas Bolger 563

315 Rocky Simpson. 564

316 Venkatesh Anandasayanam. 565

317 Michael Isenberg. 568

318 Carol Miller 573

319 Chris Waters. 574

320-321 Cara Bale and Brandon Green. 575

322 Jessica Christianson. 577

323 Graham England 578

324 Johnathon Frericks 580

325 Andy Driscoll 581

326 Rashonda Hunt 585

327 Wade Brown. 586

328 Nate Butler. 589

329-330 Walter and Empress Freeman 590

331 Barbra Espey. 592

332 Willie York. 594

333 Suzette Boulais 595

Conclusion 599

Editor's Note

For a variety of reasons, some names were changed at the request of the interviewees.

Acknowledgements

I wish to thank all of those people that were kind enough to speak with me…kind enough to let me listen.

Introduction

Like Edgar Lee Masters' *Spoon River Anthology, My Pryor Year* draws it's substance from the names, personalities, activities, and events of the Central Illinois region now known as the Heart of Illinois. In contrast with Masters' collection of fictional post-mortem autobiographical epitaphs, the souls in this anthology are very much alive.

From Willie Smith, who grew up on a Mississippi plantation, to Willie York who lives in the streets of Peoria…from Joe Hott, a mortician that works both sides of the fence, to Joe Slyman, a sandwich-maker that won't treat you like just another turkey sandwich…*My Pryor Year* is a living collection of voices from the Heart of Illinois.

In the beginning of 2005, I decided to follow a similar path an uncle of mine traveled many years ago. Lennis Broadfoot was an artist who sketched people with charcoal, and as he sketched them, they would tell him about their lives in Dent County, Missouri. He was a very "down to earth" man who swapped tales with friends. The short stories that fell from their lips were written down and published in their own native dialect. He was able to "capture their souls" and provide a true snapshot of the hill people of Missouri.

Sixty years later, my own path took me through Central Illinois and my hometown of Peoria. Having no charcoal or artistic talent, I made a decision to go out and simply have conversations with 333 people, not really knowing who I would talk to or what they would say. My intention was to speak with people who lived in the area, but soon realized that Central Illinois is an integral part of a much larger world, and many of the people would be from other places…just passing through.

I had no idea that I would have conversations with a man who was awarded the Congressional Medal of Honor, a couple of Woodstock musicians, the son of a famous lyricist, a porn queen, the president of a major civil rights organization, a White House correspondent, the mother of a white supremacist, the son of a

Peoria-born actor and comedian, and the son of a United States President. I had no idea I would listen to stories from a former ambassador and civil rights activist, two men whose lives were depicted in recent movies, comedians, authors, and a woman who won an Academy Award. I also had no idea of what I would learn from the people that were kind enough to speak with me.

In the year of Hurricane Katrina, the passing of Rosa Parks, the papal transition, the war in Iraq, the death of Richard Pryor, the sentencing of Matt Hale, the White Sox victory, the "Deep Throat" revelation, and many more news stories…people spoke to me about their lives, what they thought about current events, religion, history, family…and they recalled stories from prior years.

I hope I have captured their souls.

"Name is Willie Smith...I'm...uhhh...over sixteen. I grew up on a planta-tion...one of the largest plantations in the world at the time...in Mississippi. It was called Delta and Pineland Company and it was owned by people in England, and you can find it in the old encyclopedia. I did farm work, you know, picked cotton, chopped cotton...you know, bale hay...just typical farm work. I was 25 when I left Mississippi. My parents did the same thing of course. It was our means of survival."

"The main thing was my parents...the amazing parents I was blessed with. They never showed me anything, or my sisters and brother...anything but positive. I just lost my mother in March of this year, and I'm amazed at how she worked...her work ethic. My father...and I'm almost astonished with, as lazy as I was as a kid...it hit home later on in life. I have the same work ethic as my father and my mother. Thank God I married a woman who has the same work ethic."

"But, my mom...you know, we had to be in the field choppin' cotton at 6 o'clock...not on your way there...we had to be there choppin' at 6 o'clock. That means that my ma had gotten up and fixed us breakfast, and no matter how far you was away from the field, which was sometimes a half a mile, or a mile, you had to be back after you get off of lunch at 11 o'clock. And I mean, you stopped choppin' at lunch...and you gotta go home, and be back in the field at 1 o'clock...choppin'. My mom had to fix us lunch and go right back to chop-pin'...and work with us. We also had to stop at 6 o'clock...and she would come back and fix our dinner. It amazes me that, you know...anybody would do that...and could stand and do that. You know what I mean?"

"Now, I attribute everything that has happened in my life...a lot of positive things, and I meet a lot of positive people now...and things are well for my fam-ily and me now...I thank God for my parents."

"I been with my wife 32 years, and she took belief in my dream. I always wanted to be an entrepreneur, but I didn't know where I was headed...what I was going to do. I always felt I wanted to own my own business. When we met, I sold her on the idea...and I seen her, in the beginning...break down in tears...'cuz we didn't have anything in the house to eat...and everybody thought we was doing well. I was never discouraged in any way, that I wasn't going to succeed...not saying that I have succeeded, but I'm doing well and have been very blessed. I don't think that I could have done it without her. Like I say, when she break down, I was never discouraged in any way...I always felt a person can achieve anything they want in life, if they dedicated themselves to it...to that dream. I attribute it, again...all leading back to my parents, and meeting my wife that I met."

"I worked at Caterpillar...came here...how I got here...didn't have any relatives here, but as a child, a friend...his mom left, and left him with his grandparents, which...we all lived in Delta Pineland, and 'bout two or three years later, she came back and got him. He was about ten years old at the time...so, we parted then. In 1974, he came down...latter part of '74. He came back to Mississippi to see his grandfather, and you know, people who knew him. Of course we saw each other...and I might be a smart aleck for saying this, but I always thought I was smarter than him...and he had this job, and a Cadillac, and this and that. I didn't have anything at all. So, he told me he worked at Caterpillar...and so I came here looking for a job at Caterpillar. I got the job at Caterpillar and then wasn't happy with myself. I got the feeling I was...confined...like in prison or something. That was just my...my...my personal feelings."

"As a kid in Mississippi, I always hung around old men. When I say old, they was in their 40's and 50's and 60's at the time...and I always enjoyed their company. I used to hang around an old man selling hot tamales...and so, when I came here, I noticed they didn't have the type of tamales that they had down there. So...I went back home and asked the man to sell me the recipe. He told me that he wouldn't sell it to me...he would give it to me...and whenever I got on my feet, just bring him back two hundred dollars."

"It took me awhile to get on my feet. He wrote the recipe on paper, and it didn't work out for me. I never could get my sales going...I didn't feel like I had the product right. So, what I did...after two years of it not happenin' the way I thought it should...I called him and asked him, could I come and watch him do it. I went down and watched him, and found out what I was doing wrong. I come back, and the next couple years...I got on my feet a little bit...so, I made a special trip down to pay him his money. That's how I got into the tamale business...and everything else came from there."

"I think what's going on in New Orleans...Mississippi, is a very tragic situation...the hurricane and all. But, we're the United States man...things are gonna be all right. That's just how I feel. We're the most blessed people in the world, you know, and everyday I thank God for it, personally. Now, you may not believe it, but as I cook chops every day...I look at the people that's patronizing my business...and supporting my family...and I thank God for that. I don't take it for granted. Again, I attribute everything in my life to my mother."

"You know, we were friends. I think now...what she thought...because we were friends. I could talk to her about anything, just straight above the table, you know? The most important thing I admire about talking to her...no matter what I talked to her about...she would say, "I'm not saying you are wrong...but it could be this way, and it could be that way." So, I learned...inside...not to prejudge any situation."

"My mother was 79 in March when she died. She told me that you can never give anybody too much...and so, when I see a person that needs something...not saying that I have it all...but, I'm willing to share with them. I want to see people do good."

"Just to let you know, I live by three laws that my dad left with me. I can't let you leave without you knowing these three. He always told me...he said, quote, "Willie, if you don't learn how to think for yourself, people will make a plumb ass out of you." End of quote. He also told me...said, "Willie, if you can't help a fella, don't have nothin' to do with him." And the third one, he said, "Willie, always live your life where you can speak up for yourself...because when you're wrong, you don't have no voice."

"I live my life by those laws."

2   *Ernie Harburg*

"My father was Yip Harburg. Among many, many songs…he wrote all of the lyrics in 'The Wizard of Oz'. He was also the final script editor and wrote the scene where they give out the heart and the brain and the nerve. Years ago, I co-wrote a book about his life called, 'Who Put the Rainbow in the Wizard of Oz?'"

"My father was a socialist back in World War I…and he disapproved of the war…so he went to Uruguay for a few years, and then came home. He was smitten with a woman named Alice, who was quite beautiful and artistic, and came from Boston. They got married quickly and had two children…and it was the "roaring twenties", you know, when there were a lot of things going on. Each of them was pursuing their own careers. Yip was in an electrical appliance factory and she was in…ummm…art…singing and dancing. They started having a lot of squabbles…not getting on…and so the two children were put in different places. I lived with my uncle…and I remember being five months in a school with girls…that's where they put me when I was five years old."

"Then…the depression hit…he lost his…it was 1929, and my father lost his factory. His partner went bankrupt, but Yip chose to pay the debt. But then, his friend Ira Gershwin…and he had been a friend of his for years…persuaded him to become a lyricist. At that point my mother decided that she didn't want to continue that life, because he was never home. He had three shows on Broadway in 1932…and uh…so she got up and left."

"I remember my father being dismayed, and taking us over to Greenpoint, to his sister's house…who already had five children. And that's where I was brought up…in Greenpoint. It was a low-income working family, but a wonderful family. My uncle, who became my surrogate father, really…was a tailor. He owned his own shop. So that's how my life consciously began."

"After I got out of the Army, I got married and went to City College for four years. I got a degree in history, and then I went to Wisconsin and got a degree in cultural anthropology…in Madison, Wisconsin. Then, finally, I went to Ann Arbor and took a degree…a PhD in social psychology. I became an epidemiologist…well, it's called a psycho-social epidemiologist…a social epidemiologist with the School of Public Health."

"I became very much involved in the whole civil rights movement…the history of African-Americans and Anglo-Americans in the United States, and I did some deep heavy research, and developed a proposal for a large scale research project in Detroit…dealing with how the lives of the…the African-Americans, in their conflict with whites…how it affected their blood pressure. I had an idea that it was a situation that provoked anger on the part of each group. So, the question was, "How does one handle that anger, and how is it related to blood pressure?" Blood pressure was directly related to stroke and heart disease…so my study was about the handling of anger by blacks and whites in high and low income areas…males and females, in Detroit."

"Six years later when we came out of the field…when the whole Detroit rebellion came out…in the 12th Street area, which we had picked to survey as one of our four areas…after six years…we finally got the data, and we published. Indeed, it turned out that the major findings were that black working people in low-income or high-stress areas had the highest proportion of hypertension…elevated blood pressure. They were higher than the black middle-class group. The black middle-class blood pressure did not differ from the white middle-class group…and there was some evidence that suppressing one's anger was associated with higher blood pressure. So, there were a lot of things that came out of that study."

"While my father wanted me to become a lyricist, I was very much attracted to scientific research of a social nature. But…he was in reverence of me becoming a scientist. To me…we were both equals in carrying out our own desires. I don't think I was…and I don't know how to explain this…when I was a child…you know, we're always in the shadow of our parents. Once I became liberated, I never felt that I was living in my father's shadow. He was doing something totally different and I was very good at what I was doing."

"Tory Petersen Harper, my first wife, died of cancer. During that time, I bought a bar restaurant…my wife and I…during the 70's. I am just now writing up…it's called "The Del Rio Bar—a Counterculture Experiment." We ran a collective management in the bar. Tory and I and a friend of mine, started that. I am just now writing about that. She smoked, and both her parents smoked…and when I met her at Antioch College during the war, she was smoking. There was no question about it…that it led to the cancer in her lungs…then it went to her brain."

"First I went to Antioch…and then I enlisted in the Army Air Force. By doing that, I wasn't drafted when I was eighteen…so I just missed the Battle of the Bulge. By enlisting…I actually saved my life, I think. Two of my boyhood friends were killed on that occasion. So, I was in the Army for two years…I was in for one year and re-enlisted for a year and went to Okinawa after the war, and the Philippines."

"When I came home…we got married, and she had twins…twin boys. Then, we had a third child, also a boy. We had three sons…and we raised them in Madison for about four years, and then we went to Ann Arbor where they spent the rest of their childhood lives. The twins went to the University of Michigan and the third son went to Evergreen State College out in Oregon."

"What happened after my first wife died…and she was a reporter and a social activist, and a writer…I came to New York and took over the Yip Harburg Foundation. Yip had introduced me to a young woman, Deena Rosenberg…and she and I got married, and now we have another son. She…Deena…is a brilliant kind of woman, and was the Founding Chair of the only musical theater writing program in, I guess…the world. At NYU, she created a whole new field and program to train lyricists, composers, and book writers…to collaborate and create a musical play…which is astounding when you realize the number of people involved in a play. To teach it…to train people to do that is a wondrous thing. To create that field is even more wondrous."

"The Freedom from Religion Foundation…I just became involved in that the last two years. I have lived out my life…sold my bar last summer…I had three restaurants and sold all of them…and moved to New York. We now have a condo on Tenth Street and First Avenue…four blocks from where my father was raised a hundred years ago. I then began doing research and running the Yip Harburg Foundation…and it was only last year that I became aware of the Freedom from Religion Foundation. For years, I had just kept my own beliefs inside…to myself. My son…I have four sons now…my son is a non-believer as I am, and as my father was. He's a physician. My other son who is a psychologist…he became Catholic. A third son…I don't know what you would call him…a new wave spiritualist or something like that. I don't think he believes in a supernatural force. My fourth son has a language disorder which saves him from all of the difficulty in deciding about such things."

"I have four sons…I love them all…and they are all different parts of me. They resemble…each one of them resembles me in a different way. I couldn't tell you which one I loved the best…and it's the same way with my research…I couldn't tell you which study I loved the most. Similarly, with Yip's songs, his lyrics…there are some that are just plain great. And now, my fourth son is singing them in a wonderful, wonderful mode. But…I couldn't pick one…there are just a cluster of them…"Brother, Can You Spare a Dime?"…"Paper Moon"…"Over the Rainbow"…which, that is obviously the most globally received poetry."

"In my book that I did about Yip…I started it out…he gave a talk at the "Y"…the 92nd Street "Y" in 1970. He thought very deeply about that talk because it was the beginning of a lyrics and lyricists series…and he was being asked, as an honor, to be the first lyricist. He did a lot of thinking about that…and I remember talking with him…and he developed the idea that…a song is of course composed of lyrics…words, and music. Words make you think thoughts, and music makes you feel feelings…but putting them together, merging them…creates a song, which is a new entity. A song makes you feel thoughts. That is the artistic process…and he first delivered that at that time, in 1970."

"I have conveyed that to various audiences since then. I always loved that formulation because it's very difficult to have an example…and I always use H20. If you have oxygen gas and hydrogen gas…and if you combine them with the proper pressure and temperature, you create water. Water has its own being…entity…and properties that is different from the hydrogen and oxygen separately. It is the same as a song…it is bigger than the sum of its parts. A lyric is one thing…like poetry, and music is another. Without the two being together, you couldn't have a song. I always objected to using the composers name to say that they wrote the song. It is not true. The two people merging their crafts wrote the song. But, that was before the Beatles came over."

"Most of the money from the foundation has been given to political documentaries…movies. Also…equally, money has been given to…quote…"scholarships for minorities"…although I don't like that word. African-Americans, Chinese, American Indian…low-income recipients. The scholarships and documentary films is where we have put our money. Some of the documentaries have become quite well known. We take much pleasure in the kids going onto college and doing good works. Of course some money is spent supporting Yip's reputation.

My wife Deena, helps to produce some of the small shows we put on as a tribute to Yip."

"In the beginning, my father and me...we had quite the rebellion, you know...and it lasted for quite a long time. I was very stubborn, and he was also. Finally...oh...and I would say, when I got my PhD...I was 35...and he was being investigated by the House Un-American Activities Committee...he became a little more soft, and I became his "confidant". We began then to have a deeper friendship then we had ever had before...and so on to the end of his life."

"When I was a kid, I read a poem in which the last lines were "footsteps in the sands of time"...and I became struck by how...how huge the human effort on this planet is...and how many things have gone on, and how each of us contributes in different ways...some in small ways, and some in larger ways. But no matter how large you contribute...it's still pretty small. It will, too...disappear in the sands of time. Even knowing all that...I still think my study in Detroit was one of the trailblazers in that area...and also our efforts to have a collective democratic bar in Ann Arbor. Of course, the four sons which I have helped father, have also made me very proud."

"I always thought at the end of my father's lyrics, "Over the Rainbow"...the phrase, "Why oh why can't I?"...I always thought, well of course...you can...you know?"

3   **Sally Stone**

"My husband and I happened to be…he had…he was on an internship for the summer. We were living in Scotland…and did some traveling down into England. He had a migraine headache…and so, I went exploring through this little town. I think it was the town of Rye & Winchell. Well, they were two towns that I think were together. I don't remember exactly."

"I walked into this little church, and the afternoon sunlight was just streaming through the windows…through the stained glass windows, where much of them had been destroyed in the Second World War. There was a small group of musicians playing there. The sound of that music…in that setting…was just…it was just…exquisite. It was that afternoon light…you know how the light will just filter in late afternoon and create that long shadow? It cast patterns on the musicians…and it was just one of those moments that's hard to capture again. Beautiful. It was very special."

4   *Michael Arthur Weinstein*

"I am Michael Arthur Weinstein. I'm sixty years old…wanna see my I.D.? I'm serious."

"I was paroled here…Illinois River Correction Center. Which…I was here before…paroled here. I'm livin' in the streets…just watin' for my social security check to kick in, and they're givin' me a hard time right now. I've had a lot of physical problems…had cirrhosis of the liver, chronic arthritis…do you wanna hear all this? I have chronic rheumatoid arthritis, which has spread to my bones. I had a massive stroke, which you can see…I've had brain surgery…right here. That was in 1988. I've been on social security since then. This last time I got arrested, they stopped my check. I'm in the process of getting it back. I've been waitin' six months, and stayin' at the Peoria Rescue Mission, which is a good place, in a way. But, after you've been locked up for six years, you've got no privacy. You can't take a bath…everybody is always around…same thing as prison."

"So now, I'm out in the streets now…which…I shouldn't be out tonight. I'm on parole, and I could get violated and go back…but I been there seven months waitin' for my social security check, and I really don't give a damn anymore. But now, I've got a lawyer that's gonna take my case. They been making me wait six months…and I'll get a lot of money, but hafta spend six months livin' in a mission with no privacy. I'm on the streets every night here…and uh…nobody will help me…which I don't really blame 'em. I'm eating out of the garbage…got a whole bag of sandwiches here. They're still good…you want one?"

"There aren't very many lawyers at the…but this guy on this card is rich and he will do it…he's a good lawyer. I hope so…he said he would be. I've got $3000 coming so far, and he said I don't have to pay him…which is good. I would, but I don't hafta."

"Now, the government has been messing me around…'cuz, I had a stroke in 1988. I had a massive aneurysm. A vein exploded in my nose and paralyzed…for a long time I was walkin' the streets, got thrown out of a hospice…didn't have any insurance. But, they operated on me, which I'm grateful for. I can move around, but can't work. But, I've been goin' to prison 'cuz I'm stupid…been roaming the streets. I been doin' drugs until the…what I call the "misery hour". I don't know if you understand how it is. But…you have to…you're out here every day, you have no food, you have no money…and I won't beg people…and stuff like that."

"I only get a $564 social security check anyhow, and that would pay my rent of $130 and I…I get the food stamps. Here's the lawyer that's gonna help me…his card…and I believe he will. Prairie State is, excuse me…full of shit. This guy is a big time lawyer. He's over here in the Commerce Bank Building…Robert Strodel…I don't know if you know him or not. He's a nice guy. He's away two weeks and didn't get in touch with me."

"But the thing is…I been sendin' my medical records…I got cirrhosis of the liver…I'm supposed to be dying…there's no cure for that. Now, I'm in the streets…I can't get a damn job. I can't even get a medical card from welfare…and I need medical attention…pills…stuff for cirrhosis of the liver. Chronic arthritis…it hurts. I never understood it would hurt this bad. It doesn't stay in one spot…it moves around. Wanna see my feet? They are so bad…they swell, and I got blisters."

"I'm a criminal. I been locked up half my life. I've never been arrested for drugs, but now I'm sixty years old and I'm arrested on drugs. I'm walkin'…it was stupid…I don't even do crack cocaine, but I had one in my pocket…they pulled me over and I got busted. I smoke pot, and I admit….I'm a hippie. Shit…in the 60's and 70's…I'm sixty…I was there when the world was nice and everything, you know? Never had to worry, but it ain't like that no more. Now, everybody wants to kill you. It's back to the gangster killers. When you're on the streets now, and you got money in your pocket…they'll kill you."

"I ain't been inside my own place in seven years. Before I got busted, I had a nice little place…nice place. But what you have to realize is, I'm a criminal. From the time I was seventeen…on my 17th birthday, I was in the penitentiary. I been in the joint seven times…before that, reform school. I've had mental problems…but now the mental people won't help me no more. I'm not crazy mental, where I hurt people…I just hurt myself. I don't commit suicide…I just don't think straight. Somebody says go rob a bank, and I'll do it…stupid shit."

"But now, Peoria…three years ago, it was better than it is now. I was on parole here three years ago and Human Services took me in. They were real nice to me and everything…and now they won't help. But look, there are so many crazy people livin' on the streets that need to be…really need to be taken care of. Half of them, they…they cut their checks off. They're really crazy, and Human Services used to find them a place to live. They'd ration their checks out to 'em, but they did it for their own good. You'd have a place to live; a place to go…you'd have privacy. You got food to eat. You got a LINK card. I got one right now…you wanna buy it?"

"I'm from Chicago. I had a bad childhood. I learned to grow up quick. When I was eight years old, my parents locked me out. When everybody said it was time to go in, I'd go to my door, and it would be locked. They made me sleep outside. I was a kid…a fuckin' kid. I would say, "Why don't you let me in? Let me in…please…please. The lights are on…I know you're home." But, you see, I was not ever really wanted. My parents were nuts…Dad was an alcoholic. He spent the welfare check and never came home with the food. I know, you don't want to hear a hard luck story…but I was walkin' the streets of Chicago, and you know how the perverts get you? You learn how to survive really quick…or you die. Some perverts will kill you. There are some here in this town. Some of them are homosexuals…and I'm not against that…but…I did all that…and I'm not ashamed of it. I'm not a homosexual, but I did what I did to survive. That's a fact…I had to…I have to."

"You know, the minute you get out of jail, you want a woman…and even if they make you quit smoking, you want a cigarette. I'm not a heavy drug addict…I smoke weed. But the women…there are so many on the streets. They live at the YWCA…and they're really good looking…and they hustle. But, they're not hustling because they want money…they're hustling because they have nowhere to go, and they're hoping they'll find a guy who will take them home and keep 'em. That's the way the world works. Just like me…I'll hustle…and if you're rich, take me home and keep me. Do whatever you want. I'll tell you, I'm not a homo, but I'll sell my body. I'll sell anything to survive. I'll sell my body, but I won't beg…I won't beg"

"I'm sixty years old. I'm too weak to stick anybody up anymore…but I didn't do that anyway…I'm a safecracker. That was back in the old days…in Chicago. I would never go into a person's house and steal their TV, 'cuz I'm not that kind of burglar…I'm a professional. That's the kind of person I am. I'll steal from a company, 'cuz they can afford it, but I will not…I will not go into a person's house and steal, because I know they worked their ass off to get their own stuff. I'm a professional."

5 *Betty Gerber*

"This was the time before "ladies". I made exactly what men did. I sat between two men, and I worked twice as hard. I had to prove myself every day. I became the first woman bank officer at Peoria Savings…the first woman at a bank or savings & loan."

"I always said that I was lucky to be a lady and did what I did…but I was never into the woman's movement. I like to have doors opened for me, and so forth. Betty Freidan, who started the National Organization for Women…from Peoria…she was a Goldstein. The Goldstein's had the best jewelry shop in Peoria, until the 50's…then they went out of business. She was definitely an individual. She grew up just around the corner from Bradley."

"When I went to Bradley…my last test that I ever took in my life was at Bradley University, and it was in history. It was at 8 o'clock. My girlfriend and I had studied all night long…and we didn't have the radio on that morning. We were lucky to have a piece of toast in us, because we had to take the test. The first question…I will never forget…my last, first question on a test. The question was, "Who of prominence died this morning?" I didn't know that answer because we didn't have the radio on. Do you know who it was? Mahatma Ghandi. He was assassinated that morning."

6   *Karen Slate*

"I'm Karen Slate...and I'm 46. Born in Midland Texas...but, from six months on, lived in Dallas. I lived there until a year ago...and moved here for a relationship. That relationship quickly went south."

"I was a project manager for Lucent Technologies...or Tyco at the time. He was an installer, working in Guam...that I was the project manager over. He and I developed a friendship...a relationship. Six months after coming back, we started seeing each other long-distance. We'd meet halfway, or he would go there...or I would come here. It turned out that there was nothing there between us as far as a long-term relationship...yet, that's what I wanted. I don't know why, because we really didn't click when we were together...it was basically a physical relationship. I just thought...well, anyway...I lost my job at AT&T after 24 years. I got laid off. And so, at that point, we decided we would try the relationship full-term, in the same town...you know, living together. So, I sold my house and moved up here."

"Then...two months later, he met a girl and put me on the street. I mean...within five minutes, put me on the street...locked me out. He lied to the judge, got a court order, and had me removed. So, for fifteen days, I was 800 miles from home, had nowhere to go...knew nobody else in the whole state."

"I drove to Dallas to get the few things left before my house closed...it was closing within a week. I drove back up here not knowing what to do...sleeping in different hotels or truck-stops. Then I drove to Seattle, Washington...and back. I put 8000 miles on my car that week. I had a friend that lives in Seattle, and I told him that I had to find a place to live...and in order to do that, you pretty much have to have a job."

"They don't want to lease to somebody that doesn't have a job...and I'm currently unemployed. "Can you put me on your payroll?" He said, "Yes." I said, "Okay, I'm...I'm coming up." And not realizing he didn't need me to come up...all he had to do was tell his secretary...if anyone calls, I was on his payroll...I went. I had the money...I just didn't have the means for more money. I drove up there...got there about three in the afternoon, and the court order required that I be in a hearing fifteen days after the order. This was three days away and I figured I don't need to be there, that they would just extend the order of protection, which didn't serve a purpose anyway. I just wanted my stuff...so I didn't see any need to be there. After getting to Seattle, and thinking all the way up...I thought that maybe I did need to be there. So, I drove 3100 miles straight back...straight through...to be here for the hearing. I rented a place the next day, after the hearing."

"The key thing that came out of this was "forgiveness", and that didn't happen until four weeks ago. I spent a year, in my mind...just wanting revenge. I wanted to right the wrong somehow...I mean, I was angry. Without this experience...I mean everything that he did...the horrible, horrible things that he did...it took that for me to know, what forgiveness is. Maybe that was his role...maybe on a soul level, we had an agreement that I needed to learn forgiveness...and that was to be his role...in his life...to teach me that."

"Four weeks ago, when I had this release from all this anger, and hate and rage that was driving me, was one of the better moments in my life. Isn't that weird? I've had a great life...I've been to Cozumel over thirty times. I have two older sisters, and Mom and Dad...a very normal family. I grew up in a neighborhood in a nice house...lower middle-class maybe. I rode unicycles."

"All three of us in the neighborhood...all three of us girls rode unicycles. There was a new girl that moved into the neighborhood...Karen...Karen T...Karen Thompson. We called her Karen T because I was Karen S. We were like, twelve years old. "Well, what do you want to do?" "Well, we can go to my house and ride a unicycle." "What's a unicycle?" So, we went over there...and within a week, we all had one. And, even at sixteen, seventeen, at the local park...White Rock Lake...I rode a unicycle. They had musicians come out...a place where people come out...throw Frisbee...and there would be another guy with a unicycle, a six-foot unicycle. I'd ride out there, and then I'd listen to the musicians. The music...the music was my passion."

"I'm from Texas...and they've got the greatest singer-songwriters. They've got Guy Clark...I mean, I could name a billion of them...Stevie Ray Vaughn...lots of them. The people I would go see live, it started out...I was just real shy. I would never go or do anything by myself, and I was always very self-conscious...still am. But, I got lost one day looking for a place called "David Frames Dallas"...just looking for a picture frame. So, I pulled into this little place called

"Lilly Langtry's" and asked if I could use the phone. It's just a saloon…a little, skinny, dark hallway…and I go back and use the phone…come back…there's a girl sitting at the bar…the only one there. She said, "Well, sit down and have a drink with me." So, I did a shot of tequila with her, and basically, that became my "Cheers"…my home away from home."

"From that point forward, I did everything by myself. I had friends everywhere I went…but, I would go to the movies by myself…fancy dinners on Valentine's Day by myself…and I was very comfortable with that, because you always meet people that way. People would see me and say, "Buy her a drink, bless her heart…tell her to come join us." But, that's where I learned about music. That's where I met some of the really great singer-songwriters. John DeFore, David Lutken…who is coming Monday to stay with me for two days on his way to…he now does what they call "guitar theater" in New York, off-Broadway. He wrote and directed "The Life and Times of Woody Guthrie"…and starred in it. On his way through, he's going to stay. He's got three CD's…which is great…well, albums…vinyl…it was way before the time of CD's."

"Why am I staying here? I don't know. I have plenty of friends and family…mother and sister saying, "Stay with me…stay with me. You can stay at the farm…fourteen dollars a month…electricity is all." And they got a hundred fifty acre farm. But, I don't want to stay with anybody…mainly because of my cats. There's something else that's telling me to stay."

"I worked for Caterpillar for four months. The day that I got kicked out…the next morning I had a job interview with Caterpillar. The following day, I was supposed to start school at New Horizons…paid for by the government through NAFTA. So, every day working at Caterpillar, I was almost having an emotional breakdown going to work…crying…didn't know why…I was just losing it. I called my sister and said, "I've got to get the blank out of here. I'm coming home." She said, "Come on girl." So, I started packing. Then, the next day, I got something in the mail saying that they had moved the TTA program…to call them. I thought I had forfeited that option to go to school when I started at Caterpillar. I thought…I blew that. But they said, "No, that's always available, as long as the funds are there." So, that's one reason why I stuck around…because New Horizons had already accepted me when I got the job at CAT. I loved the job at CAT…but I…I just…wasn't right."

"Everybody that I know…my family and everything is in Dallas. I still, to that point hadn't made any friends. But now…I have a couple now…people that I met at Caterpillar, and a few others."

"Instead of studying to get my certifications, I've been reading books to kind of get some peace of mind. I've been reading Buddhism, and this "Course in Miracles". I'm only four weeks into it. It's the ultimate in…God being the creator…and Jesus being the son of God…and so are we…we are all sons of God….the Christ, which is the highest form you can achieve. We have different incarnations and we keep coming back to…learn lessons. We are spirits, souls on a path…and until we reach the highest, which is the realization that we are all *one*, we keep coming back. The book is broken into text…just reading material…and then there is a workbook, and then you live that for the day, and there are 365 lessons. Basically, in the course…we are all teachers, and we are all students, and the teacher generally learns more than the student."

"I knew before I ever moved here with this guy…that we weren't meant to be together…but something was driving me to come live with him, for whatever reason…so much so that I would sell my house and uproot myself. I believe that through this…and twenty years ago going to Unity and always having this belief…possibly I met him prior to this incarnation, and said, "Hey man, I'm fixing to go back…and I really need to learn forgiveness this time, can you set me up…can you hook me up?" So, he took time in his lifetime to come and set me up for the biggest opportunity to learn forgiveness. He did a good job…if you want to look at it that way. Then, when I see him in the afterlife, I'll just give him a high five and say, "Sorry you had to be such a horrible scumbag on this earth…must have been painful for you, but you did a good job." He waited until I had everything…everything that could be taken away…and he took it away. He knows…he knows that he did wrong…on the soul level."

7   *Cory Cooper*

"I found God. I had these dreams of burning in oil…a lot of oil…and it brought me back to Christianity, and how I should live. It opened up my life to being more spiritual…on a more spiritual level…a more personal level than based on how most Americans think they should live. It has made me more…peaceful."

8   *Staff Sergeant Minter*

"I just got back last Thursday, from my second deployment in Iraq...and I get out of the "suck" in April. I don't have my rifle strapped to me, so I feel a little naked. This last deployment was a whole lot easier than the first...not nearly as violent...but I believe I got lucky in where...in where I was deployed. The first time, I was just scared shitless...scared shitless. But this time, I grew to appreciate the people."

"On my way home...I was like Morgan Freeman in "Shawshank" as he rides the bus towards Mexico. Thoughts were running in and out of my head at a hundred miles an hour. I could barely stay in my seat."

"I was able to see some of the beauty in Iraq this time. It's a different type of beauty...a simpler type. I remember...excuse me...I remember I was sitting on a crumbled wall, looking out at the shadows of the tanks and BFV's...and this was late at night. The sky was full of these bright stars...more stars than I had ever seen. I could hear in the background...someone was playing Pink Floyd. I could see the outlines of the tanks and BFV's...which were these huge...ghosts...that swallowed starlight. A chemlight lit the faces of a few soldiers sitting on the ground. It was so quiet...so surreal...so beautiful."

"It's definitely a different world here...back home. I didn't expect to have fifty degree weather in January. I'm really amazed at how blue the skies are here, and the days are much shorter."

"I really like being home. I didn't die...like I promised my wife. I'm not sure how you keep a promise like that...but, I'm just glad I was able to keep it."

9-12   *The Margarita Sisters*

"I am here with my three sisters having a planning weekend. We are the Margarita Sisters...and we have some daughters and daughters-in-law that we are going to take on a trip with us...and we call them the Petite Margaritas...and we are also planning a family reunion which is happening in Iowa on July 4th. My name is Mary and I live in St. Louis, Missouri...and I'm 59."

"We pick a different location that we meet, like Galena, Illinois...Chicago, Illinois. We have been to Kansas City...we've been to Bend, Oregon. Our last trip was to...ummm...Margarita Island, off the coast of Venezuela...and that's why we call ourselves the Margarita Sisters. We have Margarita contests to see who can make the best Margarita."

"And I won this year. My name is Janet Kennedy and I live in Cincinnati and am about to move to Lincoln, Nebraska...and I am sixty years old."

"And that's why we went to Margarita Island...to celebrate Janet's birthday. I'm Elaine Kirchoff. I am 54 and I live in Boone, Iowa...and we just have a great time together...we just love each other so much, and this is still a great way for us to kind of still bond together. Peoria is kind of a midpoint for all of us. We heard it was a fun city...so that's why we're here."

"I'm Darlene and I'm 57 and I've been married for 37 years to the same wonderful man, and I have two daughters who are going to be Petite Margaritas."

"We have Margarita banks...that we save our money in. We save all our change, and sometimes my husband will put a twenty dollar bill in there, and we save it for our big trips like Margarita Island. We always have a really good time saving and planning where we are going next."

"And our Petites have banks also...we are all supposed to be saving. All change must go into the Margarita jar...which is a savings plan for our trips."

"If my husband leaves his change on the dresser for more than two days...it goes in my bank."

"If they take the change out of our jars for some reason, they have to pay it back...double what they took out."

"We think next...possibly we might go on an Alaskan cruise."

"Our mom used to make us outfits in Webster City, Iowa...she was a wonderful seamstress...and we had matching outfits...so that made us feel really special because we all matched."

"On our trips, we always get in an outfit so that we look alike...but they are not always classy. We've dressed like little old ladies and had tea parties. We've dressed like...oh...we've been in a gay bar and didn't know it. We didn't know about it until we got back to our hotel, and we were on the elevator, and we mentioned going to the Mashed Potato Club...to a couple on the elevator, and they said, "Oh...the gay bar." We wondered about all the naked pictures on the wall."

"We lived on a farm as children...and my dad was older when he got married. He was 41 when he got married. There were thirteen years difference between our parents...and they had four girls...and we were definitely the apple of his eye. He loved every one of us...treasured us."

"We had no brothers. I remember how Dad used to get himself off the chair...when he said you were being a little bit ornery or silly, he would take off his belt, smile at us and say, "You'd better behave, or I'll use this belt on you!" Then he would giggle at us, snap it, and put it away! He was the best dad ever."

"We take turns every year...one sister plans the trip, generally speaking, and they get to choose the place...make all the arrangements...make all the big plans. We do elaborate planning. Elaine and Darlene, we are the youngest, and we would like to both go to Italy, Venice, Italy for our 60th birthday."

"We had a Margarita contest this weekend in our hotel room, and it was between Janet and Darlene, because Mary and I have both won. I have to tell you that, although both Margaritas were very good, we had to give the prize to Janet because she came out in this outfit...black tights...and a black kind of a tank top and a green skirt...Margarita green skirt with fur on it. So, they were just one point apart...and the reason she won was because of the outfit...it was just outrageous...she looked like Madonna."

13   *Amber Padillo*

"My mother wanted me to pick up a prescription at CVS…and they've apparently designed this pill bottle for older people. It's now square with a big label on it. They flipped it so that now the top is the bottom, and the bottom is the top. My mom couldn't figure it out…just like the Heinz ketchup bottles. I mean…you go for sixty years doing it one way and then you make it completely opposite. It's like a practical joke for seniors."

14   *Fred Sturgis*

"My name is Fred Sturgis…that's me. I got me a 2001 Road-Glide. I just got back from Sturgis…that's my name also…and I just got back from there…a week ago. It's just the biggest goddamn bike rally there is. It was the 65th year. Everything goes on in Sturgis…even things you just want to leave there too. A lot of shit happens. It's in South Dakota…all the way across…it's all the way across….a long fuckin' way. It's just a good time. Three or four hundred thousand people show up. It started 65 years ago, and it's near the Black Hills. The closer you get…the more you're surrounded by Harleys…maybe a few Indians…and a BMW. There are also a few goddamn rice grinders…but they only come out at night."

"I'm a construction worker here…on the 74 job. Don't know when it'll be completed. Hell, they don't even know…but it's getting close. I'm putting all the steel and concrete out there on the roads. I been a construction laborer for the last thirty years. Expect I'll be doing it a few more…even though I should be retired."

"I was on bridge repair before. The bridge crew…they do maintenance on all the bridges in about five counties. They almost go to the Mississippi…Monmouth, Galesburg, and so on. We fixed potholes in the bridges…bridge railings…took care of light structural damage. We took care of the lights on certain bridges. The river bridges have these navigational lights under them…so the boats can stay in the channel. It's a big job. We covered a pretty good territory."

"This summer has been pretty fuckin' hot, so I ain't been out on my motorcycle as much. When it's ninety degrees, it's too fuckin' hot on the bike. But, we go out with our friends…fifty, sixty miles…ride somewhere and have lunch, or breakfast, or dinner. On the weekend, we might just take a ride and get the hell out of Shiloh. We might go to Galesburg or the Quad Cities…might go to Starved Rock State Park with a bigger group. Usually, we ride with five or six others."

"I'm getting older, but I still like to party a bit. There's a saying, "Live fast…live hard…and die young." I like to ride my bike…like I said…I've been out to Sturgis. It's a big-ass motorcycle thing that lasts two weekends…and they'll have four hundred thousand bikes. It's just unbelievable. The whole town…well, the whole area, just turns into motorcycle heaven. There are a lot of places to ride out there. It's just some really nice riding out there...national monuments...badlands. You just get up and take off and go riding to some of these places. It's pretty interesting...and just about anything you want to see, you'll see...gets pretty wild in some of the campgrounds and that. It's pretty nonstop for about a week."

"Me and Jo...we just live together...she's my little sweetie. I met her when I was down in Florida. Jo don't work. She used to live by Lake Okeechobee...right across the street. She used to go fishing there...and alligator hunting. She has five kids...and I don't know how many grandkids...even has some great-grandkids. She went with me this year and got a really sore ass. I got a sore ass too, but that's just part of the fun...getting Sturgis ass."

15   *Dorothy Berkel*

"I'm seventy. We lived in Louisiana when my husband was in the Air Force. We called it the "Swamps of Home".

"I worked for Firestone Tire and Rubber Company. I was a secretary there…and there was this bridge that went over a swamp. Firestone was out in the outlying area. I had never driven a shift car…and my husband had a shift car. So, I would drop him off at the Air Force base…and I would dread this high bridge that went over the swamp, every single day. I remember thinking, "Am I going to make it today, or…am I going to roll right back down after I shift into second? After I get up there, am I going to roll right back down and end up in the swamp?" For a girl from Illinois, that was a pretty dreadful thought."

"The first time I had coffee down there, I didn't know it was chicory. It had chicory in it. You know what chicory is? It's a root. I can't describe it to you…but, if you're raised down there, you love it in your coffee. You love chicory coffee. But, if not…then you have northern coffee…or "no'then" as they called it. This was in 1955…1956…and the Berlin Wall…that had just occurred."

"I wish I had done more when we lived in Louisiana…but I was only twenty and I wanted to get back home to Illinois. I was homesick."

16   *Harold Quinn*

"I'm 86...be 87 in a little less than a month. I'm from Trivoli...but I'm living in motel. I been living in motel for nine years. Everything I got is in that one room. My business, and everything I got...my briefcases...all my clothes is there. It ain't bad there...and I don't like fancy stuff anyway. I got two houses and a mobile home out there in Trivoli. I got a show place there...all fixed up. All it takes is work. I go there every afternoon in the summer. You see so many places, and they got old farm buildings that need painted...things falling down...weeds growing up. It's just work that makes my place look nice. A lot of people lets weeds grow...I don't. I don't let weeds grow. I got 140 acres and grow corn and soybeans. I been doing it for years."

"I used to farm, and then I quit...in 1958, and moved to town. In '58, you know...a 500 acre farm was a big farm...in them days. I farmed 500 acres and raised hogs...cattle. I drove a school bus...dump trucking...I had a pickup and a station wagon. My wife hauled kids to a little school. With all that, I still wasn't making nothin'. Then...I worked on Ready-Mix plants for forty years...loaded trucks, drove trucks, built walls. When I was 76, I retired. I went to work for Staley...but they didn't want me...I was too old. I was loading trucks...and it's like baking a cake...you make some little mistake, and it costs them money to replace stuff...and they were fussy with my loading. I was down there at Raber's...Raber's Meat Packing. I built all them walls down there. One wall I built...from the ground up, 44 foot high. I formed it up in my spare time...took some left over cement...and dumped it in the wall."

"I come here to Kirsch's...'cuz...you live in a one room place, you gotta get out...three or four times a day, and have coffee. I go to Stewart's every once in awhile. I don't eat no breakfast...but lately at noon I been eating mashed potatoes and gravy. I just ain't got an appetite. So...I stopped in there the other day, 'cuz I pick up my mail out there in Trivoli every day...or every other day."

"My wife died three or four years ago. She was in a nursing home for nine years...in Peoria. She didn't know anything...anybody. Oh...I got friends...girlfriends that call...but as far as gettin' married...I ain't gettin' married again. If you get mad at a cow...you walk out. But...if you're married to the cow...you can't do that. I got kids, you know, and I don't need some new woman takin' my things."

"I was twenty years old when...this happened. It was a corn picker. I was just out of school two years...and you know, the bevel gears back in there...you listen to the sound when you're up on the machinery...and I hear it rattle. I went real slow and listened. She's a rattlin' down in there...there was a stalk down in there...in the gears. I grabbed for the stalk...it grabbed my leather glove and pulled me in up to there...and it killed the tractor while it was squeezing down on my fingers. Well...you think, after that, "Well shoot, I can't do nothin'." But then you just make up your mind...and you're gonna do it. I can't do a type-writer or other things...but, I can shovel anything with it. Iit's like plyers, in a way."

"It's just one of those things...you get in a hurry...don't take caution. Like...there was a sign on the shield door that said...don't raise it up if it's run-nin'. I raised the shield up and...and well...it saved me from gettin' in the Army. It happened...so...nothin' I can do about it. The biggest trouble I had with my hand after that was bein' self-conscious. So...I carried it in my front pocket...or I had a glove on...because I was ashamed of it. Then, I said, "The hell with it." Then, I found out...I was around people for several years...they didn't even notice it. I ain't noticed it myself for years."

17   *Kunjali Padahya*

"I spend all my days with my family…we hang out together at family functions, weddings…Christmas, Thanksgiving. We can be silly and act retarded with each other, and nobody cares. We eat and sit around and joke with each other…make fun of each other. We have religious ceremonies with the family…it's nice. We are Hindu."

"We were on the Island of Capri, off the coast of Italy…and went to the Blue Grotto. It was amazing. They sang Italian love songs in the grotto. It was very peaceful, and the water was the bluest we had ever seen. It is the deepest, deepest color you have ever seen…just glistening…and you realize, you know…you're in Italy, and it's sunny…bright…you're with people that you love…and you realize that there are some really good things in life."

18   *Earl Flatt*

"The name is Earl Flatt…Earl E. Flatt. I was born and raised here. This is First Street right here. I got turned around myself…but that's First Street right here…where First Street was. There's nothing here now that used to be here. This used to be Spencer…and it's Richard Pryor Place now. Richard Pryor, he live right over there…on First Street."

"I knew Richard Pryor back in the day before I-74. It wasn't here…74…it wasn't here. There wasn't no 74. I used to live at 303 North Adams Street. Richard Pryor's granddaddy…his pool hall was next to where I live at. He had three pool halls…one over there on Sixth Street…had one over there on Spencer Street, and one on Adams Street."

"His granddaddy raised him…he lived with his grandma Gertrude, and grandpa. I don't remember his grandpa's name…I called him Pops. It used to be Pop's Pool Hall…and I always called him Pops. I hang out there all the time when I was a kid. He brought me in, and then…he run me out of there."

"Richard Pryor, when he go out talkin'…he'd make you so damn mad. He'd talk about you like a dog, and then turn around and you'd be laughin', 'cuz he cracked some jokes. He was his own comedian…he didn't care what he say, he just told you how he feel…and he should have something more than…what, this one, two…this three block street?"

"When he come here with "Jo Jo Dancer"…he was giving out…I bet he give out twenty thousand dollars to guys he know…hundred dollar bills…and Barta May…he gave Barta May about ten thousand. She dead now too. Barta May was his girlfriend. Him and Monroe sat and talked…they talked about back in the day when they drink wine and shit…and clown like a fool."

"But…I was always working and hustling. Monroe…he never did have no forty hour job. He ain't never got married. I retired from Caterpillar after 35 years. I'm 59 now. Monroe…he's sixty. He's a year older than me, but I always been the big brother. I was always the big brother because I would hustle up…buy my sisters and brothers Christmas presents…birthday gifts. For about ten years I did that. When I was fourteen, I was bringing food home and helping my dad out. I always hustled. Monroe…he lived with me for seven years…you know what I'm saying? Now…he got his own place, and you can't tell him nothin'. Pam got a little money…and you know, money make you funny sometimes. Money ain't nothin' but the root of all evil. If you got it, you gonna take it to the grave with you."

"I started shining shoes on the streets when I was six years old. I lived in Taft Homes before it was Taft Homes…put it that way. Then I moved to Adams Street. That was back in the time when prostitute houses was all over the place…and there wasn't no 74…I lived right there where 74 is at. It was Route 66."

"My father…he built a lot of houses all over Peoria…he built a house from the ground up…electrical, plumbing…from the ground up. He was a carpenter for fifty years, and he still didn't retire. He worked at K-mart for awhile, until my mom made him quit. He was 85. My dad…he was a hell of a man…he raised fifteen of us. He was 93 when he died…and his name was Monroe Flatt. He built the old John's…you know Big John's? He built the original one…the old one and the new one."

"John shoulda been filthy rich, but he messed up a lot of money…that's all I can say. I remember when John had a little garage that he served meat out of. I used to…I'd go get me, for fifty cents…a whole bag of tips. That was when I lived on Seventh Street…its Martin Luther King now…and it's torn down. That house is all gone now."

"You should go talk to my brother Monroe…he like to talk. I'm having a transmission put in my car, that's why I got one of his trucks. That's his truck right there. Monroe always haul stuff…refrigerators and stuff. That's why I call him "Sanford and Son". He weighs about three twenty now. He's got it made really, but he try to lift a refrigerator off his truck and he hurt his back."

"I'm the only one that took up after my dad…I got thirteen kids. They all grown…one teaching in Chicago…one the head of a clinic…Bernetta, she's a supervisor. I see 'em all the time. They gotta check on daddy. Dion…Earl…he's got seven more years in the Marines. He was in Iraq four times. I'm glad he's home now…in Atlanta.

Dion…he was in the Marines for ten years…and he's in college now. He's gonna get a masters degree and make $350,000 a year being a computer engineer."

"Over there…that's Carver Center right there. Richard be there all day. He should have a statue right there…but Illinois…it's full of shit. I know Illinois…I was raised up here…I know how Illinois is…how Peoria is. They should be honoring him. They didn't even want to name this street after him…but he put Peoria on the map…you know what I'm saying?"

19-20   *Kailey and Robin Lemons*

"I'm Kailey…and I'm sixteen. I remember the first prom that I ever went to. I was going out with a senior…which really boosts your status in high school. I was a freshman. I had this gorgeous dress on…and I got it for twenty bucks, too. It was great. We went to "Lindsay's on Liberty" for dinner. The only bad part about it was…every time you'd jump, the DJ's CD's would skip…so whenever you did the Cha-Cha slide, or whatever…you would have to just jump a little bit, or it would skip. Then, after that, we went to "In-Play" and got unlimited cards for the whole place. That was a blast…and then sometime around 3 o'clock in the morning, we started truckin' home."

"I'm forty…originally from Phoenix, Arizona. I moved from Phoenix eight years ago. I work for Caterpillar…and am a systems analyst. I also work as a waitress in a café…in a small town, on the weekends. I am a single mom of two kids and I own a farm…a ten and a half acre farm. I was born and raised in Arizona…and what I used to do there…I used to…sweat. It was very hot. It's horribly brown there…nine hundred different shades of brown. When I was there, I was in "Fire & Rescue"…"Search & Rescue"…and when I lived there I was an office manager. And so…and then…we moved out here."

"I was raised on a horse ranch in Phoenix. We only had seven horses…and I barrel-raced, which is basically high speed "running your horses around barrels". It's fairly intricate…but the big thing is to just stay on. I haven't done that in years. We have horses now, but I don't do that any more…we just pleasure ride."

"My first job, I worked for Kentucky Fried Chicken, at fifteen…for three years. I slung chicken…and now…I hate chicken. It was $2.56 an hour, and I thought I was the "cat's meow"."

"I started raising and showing dogs at five years old. I had champion Pugs…but now I breed Great Danes. It's another one of my sidelines."

"We've got three Great Danes. Oden is our sire…Lucy is our bitch…and Butch is our puppy from last year. He is so beautiful. He's a "merle". Merles have a genetic…or a gene in their system where if you breed them with another Great Dane, you're liable to get "deaf whites"…and you can't sell those."

"A deaf white is a hundred fifty pound dog who is white...pure white...and deaf."

"Butch...he's a gray color with black spots...his feet...and the tip of his tail is white. He's got a white blaze and a white chest...and a white collar around his neck."

"We breed "Harlequins"...white with black spots. They look like Dalmatians with big spots."

"We left at 5 o'clock this morning and went to Peoria...helping with registration for the "Diabetes Walk". They do a "Kiss a Pig Gala" in the fall. They raise money...get sponsors, and the sponsor that raises the most money, at this huge black-tie affair...they have to kiss a pig...a real pig."

"I love the Midwest...low crime...it's a great place to raise your kids. I'm a single mom, and I don't think I am constantly chasing myself in circles here. The pace in Phoenix was so fast, compared to here. The pace there was almost impossible to keep up with."

"Your kids, unless they're specifically supervised...they have to stay inside. You really can't let kids outside their own front doors. They've got the chain gangs that clean up the alleys...and all that. The wardens are always standing out there...with their big old rifles and everything."

"In Phoenix, the roaches come out at night, if you know what I mean. There is a high crime rate there."

"One night, my husband was just drunk...coming off being stoned or something...and we were separated...and he...he shot into our house, quite a bit. Most of the windows got shot out...and we hid in the bathtub. It took the cops fifteen minutes to get to us...and by the time they had gotten there, he was gone. He never got charged with it...and we moved here shortly after. He's not in jail now...he never got charged for it. He ended up going to prison for something else...but got back out in very short order. He didn't serve very long."

"He played his good behavior act."

"Here...I want my daughter to meet and marry a good man...and have children...and be happy. I want my son to do the same. He is eleven."

"Except...you know, we hope he doesn't marry a man."

"Yes, I would prefer a woman, but you know...you go with the flow. You don't make it as far as I have without going with the flow."

"I want somebody to take care of my little brother...because he's not exactly the strongest person in the world. He grew up when it was very difficult for the both of us. My mom was pretty much going back to college and all that...so we had to raise him together...and he needs...he needs help along the way. He's very sensitive."

"He's never really been around a man. He's living with my folks right now in Kansas. My dad is a good man. He's a good man. So...my son is with him right now, so that he can learn to be a good man."

"He's like the best man ever...patient. You can hardly ever get him upset. He is so patient...but when you do get him upset...watch out, you're getting it. But, he is so patient. He's god-fearing, fair...kind...and will give you the shirt off his back...no questions asked. He is a good man."

"We live in rural Ellisville. You know where London Mills is? It's perfectly south of London Mills. Mt. Pisgah...it's on the Spoon River Drive. It's near there."

"You know, the Spoon River Drive is fun. It's a shame more people don't know about it."

"There's nothing like this in Phoenix. This would be courting disaster there. There would be robberies...killings...you just couldn't do something like this in Phoenix."

"In Ellisville, a good day in my life is waking up...going to work...coming home...no excitement, no thrills...just everyday life. To me, that is a good day. Every day that God gives me...that is a good day...no stress...or minimal stress...that is a good day."

21   *Mary Ann Shea*

"One time I found a letter in the ladies room at Bergner's…and it said something like, "Janice….here's some money for your toaster. I don't really need anything tonight, but could we make a deal where you can sleep with me all night, at a price I can afford? I wouldn't need sex that night either. I'll take you out that evening also…after I drop the kids off." So then I wondered…what's up with the toaster?"

22   *Ralph Edmunds*

"My name is Ralph Edmunds…81 this month. I'm from…uh…Macon, Missouri originally…that's where I went in the service from…and uh…but I've lived in Silvis, Illinois for 55 years. Uh…I'm retired. I worked at American Airfilter in Moline for 34 and a half years, and retired from there. At American Airfilter, I worked product repair…and uh…a lot of heating and air conditioning stuff…electric heat…all kinds of heating equipment and cooling."

"Well…I…the day I graduated from high school, I got my notice to go to Leavenworth, Kansas for a physical. I went to Leavenworth and passed my physical, and uh…they said uh…you got a week to go home and get your stuff in order…and I said, "Well I don't have much in order 'cuz I haven't done nothin' but go to school." So I went back to Leavenworth and they shipped me out to Colorado, and because I was a Missourian, I happened to…they put me in a mule pack team out there. Yeah, and it was part of the10th Mountain Division…you see them on TV quite a bit…a ski troop."

"Anyway I was in there for long enough to go through six weeks of basic, and then they said…uh, they come out with an order that if you wasn't 5'8" you wasn't big enough to pack a mule. So I went into the…uh, they transferred me into the Medical Corps in the 10th Mountain Division. So I went through some medical training and…uh, then I uh become attached to Company C of the 10th Mountain Division…ski troops in Camp Carson, Colorado, where they…where they started, and then…I believe that's where they started. Anyway, we shipped out to Camp Hale, Colorado just outside of Leadville and I was there for about almost a year…uh, learning how to ski…and we was the first ski troops that was there…and they sent to Sweden to get a few…uh…skiers to come over and train people…so they could train us."

"This would've been '43 & '44. I went in, in May of '43…and uh, I uh…Medical Corps was a pretty good job…and uh…we never carried a gun…only on the firing range, just in case something turned around…and uh…I was a pretty good shot and I…I got a marksman badge, and I hadn't had any military training with a gun. I was an old Missouri squirrel hunter, and I could shoot."

"And uh…so we went out a lot of nights…and we'd camp out or go out and stay for a week…and up in the mountains with forty inches of snow and forty below zero sleepin' out in a tent. But you didn't get cold 'cuz you had the equipment to do it. The only time I ever got cold is when me and my partner decided to…uh, not to put down pine branches…and uh…the next morning we woke up shivering in a foot deep print in the snow. It had snowed another foot…and uh…so we didn't…we didn't do that anymore. We always…uh…put down pine branches on the snow and pitched a tent on it. But they had…uh "down" sleeping bags and you couldn't…uh you just couldn't hardly get cold in them."

"And uh…so after all the training…uh…we all learned to ski and they had a place called Cooper Hill just outside of Leadville, and if you come down the hill and you didn't…didn't try to hold back your speed, you'd be hitting ninety at the bottom. I never got on that hill because they give us a free last day of skiing to get some of our buddies and go out and ski. So we went up in the woods and up through the side of a mountain and up behind. I come down through there…and I was like Sonny Bono. Here was a tree in front of me…so I…the only way I could stop was hit that tree. I went down…and uh, my body rolled, but that seven foot ski twisted my knee up…and uh, in them days you didn't know if tomorrow they might put you on a train…and then you're gone. So, I was in the hospital for a couple weeks with my knee."

"I was on crutches when the order come to ship out, and they didn't…they didn't let me go…and that kinda broke my heart, 'cuz I worked with these guys for, ummm…all the time, you know…and uh…I didn't get to go. So, they transferred me into a…ummm…into the medics. They transferred me into hospital training and I went through eighteen months of training for to be a surgical technician…and uh…I worked in the operating room a lot. By the time all the training was over and we had our MASH type hospital ready to go and…down in South Carolina we was there ready to ship out…the war ended, and we didn't go. So uh, I was turned out…in '46, I guess."

"In the meantime I got married down there…in uh, Lexington, South Carolina by uh…by uh…Justice of the Peace, Sarah Boozer. But she wasn't drunk that day. She wasn't really a boozer at all. Anyway…ummm, just last month we celebrated our 60th wedding anniversary…so uh…it's been a good life…but I had quite a history in the service…and uh, I had a lot of fun."

"About sixty miles west of Hannibal...me and my brother we still work together. We put in a furnace and air conditioning once in awhile. In fact next week we got a big furnace and air conditioning job...uh, but anyway...after I retired from American Airfilter...about two months after I retired...uh, they declared bankruptcy and we lost our company pension...and with the Federal Guarantee Board they cut $200 and what...about $260 off the original pension and uh...so that made a difference in surviving and having something to enjoy in life. But I like to work and I still do some work. I do lights and electrical...lights and heating and air conditioning...but, you know...I just like to do something. I like to keep busy."

23 *Mike Hammes*

"I was born in Peoria but grew up in Iowa...lived in San Francisco, Phoenix...went to college in Arkansas and Missouri, Iowa, and California. My mother had abandoned me, and that's when I went to Iowa. That's when they took me over there. That was 59 years ago."

"I have college degrees to teach chemistry, physics, and biology...anatomy, kinesiology, physiology...and dance. I never used any of them because I love this so much. I worked my way through college shooting pool and playing poker. I also got a couple of track scholarships...I was a good athlete."

"I was always attracted to old stuff that was well made. I love the unlimited amount of challenges. The diversity of it has challenged me. I've been doing this for 38 years. I work seven days a week...fifteen, eighteen hours a day. I eat, sleep, and drink it. I will never, ever retire...because this is what I enjoy doing. This is...this is what I love."

"I have a painting by Paul Gauguin...and another by Metcalf...who was the leader of the "New York Ten" impressionists. His major painting hangs in the Chicago Art Institute, called, "Winter Thaw". I have an artist study, done in 1908 of the big painting...which I am going to try and trade to the Chicago Art Museum."

"I used to run auctions, 25 years ago...I am an auctioneer as well. I've sold in my lifetime, over $200,000,000 in antiques. I made it big...I've lost money...made millions, lost millions...several times over...and back up again. My middle name should be "yo-yo". I am a high-risk taker...there is no deal that I will not try and get. I love great deals...I love risk-taking. I just...can't stop."

"I still do all my buying here...in America. When I started out, most of my deals were in New York, Connecticut, Massachusetts...the high-end stuff. Now...most of my buying is here in the Midwest. The market here is...cheaper than anywhere else in the country right now. That's why I'm here."

"I came up through orphanages...and most people get crushed by it. I didn't. I just love life...livin' hard and fast...right every right, drink every drink...and don't step away from nothin'."

24   *Rhonda Foster*

"I'm Rhonda Foster...Rhonda with an "h", and the middle initial is "J". I was born in 1960...at least that is what I put on every Internet form. I have written my entire life, from the time I was little kid...carried around journals...since I was eight years old. Grownups would say, "You...you want to be a writer?" I would say, "No...I *am* a writer.""

"I graduated college in Ohio with a degree in English, and I was a very good writer, and won some contests. I won every prize at the college level...but couldn't get a job writing. At the time, Stephen King was my hero, and as I said back then...we don't all make the money Stephen King does...especially the first year. So, reality intruded, and I sent off an application to one law school...Ohio State, because it was the cheapest. It was only ten dollars. Harvard and the others were like, fifty bucks. So, I got accepted...I got a partial scholarship...and I went to law school for three years. That was fun, you know...had friends...didn't care about my grades...like, "B" averages. Graduated from law school...came out here to Illinois."

"The only job I could get was in the Public Defender's Office...which was not something my heart had always longed to do, but I worked there for ten years. I represented juveniles...abused, neglected...delinquent kids. For me it was very emotionally draining...not satisfying...exhausting. At the end of my day, there was nothing left. I was a vegetable on the couch, staring at the TV. There was no writing."

"Finally, I got desperate to get out of that rut after ten years...and they advertised for screeners at TSA, at the airport. I went and signed up, and did that. It was interesting...a good way to describe it. They were suspicious of me because they couldn't understand why an attorney would close down a law office and go to work at the airport with people with high-school level educations. So, I wasn't really popular there...didn't quite fit in. Eventually, I resigned, and then developed fibromyalgia...spent a year and a half just crippled at home. During that time...began writing again. I kept journals every day. Now that I am recovered, I've gotten published. I'm working for a magazine in New York, and I think I am going to follow my dreams a little more closely in the future, and a little less with the successful lawyer image."

"The magazine is called "Stylus". They...they publish articles and stories about fine writing instruments and fine papers...and since I collect pens, I'm pretty knowledgeable about it, and seemed to have just found my way into that...old fashioned dip pens that you dip in inkwells, old fountain pens, like your parents used. Pens and writing...it seemed like a good collection for a writer, and it's something I have always done."

"Getting my first article published...it didn't seem real. I carried the check around for a month before I finally took it to the bank. I made a color Xerox of it, so I could frame it. It just amazed me...because, through circumstances of luck, the magazine was short-handed, people had left, and so I didn't have to send out queries...I didn't have to work for it...I lucked into it by helping somebody out. I am happy for that, because...it is work...and it makes me happy because there is a huge difference between doing something you love and doing something just for a check."

25   *Dennis Ronk*

"I am 58 years old. I just retired form the City of Canton, where I live. I used to work for the water department, and did a little bit of everything. I mainly…shut people's water off that didn't pay their bills. I read meters…water meters…made water taps for these new homes. I cleaned sewers by hand, before they came out with the new machines."

"I'm still living in Canton. Spent six years in the Marine Corps. I was at Camp Pendleton…in '63…went to Vietnam…then came back to Camp Pendleton. I got out after four years, and then spent two years in reserves…inactive reserves. I'm a Motor-T man…hauled troops and ammo…dead bodies. I was mostly in Chu Lai…that was back in, what was that…back in '65."

"We hit the beach just like a John Wayne movie. The night we landed in Vietnam, it was raining…and it was January 28th, my dad's birthday. We got off the ship, went down the net…the rope net, down into a "mike boat". We took off and got hung up on a coral reef. We was way out in the water yet…and they couldn't get us off the coral reef, so we had to wade into the beach. We had to hold our rifles…we had to hold our rifles above our heads. I fell down a few times and stuck my rifle full of sand. That night we had to dig in…and then the next morning woke up with water about halfway up my body in the foxhole. The next day, we took off walkin'…drying our clothes out…and that night it rained again in my other foxhole."

"During a firefight, I got to watch F-4's come down and napalm a village. We got to go through a village and look for VC…and we found a few. There was a day we was gettin' ammo out of the ammo dump at the end of an air strip. An F-4 Phantom took off, went up in the air. All of a sudden…I looked up and could see the ejection seats come out…and the plane came right back down and exploded. It scared the crap out of everybody. But, the pilot and the RIO got out."

"I once got to go to the PI for five days…and I can only remember a couple. I got hooked on that San Miguel beer. I had a good time there, if you know what I mean."

"I just came back this weekend from a forty year reunion...with the boys I was over there with. I hadn't seen some of 'em since I was seventeen. I went down to the Hyatt Regency Hotel over there in Indianapolis. Eight showed up...and fifteen was supposed to come. Eight showed up, out of...about forty. There's just a lot of 'em we can't find."

"The day I got out of the Marine Corps, it felt like I lost a hundred pounds that day. It was a big relief. I came back to Canton...and I wasn't going to stay. I just came back to see my parents. I had married a Woman Marine...a WM...and we were going to go back to California and live...but that, that didn't happen."

"Since 1972, I've been a bodybuilder...about 33 years. I was just watching TV one day. I saw these weightlifters on TV and thought, "I'd like to do that." I got a set of weights from a buddy of mine...put them in the spare bedroom and started pickin' 'em up and puttin' 'em down. I remember one day I was gettin' my uhhh...I had my garage turned into a room. I had a guy close it in for me, and put all my weights out there. I had my bed shoved all the way against the wall...and had my weights spread out. I started buying all these plates and stuff...and turned the garage into a weight room. I got a lot of stuff out there. I got a lot of machines."

"1972 was a good year for me. I got my job with the city...I got divorced from my wife that year, and started lifting weights. She went back to California where all her...she was from Rock Island originally...but all her brothers and sisters lived in California. So, her and my two kids are out there. I have a 38 year old daughter and a 36 year old son."

"I'm still lifting weights, as you can see...but I'm going to the show here pretty soon with this lady that I ain't never been out with before. I like to go to the show. There really ain't much to do in Canton...so I come into town and go to the show."

26 *Kelly Billington*

"It was opening night for "Picnic" at Spoon River College. It was a play about a young guy coming into town, and a young girl falling in love with him. I played an old lady...pretty funny...and really, really sweet to the neighbors...but horrible to her mother. She had a horrible mother that made her get divorced when she was young. She still wore her wedding ring. She was just the sweet old lady next door that screamed at her mom every time she talked to her."

"That was the first time I was in a play...with that wonderful adrenaline rush...and everybody getting a standing ovation. I will never forget."

27   *Noriko Yasui Fenald*

"I am 36. I am from Japan…called Hyogo Prefecture…near Osaka and Kyoto. First time I came here was 1990, and stayed here two years…went back to Japan, and worked for four years. Even after I came back to Japan, I still wanted to come back to United States to maybe go to more school, so I can work in the future…here in the States. That's why after four years work in Japan, I saved some money…of course my parents helped…but I came back to Florida to go to university there…to learn business. I met my husband there, and got married. He's from Central Illinois…here."

"I work at PNP, and mainly translate…interpret Japanese, because my bosses are Japanese people. I always wanted to do that…be a translator…since I was in junior high. In Japan, we usually start learning English in junior high, and I like learning English…to communicate with different people. I learned and I could then speak with many people. Since I was little, I wanted to do that."

"Here…Christmas is like a family get-together. Over there, I'm not from a Christian family…they are Buddhists. Generally, first…New Years is the biggest celebration. We have three days of celebration. People, relatives…some family comes…and for children, instead of Christmas gift…they get money in envelope. Always, when you are little, your family comes and gives you money. We have a very special meal for those three days, and traditional things. And then, the next biggest is in summertime…actually like right now, called Obon. Again…family comes…has parade, and visits ancestor's grave. Most of time, family leaves something."

"Biggest difference in Japan and United States is land. Japan is smaller country…everywhere is crowded…people are busy, people are hurried, people are scheduled…you carry a watch. Here…I don't carry a watch. I leave for work before 8 o'clock…maybe 7:40. Of course I look at watch at home…but there is not much pressure by time. So, that is biggest difference…country is smaller…space is smaller. Here, there is more room, so I think you can relax better."

"I am glad that I found the job that I like, and I always wanted to be a translator…using my abilities. I utilize that a lot now. But, also…what makes me happy is…my kitchen…remodeled…total remodel. We've been living in this small Cape Cod house for six years or so. The kitchen was okay, but we been thinking to remodel for about two years…and finally we did it last winter. Kitchen looks like, uh…I like the contemporary look, so it's not country kitchen…it's not traditional kitchen…it's more contemporary looking."

"I cook almost every night for dinner. I cook Japanese, and my husband doesn't really mind. He sometimes…he jokes a lot and says, "Oh…again…rice.""

28   *Gene Muehrig*

"I an originally from Hannibal, Missouri, but since then, I've been all over. I came back to this area seven years ago to…get married. I will be 68 next month."

"In Hannibal, we moved to the farm when I was nine years old. I think we were pretty poor then, but I didn't know it. My father was a…worked for the shoe company there in Hannibal…at one of the three plants. International Shoe Company had three plants in Hannibal. He was making a buck and a quarter an hour, or something like that…and when they closed their doors, he was nearing retirement…so he worked another couple of years as a night watchman. I think he got about sixty bucks a month in retirement after 38 years at International. We moved to the farm, and that was interesting…didn't make any money, but it gave us boys something to do…raise some stock, and things like that."

"Always enjoyed playing baseball…sometimes the farm work didn't get done…but I played junior league…high school ball…and I played on a semi-pro team for awhile…and I even tried out for the Cardinals a couple of times. I was a pitcher. I really loved it, and when I get a chance, I still root for the Cardinals."

"I graduated from high school and went to the junior college there in Hannibal. I ran out of money and worked for the railroad for a year…plus two summers…before I went to the University of Missouri, and got a degree in engineering…industrial engineering. I worked for Dupont in Circleville, Ohio for about a year and a half. Then, to escape the draft, I entered the Air Force. I had to enlist to escape the draft, and then I got into OTS later…about six months later, and became a navigator…flew C-130's, 141's, and C-5's…before they eliminated navigators with all their modern equipment."

"I flew three years with the Hurricane Hunters. The C-130's that penetrate hurricanes, that was our outfit that was doing that. We were flying out of Ramey Air Force base in Puerto Rico…the 53rd WRS. I did that for three years, and that was interesting…interesting work. After Ramey, they sent me back to get my masters, and of all places, sent me to Champaign/Urbana…the University of Illinois. I got a masters in operations research. This was back in the days of McNamara, when he wanted scientific management…and I never did use the degree."

"The worst part of my tour was...Vietnam. After getting my masters, I had not had an overseas tour...or an isolated tour, they called it...so I knew I was going to Vietnam. I went to CCK, Ching Chuan Kang Air Base in Taiwan. From there we took two-week tours in Vietnam...and so I got over 200 days in country. I left a sixteen-month child. I got married before I went to Puerto Rico...had a sixteen-month baby...and I got back once to see them."

"We were...they called us "trash haulers". We would fly in there...fly troops in...fly a lot of body bags out. We flew between the bases in Vietnam and Thailand. That's what I did for fifteen months over there...a little long, being isolated over there by yourself. A typical stint in country...and I had 208 days in country...we would go in for fifteen days at a time, because we had to be gone over two weeks in order for it to count. If we were in for thirteen days, it didn't count toward the Southeast Asia tour...and we were anxious to get six months in, so that we wouldn't be eligible again. So, that was the object of it. We flew every day...no...we had one day off in the two weeks. Otherwise we flew every day...and we would fly twelve to sixteen hour days. The Air Force had a limit of sixteen hours with a single crew. If you had an augmented crew, you could go 24 hours...but you had to have two navigators, and an extra pilot."

"You'd get alerted about three hours before you actually went on a mission...so you're talking fifteen hours, even if you have a twelve hour mission. We would do that every day...day in and day out. When you were in country, it was pretty intense. One time, at night...we were going into DaNang and the pilot asked me if we were over water. I said, "Yeah...we're over water." I thought it was kind of curious. "Yeah, we're over water." Pretty soon, I looked around, and he was descending, Well, what he meant was, "Is it safe to descend?" Well, being sleepy, I said, "Yeah, we're over water." Luckily, I looked at my radar...and there was a mountain coming up...so I hollered at him. We were within about fifteen seconds of...oh, and we were in the soup, in the fog...fifteen seconds of flying into the mountain. That scared me...and I realized it happened because we were all just worn out...tired. I thank the good Lord that he helped me escape that one."

"My first wife...we was married 32 years. She died of a brain tumor. It was kind of ironic. She came home from work one day...and she worked out...and said, "My foot would slip on the stair climber...and there wasn't a good reason for it." So, at my insistence, she went to the doctor, and he couldn't find anything wrong. They then sent her out for additional tests at the hospital, and gave her a brain scan. They found the worst kind of a brain tumor…not encapsulated…and they just don't give you much hope. Radiation didn't help…and she was…she was sick…one year to the day…and then…passed away. Her name was Judy."

"I came here in 1998…got remarried July the 4th of 1998. So, I moved here and haven't been sorry. I came from Travis Air Force Base in California. I like the weather better there…don't like the winters here. My wife works for the Social Security Office…and I'm looking for a way so she can quit…she's younger than I am…and I haven't got her financial future all secure yet. So, I'm working on that."

"I accept responsibility…the people that I am responsible for will be taken care of. So many people these days don't accept responsibility…declaring bankruptcy…and don't have any trouble stepping on toes if it will further their career…and I just don't agree with any of that. That's not what I am. I have a responsibility to get people where they need to go."

29   *Richard Pryor Jr.*

"I was born in 1962…I believe it was Fourth Street, the old Fourth Street. It's all different right now. It's not the same as it was in prior years."

"I tried to be a comedian, but it didn't work out. I was constantly compared with my father…where, people wanted to see that, that same type of humor…the exact same thing…and I couldn't give that to them. My comedy was totally different. Even other comedians wanted to see that. They wanted to see "Richard Pryor Onstage", and I was totally different. I couldn't stand the pressure of livin' up to that. You can't live up to that. So, I thought, "I'm not gonna do this any more.""

"My comedy was cleaner. You didn't have to worry about your kids leavin' the room. I did things from movies, and talked about my family. I didn't…I didn't have the life he came up with…as far as the brothels and all that stuff. It was pretty clean, compared with what came out of his mouth. Totally different."

"I'm living in Altoona right now. I used to work for Qwest…that's how I ended up here. I used to do customer service…I was an operator. I answered phone calls…when people would call in about their bills or whatever. I moved out of Peoria…I been here four years…so…probably five years ago. I was married, and me and my wife separated. I was working at a company called AFNI. I was working there as a supervisor…and I took a job in quality development in Alabama. So…I transferred down there and I wasn't there very long before I missed everybody. So, I wanted to come back up here to AFNI…and they didn't have no more openings. They said I would have to start back on the phones and stuff. I figured…I'm not gonna do that. I got on the web to find a place close to Peoria…and Qwest came up. I went to Des Moines and did my interview thing…and two weeks later, I was hired."

"I now live in a suburb called Altoona…which is really nice. I love the people. I went into a bar and started doing karaoke…and I ended up running the karaoke and then started bartending part-time, while I was with the phone company. I been working there ever since. They're my friends…they take care of me…all the good stuff. That's why I like it here so much."

"I've mainly done customer service work, and then I've done...I've worked in the restaurant business...I used to be a waiter. I worked at trying to be a stand-up comic. I did production work on movies...I did "The Color Purple"...and some of my dad's films. I've done from one spectrum to another...some commercials, one spectrum to another.
I used to be a minister. I was married, and I have a son. Before that I did all the stuff that the tabloids talked about...which I'm not proud of, but it was part of my life."

"I didn't really like high school that much...I had hard times in high school. High school was so...not really competitive...but it was really..."this is what I have"...you know? A lot of the kids...I went to Richwood's, and a lot of the kids at Richwood's, where I had my most trouble, and it was kind of a tough thing, a lot of the kids were either bussed in or they were like...real wealthy. So...I didn't really fit in because the ones that were wealthy...they were jealous of me because of who my dad was...and the other ones didn't like me because of...who my dad was. I felt like a kid lost in the middle, with nowhere to go."

"My mom, Patricia Price...she died two years ago. I still miss her. My mother was awesome. She always done jobs that were...not really beneath her, but...being married to Richard Pryor and then...and then, you're doing house care work, and home healthcare work...which she loved doing...loved taking care of people....but having to do that...it just didn't phase her at all."

"When I was coming up, my child support when I was real little was $300 a month. When my dad started making money, she would not go back to court to increase it. She said, "It's not a problem. I don't have to do that." So, the whole time, until I was eighteen...my child support was $300 a month. She could have went to court and had it increased...but that wasn't her. She was a "Get out and work and take care of yourself." That's the kind of person she was. She always thought about herself...last."

"I had to have been...and Rain is six or seven years younger than me...I would say it was the middle to late 60's when they were divorced. If you go on the Internet, it says they were married from 1961 to 1962...which is inaccurate. They were married for seven years, but not together the whole time. His thing was, "I'm going to go out and find my dream, and I'll be back in a couple weeks." She didn't see him for three years. That was his dream when they were younger...he always wanted to be a comedian. Her dream…my mother's dream was to be a mortician."

"I think Whoopi Goldberg was a mortician at one time. I haven't talked with her in a long time. I worked with her on "The Color Purple". I had done production work before…but it was kind of nice being away from my dad's films and doing it on my own. It was actually about the same time we did 'Jo Jo Dancer.'"

"My future is in singing. I sing out here…do weddings and things like that. I sing with a couple bands that come into town. There's a big band that comes in, and I sing with them. I travel around the vicinity and sing in bars. I went out for my dad's funeral and we had a memorial luncheon…and I started singing there. My dad's wife, and different ones there, didn't know I could sing. It shocked them a bit. I'm going back out there for another memorial thing, and I'll sing at that."

"My stepfather…only had one stepfather…his name was Harry Price. He died a few years back. He was pretty much the only father figure I had. I saw my dad in the summers and all that…but Harry was the only man that was actually there for me. I called him Dad. Even to this day, I still call him Dad. But, he still didn't take a lot of time with me as far as…things that you think a dad would do…baseball…and showing you how to do things. I didn't get that from him. I got that from my mother. My mom was my mother and father. She used to joke about it. I remember one year I sent her a Father's Day and a Mother's Day card…you know…'cuz…she did it all. Harry was a disciplinary person, but that was about it. My mother…she did it all."

"I didn't have any real relationship with my dad, Richard…not until I got older. When I got a little older, I would tour with him during the summer, when he did stand-up. I would introduce him on stage. When he did movies, I would go with him on the sets…things like that. He would take all the kids with him to Europe…we did things like that. I never really lived with him 'til I got older. It was after my high-school period…I actually moved out to California and moved in with him."

"Our relationship was kinda weird…not weird, but…I was kinda quiet and shy…and my dad was kinda quiet. Communicating together was…and I think about it now…it was hilarious. We talked to each other and it was like, "What are you saying? I need you to speak up." "What?" "I can't hear you." He talked real quiet and soft spoken…and I was very soft spoken as well. We'd be in the same house and sometimes not speak for several days."

"I did a…years ago in high school…I was at Peoria Heights High School, and I was in a talent show. Back then they had talent shows…I don't know if they still do that. I was dancing with a girl named Monica Patterson. We were doing this dance skit, and my father was actually there. He happened to be in town during that time, and came to the talent show. That was…that was a big day for me. I was a freshman…fourteen or fifteen years old. My dad, actually being in Peoria and sitting in the audience at my talent show…that was wonderful. It all ended up being in a magazine…Jet Magazine."

"There was also a show back then…it was called "The Midnight Special" with Wolfman Jack. I was on that show with my father. Those were good…good memories. I think about those times because…I didn't really have a lot of time with Dad, except when I got older. But, when I think about my younger years…I think about that. I also think about…and this is gonna sound morbid…but another great thing was…being with my mother when she passed. I mean, it's not nothin' I'm happy about. I was just happy I was there."

"My son Randis is in New York City right now. He lived here with me for a year when he was in 7th grade. He lived with me for a year…but he's a freshman now. He lives in New York City with his mother. I try to spend time with him when I can…and we talk all the time…almost every day."

30   *Steve Kiesewetter*

"I sell insurance. We've had some tornadoes here in Farmington. I saw the roof roll off the top of that building over there...June 30th, 1998. The fun part for me...there's this State Farm guy across the street...he's our competition. It wasn't this particular State Farm guy...another guy...but, the wind blew his sign off and we saw it shooting down the blacktop...clear down the street."

31   *Adam Kessler*

"I'm thirty…thirty years old. When I was seventeen, it seemed like a really cool idea to join the Marine Corps. I knew I wasn't ready for college. I was too stupid to take it seriously. I was smart enough, just not serious enough for school. I watched too many war movies, and thought it sounded like fun and adventure. It's not. You end up spending four years mopping floors, and picking up debris out of parking lots."

"But, the summer of 1995, we were on the U.S.S. Kiersarge…floating in the Southern Med. There was…you know, all that stuff was going on in Bosnia…former Yugoslavia. An Air Force pilot, Scott O'Grady…he was flying an F-16 or something. He got shot down, and was there on the ground for three days before he finally made radio communications. We were the closest ship in the vicinity with people that could go in and get him."

"They got a group of guys together…hopped on some helicopters, and flew to some clearing in the woods where he said he was going to be. These guys came down and…well, first of all…like, everybody and their brother wanted to get on the helicopter. It was like…I was in during peacetime…so it was like…the only action any of these guys were ever going to see. So, we had the battalion sergeant major, the battalion commander…the battalion XO…I mean everybody hopped on this helicopter to go get this guy. They wanted to do something…go get medals, or just say that they were there."

"On the way in, they started taking small arms fire. The rounds were coming through the skin of the ship…the helicopter. I wasn't there, so I heard of all this afterwards…but, this one kid was sitting there…and this round came up through the skin of the aircraft…went through his canteen…kind of rattled around inside, and the projectile fell onto the deck. The battalion sergeant major reaches over and picks it up, gives it to the kid and says, "You're one lucky son-of-a-bitch."

"So, they go in, they bring down the helicopter…well, also…from what I understand, they also took some SAM fire too. I don't know how in the hell a helicopter evades missiles…but, I guess they did. So, anyway, they come down into a clearing. O'Grady had said he was going to come out at their 3 o'clock position…and it was a hot landing zone. There were Bosnians chasing the dude and shooting at their helo. But, instead of coming out at their 3 o'clock…he comes out at their 9 o'clock. They turn around…and the guys that I talked to afterwards said they nearly turned around and shot on the guy because he was coming up from behind them and wasn't supposed to be there. So…he nearly got his ass waxed by some of our guys going in to pick him up. They finally got him on the helicopter and brought him back to the ship."

"At the time, being a lance corporal, I had to pull extra duty on the ship…and instead of going to work on the mess decks…I lucked out and got laundry room duty. I worked a twelve-hour shift from six at night to six in the morning. Now, this happened at like…two or three in the morning. But, they get him back on the ship, and the Captain announces on the 1-MC that they had picked him up and he was safely aboard."

"Not more than an hour later…down comes this load of laundry…and it's his stuff. They've got him changed out of his clothes, and they sent his laundry down to us. Now, on the laundry deck, you've got these humongous washers and dryers. People don't get to wash their clothes individually. Everything goes into one great big bag for the entire platoon, and it gets tossed into the big washer. But…the captain has his own Maytag washer and dryer…you know, just a regular home-type deal."

"So, they sent it down and said to wash it in the captain's Maytag. So, I did…I got to wash Scott O'Grady's shitty underwear. After three days out there…they were pretty bad. The rest of his clothes were pretty stinky also. That was my military highlight…washing Scott O'Grady's skivvies."

32   ***Elaine Lindsey***

"It's just barely snowing…hardly a whisper. The weather has been fairly mild here this year. If it continues…and I hope it does…I'll have to mark this as one of the easiest winters that I've seen. We're gettin' caught up with the chores…and Dan's taking care of the hogs."

"My office right now is full of corn. I've been on a roll. I just sit here shelling corn, listening to bluegrass music most evenings. I learned more about different style corn cobs these last few weeks than I did my entire previous life. One thing about open-pollinated corn…them cobs aren't all the same. There's all sorts and it's kinda interesting seeing them all, not to mention handling them. I would have to say that this next year's corn crop is going to be a different experience."

"My life is so much better nowadays then before. It's a constant adventure, and it won't end with my death. But, before I die…I need to shovel out my office because, the tax man is just around the corner."

33 *George Manias*

"I am 74. I been in this business…be sixty years. I been shining shoes sixty years this coming December…the 6th. I was born here in Peoria…was born in Proctor Hospital…the old Proctor Hospital…before your time. It was on Second Street up here. You didn't know that, did you?"

"My dad and mom were born in Greece. My dad came here in 1910…and I was born in 1931. I been doing this, like I told you…'bout sixty years. Back when I started…downtown…there was all the stores, all the restaurants, all the theaters…everything downtown. Everybody would just be downtown. You have to eat, you come downtown, you go to the show…you have to come downtown. Now…all the stores, everything…you have to go to shopping centers…so it's different than it used to be, back in the 50's, 60's, and 70's."

"I opened my store in 1946…and I moved four times, 'cuz every time I move someplace, they tear it down. I shined shoes…oh, about thirty years ago, of President Ford. I shined shoes of Reagan, 'bout 1982. I shined congressmen…mayors…man from CIA, George Tenet. He was here…that's his picture right there. He was the CIA guy, you know…the CIA guy that just resigned…'bout a year ago. Everybody come through here. You know this guy…Obama? He was here. This is the chief of police…this is the chief of police used-to-be. You remember Edgar…Governor Edgar? This is my mom and dad right here. There's a lot of history here."

"My dad was in restaurant business before I was born. He came here in 1910 and went to World War I in 1917…1918. He came back to Peoria and opened up a restaurant. Meantime…he went back to Greece to see his mom and dad. That's where he met my mother…he married my mother in 1930 and came back here. I was born here, and my sister was born here. Meantime…his mom and dad got sick in Greece…so, he took me and my sister and my mom back to Greece…1934 I think it was. I was just a baby then…a small guy, you know?"

"So, meantime…his mom pass away…his dad pass away. We get ready to come back…and World War II started. So, we got stuck there. We didn't come back until after the war, because Germany came down and took over Greece. I was there for over eleven years…twelve years. When we came back here in 1945…1946, you know…we have nothing. You know, Germans came down and took everything we

have. We come over here and have no place to stay. So, we stay down at Harrison Homes…four years.
We have nothing…nothing."

"In Greece, I have no shoes for five years…'cuz, we didn't have no money…we didn't have nothing. Germans took over Greece, and you couldn't go nowhere. You have to stay right there at the house. You cannot be out on the street after seven at night. You couldn't be out in the morning…you know, daylight wasn't until eight o'clock. No lights…no nothing…you have to be inside house. If they catch you out there…they kill you. I was right there…I watch them come down. My mom and dad was from Crete, and the Germans came down in parachutes, you know?"

"My dad was telling me…he said, "If you want to make some money, you have to work. You have to work, and save your money." So, that's what I did. I started with one chair…in barber shop, you know? I had a chair in barber shop, shining shoes. In 1950…I bought this up here, you know…not here…it was up on Jefferson Street, but they tore that down. I worked twelve, fourteen, sixteen hours a day. I still work almost that much anymore…you know?"

"My dad passed away in 1965, you know? I lost my mom in 2000…November 3rd…five years ago. My mom was 93…and it's kind of hard, you know…because my mom…she stay with me all that time. She had a stroke about nine years ago, before she pass away. It's hard because…you know…I was real close to my mom. A lot of people…kids, aren't close to their mom and dad. But…I miss her, and it's kind of hard. I was never married. I never have a wife."

"I shine shoes. I don't smoke and drink. I don't go to…too much taverns or anything like that. Tell truth, I don't go out much…mostly I stay home. I eat at home. I don't retire. I keep going as long as my health is good. Today…Martin Luther King's birthday…not much business today. People stay at home and don't go out."

34   *Jack Brogan*

"I was born in Peoria…lived in Chicago, and moved around a lot…Iowa…Pennsylvania, but I always ended up moving back to this area. When I was a kid…I read. I can show you some of those kids books over there that have my name in them. They were my books. I really liked reading Sherlock Holmes…the Sherlock Holmes stories. It was fun figuring out the story…but, it was also where they were set…and imagining London at that time."

"I like Kurt Vonnegut. My unsolicited opinion is…he's turning into…replacing Jack Kerouac as the touchstone for a younger generation to an older generation. I get…almost daily, "Do you have any Kurt Vonnegut?" Yeah…I still do, but I'm constantly searching for more because, young people…it's the first thing they ask for. I'm constantly searching for…any crappy paperback, because I know I'll be able to sell it."

"I had a book store before this one…and there's a joke about a man who owned a used book store who wins the lottery. The paper comes to visit him, and they say, "You've just won this fabulous amount of money. What are you going to do with it all?" He says. "I'll keep selling used books until that's gone too.""

"There isn't a lot of money in this business…as you can tell by the way I'm dressed. I've already decided…the day I die…all books…fifty percent off."

35   *Theresa Shane*

"I'm from Princeville now…but come from New Hampshire. I'm from Chester-field, New Hampshire. It is very beautiful there, and I moved away when I was eighteen. I am 51 now. It's been a long time."

"I was very fond of the apple orchards there, and that's why I am so impressed with the apple orchards here. As a part-time job, I would pick apples. We would go as a family and pick up the dropped apples, and have picnics there. I also loved the mountains and the trees there. We would hike…and hike…and hike. There was Mount Washington and Mount Monadnock…and we would hike and climb the mountains. There were lots of lakes. It was very beautiful. Then, I was married to a military man who was sent to Canton, Illinois. We got a divorce…and I stayed here."

"The Community of St. Johns is a group of sisters…they are nuns and priests and brothers. They have a monastery there in Princeville. They are right in Princeville on Legion Hall Road. For them to survive…they are helped by the diocese, but mostly self-sufficient. They harvest their own honey. They make salsa. They make rosaries…and everything. They have their own gift shop, and I thought this would be a good thing for them to sell…they have a lot of honey…so I suggested we sell honey on the Spoon River Drive. This is the very first time we are doing it."

"We are lay people, and later on two more couples will be coming. We are doing it because today is the feast day of St. Therese…and that's a very special day for the sisters. So, they are staying and celebrating at the convent. St. Therese of France…she is the patron saint of the sisters. The sisters will be out tomorrow and next weekend."

"It began in France. Father Philippe was the founder in 1993. He is still alive. There are two learning schools in France…and there is a priori in Princeville. It's called a novitiate as well. That is where young men from all over the United States go to determine if that is something they want to do. The brothers have their chapel there, and their school right at the intersection. The sisters are a little bit down the road, and they have their own chapel and their…cells, right there. That's where they learn. They just determine if that is the right life for them. If they decide that it is, they start their formation...and when they receive their habits, they are sent to France. That's where they have further studies...usually two years...and then they go throughout the world...all over the world."

"They are just starting to raise funds to build a conference center by the brother's chapel. The conference center just broke ground last month. People can come and start learning and hearing the words of the brothers."

"Myself...I just moved to Princeville...right behind the brothers. It's wonderful for me because I can just ride my bike and go to daily mass. I help cook for the brothers and sew their habits. I am very involved. Being a part of that community has made my life so much better. My life has really changed since I have come to know the brothers and sisters. It is much nicer. I know what is more important now. My life is straight now...and I know what I have to do to go to heaven. I just want to do good. I know that more of the simple, basic things in life is what is important...and I don't worry about materialistic things so much. I am just more peaceful and happy, and I enjoy life more."

"I try to think more about the Lord now. I think our goals should be...more...helping other people, and not be concerned with all the extra stuff that we have accumulated...just being comfortable with simpler things."

36   *Louis Naseem*

"I admire Malcolm X....and Louis Farrakhan. I like people that stir up the shit. In the end, it's good for everybody. I may not agree with people that, you know...have unpopular things to say...but it stirs things up and makes people think. You know Matt Hale? He lived right over there, across the river. I don't agree with anything he said, or anything he stood for...but he stirred the pot."

"Here's one thing...like I said, I don't like anything he preached...but that boy was sent to prison for forty years...and it looks like...it looks to me like, he was railroaded. It points out that there is something wrong with our justice system when they pull something like that. Matt Hale...he may be a racist and...and a...a nut...but, if you read about what happened...justice...in this case...wasn't blind. You fuck with a judge, or if they think you fuck with them...you go to jail...whether you did anything or not."

37   *Robert Jackson*

"My name is Robert Jackson. I've worked in the restaurant industry most of my life. That's what I did in the Army, too...down at Fort Leonard Wood."

"When I was fifteen, I used to bus tables at a restaurant...and then I started working at McDonald's as soon as I turned sixteen...and then shortly after that, I...I quit high school. I think mostly because I felt like an outsider. I was always very careful not to let my manager know that I was a dropout. I felt ashamed...as most of the people that I worked with still went to school...most went to Manual High School. They all seemed, better than me...you know what I mean? They joked around a lot...most of them knew each other...and again, I got to feeling like an outsider there. Being an outsider is kind of the story of my life. I probably feel like an outsider even when I'm alone. It's just the way that I think."

"I went into work one day...a Saturday. I drove my dad's car, a brown Rambler station wagon. It was the kind that still had the pushbuttons instead of a gear-shift. My dad was always working on that car. My dad worked at Keystone...and was always working on different cars that we had. He always bragged about putting a lawnmower piston in an old Renault he bought, "The hell with those high prices at J.C. Whitney. I found a lawn mower piston that fit perfectly. That car has a lawn mower piston in it...and it runs perfect. Don't tell me what part I have to use.""

"So, I went into work, and it was a day that things didn't feel right. I can't say exactly what was different...but I felt like more of an outsider. There was a new manager in training, and I was showing him how to cook burgers. He was a pudgy older guy with one of those thin mustaches that leaves a huge space under the nose...and when I say older, he was just in his 20's. I don't know if he looked at me wrong...I don't know if someone said something to me...all I knew was that I had to get out of there. Things just didn't feel right. I decided to just walk out and not come back. Actually, I still feel that way sometimes...I just want to walk out of a job...a marriage, a situation...and not come back. I don't know why...I just have this self-destructive thing, I guess."

"I went out to the car and took off, still wearing my greasy blue smock and paper hat. I went down University, cut over to Sterling and was pulling up to a stop sign, when this guy who was standing there hitchhiking, asked me for a ride. I was sixteen years old...I didn't know how to refuse, so I said, "Okay." He got in and...and started talking...I don't even remember what he was saying. I couldn't take my eyes off his shoes. His shoes were shiny and white...really, really shiny...really, really white. I had never seen shoes like that before. They almost blinded you. It suddenly hit me...this guy is a homosexual, a queer. I have a queer in my car. Now, I really felt like an outsider. I couldn't focus on anything he was saying...my eyes were on his shoes, and I was just trying to think of a way to get him out of my car."

"My dad once tried to tell me about queers before...he was giving me a haircut, but just couldn't bring himself to be descriptive enough to tell me exactly what they did. I knew they kissed other men, and had sex with them, but I didn't know how. At the time, I didn't really know the mechanics of having sex with a woman. Of course, I knew what was supposed to go where, but I didn't really know what happened after that. I was naïve for a sixteen year old. I just knew that whatever queers did...it wasn't a good thing...and I didn't want anything to do with a queer."

"As Pierson approached Farmington Road, it turned into a steep hill...and at the bottom of the hill was a bar called "Maroon's Hitching Post"...right across the intersection. Now, when I was younger, my dad always joked every time that we came down that hill, that his...brakes failed. He would dramatically pump the brakes and scream, "NO BRAKES! NO BRAKES!" as we got about halfway down the hill. The first few times this happened, my sister and I screamed...but then we got used to it. He would pretend that we were going to crash into the Hitching Post and all die. Every time we would go down that hill, for several years...he would do the same thing. It was funny...funny to him and funny to me and my sister. My mom would always roll her eyes, and my dad would just continue his "NO BRAKES!" production. It became a regular thing."

"I wasn't thinking about that, but while I was thinking about the queer...coming down Pierson hill...I hit my brakes...and I swear, I swear...I had no brakes. I had "NO BRAKES!" I could hear metal grinding, and a slight pulling to one side, but I was not slowing down very much. I heard myself say, "NO BRAKES!"...and I could see the man next to me moving his feet. There was a flurry of activity with his shiny shoes...but I was focused on what I had to do next. I pumped the brakes several times, and I felt it slow me down a little, but the stop sign was fast approaching…as was Maroon's Hitching Post, and all the traffic on Farmington Road."

"I swerved into the stop sign to slow down the car…heard a clunk, saw the sign roll off the hood…and jerked the wheel to the right as hard as it would go, hoping that no traffic was coming. Luckily, there were no cars coming, and I swerved into the right lane. I still couldn't stop…and I was going pretty fast…so I swerved the car into a traffic sign of some sort and heard another clunk. Now, this was at a time when Bill Butler's Trailer Court was right there by the Hitching Post…and I steered the car towards his lot…went over a small embankment, hit another traffic sign and stopped…hard. Later when my dad came to get me, he said that the car had a broken axle…that it couldn't be fixed."

"I was still wearing my paper McDonald's hat, and shaking, when the man sitting next to me said, "Whoa…Whoa…Whoa"…and quickly jumped out of the car. I could see the whites of his shoes as he jumped out. I heard him say, "Are you okay?" I said that I was. He then walked across the street to…what is now Jimmy's Bar…I don't remember what it was then…and I never saw that man again. I'll never forget those shoes he had."

"Bill Butler happened to be in his lot…and on Bill Butler's commercials, his catch phrase was "Bill Butler, The Man with the Cigar". Bill was in the lot with a customer and saw my car go through the signs and then stop. He was with another guy…and he was smoking a cigar…Bill was…and he walked over to my car. He asked me if I was okay, and offered to let me use his phone. I walked to his office and called my dad…who was always very understanding, and said he would get Mom's car and come and get me. So, I went back and sat on the embankment by the car to wait."

"Meanwhile…Bill Butler came out of his office, walked across the lot and handed me an autographed picture of Richard Boone. He said he had it left over from when Richard Boone came to promote his business. Richard Boone had been in a TV show called, "Have Gun Will Travel" years before. He was trying to make me feel better, but at the time, I had no idea who Richard Boone was…or why he was giving it to me."

"About twelve years later, right after my son was born, my father died…and after a few days…I went to clean out his locker at Keystone. I don't know what I was expecting to find…but, it was mostly just junk. I found a $35 receipt from the Page Bus Company from when I was in third grade…empty Half & Half cigarette wrappers, and taped to the inside door…was that picture of Richard Boone. It was kind of torn up a little, but I still have it. I still have that picture."

38   *Darren Mobry*

"I was behind this lady at that Sterling Avenue stoplight…on the other side of the mall…you know, where they have that new on-ramp. The light turns green, and she's still doing something to her eyebrows in the mirror. She doesn't have a friggin clue that she's holding up traffic. I honk a couple of times and she's still screwing with her face. I wish I could tell all women to leave their eyebrows alone. Do they have any idea how much men care about eyebrows? Do they have two of them? Okay…that's how much we care."

39   *Greg Williams*

"Name is Greg…Greg Williams…I'm 55. I went to Spalding when there was a Spalding Institute downtown. I was in the school band…the house band you might say. It was a four piece rock band at the time. They were doing some popular stuff…radio stuff, and they were called "The Shamrocks". The thing that is different…I think most people my age, almost everybody would tell you, the Beatles on Ed Sullivan, inspired them. They saw them and their whole lives changed…they had to get a guitar the next day. And although I did see the Beatles on Ed Sullivan, it was long before that, maybe seventh grade, I saw a band play in my grade school gym, St. Bernard's…and that changed me forever…just the sound of the band. The sound of the bass guitar…the two guitars playing together…it sounded like something that I would like to be part of. I didn't even care if I got paid. That's how I got started."

"I've been playing right here at Jonah's for about three and a half years. I did the cliché…"go to the west coast and try to be a star" thing, in the middle 70's. I was about five, six years too late. The hippie movement in the late 60's…not that I thought I would take a band out there and get signed in the midst of all that…but that is what everybody was thinking of in those days…you know, that you get your little band together and go on out to the coast, because this area didn't have the large record companies. Those days the thinking was that you had to get signed to be a success, which has changed, of course. So, I tried that…failed miserably…went out there with a three piece band…friends I had played with for years."

"Had a buddy who came back every year and would say, "You guys have gotta come out." We finally called his bluff, and he said he would put us up, get us the equipment we would need…and in retrospect now, it was ridiculous. He said he had about fifty clubs we could play. We were tired of playing in our little tiny holes in the Midwest, and so we went out there, and by the time we did, this guy had blown through all of his inheritance…and it was a nightmare. We lasted about two weeks…we had no money because we expected to play right away. We were naïve. We thought we could fool these California people into thinking we were something different. We didn't. I actually had fun out there though…it was a buzz. It's just that we weren't quite ready."

"It's a good feeling to hear people say, "I dig your stuff." I have a lot of original songs I can play, and on some nights, I do…I make it a point to play every song I have written, and it's cool when you get a reaction. My songs may not get played on the radio, but that's not really the point at this stage of my career. It makes me feel better knowing that I am doing what I promised myself I would do…and that's not play other peoples songs every minute I am onstage."

"I've been playing for 39 years. I've done the tables and chairs tour. Some nights, playing empty rooms has been some of the best musical nights. It's ironic that it can happen…you play your ass off to no one, or maybe a couple of appreciative people."

"Right now, I'm doing this, and teach guitar six days a week. That takes up a lot of my time, and has changed my life for the better. In my younger days, if you miss a Friday night, you then say to yourself, "My God, now how am I gonna pay the utility bill?" I did that for years and years."

"I am finally at a point in my career, where instead of being judged on how closely you sound like such and such, like George Harrison's guitar tone…if you could make your guitar sound like George Harrison's guitar, or sing like John Lennon or Paul McCartney…you were the best band anybody ever heard. That was the litmus test. At this point, it is more important to me, to have someone come up and say…and even though I am doing cover stuff…to say, "I like what you did with that song.", or "I like how you spun that song." That…*that* is the ultimate compliment. And after that, if I can get those same people to listen to my original stuff, and then say, "Well, I dig your original stuff too."…that's about as good as it gets."

40   *Sara Zielke*

"I bake for the Coffee House, and go to school. I'm going to be a pastry chef. Are you going to ask me about why I'm sitting outside in the cold with a cigarette? I'm tired of people asking me that."

"This last Halloween, I went to the Canopy Club in Champaign. I saw the "Yonder Mountain String Band". They're wonderful...and I'm really into bluegrass. Me, and two other friends went all out with the costumes. I was the "autumn wind". I painted my whole body gold. I had all these shawls...and had all these leaves in my hair. It was awesome. I could smoke in the Canopy Club. I was autumn wind with a cigarette."

41   *Latonya McClain*

"She was like, "You wanna come over to my house and have a barbecue?" She don't have a grill...or charcoal...or lighter fluid. Why would you invite somebody over if you ain't got no grill? "Come on over for a barbecue, but I ain't got no grill...can you bring a grill? When you bring your side dish, can you bring a grill? Can you bring some meat, too?""

"I'm Latonya, and we was just talkin' 'bout my niece that can't talk. Well, she can talk, but when she talks, a little spool of dribble...slobber, comes down her mouth. So she starts laughin' and tellin' a story...and the slobber just starts coming out...it's just like a drool of spit that comes down her front. We have to stop and go get her a napkin. But we, just continue to laugh at her. We laugh with her, not at her...no, no, we laugh at her."

"This weekend is the 4th of July and we're havin' a barbecue...you wanna come? Bring a grill. We got the meat...we have everything...but we don't have a grill. We don't have any place to put a grill either. We could go over to the Watson's house, they're gone. Maybe they got a grill."

"We was at church...and so my husband locked the keys in the trunk. He had his keys at home...so we had no keys to get into my house. I have my spare keys to my car in the house...but we couldn't get into the house. So, my sister had to break into my house, so we could get my spare keys, so we could go back to church, so we could get into my trunk...to get into my car. Then, come to find out...my husband has a spare key to my car in his wallet."

"I bought him a new wallet for his birthday. He ended up going through his old wallet, and we found this pouch...with all these keys in it...and I was like, "That's the key to my car." Besides that...men don't have pouches. Why do he have a pouch? Men don't wear pouches. Why do he have a pouch?"

"Luther Vandross passed away today. He was 54 and he died today. I'm very sad. I came here today to get a funnel cake, to ease my sorrow, and they were all out. Then, they were out of Pepsi. First Luther, then no funnel cakes, and then no Pepsi. They said they only got Coke products. It was like, "Waaahhhh, stop the madness.""

"My granny, she's kinda older. She don't be thinkin' all the way...so, she was drivin' down the street the other day...drivin' her car. She just left from Coker's and was drivin' her car down the street...and then she couldn't find her keys. She pulled over...and got out the car and looked in the trunk...she looked in the door...she couldn't find her keys. They was in the ignition. It was like, "Where are my keys?" They're in the damn ignition granny."

"Now, I'm not gonna say somebody at the church stole my keys one time...at church...but they did. They made an announcement that if somebody find my keys, she lives at blank blank blank, and has a red Exposition. I'm like, "Just tell the thieves where I live...they got my keys...they know what kind of car I got. Thank you Sammy...now I won't sleep at night."

"All I know is Luther Vandross is dead and I ain't got no funnel cake."

42   *Megan Davis*

"When I was like, nine…my dad took me fishing on our little two-seater boat, really early in the morning…when the sun came up over the lake. It was at Banner Marsh…so there was all these, like…trees. It was in the spring, so they were just starting to get green on them. When the sun came up, you could see it through the trees…these…like, these little…these little half-circles of the sun streaming through the sticks and the green leaves…and it turned the color of the water into the colors of the sky, like a mirror…and there was this…this fan of branches…reflecting itself on the water. There were vibrant colors all around…and me and my dad…we just sat there and watched it."

43   *Wendy Blickenstaff*

"My grandmother's back porch, off of her kitchen...I can describe that kitchen very well...I knew exactly where everything was in that kitchen. At the time...my dad was still an officer in the reserves when they got me. He was headed off for the Korean War. So, my mother had been living with her parents while my dad was in the South Pacific...and that's where we were, down on South Blaine Street. My grandmother's kitchen had these great smells...and I couldn't have been very big, because the cat was taller than I was. There was a high...high chair...and a window...and I suppose it was a high chair that my grandfather had built for their kids. It always sat under that window. Super Snooper, the big hairy cat would sit on there, and my grandma would throw him scraps...treats, as she was cooking."

"I'm 54. I walked through the doors of Woodruff High School when I was four years old. My main goal in life was to be an actress...that's all I ever wanted to do. So, I started taking dance lessons when I was four...and my dance recital was on the old Woodruff stage. The first time I came through these doors, I was in my tap shoes and tutu. I graduated from Woodruff...went away to school, the U of I...putzed around and did my student teaching...and came to the realization that there wasn't a large market for actresses in Central Illinois. I applied for a job in the district, and this is where I was assigned. Now I am a counselor here at Woodruff."

"Toward the end of the 60's...early part of the 70's, this became a very rough place to be...with the assassination of Dr. King, and Bobby Kennedy, there was a lot of upheaval and racial tension. There were a lot of fights and riots...police."

"We just had an incident this January that was...dumbfounding. The child had only been here for one or two days. Nobody really knew the kid. Kids are randomly "wanded" when they come in the door, to check for guns, and we all keep an eye out...but...there was a shooting. Luckily, nobody got hurt."

"Marty Sauccer and I, our birthdays were two days apart...we lived in the same neighborhood and were joined at the hip from second grade. She was in my wedding...I was in her wedding. In fact, when I got married, she was in France studying with Marcel Marceau, and we had to put out an APB to get her back...and we had to wire her some money. We both went to the U of I and majored in theater...Dan Fogelberg was with us...there were four of us that did that. Martha got involved in some goofy stuff...got involved in some Christian religious cult stuff, and she eventually took her own life. Her parents did everything they could think of to deprogram her."

"In the Dan Fogelberg song, "Same Auld Lang Syne"...the girl referred to in the song could have been Marty. It could have very well been her. They were very, very close friends. It really wasn't a huge love affair...but it could very well have been her. She and her husband, Allen, and Allen was an accountant...they lived in Minneapolis...and she came home to visit her parents at Christmas time. It's entirely plausible that it was her."

"Marty and Dan...they were both kind of lonely. Dan was kind of, always the odd man out. He was so artistic...so intelligent...but, this was the pits to him...a necessary evil. He really has no fondness for this place. There weren't good memories for him here."

"It could also have been Susie Shelly...she was Dr. Shelly's daughter. That was a love affair...and they were very, very fond of one another. Her parents don't live here any more, but last I heard, she was back in town. She's divorced and lives here with her daughter...but, Dr. Laura Shelly is still in practice...her sister. Susie and Danny were very close. Very close."

"I remember I ran into Danny at the U of I. I lived at Fourth and Gregory and he lived at MRH...a huge building behind us. There was a...malt shop...I don't know what else to call it, they had hamburgers, and people would go in there to study. I ran into Danny and he told me he was quitting...quitting school. I said, "Why?" He said, "Well, I don't like it. I don't want to do it. I don't need it." It wasn't long after that...that he headed out to California, and got hooked up with Stephen Stills and all those guys."

"I sang in a show in community theater and...ummm...I love 40's music. I got to sing *Big Band* music...and I got to do it kind of *torchy*. Being on that stage and knowing that...as a performer, you open yourself up and pour your guts onto the stage...and knowing that, to sing that song, and get that response...that was the highest I've ever felt. After that, probably the hardest thing for me was coming to the realization that...I am where I am. I'm not going to take Broadway by storm…I'm now too old. Not that my life isn't great, but it was hard to give up that dream."

"I am adopted. I don't know who my birth family is. When you are an adopted child…and I have had great parents, and had a wonderful childhood…but, when you are adopted, there is always a piece of you that is missing. I think I'd like to know if I'm Irish or Scottish, or whatever. Right now, I'm a mutt dog. My husband teases me and says, "And then there's your mother…the mutt dog."

44   *Joshua Seldeck*

"I think I've already convinced myself that I'm dead…even before getting there. I think it's the only way I can prepare for the deployment. I've been searching the web…reading blogs and trying to find out what I might need there…in Iraq. I don't think I really care if this is a good war or not…other people can argue that, like…like my mom. My thought is that…I'll be there in a few weeks…my job is to help train the new Iraqi military, and then come home. I'll be teaching a course called "Iraqi Platoon Leader Course". If I do get killed, I just hope that, like those that went ahead of me…my life made a difference."

"So, my main job right now is trying to figure out what my job will be like over there…and how I can make a difference. One good thing…I'm hearing stories about Iraqi people helping locate IED's. I hear about more and more Iraqi kids marking the spots where the IED's are. I was told it's a good idea to take toys with you…to give to the kids. I've got a bag of plastic soldiers I'm taking with me. I hope they help."

45   *Lane Knouse*

"I am a Lutheran minister, and I am 55. I've been here for about thirteen years. I am originally from Minnesota...north of Minneapolis, about 25 miles. I grew up five miles from a town of fifty people. The town is Soderville, directly north of Minneapolis. Central Avenue becomes Highway 65...and my folks bought a lake home there in 1960, when I was ten."

"I have married a couple hundred people. There was a time when I forgot the wedding vows for a couple I was marrying. It was before the wedding, and I was getting ready...and I had been there for a number of years. I had been in the upper peninsula of Michigan for fourteen years before we came here...but we escaped. I was getting ready, and I was talking with the organist, and I was talking with the gal that does the altar, and I said, "Gee, I feel like I have forgotten something...can you think of something I might have forgotten...I've got the bulletins, I got the candles on the altar...I just feel like I have forgotten something, can you think of anything?" She said, "No, Pastor, we can't think of anything.""

"So, the wedding began, and the bride and groom started coming down towards me, and she takes one step and I look in her eyes, and I thought, "They wrote their own vows...and I don't have them." She took another step and I thought, "They're in the parsonage, in the basement, on my desk." She took another step and I thought, "Okay, it's about fifty yards from the back door of the church to the parsonage. I used to do the hundred yard dash in eleven seconds...and I figure twice that for half the distance at my age...there's a solo coming up right after the opening prayer...I could get over there, get it, come back in about a minute and twenty seconds...and the solo is three and a half minutes. I can do this.""

"They get up to the front and I lean over to the organist and say, "Stretch out the entrance to the solo, because I'm going to run over and get the vows that I forgot." So, I did the prayer, the soloist starts, and I'm smiling and everything...and I'm kind of fading out. The only ones who could see me were the bride and groom as I dashed down the back steps. They didn't say anything at the time, but the video of the wedding has them turning their heads and their jaws dropping. As I disappeared down the steps, they said that all that they could see was my robes flying behind me."

"I get down there, find it right away, and come back...I'm way ahead of schedule. I'm feeling good, coming across the parking lot, and just then...a gust of wind comes up and blows the vows out of my hand. So, now I'm running up on them, trying to stomp on them...running and stomping, running and stomping. We had three windows on that side of the church, and people were looking out, "What...what's the pastor doing out there in the parking lot...he's not dancing, is he? What's going on there?" So, I finally get back and do the rest of the service. I'm out of breath and everybody just thought I was being emotional. After the service, the groom came up to me and said, "Pastor, I had this nightmare that my bride was going to run out on me...but I never thought you would."

"We also had two guys in the parish...the same parish where I did the wedding. Mike Pietro and Martin Wuoremaa. It took me four years to learn how to say his name. Martin is in heaven now...he was quite a character. These guys never came to church before their wives died. Some places have Norwegian Bachelor Farmers...we had Finnish Widower Miners. These guys worked underground...wore no earplugs when they were blasting, so they were pretty hard of hearing. They sat in the back of the church, and weren't really familiar with the service that much, and would ask each other questions as the service went on. It was sort of like having a play-by-play going on in the back of the church while I was trying to do it up in front. Martin, in particular was very colorful. I met him when he started putting berries on our doorstep. I caught him leaving the berries, and I said, "Martin, where did you find all these berries?" He would say, "Nort...nort." He wouldn't get any more specific than that."

"I bought a chalice with a little pouring lip, and got some glasses and thought, "We're going to try this...it will make things more sanitary, and we still have the symbolism of the chalice up front." I told the altar gal that we would need more wine up there, to put a bottle under the altar...but she apparently never got the message. So, I had about seventy people for communion that Sunday. By the time it got to Martin and Mike in the back, they got only about three or four drops each. So, I got up to do the post-communion blessing, and Martin turns to Mike and says real loud, echoing throughout the church, "He really gypped us on wine today, didn't he?"

46   *Lorna Smith*

"I grew up on a dairy farm near Galena. I milked cows…Holsteins…days and
nights. My mother raised geese, and I was part of both. I would get the cows in
for Dad, and gather the geese up at night for Mom. I let them into the hog house,
so that the coons and mink wouldn't come and kill the geese. My mother had
two incubators in the basement. The geese would hatch…she raised Pilgrim
geese…and the ganders were white, and the geese were gray. But, when they
hatched, the ganders were yellow, and the geese were kind of a green color. She
sold them…advertised them in "The Prairie Farmer", and shipped them by rail.
One customer would come in a plane…land in the north field…and we would
deliver the 25 goslings to his plane. People would also come by car and get
them."

"As a carryover, in my fourth grade classroom…we hatched chickens, every year.
We had an incubator and hatched chickens. I think all children need to see that.
All children need to have that experience."

47   *Dan Martino*

"I'm 53. I live here in Peoria, but I'm originally from Roanoke. I moved here to be closer to work. I work in Mossville, at the AC Building…for Caterpillar."

"Carol and I actually met while we were married to someone else. She was a friend of my ex-wife's…they played tennis on at least one occasion. They are also both writers. Years went by, and we had both been divorced. I was playing in a band, and she came to see me with a friend of mine…they were dating. We sort of met up again and I asked her out…and a few years later, we got married."

"Carol and I lived in England for Caterpillar, for two and a half years. I also had responsibility for our Kiel, Germany plant…so I was over there quite a bit. There's a little airline…a low cost airline that flies between a small London airport, to an airport about an hour and a half from Kiel, Germany. It's called Lubek. Ryan Air is the airline…and they say it's Hamburg…it's actually about forty miles from Hamburg, and they call it Hamburg-Lubek. It's a little airport that is very easy to get in and out of. This city…which was pretty much destroyed in the war, has been rebuilt, almost duplicating what it was, you know…a thousand years ago. It's a beautiful little seven-spire city. It's surrounded by a canal, and if you look at it from the air…it's almost a round city with these seven beautiful copper spires. It's just a great little city, and I had been there a couple of times. Finally I told Carol, "I'd really like to take you and show you the city." So we did, a couple of different times."

"I think the second time we went, it was in September…and there was an Oktoberfest. Now, this is not a tourist city. It's just a little German city where hardly anyone speaks English. So there was this Oktoberfest…and I thought, "Great, we'll go to this Oktoberfest." So, we're sitting there in a tent…or was it a tent? Was it a building or a tent? Yes…it was a blue and white tent. We sat right up near the front, off to the left side of the stage, and they were playing…they were a bunch of young guys dressed in German clothing…traditional outfits, and they were playing the tuba and everything. The whole first set was great, and we're thinking, "Oh, it was great…just beautiful.""

"They started the second set with "Wooly Bully" by Sam the Sham and the Pharoahs. Honestly. Nobody danced the whole first set. They just sat there and did the "hoi, hoi, hoi"…and all that stuff. Then after that, they did "Satisfaction". They started playing 60's rock & roll from England and America. They were singing…they were singing in English. You could tell they didn't speak it, just mouthing the words. It was unbelievable."

"So we go to this, what we think is this traditional German Oktoberfest…in a little town in Germany, and we get to hear the Stones…the Beatles…Dave Clark Five…and it was…great. We were so fascinated that people weren't dancing in the first set, but we didn't know that they were waiting for…this."

"I once had some music that I had done, played on the radio. I was 25, and I had done an album of songs that I had written with a bunch of friends of mine. A friend of mine had made an album…and my family said, "Why don't you do that?" I said, "Well, it costs a lot of money." My aunt said, "I'll pay for it." So…she did. I did the album, and there's a little local radio station in Pontiac, Illinois. Somebody said, "You should take your record out there and see if they will play it." So, we went out there…took the record out there and met the disc jockey. He said, "Yeah…I'll play it in about ten minutes." So, we went out and sat in the car…rather than sit in there…and sat there in the car listening to the music I had done. We all sat in the car listening to *my* music. Since music was a big part of my life at that time…it was definitely a major highlight."

"Of course the best thing that ever happened to me was when my wife left. It was also the worst thing that happened to me. It was definitely the best thing, and changed my life in a way that was probably necessary. She actually…I found out later…was somewhat afraid to leave me, because I was in counseling at the time. Then she figured that it would be a good time, for the very same reason…and so she left. I then stayed with that counselor for several months. I got through it by going to counseling and didn't take any drugs. I probably should have done some drugs…but I didn't. It took a long time for me to get through it. I remember the guy telling me, and ironically, he actually married us years later…Carol and I. He was a minister, and actually married us later. He told me, "Somewhere down the road, and you're not going to believe this now…but somewhere down the road…if you saw your wife walking toward you with a group of other women…she would probably not be the one you would be most interested in." And…he was right. It goes away. It takes a long time, but it goes away."

"Look…right over there. There's a guy right over there, from Pontiac…and he lives here now. But, when my wife first left me, she left me for a married man. That's him. She couldn't be with him in public at the time…but I knew. He was in my band at the time…and he would be hanging all over her, all the time…which I thought was a pretty classless thing to do. I hadn't seen him in years, but there he is right over there. What a coincidence…very strange."

48   *Michael Reagan*

"My mother was having a birthday party at the house. My sister and I decided to go to Rodeo Drive…to buy her something. I had picked out a…a tray that had a layout of Marilyn Monroe. I tried to convince my sister that…that is what we should get for Mom, for her birthday. My sister thought that maybe it wasn't a good idea, so we got something else. But, that day, I was in charge of the door. So, while I was opening the door, and people were coming to the party, the door-bell rang. I opened up the door…and I was looking at Marilyn Monroe."

"My wife is a little farm girl from Nebraska…one room school house. She got indoor plumbing when she was like…twelve. Electricity when she was fourteen. I told her, "You know…I didn't really have that problem." I told her I had extra bathrooms at our house in Beverly Hills. I had plenty of lights."

"I grew up the son of Ronald Reagan and Jane Wyman…which should have been the perfect…perfect life. I was adopted into the family…my sister wanted to have a brother…and I found out at a very early age that I was adopted. I took that to school and told kids that I was adopted…that I was chosen. Kids began to tease me, that I was kind of the illegitimate Reagan. Children will do this…start to internalize and think that they have all the answers…but they have none of the answers. So, I started to think that maybe my birth mother gave me away because I wasn't legitimate…so, I better not tell Jane. I started keeping secrets from my mother."

"Being in boarding school at six years of age…it was pretty easy to keep secrets from both parents. Here I was in boarding school in first grade, second grade…and in third grade I finally get out. My mother put me into a day school…but at the same time put me in an after-school program. She was work-ing pretty hard and couldn't be there 24 by 7. The after school program was run by a man who gave me all the things I was missing, from not being with my dad 24 hours a day. He taught me how to throw a baseball…a basketball…he taught me how to be a young man. Every young girl and boy needs affirmation of who they are…and I was looking for that affirmation. I wasn't getting it from my dad…not because he wasn't giving it to me…but because he wasn't in my house…because my parents divorced when I was three."

"When I was with Dad, I was in awe of him...swimming, riding horses, all that stuff. But...Don...taught me how to throw a football...a baseball. He taught me how to be a young jock. I was winning gold and blue ribbons in swimming and all these things...and my dad was a big swimmer. What he didn't know about Don was...he was also a pedophile. So...about a third of the way through my eighth year, he began dropping me off last...at home at night. He began to sexually abuse me. And...by the end of my eighth year, he took me up into the Santa Monica Mountains and had me strip down, and took photographs of me...and back to his apartment a couple of days later. He took me into his apartment where he had a darkroom. He took a piece of paper, and using tongs...he moved the paper from one pan to a second pan to a third pan. In the third pan, what came up was a picture of the Santa Monica Mountains."

"As a boy...it was magic. It was the greatest magic trick I had seen in my life. He asked me, "Would you like to do it too?" I said, "Yeah." So, he put the tongs in my right hand...and moved my hand from the first pan to the second pan to the third pan. What came up from the third pan was a nude photo of me he had taken just a few days earlier. He put his hand on my right shoulder and he said, "Wouldn't your mother like to have a copy of this?" It was at that point...I thought my life was over. I knew my mother couldn't see a copy. I was afraid that if she saw a copy, she would throw me out."

"So...I began this process of trying to get away from my mother...because I thought I was dirty. I thought I had done something terribly wrong, and if my mother or anyone else found out...they would give me away like my birth mother did."

'I didn't know if I was homosexual...how I was perceived...or how I should perceive myself...because I had been touched by a man. Every year that went by, there was more fear...to share with anybody, what I was going through. As Dad got more political, it got scarier for me, because I worried about the photographs coming out. People would see the photographs...and I would be the Achilles heel that would stop my father's growth...to the governorship, and ultimately...the White House."

"During that time, my anger and all that frustration would take place. I had to hide these secrets within me. You know how you have friends from your childhood? I don't really have friends...I didn't think I deserved to have friends...and

I didn't want to have them around, for fear that they would find out...and walk away. My anger got so bad at times. I wouldn't kill people...but...I would destroy things."

"My mother gave me a bike when I was ten...made me earn a bike. She made me get a job when I was ten years old. The chain came off the bike, and I thought the bike hated me too. So, I took a ball peen hammer and destroyed the bike. I put it over my shoulder and walked out to Newport Beach Pier, and threw it in the ocean. I told Mom it was stolen."

"In 1965...I had a '65 Oldsmobile Cutlass Supreme. I was out at the ranch, and the battery went dead. I thought that the battery hated me...everything hated me. I thought Don hated me...and I was going to hell. I was doing everything I could to get there...because I wanted to earn my own way there rather than have someone else push me there. I was doing everything that I could to really truly, earn my way there. When the battery died, I went to the barn and got a sledge-hammer, and it took me thirty minutes to destroy the car. I called my dad and said vandals did it. The insurance took care of it...but, I destroyed that car in thirty minutes. Then, I sat down for thirty minutes and cried my eyes out...and never told anybody."

"My wife and I were baptized in 1985...and she was already a Christian...she got baptized with me. It would still be two years before I could share with her about my molestation. I was fearful that if I told her...she would leave...walk out the door. By that time Ashley was four years old...and I told my dad too. The hardest thing was telling my dad. I was looking at his boots...and...have you seen "The Exorcist"? Linda Blair? Linda Blair looked like I looked. I was describing what this man did to me when I was eight years old...and I'm puking on his boots. I'm thinking he's going to be mad because I'm puking on his boots...and when I'm all done he says, "Well...where is this guy? I'll kick his butt." Nancy says, "I don't think he has a butt anymore, he's 79 years old and lives in Cedar Rapids, Iowa." So...I told my dad in 1987."

"The first time I told my father that I loved him was in 1991. I had never told him in my whole life that I loved him...until then. I blamed him for not telling me that he loved me. God said, "Listen Michael, when was the last time you told him, you loved him?" I realized that I never had. God made me promise that the next time I saw my dad, I would give him a hug and tell him I loved him. Next time I saw him was at my radio show…and I fulfilled my promise. I told him that I loved him…and gave him…this…this hug. That began our relationship for the remainder of his life."

"One story…going into the 1980 campaign, I was in my room there…in Detroit, and I was told that my dad wanted me in his room. I said…and I'm thinking, "Oh hell…what have I done?" I went down there…and my dad is in this room leaning up against the couch…and said, "Come here." So, my dad and I are leaning up against the couch…and what's going on is…him deciding who the vice president is going to be. Gerald Ford is three floors down…and Lynn Nofziger is talking to him. Gerald Ford wants to be the vice president, but his negotiation is…he wants to be a co-president. Dad's going, "That's not gonna happen.""

"Ed Meese walks into the room…and Dad says, "Ed, come here." I'm just taking all this in…and he says to Ed…looks at his watch…by the way, my dad wore his watch this way…a little history for you, because…he rode a horse…holding the reins…and so my dad looks at Ed Meese and says, "Ed, call down and tell Lynn Nofziger that Gerald Ford has three minutes to make a decision or forget it." My dad then just leans against the couch. Nancy walks in through the kitchen…and if looks could kill, Dad would be dead. She says, "You're not really going to take Gerald Ford, are you?" Dad didn't say a word to anyone. Three minutes later, he looks at his watch and says, "Ed, call George Bush…he's my guy." Ed calls and Dad picks up the phone and tells George Bush, "You're my guy." That's the first George knew about it…that's the first anybody knew about it. That's how that decision was made."

"I met George W. Bush at the same time I met George H.W. Bush. Back then…George W's wife was pregnant with the twins…at the inauguration in 1981. H.W. was great with my kids. I'll tell you…if I had to vote for a guy for "Father of the Year"…"Grandfather of the Year"…"Nicest Human Being on the Planet"…George Bush's dad would probably be it. He is that kind of a guy…just a wonderful, wonderful human being."

"My dad…always knew what he wanted to do. He knew who the enemy was, and he knew what he would do if he ever got into a position…how he would treat the enemy. My dad knew that you always had to be tough with the Soviets. He knew how to bring pressure on Mikhail Gorbachev. To tell you how bad, things were, in the Soviet Union…when I got together with Mikhail Gorbachev this past year…he said, "We were so broke, we could not spend and keep up with you all. We were so broke that the ladies in Russia were mad…because they could not get panty-hose. So, I had to go out and get a Czar of Pantyhose, in the Kremlin. That man's job was to go out and make sure women in Russia could find panty-hose."

"Mikhail and I…he and I have become friends. My wife and his daughter just sit back and giggle when we get together. My father…and I think we've lost this somewhat in the America we live in today…my father made friends out of his enemies. I think that's what's missing today. Mikhail Gorbachev and my father…their relationship…truly became a friendship over the years."

49   *Colin Boland*

"I'm from Dublin, in Ireland...originally, but I live in the middle of Ireland now...in a county called...called Westmeath. I live outside a town called Delvin...about a mile and a half. I moved there in December of 2003, and I've basically been touring ever since. It is a small town...has a couple of pubs...three or four shops, and a butcher's. I grew up in Dublin...I suppose a fairly standard, sort of upper middle class background. My father was a doctor...went to good schools...very, very normal and uneventful."

"I am the sound designer and sound operator for "Celtic Woman", now playing here at the Civic Center. This show started in July...we came over on the 13th of July. At the moment, they seem to think we'll be touring until next July...and probably beyond. I will miss my partner and my six dogs."

"This show seems to be a bit of a phenomenon. Basically, about four months ago, it didn't exist, and they made a...a...DVD, from a show in Dublin...and it went out to PBS, and it's been remarkable...a phenomenon. Everywhere we've gone, it's been sold out. It's actually incredible. I personally quite like the show. I love working with very slow types of music, so those sections of the show are...there is a section in the second half, second song is "Harry's Game", then "She Moved Thru The Fair", "Send Me a Song", and "Soft Goodbye". I love that section."

"I never really learned how to do sound. I started off very young in the business as a musician, and then being in recording studios and that...I decided one day, that being a musician, that I was sick and tired of bad sound, and thought, "I can do better than that." So, here I am thirty years later. I've worked with other artists...recently, most recently Sarah Brightman, Jose Carreras, Placido Domingo...people like that...Katherine Jenkins...those type of people...if you like operatic or semi classical. I'm actually doing this show because my brother produced the album. So he asked me if I would come and do this, and here I am. My brother is Andrew. His name is Andrew...Andrew Boland. He recorded "Riverdance", and "Lord of the Dance". A lot of the people in this show are ex-Riverdance people."

"I have it very easy, because...basically, I just do the...operate the sound, and so my day is...I'll come in with the guys about halfway in the morning, I'll have some breakfast, and then I'll usually sort out all of the IT stuff…make sure the Internet is happening, and get the wireless systems running…while all the guys are setting up the stage and the sound equipment and lights, and that sort of thing. I sort of wander around during the day…up until about…3 o'clock, and make sure the system is set right. We do a sound check from about four to five…ummm…go and have dinner…relax for awhile, and do the show. As soon as the show is over, I have five cables I wrap up…and then I go and hang out. It's quite easy, really."

50   *Marc Zoschke*

"I don't have a hometown...I grew up all over the world. But, the closest thing I have to a hometown is Litchfield. I am a professional photographer. I've owned an art gallery for twenty years. I started in photography mainly as an amateur."

"The day that I knew I was a professional was the day I was in Tennessee, hiking in the mountains...and I took this one photograph that I knew...at that moment...and if everything worked out right...it would be a defining photograph. When I got back and everything developed, it was the one of best photographs I ever took. It wasn't my best photograph, but it was the one that defined me as a photographer."

"I had always felt like...less of a photographer than others that I looked up to. But this photograph...this told me that I was really good. A lot of the great photographers in the world would say, "This is really, really good." I could look at it and see that it was exactly what it needed to be...and I knew it when I took the picture, because I could see it in my mind...how it was going to look."

"This particular picture...I'm hiking out in the woods by myself, with nobody else around, and it was really an ethereal moment to go somewhere...look at something...picture it in my mind...and then capture it...exactly the way I thought it would look."

51   *Pat Lingon*

"I'm 55 years old. I work for the water company. We treat the water…take river water, and we have to treat it, chemically, to make drinking water."

"I was born in the south of Peoria. There are just so many memories when I was a kid. Glen Oak Park had this great playground, and we'd ride our bikes there…we just rode our bikes everywhere…everywhere in the city. One of my favorite things in Peoria when I was a kid was the Santa Claus parade. Going downtown every year…with Block & Kuhl, Carson Pirie Scott, and watching the parade…that was really, really something.

"I left in…I was drafted back in 1970, during the Vietnam War. I went in with some friends I had here, from Chillicothe mostly. I went through and ended up in Special Operations, in Vietnam. We worked with the Vietnamese Special Forces in '71 and '72. I was an Airborne Pathfinder, actually."

"I guess I wanted to think I was better…wanted to do something more and the regular Army just wasn't enough. So, I went to Airborne School, Pathfinder School, Language, and Weapons School…quite a number of them actually. We always worked with the Vietnamese…never worked with Americans very much. We mainly did missions. We would take them out and work with them. We did air traffic control for them and bring helicopters in…talk to the pilots, and that type of thing. We basically trained them in many different ways."

"We worked in different areas…Cambodia and Laos, but mainly, the mountains. It was cool up there, but then you get down to a lower elevation and it was hot…high temperatures and humidity. Up in the mountains, it was nothing to see snow."

"One Christmas day, we were back at base camp. We were told that we had a mission to go on…and we knew Bob Hope was coming. We didn't know what the mission was. They took three of us aside and told us to get ready. They told us to get ready…a helicopter was coming in and we were going on a mission. I was disappointed because, you know, I thought…Christmas day…I thought it should be different."

"Well, the mission was to go to Eagle Base Camp where First Airborne was and bring Bob Hope in…bring in his helicopter and secure the area. So, I met him then, after we brought him in and he stepped off the helicopter. We were on the airstrip, and all the other individuals had already gotten their seats and were waiting for him. But, the three of us…we were there with Bob Hope, and he said, "You three come with us and sit on the stage." So, we actually got the best seats in the house."

"An interesting thing is…I have a son over in Iraq, and he's in Special Forces also. He'll be there during Christmas this year, but…no Bob Hope."

52   *Harold Petersen*

"I think that a lot of us are looking to go down a different path. People are hungry for a simpler life. There are so many people just gettin' tired of the rat race. When I was younger…I remember folks gettin' together and all workin' together, helping each other on their farms. I think we need to do that again. It's just a natural thing in a farming community. Talking with other people…it always seems to come out that we all need to come together and help each other like we used to do. If you're a kid…it's just a wonderful way to be brought up. Kids can have fun like they're supposed to. My family loves spendin' time together…as a family working together. We have the greatest time and learn so much during those times."

53   *Joe Hott*

"I started out working in the funeral business in Springfield, and a classic thing that happened at the time in the funeral business…I had been promised a job for life at a funeral home. They basically sent me to mortuary school, and I came back, and the owner's son-in-law said that he wanted to go to mortuary school…so that meant I no longer had a job. The next job available for someone with no more experience as I had, was in Peoria. The funeral home in Peoria used to take care of this funeral home in Princeville, when they would go on vacation…so I became acquainted out here. So when these people decided to sell, I stepped up and asked if I could buy the funeral home."

"I started out majoring in elementary education…ummm…with a minor in special ed. In two years of college, I was working for that funeral home in Springfield, and basically, teaching jobs were not available in the early 70's. There was a glut of teachers, and working for the funeral home…it just kind of evolved. I started doing more and more for the funeral home. I ended up going to mortuary school and getting my funeral director's license."

"I've got a 1972 Volkswagen Bug…which is interesting, as you don't see too many of those any more. This is the vehicle that I learned how to drive stick shift on. This belonged to my great uncle who died a number of years ago. When he died, my cousins got the car, which was in mint condition…always garaged and whatnot. Then a couple of years ago my cousin said, "Remember Uncle Tom's old bug?" "Well, yeah…whatever happened to that?" "Well, if you want it, here is the title." They said, "You can't sell it…its got to stay in the family." So, I have that…and it's brought back a lot of memories learning to drive…Uncle Tom smoking his pipe and telling me how to shift, "You shouldn't touch the brake until you've shifted. Let the transmission slow you down. Unlike a V-6 or a V-8, it's a Volkswagen…an air-cooled engine, and you need to run it as high of RPM as possible." Of course that's pretty lousy on gas mileage. So anyway, I been kind of tinkering with that thing…and that's bringing back a lot of memories."

"When my wife and I first dated, my dad had a Volkswagen…not the same one. In the course of our first date…with the woman who I am now married to…I found out a Volkswagen really does float, until you open the doors…then they sink like a rock. We were out on our first date…I don't remember where we had been, but there had been some flooding north of Springfield, around the airport. I had some friends that lived in the area, so we went driving out. There was a creek that was flooded over…and I said, "Don't you worry, I know exactly where the bridge is." I stepped on the gas and found that the bridge was no longer there…it had been washed out. So, as we bobbed in the water, we were fine until I decided that we had better get out. I opened the door, and that's when it sunk. After the tow truck driver got it out, and picked it up from the front…the water drained out…and within five minutes the engine was running. I drove it home."

"Buying the funeral home and knowing that I was no longer accountable to anyone else was a great day…February 1st, 1994. I walked out of that bank, and it was like I had a hundred pounds taken off my shoulders. It was a really good feeling knowing that I no longer had to work for someone who I didn't respect, or someone who I felt was not treating families as they should be treated. I could now do things my way. I am finally on my own. It was an established business, and I had already been here for two years, and some people already thought that I owned it. It was a pretty smooth transition. I'm 49 now, so I was 38 then…and not a kid."

"This is something I'm never going to get rich doing. My wife is a schoolteacher, and we bring home almost the same salary. I think people are surprised at that. It's a good living, and I'm very comfortable…like what I'm doing…and I am my own boss. I call my own shots. I am not in this for the money. I am in this because I like what I do."

"I get a real charge from people in town, because I am also an EMT…in the ambulance. I get a lot of ribbing that I'm trying to…ummm…drum up business…what's the word? It's escaping me at the moment. But, it makes me feel good…the number of times I have walked into a house with the fire department, with my bag. I kneel down next to somebody and they say, "Oh good…it's Joe. We know Joe. Joe will take care of me." And…that makes you feel good. It's all volunteer. So, I kind of work both sides of the fence…the living and the dead. I think the toughest thing for me is to go out on one of those calls, and then getting a call a couple hours later to come get the body. That's…that's…gotta be…I've almost baled a couple of times on the ambulance…because it's gotten to a point where I almost can't take it any more. But, there are just a few of us in town during the day as EMTs to respond…so I stick with it."

"I had a young man, just a couple of years ago…and I'm getting choked up…he was supposed to come and work for me. He was an embalmer who had been to mortuary school. He was to come to work for me in two weeks, and he found he just couldn't take life any more. He ran his pickup truck into the side of a train right out here. That's been…and of course, they called me. That was tough…that's probably my worst. It still gets me, because he was like a son. My son is not interested in this business, and my daughter isn't interested…but this young man was searching. He had kind of a rough time in his life, and I took him under my wing."

"He was just a neat kid. He was active with the fire department, and the kind of a kid that the younger kids looked up to. He hit a point in life where he just couldn't take it any more. He had demons working him that nobody was aware of. He was talking to someone when he did it, and there was no doubt it was suicide, and not an accident. That was about my darkest day."

54   *Richard Greene*

"Richard Pryor...he died this morning. I went to his website yesterday, and it show a picture of him with one of them...cartoon clouds that says, "I ain't dead yet, motherfucker." He also got a posting...he kept a diary, and the last thing he wrote was, "Nothing kills me...happy fucking birthday to me." That was on his birthday."

"I just sent him an email two weeks ago. He never answered it, but I didn't 'spect him to. I know he been pretty sick...you know what I mean? You remember a few years ago when they had that big deal with the city council? It was about renaming a street after him? He's like, the most famous guy from here."

"They had a big fight about naming a street after him...and it wasn't even a whole street.....it was the end of a street. Bunch of fuckin' white guys fighting over naming a street after him. If it woulda been Elvis, you think they woulda been fighting over that? Hell no. Elvis woulda had a whole town named after him."

"I got his record at home..."That Nigger's Crazy". It's all scratched up, but it still work. I bought it when I was in the Army...and we used to listen to that record in the barracks...and laugh...and it was white guys and black guys in the barracks. We had this one guy, his name was Alfred Thomas. He was one ugly motherfucker, but he could do Richard Pryor almost as good as Richard Pryor...'cept the boy was taller and uglier. One time he hit me on my jaw when we was fuckin' around with the floor polisher, and we didn't get along too good after that...but he could do Richard pretty good...you know what I mean?"

55   *Larry Melaik*

"I come from Eureka...but, I've been here for about fifteen years. I'm a retired dentist. I've been retired about two years now. I had my practice In Eureka for about 22 years...took a sabbatical for about five years...then had a practice here for about seven years. I got tired of doing dentistry in Eureka, so I went back to school for awhile and became a chemical dependency counselor. After awhile, I decided I was a better dentist than a counselor."

"You know, I saw that Johnny Cash movie yesterday. He had a rough way to go...was an addict for years and years. It was really good. I didn't want to go, but my friend did, and I'm glad that I went. I listened to Johnny Cash when he was alive. I wasn't a huge fan, but I listened to him."

"Yes...I was born and raised in Eureka. I go back every once in awhile to play golf with my buddies, but I wouldn't want to live there again. There are too many Christians there. My dad was an Agnostic, and my mom was an Atheist...I mean...really an Atheist. She was brought up in a fundamentalist Methodist church down in Southern Illinois. It really turned her off of religion, and she would become really emotional about it. She would cry when she was talking about it. She didn't really talk to me about it until I was older, but she was just...very angry. Her religious experience was just terrible."

"I didn't hear a lot about my parent's beliefs when I was younger, but I knew they were not believers. They did send me to Sunday school on occasion...just in case I guess. Then, occasionally when I went to college...I went to Murray State College in Kentucky...and I lived with my aunt that taught down there in Kentucky...and she encouraged me to go to church at that point. So, I went then, and I didn't really think a lot about it, except that it didn't seem to make much sense to me. I stayed that way for awhile...as they say, in limbo, as far as religion was concerned."

"To get to my aunt's, I used to ride this train when I was a kid...it was called the "City of New Orleans"...and I would catch it in Champaign and ride it to Fulton, Kentucky. I was this little kid...and the dining car...the dining car was just beautiful. We got on the train and it was so exciting, and we were on there long enough, that we got to go to the dining car. The tables had linen...white linen, and really good silver...it looked good to me anyway. They had china...nice china. That's the most memorable thing about that train to me. I probably made that trip ten times and always liked going to the dining car."

"I was married at an early age, when I was in dental school....and stayed married for thirty years. I got divorced, and was single for five years, and then married a Roman Catholic widow. That, kind of started me on whatever journey I am on now. The easiest way to marry her was to join the Catholic Church...so I did that. The whole time I was doing that, I was asking myself. "What am I doing?" I didn't really believe much of anything anyway, but I started going to church on a regular basis. The more I heard, the more I thought, "I can't...I can't do this any more. I'm being dishonest with myself." So, I quit doing that, and we've been divorced about a year now."

"After this last divorce...I felt really free. My first wife was an alcoholic and could just never get sober...so I left that marriage. Then my second marriage, I just quit pretending that I had a religion at all."

"I hooked up with the Freedom from Religion Foundation and joined American Atheists...although I'm not sure I'm an Atheist. It's hard to put a label on my beliefs. For me, and I don't know where I am exactly...but, I don't believe in a personal god. It doesn't make sense to me. I am Atheist in the respect that I don't believe in a personal god that has any control over my life, or anyone else's life."

"I have become somewhat of an activist lately, because I am really worried about this country. I'm worried about...and I've been a Republican my entire life...the Republican Party is being taken over by the religious right. I read in the paper where they were praying in the city council chambers...here. That really, really pissed me off. I wrote to the mayor...I called the mayor, and didn't get any response at all. So, I contacted that Freedom from Religion Foundation and told them what was going on here. Annie Gaylor, the president said, "I'll write the mayor, and I'll write the Journal Star." So...she did."

"I'll tell you...I saw Ellen Johnson, the President of American Atheists, on FOX, and this was about three weeks ago. I am really very impressed with her. She is very articulate...she comes across very well. So, I also wrote her a letter and told her I appreciated what she is doing. She emailed me back, and apparently she got tons of hate email...but she emailed me back and was very nice."

"I still volunteer at Proctor a couple of half-days a week. That's really…entertainment to me…and another thing is, I'm the youngest guy there. Most of them are World War II veterans…and listening to them is just…just wonderful. I also volunteer with the Heart of Illinois Harvest. Are you familiar with them? We have a little office in Pioneer Park, and we have a couple of trucks we keep at the Metro Center. What we do is…we go out in the truck and stop at grocery stores…Kroger's, Schnuck's, and a number of restaurants…and pick up any food they might have. We then take the food to several food pantries. I suppose there are fifteen different food pantries in the area."

"Thinking back, had I made my religious views known to anyone when I practiced, it would have adversely affected it. There are lots of Apostolics in Eureka…and those that aren't Apostolic…I would guess 90%, are theists. I just would not have ever talked about that. But now…I don't care. I'm being honest with myself. I am finally being honest with myself."

56   *Rhonda Stephens*

"I'm 33. I was born in Albuquerque, New Mexico. I was eight months old when I left…but we went back. My dad was in the military for 21…26 years. When he retired, we moved back to Albuquerque and I graduated from high school there. I went to UNM, and then moved away from there."

"My grandparents lived in Yates City, Illinois, and when my husband got out of the Army, we moved up here because my parents moved here…because my grandparents lived here. So, it's a whole family connection. I'm currently a waitress in Elmwood at J&G café. The Elmwood Brewing Company is there, and they have a Strawberry Festival, and a Fall Festival. Elmwood is nice."

"My son won "all-tournament" for Scholastic Bowl there. He actually did it two years in a row. He was on Scholastic Bowl in Yates City, his name is Joseph…and he's been on Scholastic Bowl since he's been in fifth grade, and went to the Peoria County tournament. There was 255 students…and he was in the top five for answering questions. So, he won a medal for being "all-tournament". The next year, we moved. They closed Yates City School down…so we moved and the kids started going to Spoon River Valley. He was on the Scholastic Bowl then, and went to a tournament in Fulton County. Again, the same number of students participated, and again he won "all-tournament". He got another medal…so that's kind of neat. The boy never brings a book home. His lowest percentage is what…93? In Algebra, what…93%? That's good."

"There are four kids altogether. I hope they all graduate high school and move out of my house. I hope they go on to college and do whatever it is they want to do. I know what my girls…my twins want to do. This one, she's got a little bit longer to go, she's only ten now. She doesn't know what she's doing yet…but that's fine."

"The only things I really do are go to work, and go to ballgames. They all play basketball, baseball, softball…those kinds of things. That's what I do…I do sports. If it's Sunday afternoon, I'm watching football. Sports is my thing."

"My husband, when my youngest daughter was born…ummm…I was pregnant with her, and we were on our way to the hospital…I was going to deliver her. We got to the hospital…my husband…I have to precede this story by telling you that he had been up since 6 o'clock the previous morning. So, it's 4 o'clock in the morning and we're heading in to the hospital. We lived about 45 minutes away, and he was in the Army at the time…and we get into the hospital and I had to…ummm…use the restroom. My husband had made a big breakfast, and I went to the bathroom and came back."

"My husband is sitting on a stool…and he's got a sheet over his lap. I'm thinking, "What in God's name is going on?" So, I get up on the table and say, "Okay, let's get this thing out of here…this is baby number four, and I'm done…let's get it out. I'm ready." So, I looked at my husband. I look at him and go, "What are you doing?" I look at the floor and his pants are folded up, sitting on the floor…on top of his tennis shoes. I said, "What are you doing?" He goes, "Well, the lady that was in here just a minute ago, told me to get undressed from the waist down, and put this sheet over myself." I said, "What!" So, he said…and he repeated the story. I said, "You've got to be kidding me." I go, "Are you sure she didn't say…*me?* Are you sure she wasn't talking about *me?*" Oh my God…he jumped up, threw the sheet off, and pulled his pants on. About that time, here comes the nurse walking in. I'm in tears. I'm laughing so hard…in hysterics. The nurse just looks at me and goes, "Oh my God honey, are you okay?" My husband just looks at her and says, "Yeah, she's fine…she's just laughing at me."

"It's hard to believe the Scholastic Bowl kid came from him."

57   *Gary Perkins*

"Farmington is kind of a hub for a lot of the smaller communities...I'm from down the road...Trivoli. I always like to say...going into Peoria...well, one time I was in Wyoming and I kicked an ant hill over...and I saw all these ants scurrying all over, you know, to do their jobs. That's what it's like for me when I go to Peoria...all these ants scurrying."

"In 1987...about two months before graduating from high school...my daughter here was struck by a car while riding a bicycle. She was in a coma for six weeks, and we didn't know if she was gonna make it or not. She'll be living with us the rest of her life...but she's made a lot of progress. They thought she was gonna be a vegetable...but, you can see, she's not. She's got a bad left side...caused by a right side head injury, but...the biggest thing is her memory...has trouble with long-term memory. That's been the worst thing for me outside of Vietnam."

"In Vietnam, I was just overwhelmed...totally amazed when I got off the plane. I thought, "This looks just like...earth." I was so...I didn't know what to expect. That was the main feeling that came over me, "Man, this looks just like...earth." First thing I did, and this was late at night...first thing they did was take us to the morgue and said, "Half you guys have appointments here." That was a big shock for me."

58-59 Rich Waschek and Katy Rose Gabriel

"My name is Rick Waschek...I'm 43. Katy Rose and I came for the TT races, and the big party beforehand. We came down from Minneapolis, Minnesota. I'm general manager of a trucking company called CW Logistics. They do expedited deliveries, third-party logistics, and general airfreight...a little bit of everything."

"We both race flat track motorcycles...me and Katy Rose...and my two oldest kids. The youngest one wants to. Every chance that he gets, he wants to get on the motorcycle with daddy."

"That's how we met...we fell in love with each other in the pits...a dirt track romance...and we just got married...June 26th."

"Our son was born almost, a little over a year ago...my youngest son, Levi. I've got three...my son Travis, he's seventeen, my daughter Natasha is fifteen...and my youngest son Levi, is thirteen months."

"And...I'm Katy Rose. I'm 29. I've been a waitress for a very long time...up until recently, and now I'm just mooching off of Rick. I waitressed up until I was like, eight and a half months pregnant, and right to the end, I had a belly out to here...and I was hosting."

"This one guy came in yelling at me that he was waiting too long for a table, and started getting up into my face...calling me swear words and stuff...so, I just punched him in the face. Then some guys threw him out and everything. He actually had the nerve to call the next day and complain about the way he was treated there. The managers just kinda laughed it off...I mean I was eight and a half months pregnant, for crying out loud."

"Last year, at the end of the season...I had been out for half the season because I was pregnant for most of it. So, it was my third race, at the end...and I got into a three bike pileup with another friend, and she broke her neck, and had to have a halo on for like...six months, I think. It broke a vertebrae in her neck...the same vertebrae that the superman guy broke. So...it could be fatal, or cause you to be paralyzed from the neck down. I broke my foot in three places...sprained a muscle in my shoulder...had a

huge black eye…plus I had a two and a half month old baby. So, I had a huge cast on it, and had to go all around my house taking care of my baby."

"The house that we lived in…from the street level entry to where the bathroom was and everything, was 29 steps. For the first two and a half weeks, I carried her up the stairs."

"There are probably fourteen friends of ours that are from Minneapolis. We all stay here with a friend of ours…up in Chillicothe…and we have friends that come from all over Illinois. It's a big gathering…a lot of fun. It's kind of ironic, in that we have friends that live in Minnesota, and this is one of the few weekends that we see them. Every time I come down here, it's kinda like a homecoming deal for me because…I had no interest in dirt track motorcycles whatever, until a friend of ours in Chillicothe…we'd go to the road races together…and I thought racing on asphalt, that's where real men race. Anything in the dirt was for little kids, old men, and sissies…that they couldn't handle the speed on the asphalt. He would go on and on about the Peoria TT. I'd basically say, "Shut the hell up. Go get another beer and quit yakking about it." Finally, one weekend, he had a motorcycle he wanted to buy, and I had nothing else going on…and just out of curiosity, I thought, "Okay, I'll come down and check out this race." I think it took me about a lap and a half of practice, and I was instantly hooked. I immediately thought, "This is the coolest thing I have ever seen in my life."

"The race is phenomenal. The skill of these guys is just above anything around. The whole thing just hooked me…and I been coming down for eight years now. I think every year, I bring two new people with me. It's the reason I started dirt track racing. I found out what a wonderful sport it is…and got my kids into it. I don't possess the skills to do what these guys do…but I love it."

"The first dirt track race I did, I crashed. I didn't really do much…sprained my thumb. Two weeks later, I ran over a really good friend of mine, and I was knocked unconscious for about a minute. I broke my collar bone…and my buddy that I ran over, I broke his leg. If you're gonna race motorcycles, you're gonna crash. It's not a matter of *if*…it's a matter of *when*. The best way to minimize the damage is to be aware of that. I haven't suffered any major injuries, but, you know…just broken bones and everything else."

"Usually when you go to the emergency room after a motorcycle accident it's not real stellar, because, they take the attitude that you kinda brought it upon yourself. When Katy Rose went to the emergency room, she was talking about it. They were very kind, very nice, very courteous, and everything else. At the end, the radiologist that was there…I commented to him…I said, "I appreciate the care and the kindness you've extended here. When you get hurt racing a motorcycle, it's usually not like that," The radiologist said, "Yeah, I know exactly what you're talking about." Four years ago, he was riding his street bike, and a car ran a red light and *T-boned* him. He worked at the hospital that he got treated at…and he said they treated him awful. They were yanking him around, and telling him to quit his complaining…that he did this to himself, and he wasn't even at fault. He said, "I know exactly what you're talking about. I feel your pain."

"This race…this weekend…it's kind of like Christmas for us…dirt track Christmas."

60   *Jonathon Wells*

"I was born in Paducah…but I'm from here actually. I was here from the time that I was four until I was eighteen. I don't remember Paducah. I'm 46 today…today. I'm here at Skippy's and Floyd's to get a haircut."

"I want to talk about…judges. Judges need to be screened a little bit more thoroughly, and their judgments scrutinized more because they don't always make rational decisions. They're only human, so you know…they are subject to error. The reason I came to that conclusion is because of one judge in particular."

"I'm currently in the process of some child custody battles, and I been through some domestic violence cases with him. My primary concern is my child custody battle, which concerns my one year old daughter. Her mother is a…to put a long story short…not up to par in raising a child properly. It's been proven…I proved it myself and I had a lawyer prove it. And in the process of proving this, drugs was brought up…drugs and alcohol. And, what struck me the most was a statement that this judge made one time during one of these court proceedings. He said, "What does being a drug addict have to do with good parenting?""

"Hey…hey…wait a minute…what was that? Is that a mouse? He just come in. If he fuck around and bite me, I'm gonna have to change this whole story to "Why I sued Skippy and Floyd." Okay…okay…sorry about that interruption."

"Okay…okay…he made that statement, and I just could not believe that, because, you know…that's just inconceivable. And then this guy…to me…what struck me was…he's in a position to control people's lives. If he's thinkin' that irrationally…I don't know."

"An Order of Protection…they give 'em on anything. The woman I'm talkin' about…she's got them by word of mouth…with bogus lies. I mean…shooting tires…beat me up…false police reports…I been through that "whole nine" with her. But my whole concern, like I said was my one year old child, because I know her history. I know her drug history, her background…I know all that. She's got three other kids that was lost because of her problem…and for this judge to sit there and say that, just…blows my mind. This guy, he has the power to determine people's lives…especially a minor child who has no control or ability to take care of their self. And he placed my child back in her custody."

"Lo and behold…they say the truth is the light…and good things come to those that wait…the DCFS caught her with her drawers down out on a drug binge, and left two kids in the house by their self. So, lo and behold, DCFS came in before anything happened…this time. But, just that statement right there has stuck in my mind more than, I would say…more than my first popsicle. That statement, "What does a drug addict or alcoholic have to do with good parenting?" I don't see how a man of the clo…a man like that, can say that."

"Every judge in Illinois…they side with the woman. We can thank O.J. for that. Nine times out of ten, they're going to be on the woman's side…and you know, with all this battery stuff, women have just flipped the script. It's like…you got women in penitentiaries that's killed their husband…all they gotta do is say, "He was abusing me." They're gettin' paroled….they're gettin' clemency, gettin' forgiven…you know, all that. But…yeah…due to the fact that OJ got away with that…they have intensified the domestic battery laws and all that. But, you know, too much of anything ain't good. You can over-do stuff. I think they went a little bit too far with that."

"This female in question…I dealt with her from both sides. She would call the police on me, and they would come out with billy clubs and handcuffs. Being as how I am aware of the law as far as that stuff goes, I call the law on her…and it's a joke. It's a joke. "Can't you handle a woman?" They look at you like you're a sissy. It's a joke. They don't take you seriously. Whereas…women…any grown adult can do just as much damage as the next one. This same woman in question came to my house with a knife and threatened me and my fiancé, and they didn't even arrest her. They said they would go talk to her."

"She was calling them from another place, and I was in the bed…and they came and arrested me…and I was in bed with a witness that stated that I had not been nowhere. The guy seen me wipe the sleep out of my eyes, but he arrested me anyway because of a phone call she made…word of mouth. So, why is a female's word any more valid than mine? That's justice…that's justice."

"I been in his court, in the last year…a good eight to ten times…eight times for sure. Now, when I reminded him of that statement, he said he didn't make it.

The statement about the drug addict and parenting thing...he said he didn't make it. He also threatened me with, "Shut up, this is my house, and what I say...go." I seen that on several court programs on TV. So do all judges think like that...that they are God? "Whatever I say go, whether I am right or wrong."

"The old cliché, "innocent until proven guilty" is actually the opposite of that...unless you got Johnny Cochran or Perry Mason to prove you innocent. And...both them guys...one's fictitious and one's dead."

61   *Daniel Lane*

"My name is Daniel Lane and I am 33. I'm an engineer. I got into my line of work completely by accident. I wanted to be an engineer since I was as young as I can remember. I wound up doing chemical engineering because I had been convinced by friends…friends of my parents, that aerospace, which was an interest of mine…if you couldn't find a job as an aerospace engineer, the next best thing was working as a taxi driver. But…I liked chemical engineering, so I just started doing that, and worked my way, working through paper mills and consumer products…and wound up working for Specialty Chemicals. I did my undergraduate at Vanderbilt and graduate work at the Institute of Paper Science & Technology at Georgia Tech."

"I grew up all over. I was born in Puerto Rico…from Puerto Rico to Pensacola to Spain to New Jersey. I think one thing about my parents…I never really thought they were as great 'til I got as old as I am now. Everybody seems to do that. The joke is, in the Navy, that the Navy wife is the toughest job in the family, and to this day, I can't…to this day, I really have a lot of respect for my mother being able to raise a family overseas. My father would be at sea for six months at a time. It was hard on my mother."

"My dad, when he was in Vietnam…you've heard of the Pueblo…U.S.S. Pueblo? Well my dad was on the U.S.S Jamestown, the sister ship. After the Pueblo incident, the story he tells…they didn't want another ship taken intact with all of the codebooks and cryptographic equipment, so they equipped the ships with explosives, all along the waterline and the gangplank, and on top of all of the equipment. They didn't have any weapons really…shotguns, but no guns to keep a ship away. So, if they were captured, they were supposed to let the ship come up next to them…and once they started to be boarded, the captain was supposed to push a button and blow out the waterline and the gangplank and kill all the people boarding…and then it was every man for himself."

"The ship would sink instantly. My dad always said it was amusing, because they were in the Gulf of Tonkin, and I think from the deck to the keel was thirty feet, and they had about a twenty foot draft on the boat, and about five feet below that to the bottom. A lot of the time they were in shallow water, and so he was amused at the idea that you would push the button, blow out the waterline, the ship would sink, and then they would lower the lifeboats five feet...jump in and try to get away. They hadn't thought about the water depth when they made the plan."

"I'm only married for one month and four days now. We met in graduate school. I had just come back to work on my doctorate, and she was back working on her masters degree. We worked together for a year and a half, and when we left, realized we wanted to keep seeing each other. So for the last five years, we have been seeing each other...at least four hours apart. I finally married her...we ran off and eloped to Hawaii...and now I live in Mobile and she lives in Minneapolis during the summer, and St. Louis the rest of the year. We're trying to figure that one out...eventually...but only one more year...then we'll be living in the same city. We both respect each other too much to say, "Well, I think you should quit and come be here". So we're trying to figure out how we can be in the same place together, and have a long and fulfilling wonderful relationship, which is the American dream."

"Oddly, I have never been to Minneapolis, but will soon. She is doing an internship with Emerson. They have a box...so the Twins are playing and I'm going to go up there so that I can get the full experience...box seats to see the Twins. I have been everywhere it seems, but not Minneapolis...never Minneapolis. I've never been to Chicago either...but having never been there, and having no explanation why, I have been a Chicago Cubs fan for fifteen years. Maybe that's why I went to Vanderbilt. I like the underdog teams."

62-63 Marie-Jo Schneider and Lois Becker

"We are neighbors...we are looking at books. We went to get the New York Times and to have dinner. We don't live together...we live two doors away...and quite often we spend time together."

"I'm 82. I was born in Paris...and, uh...when my pilot, during the Second World War...pilot-husband brought me here in 1948...I have been here since. He died...we were married all that time, and he died three years ago. When I was back in France...they...they didn't live that long, and my mother died when she was 76...and my father...he was...he was seventy."

"I used to jump horses, that was my specialty...and I fell many, many times...didn't break anything...and won several competitions. I have been to the Louvre many times...many times as a child, as a student, and even as a tourist...when I would visit. I like the Renaissance very much, and also the modern impressionists. I have...I have grown to like Picasso..."Les demoiselles d'Avignon"...yes. I am going back this summer, and I am very excited about that. It has been five years."

"I am Lois Becker and I'm 81. I was married and divorced, and then I came to Peoria...my folks were here, and I took care of them in their elder years. I stayed here and enjoyed it...I lived here once before. My dad was a doctor here—Dr. Dunseth...good Scottish name, and was in general practice 'til he died...about 94...and my mother was ninety when she died. So, I expect to live to a ripe old age."

"My great-grandfather Brown, that was on my grandmother's side, was in the Civil War...and he had...uh...did a couple of diaries...had a couple of pocket diaries, and so when he got home, I read one of them once...and it was interesting...'cept, it was a little hard to read...but then it went to some people...to the family. Then I found out from my cousin that this boy that had the diaries gave them to the Elmwood Historical Society. So, we went over there and looked at them again...so that was fun. Then I gave them a picture of my great-grandfather...so it was interesting. So...we kinda looked around in Elmwood...my niece, my niece and I, and found out a little about our family history. It was very easy to do, and my grandmother had written enough that you could tell it was her talking."

"I was born in Streator, and grew up in Peoria…went to school here, and when I got married, went to other places around the world…around the U.S., and everything. So, and I was just thinking…my grandfather in Kickapoo…I guess he was born in Kickapoo…used to train "break horses". Arthur Dunseth was my grandfather. His father, Arthur's father…that would be my great-grandfather, married Elizabeth Burnside. Elizabeth Burnside was General Burnside's sister. He was a general in the war…the Civil War, and ever since then they have talked about Burnside. That's where they got the idea for sideburns…you know…sideburns."

64   *Omar Terrie*

"I'm 21. I'm a senior and have a double major in political science and speech communications. I'm getting ready to finish my senior year at Bradley University. I have recently taken a liking to fencing, and Bradley offers a fencing class. I haven't taken it in, like...the past year...but I was really active in it the year before. I'm going to try and get back in it...getting active with it in the next semester."

"My family is retired military, and I was born in Alaska. Then, my childhood was spent in Germany. When I was ten or eleven, we came to Illinois. I've been living here in Illinois for the past ten years, near Scott Air Force Base, which is about 25 minutes east of St. Louis."

"My folks are originally from New Orleans, and we went down there to see how my grandma is doing. I go to New Orleans about once a year...and I went there this past August for a vacation. It was a family vacation. I was there before Hurricane Katrina, so it wasn't too bad. New Orleans food is great. I love the beignets. They are a French donut made to be porous...so they are a lot fluffier. You wouldn't think that three of them would fill you up, but you could never eat more than three. They come with powdered sugar on top...and they are so good."

"Over in Germany, because we didn't have much TV over there, I would go out with my friends, bike riding and running. There was a field where we would go to play. We built a fort there, where there was a thicket...and that was really cool. Germany is really cool. I just love the people there. They are extremely friendly. The food is far superior than anything in America. I love it. But, they have been at it a lot longer than we have. I'm really big into history...politics and history...and I think it was because I was introduced to different cultures at such an early stage. I got to see all the castles, and learn the history that went along with them. I loved the countryside, and the food, and the people."

"Coming from a military background, I never had friends that I grew up with, like, from kindergarten and stuff. I've always had to adapt to the situation at hand. I would make friends for one or two years, and then move on. It's fairly easy for me to make new friends."

"With my poly-sci degree, I hope to go into either corporate governmental lobbying…or run for elected office, or possibly work in the government itself. I prefer Washington, D.C. over any other place. I just got done with an internship at the Pentagon over the summer, where I worked at the Public Affairs Office at the Department of Defense…and I handled correspondence for the assistant secretary of defense for Public Affairs. I handled letters, emails, phone calls from the public…and NATO, and things like that."

"I'm a very social person. I love being in a social atmosphere. I go out with my friends, and tonight I'm going out to a bar. After that, I'll go to a movie. I usually go out to clubs or bars on the weekends. Although, if I'm not feeling in a party mood, my friends and I will get together and order some pizza, and watch a movie. I'm a person that…I love being around people. I love being social, and talking to people…getting involved with them. When I'm with people, it's great. It's very seldom that you would see me by myself. If socializing was a hobby, that would be my hobby."

"I recently beat my old computer with a baseball bat. I got a new computer, and it was taking up space in my room, so I took it outside, and my roommates and I beat it up with a baseball bat. It was a fun social event."

65-66　　　*John Wateler and Bill Snyder*

"I'm retired now. I was a security guard at Pabst Blue Ribbon…and I put on aluminum siding."

"I shot a big deer one time…in '77. I do a lot of huntin'…and he does a lot of huntin' too. I killed a lot of coyotes…a lot of coyotes. If we get a good snow, we go out…but if you ain't got a good snow, they're hard to find."

"I work for the City of Elmwood. I do labor for the city…repair water leaks, fix the streets…like that. I've always been around here…and there's good huntin'. I've never really been anywhere else…been here my whole life. I did go to Wyoming…got relations that's got a cabin out there. I been out there a couple times…deer huntin'. It's nice there…bein' up in the mountains…nice."

"This is the first time I seen John not wantin' to talk."

"Well…I got a lot of tales. I was rabbit huntin' one time…and I can tell you this…there was a spring down by the dump, and nobody ever believes me…but I seen a mountain lion. He was a drinkin' from that spring…and my dad told me never to shoot one, because if I shoot one with a shotgun, it wouldn't kill him. So, I took off runnin'. There was a big ditch. I jumped the ditch and jumped the gate…and turned around to see if he was coming or not. Later on, I went back to jump that ditch…and I never could jump that ditch again. That was back in '56…the good old days."

"I had lightning one time, 'bout got me…and nobody ever believed it. I was coming up over a hill, and there were two trees and two picnic tables between them…it was raining like everything…lightning. Just about the time I got almost there…lightning come down through the tree, and there was a cow standin' over there on the other side. The lightnin' hit that cow, and she went "POOF!"…just like that. Dead."

"I walked up to her, and her horns…her teeth…and all four hooves were layin' there…just like she took them all off. It knocked her right out of everything. Nobody…nobody believed it…but I can see it just like it happened yesterday."

67   *Marilyn Chambers*

"I was born Marilyn Anne Briggs…and my name is spelled M-a-r-i-l-y-n. I was born in Providence, Rhode Island, April 22nd, 1952…and I was brought up in Westport, Connecticut. I had a fairly normal childhood…ummm…it's about 9 o'clock in the morning…I usually get up at 5 o'clock, but today is my day off, and so I totally forgot I was going to talk to you…no offense. So…let me get in the mode here."

"Let me see…what can I say? I was a very athletic child. I was on the swimming and diving teams at our local "Y". Then I became an AA and Junior Olympic…ummm…AH and Junior Olympic…what do you call it…it's been so long…AAU Champion in both diving and gymnastics. So, I was athletic. I was a cheerleader. I was on the field hockey team. I was a singer in the chorus…the choir…at church. Basically, I was pretty…all-American. I was up for homecoming queen, but I didn't make it."

"I was thrown off the cheerleading team for wearing no underwear. No…no…that's a joke actually. No…you know when you were in high school, drinking and smoking was cool. They said that if any of the cheerleaders or members of the football team get caught smoking or drinking, you're going to be thrown off. Well, we lived about twenty minutes from New York…and eighteen was the drinking age there. Of course, we all drove to New York state and drank. Somebody ratted on us and like, three quarters of the football team and most of the cheerleaders were thrown off the team."

"I did have…you know how they have in the yearbook section, like "Best Dancer" and "Best Looking"? I didn't get any of that. I got "Best Student Body". Myself and Bill Keschetta…we got "Best Student Body.""

"I graduated from Staples High School in Westport in 1970, and started modeling…pounding the pavement. I was seventeen. My dad was in the advertising business in New York, and totally tried to discourage me because he knew what…I know now. But, I did get with a couple of agencies…one was the Wilhelmina Modeling Agency. Through that, I got the Ivory Snow ad…where I am the mom holding the baby on the Ivory Snow box. That was kind of my big…deal. At about the same time, I got a part in the "Owl and the Pussycat" as

Barney's girl. Barney was Robert Klein…and the movie starred Barbra Streisand and George Siegel….and I was seventeen when I got that…and that's how I got my Screen Actor's Guild card."

"I don't say anything…but, have you ever seen the movie? When George Siegel and Barbra Streisand…when he gets thrown out of his apartment, into the rainy night…and they're yelling and screaming or whatever? He's trying to find a place to stay, and so he goes and knocks on his friend Barney's door…and asks if he can spend the night. He says, "Sure, here's some blankets and a pillow. You can sleep in the living room." So, I'm in bed with him, which was supposed to be a topless scene, but Barbra Streisand…nixed that. Whatever. But then they start screaming and yelling, and we're tossing and turning…and it kind of goes back and forth like that…and finally, we decide to get up and leave. So, you see me standing at the door with my long hair and pea-coat. Very brief…but there I am."

"I was also in some Pepsi and Clairol…and you know, that was in a time when…you know, there was Twiggy in the 60's…and then Cybil Shepherd became, you know…the top model. She was very healthy looking…she wasn't like anorexically thin…she was very healthy…and so, therefore I kinda…you know, my look was good then. You know what I mean? I was very healthy look-ing…very all-American. But…needless to say, the competition was very stiff, and I didn't get a lot of work."

"I moved to New York from high school, which really disappointed my par-ents…they wanted me to go to college…which now I regret. I found out that modeling is a very difficult business…a lot of competition, and the rejection is…heartbreaking."

"In being a porn star…I always pretty much considered myself to be a profes-sional. The movie "Boogie Nights" did not appeal to me at all because it wasn't a good example…to me…of what the porn business was. When I did a film or a scene or whatever…when it was over, I went home and cooked dinner and cleaned my house. It wasn't like it continued into a big orgy or anything…you know what I mean? But, a lot of people in the porn business, that's what they did. They socialized with each other…and that kind of stuff…and I really didn't."

"Back in those days when they first started making X-rated films...it was...ummm...I didn't do that many films. To do one every five years, or three or four years or whatever...it usually took a long time to do it because it was shot on film, and each scene was like, a big deal to change to, because the lighting and all that. It's...it's quite different today. With a digital camera and a Sony...whatever they are...DVD's...it's just a totally different thing."

"I'm still producing. My company is called "Chambers Maid Inc". I just did a film with my partner...it's called "Nantucket Housewives". It's X-rated and going on the...you know...cable...and DVD. It was really amazing how it was to shoot this thing...like, really easy."

"You know Sean, in Dixon, Illinois? He used to be my fan club guy...he handled that for me. Then he decided he was going to do "Insatiable Marilyn"...whatever it is...the website. I gave him permission to sell some of my pictures...so that's my link to Dixon, Illinois...you know, where Ronald Reagan grew up."

"I have a pretty good sense of humor...and dry as it may be...ummm...I think that, because I have another life, and I haven't let my film life consume me...and a lot of people have been consumed by the drugs and alcohol...the marriages and the divorces...and I've been through my own hard times...made a lot of money and lost a lot of money...but, I think that you really have to have a life. My daughter is fourteen...going on fifteen. She is the light of my life. I've gone back to college and have a few degrees...I'm a voracious reader, and I do crossword puzzles...I do about three a day. Also, I've been single for about ten years...and I'm looking."

"I've become very cynical of show business in general, and especially the porn business. There are a lot of people who are total rip-off artists. A lot of distributors that cut your films and make other films from them...and then you don't make anything off of them.
All these sleazy guys are making millions and millions off of people like myself...and there's nothing you can really do about it."

"Behind the Green Door" was my first porn film. It was the very first hardcore pornographic film widely released in the United States. "Deep Throat" wasn't released until later that year. I just said that I wanted ten percent of the gross...and I'm sure I didn't get exactly that...but they paid me a percentage for, you know, many, many years. Then, Jim and Art parted ways because Art is no longer with us. You know the whole thing about the Mitchell brothers?"

"You ever see a movie called "Rated X' with Emilio Estevez and Charlie Sheen? It's about them. The Mitchell brothers who produced "Behind the Green Door"…Jim shot his brother Art and killed him…murdered him. Jim then did some time in San Quentin. There is a book called "Bottom Feeders", which is something you might want to pick up. That caused quite a sensation in San Francisco."

"I remember…I was probably around 23…24 years old…and myself and Chuck Traynor, who was my husband and manager at the time…we were in New York City and staying at the Warwick Hotel. I was doing a show…my song and dance act…at the Riverboat Room at the bottom of the Empire State Building. Anyway, when we arrived in town, at the Warwick Hotel…we were standing in the lobby, and all of our suitcases were there…trunks and what not…ummm…in preparation for our long stay. There were tons of people in the lobby…suitcases all over the place…and all of a sudden, I hear this buzz. People were talking, and I heard this really loud buzzing noise. Everybody cleared away…and there was my suitcase in the middle of the floor…making this really loud noise. The Bell Captain said it was a bomb scare, and he wanted to get everybody out. I said, "No…no…I know…wait a minute…wait a minute." I was so mortified…so embarrassed because, I knew it was my suitcase…and I knew what was in there."

"In front of everybody, I had to open my suitcase…and there was my vibrator that had accidentally gotten turned on…buzzing very loudly. I had to take it out and turn it off…for all to see. It got quite a chuckle from everybody…but I was just mortified at the time. It might have been a bomb scare, but ended up being a vibrator scare."

"I'm a total morning person now. I wake up at five or five-thirty every morning…and I believe that getting up in a good mood is going to set you up for your day. I try to be a positive person…and it doesn't always work…but, I try to set a good example for my daughter, who is now approaching her major teenage years. Being a mom is like…WOW! It's like, one of the most consuming things that I have ever done. It's very nerve racking…and I find myself being just like my mother."

"I am a very caring, altruistic, compassionate person. I really…I really like to fight for the underdog…for people less fortunate than myself. I believe in sharing and giving. I believe that animals are the most precious creatures on this planet, besides our children. People abuse them and discard them like…garbage. I work very hard to protect animals. I go to the pound and find homes for them…I participate very much in that type of work."

"Really, the X-rated film business has been a small part of my life. I've done a lot of other stuff for cable…I've written for a magazine for eighteen years…I've done a lot of different things…although I'm known for being, you know…the 'Queen of Porn.'"

68 *Lydia Wraight*

"I dropped out of graduate school. I didn't like it. So instead, I dropped out…and went to med school. I'm going to be a doctor, but I don't know what kind yet…probably a pediatrician. I took some advice that had really been coming at me for quite some time…and I finally did something about it. I imagine it will change my life forever."

69   *Conrad Stewart*

"I was born in 1923…what the heck was the name of the town…a little coal-mining community on the Tennessee-Kentucky border, on the Tennessee side…so I am a Tennessean by birth."

"At one time, I lived in Black Mountain, a coal-mining camp, and the post office address was Kinver, Kentucky. We lived there…let's see…I went to school from the third grade to the seventh…so about five years I guess. When I moved there…on the way up…there was a lot of violence at that time with the established unions. It made an impression on me, I guess…`cuz a lot of the time, when I was walking…I remember I had a dog…a young pup. I called him Brownie. I would take Brownie with me when I would go to the grocery store to get a can of condensed milk, or loaf of bread…although Mom didn't buy bread, but she bought condensed milk and stuff like that…and I'd have to walk back home. I didn't really feel all that safe sometimes. There was a Homer Brooks…I remember the name. Oh…he was about three or four years older than me…and he was gonna beat the stuffin' out of me…he kept tellin' me anyway. Never did…but he kept tellin' me…and I had to walk past his house on the way to the store, and on the way back. So, that was something that was impressed on me. It was a time, when people…people in my age bracket…we didn't really feel terribly secure."

"In the coal mines…as they should…from my economics, that is…I understand how they operate, and why…and I think they should do it just that way. When they had a lot of orders, my dad had a lot of work. When they didn't have any orders, he had no work. So, we had gardens to tend and raise to make sure we had food in the winter time. Of course, in the winter, he was almost always busy…working…but in the summer, there was a lot of free time. He was not an agriculturist…he would clear a space off on the side of the hill, and plant corn, and potatoes, and onions…and beans. If he could keep planting, he'd put up a few tomato plants, and sometimes we could find sweet potato plants…to put 'em out. We subsisted a large part of the year, on stuff that Mom canned and dried. Apples…we would core them and dry them and slice them and string them up. It's not an easy life…I was never scared about having no food…we always had enough food…but then I always helped produce it also."

"I did accounting for the Bemis Company…primarily toward the end. The last 27 years I had worked for…before that I had worked for a number of people—The University of Tennessee, an electric company, Palm Beach County…and then I got with Bemis and I stayed. They had a paper mill and a bag factory…made paper and bags."

"Brought my family here on January 1st, 1958. So I been here forty…give or take…forty years. I have three children, all grown. One is a school teacher…daughter…ummm…as my wife was. Two sons, who are employed in the computer industry…one in the D.C. area, and one in Atlanta. The last twelve or eighteen months I have curtailed my travel, so I haven't been to Atlanta. The last thirteen…fourteen years, we always went to Florida every year, and we would spend some time in Atlanta on the way down, and some coming back. This past year I did not leave town. I told Dr. Shea that if I was going to run into trouble, I would like him to be nearby."

"Bemis has been here in Peoria…I think they started operations in…they had a plant in 1912, but I don't think they really got rolling until 1914. They started in San Louis…1858…Judson Bemis, the older, was roaming around trying to find himself and get something started…and didn't know what he wanted to do. He ended up in San Louis, and they needed shipping sacks on the waterfront. Of course the cotton growers, just a little bit south of there, wanted bags to drag behind 'em, and throw their cotton balls into. He made those…and made those in Memphis, Tennessee. I think Bemis was the only provider of bags for the cotton industry at one time."

"I been a lot of places…saw a lot of people…didn't do much…not really. I was a weatherman in the Air Corps…Army Air Corps, in the Second World War. Most of the time I was in England…near Thetford, England. Very few people recognize the name, but there is a town called Thetford in…uh…in England. It's north of…about halfway between Newmarket and Norwich. I didn't get to Portsmouth, that's down south. I got to London…and that's about as far as I could get. The people in London were wonderful…greeted me with open arms…they made me feel safe."

70   *Heather Carter*

"I'm here from Memphis visiting my dad...in Kewanee. Really...I'm from Millington, but I say I'm from Memphis, b'cuz it's close. My mom and my sister and me...we live in Millington...in a...a...a apartment. We go to Memphis all the time. One time we ate at the McDonald's right next to Graceland. We didn't go to Graceland...we just stopped there to eat lunch on our way to dance class...but, I don't dance any more. I don't really like my teacher anymore. She's not really very nice. She's mean."

"We went to the Walmart one time...in Millington...when I was...ummm...six...or seven. My sister was two, and we bought a fish. My sister ate it...she ate it after she poked a hole in the bag...and all the water leaked out. My mom looked down, and my sister was choking. After she got done choking, my mom looked where the fish was supposed to be...in the cart...and she saw the empty bag. When we weren't looking, my sister poked a hole in the bag and ate the fish. We looked around on the floor and didn't find it...so my mom said it was the fish she was choking on. It was a goldfish."

"We didn't have to pay for it b'cuz the lady at the counter said she couldn't scan it...in my sister's stomach."

"My sister is eight years old now...and she don't even like fish."

71   *Raymond Spicer*

"I'm 39 and just retired from the Navy. I just got back into town and will proba-bly help my dad in his business. He does industrial cleaning...and he also runs wire. I had a lot of experiences in the Navy...but, my first Med Cruise, my first visit to Naples kind of sticks in my mind."

"It was Randy Cunningham's birthday, and it was the day before Christmas Eve. I was nineteen. Everyone in my shop took a liberty boat from the ship to the dock. In Naples, the short trip to the dock was always...interesting. The Italians pump their sewers directly into the Med...and the last time that it was flushed, was probably when Mount Vesuvius was active. The smell was what you would expect...not exactly flowery. I don't think it has changed much since then."

"We all went to the Number One Piano Bar...that was our first stop. In the bars in Naples, they have women that come and sit with you...and sometimes they speak a little English, sometimes not. I remember the first woman I sat with said, "Do you like Napoli?" I thought, "Napoli...what the hell is Napoli?" I didn't know until the next day that Napoli was the Italian word for Naples. I guess I wasn't very bright...I just shook my head and said I didn't know."

"The women will sit with you if you buy them a drink...and they'll go back in a more private room with you if you buy a whole bottle. There is talking and touching, kissing...and more if you have enough money. I'd had sex a few times before...once, right before we left on the cruise, with a nurse in Port Royal. We met at the EM Club, and she took me home to her trailer behind the Burger King. It was great...and I knew I definitely wanted to do it again...soon. I was counting on it."

"Anyway...I sat with this woman, who seemed to be nice...and I bought her a few drinks before rejoining the guys in my shop, at the bar. Some of the older guys said that many of the women were actually what were called "benny boys". They told me to be very careful."

"After a lot of drinking, mostly Peroni beer and cheap bottles of wine...and by cheap I mean...not good...expensive, but not good...Narkun and I left the bar and stumbled outside. We were both drunk and had decided that we were going

to go up into "the guts" and find a hooker. The guts was the old communist section of Naples...and we were warned not to go there...and everybody knows that
if they tell you not to go there...you go there. We left the bar, and right outside
the bar was a man with a cart, selling hot peanuts. I think it was a thousand lire
for a paper cup filled with hot peanuts...still in the shell. When you bought a cup
of peanuts, he would fill it from a larger plastic bag."

"Being drunk and trying to be funny, I motioned to the peanut man that I would
give him 20,000 lire for the big plastic bag. He got very excited...took my
money, and handed me a large twenty-pound clear-plastic bag of peanuts."

"Jim and I walked through the dark streets of Naples going east...and up, both
eating peanuts from the bag I was carrying. Now...there is a line...and we didn't
exactly know where that line was, that we weren't supposed to cross...but at
some point, we did. We saw a group of three women gathered under a light on a
corner. They were talking with a group of sailors in a very animated fashion. We
kept going...further up into the guts. Before we got very far, we were approached
by a...a woman who looked quite a bit like the lady who lived next-door when I
was growing up. She looked almost like Betty Farrell...high waist...spindly
legs...stringy black hair...not attractive enough to be a benny boy."

"After some awkward communication...she motioned for us to follow. We went
further into the guts and eventually went into a building, through a very thin and
old wooden door. Down a short hallway, we were led into a waiting room. There
were chairs and people sitting in the chairs...mostly sailors...waiting for their
turn in "the other room". There were children...little kids running around...toys
on the floor...and one kid sitting on the lap of an elderly gentleman."

"After a short period...this middle-aged blonde woman opened the door and
came out with a young sailor...and motioned for the next guy...then closed the
door after they went in. Our hooker was nowhere, so we just sat waiting...and
eating peanuts. Several more times, the blonde hooker took another guy into the
other room and shut the door. After a little while, everyone in the room was eating my peanuts...including the kids. We were all sitting around having a good
time eating peanuts."

"When it was my turn...our hooker came back and led me into the other
room...and shut the door. She motioned for me to wash myself...and turned on

the faucet in a sink right next to…what looked like, my grandma's bed. So, I did…and the water was almost volcanic…it just about burned my skin off. She quickly took off her clothes and laid in the bed…and motioned for me to come over. What happened next was what you would pretty much expect. It didn't take very long…and was about as exciting as having sex with Betty Farrell. Not that I had sex with her…or wanted to, but you get the idea."

"Afterwards, I waited while it was Narkun's turn. By this time, I was the only guy in the waiting room, except for the old guy…and the kids were still running in and out. The peanut bag was completely empty…peanut shells all over the place. One kid had a load of peanut shells in this little toy truck with an Italian name on it…and kept shouting, "Madre…Madre…Madre." Finally his madre came and got him."

"After a few more minutes, the kids were gone, the old man was gone, and I waited for Narkun to come out. I started playing with the toy truck…and ran over a few peanut shells. The peanuts were all gone. A few more minutes later, Narkun came out and we walked back to the dock to catch the liberty boat."

"That was my first hooker…and that was my last hooker…and that's a true story."

72   *Mary Ann Watkins*

"I will be 65. I grew up on a 500 acre farm, where we had corn, beans, and hay. We grew Angus cattle and sheep...and when the Libby plant was functional, we grew peas. We had one of their pea-viners on our farm. It was a machine where the peas would be harvested in the field...brought in by truckloads and run through the machine...and it would take off the hull...and the peas would roll out."

"My father came from a family with ten children...and he just died in February...and had another uncle who died in July...and just yesterday, another of my father's brothers died. So...that's sad."

"I grew up in a family with five girls, which was unfortunate for my father. We did housework, and took meals to the men in the field. We helped out in that way. But...the summer between my junior and senior year in high school...I worked in the A&W Root Beer Stand, which was on the west...the east side of town. It's no longer there. My uncle was manager, and he hired me to work inside...to make up the orders. Then, I went to college and became a registered nurse."

"As a new graduate, I worked at Mennonite Hospital...and at that time there was an eye surgical unit. Working as a surgical nurse there was very memorable. We would be handing the surgeons the instruments, and seeing the eye surgery up close...you know, eye-to-eye, so to speak."

73-74   *Anne Siberling and Christa Stucky*

"I'm Anne…47. This book, "Why Do Men Have Nipples?"…it's all these questions. It says that these are the types of questions you would ask your doctor after three martinis. It's really funny…very funny. We can't stop laughing. I hope they don't throw us out of here."

"Christa…31. I'm from DeKalb. They invented barbed wire in Dekalb…and Cindy Crawford grew up in Dekalb as well. She was valedictorian in high school…Dekalb High School. Dekalb also has Northern…and I went there."

"I worked at McDonald's in Dekalb…that was my first job. The manager didn't know me at the time…I was sixteen or seventeen…and we were sitting in the back…and we got kicked out for laughing. They asked us to go outside. Anne and I laugh all the time. We've never been kicked out of here for laughing…at least not yet."

"I'm from Charleston…'bout ninety miles from here. I'm originally from Minnesota…near Marshall…south of Ester. I was 45 when I left Minnesota. We had some pretty hard winters there. One winter, my mom made homemade sauerkraut…in these big crocks that she kept in the basement…to make the sauerkraut in. My entire family was sitting in the kitchen, and there was this great big crash in the basement. My dad jumped up from the table and ran down the stairs. There was my youngest brother, and he was standing there with a hammer…and the crock was in pieces all over the floor. My dad said, "What in the hell are you doing?" He set the hammer down on the picnic table and said, "Well…I was just setting down this hammer." Then he quickly ran upstairs. He never got scolded because my dad thought it was so funny."

"I was married. When I first met my husband, he swept me off my feet. He brought me flowers. I had a friend who told me that when a man brings flowers, he either wants something or he's sorry for something. I suppose that's true. He took me to the opera…and he was a pilot, so we went flying…and it was a whirlwind relationship. Then, it turned out he was rather abusive, so I walked…got out of there…and it was a good thing to leave."

"Christa and I are both pastors. We always kind of hate to tell people that part, because they might treat us differently. But, I actually love it…it is the hardest work…but also the most rewarding…in the same day. Today is a good example. I started off the day with a woman who was beaten up last night, and filing a claim against her husband. I met a friend whose father has cancer…and then…a fellow pastor was killed in a car accident last night. So, that was all before noon. It is that, and the real joy of being a pastor. People let me into their lives in the hardest and most enjoyable parts of their lives. They share that with me…without really thinking about it. It's really special to be brought into people's lives."

"I like the flexibility of being a pastor…and sharing their joys and struggles. One of my favorite things is to see when that light bulb comes on. You know, they get something, and they're able to take it on their journey."

"One of my greatest gifts is listening. I don't have the answers. I'm not God…and God's time is different then our time. Sometimes I put voice to the questions they're having…which is the same as everyone is having. Like…New Orleans…where is God in this? That's a tough question. It's easy to give a pat answer that God is there by your side. He is…but it doesn't feel like it at the moment. I think the most I can do is listen to their pain. I don't fix their pain…I walk alongside them in their pain. Also, on Sunday, I get to be a ham. I always get my best jokes in on Sunday. I get a few laughs."

"I just wrote a book, called "Fully Rely on God, Pastor Anne". I was in the hospital last summer with a serious kidney infection. The title comes from a man in my church. He didn't bring flowers; he brought this really big lawn ornament frog…with a hysterical grin on its face…looks like a "loony toon". In its hands, he put a floral card…and it just said "FROG". Then he put "Fully Rely On God, Pastor Anne."

75   *Ralph Higgs*

"I taught school…6th grade in a self-contained classroom. But since 1962, I been at Melgreens. I think over the years, customers are more savvy about getting more for their dollar. I've noticed that change."

"I was always out in the neighborhood with six or eight kids…playing athletics, baseball, football…whatever season…that's what we played. You don't see kids doing that today. If it's not organized for them…they don't play. I think kids miss that. They don't know how to play."

"You know, there are old mines with the lakes and the timber, and that sort of thing…just west of here. About ten years ago, the mining company was selling some of the strip mine ground, and there was one parcel of a hundred acres with a lake…virgin timber. My family really wanted to buy it…and we didn't think we were going to be able to…but we did. We bought it. With the price of ground today, we couldn't afford to buy it today…but we were lucky enough to get it then."

"We drive out and enjoy it for the day…do a little swimming, boating…fishing. With the timber, we've got deer and turkey. It's only ten miles. The first day we went out and walked…there had been a slight snowfall. We went out there and walked…we saw these big tracks. They were mountain lion tracks…not supposed to be here, but they are. We have since seen the animal on three different occasions."

"You know, you see pictures of things on TV of certain things…like the Grand Canyon or whatever. Nothing does it justice until you are there…the vastness…the color…just absolutely gorgeous…nothing like seeing it on TV. You have to live it."

76   *Ken Smith*

"Part of my experience was to go into Chicago with my father...to the Union Stockyards...to see his cattle sold. He wanted to make sure that he was there to see them weighed...to see them on the scale...to see how they looked when they got to the stockyards. We raised livestock...hogs...and we fattened beef cattle. We bought small calves from the western ranchers in the fall, and we fattened them up."

"Being on a farm, you learn how to do chores, and that you're expected to assist. That helps to build a good work ethic that has stuck with me over the years. Folks...at least when I observe them...peoples lives seem to be more leisure oriented, rather than task oriented."

"We took a leisurely vacation this past year. We were in Salzburg...in Mozart's apartment. You know, this year is the 250th anniversary of Mozart's life? We went to Germany and Austria celebrating my wife's retirement. It was a very modest home...and he had really small violins. His apartment area...they would collect the rainwater off the roof to be used for the washing of dishes and things like that. Then, when they got done with the dishwater...they would pour it in the gutters, and it would go off into the drain system. I thought that was interesting. That's what I found interesting."

77   *Linda Labbee Howell*

"I'm 57…and was born in Desoto, Missouri…then moved to Bismark, then Tiff. We traveled a lot in our lifetime, 'cuz my husband is a preacher. We traveled to different churches. We visited the churches, and somebody would ask him if he would help out…so, then we'd move there. We've lived in Beaumont, Texas…Colorado, Tennessee…we've lived in Alabama…both north and south."

"My daughter had moved out when she got married…and her and her husband got transferred…transferred to a job from Memphis, out to Ramrock. And then in 2002, my husband had heart surgery…he got a metal aortic valve…he had it replaced 'cuz his aortic valve crumpled…and I've got sick problems also. My daughter called and said, "We're thinking of investing in a house, and we'd like you and Daddy to come up and live in it. As long as you live in it, it's your house…and you just make the payments. We got the payments low enough so's you can afford it. I'd rather have you's up here so I can keep an eye on you…and not have to worry so much about you all the time." So, she bought the house, and we moved so we could be close to her."

"We built a cabin near Bismark…what year did we build that cabin, Daddy? Was that '95? Yes…'95. We were livin' in Cherryville, Missouri, and my husband was drivin' a truck on the road. He was home about three to four days out of every four to five weeks…and I had my youngest son with me. He was still going to high school. He was graduating…and then a couple days after he graduated, he went to the Army. So, I was having sick problems…I was taking antidepressants and I had OCD and SAD…anxiety attacks and all that. So, with him leaving, I was getting upset about being by myself when my husband was gone. They put me on a different medication, and I got to where my memory was going…and different things like that…problems driving. So then my husband quit, so's he could stay home and help me work through it. So, when he did…we knew we couldn't afford the house, and we had talked for years about trying to live how people lived, you know, back in the old days…the pioneer days"

"I'm part Indian…and it's just in my blood. My mother used to cook out-side…she was so countrified. So, we wanted to see how our ancestors lived, and it was a cheap way of living too. We had planned for maybe six months to a year before we did it…and during that time we was buying coal oil lamps, and coal oil lanterns. Then, when we moved, we sold our house with everything in it. We took only our personal items that the family had given us over the years...from our children. We left the furniture, we left the pictures on the wall...we left the bed made up with the bedspread, and the curtains that matched. We left the whole bit."

"First we bought us a bus...an old empty bus. A friend of ours moved it for us. He pulled it over to this land that my husband's sister had just bought...they was eighty acres. We went out there and found us a spot by a little creek. First, we lived in the bus...just an empty bus. My husband made a platform bed in the back of it...and ummm...we cooked outside. We had a canopy thing...tent out there...and we spent all our time outside, 'cuz it was the summer time."

"A little while after that, he started buildin' the cabin. At that time, I was just get-tin' about $80 a month from the general fund, they called it...from the govern-ment, because I wasn't able to work. I hadn't gotten my Social Security through yet. And, we lived in that bus...and my husband would go out in the woods, and used an axe and sometimes a chain-saw. It would work, even though it was an old one. He cut the trees by himself...and cleaned them and carried them him-self...all the way to where we was buildin' onto the bus. Each day, he carried log after log after log and built the first room of the cabin."

"We used a little bit of cement...a lot of straw and pine needles...and ummm...mud. That's what we used between the logs. No nails or nothin'. We just put the logs together for them to fit...put them together that way. We didn't use any nails until we got to the roof, where we had to put a roof on. And then, we lived in that small place for maybe a month or so...and then he started on the other room. It didn't take him long to build em'...and we lived like our ancestors lived. Everything...everything was done outside."

"It was a great experience to live like that...like they did in the past. You had to prepare for the evening. You know, all day long you spent preparing for the evening, when there wasn't any light. You gathered your wood...filled your lan-terns for the evening, and got everything ready. My husband would cook out on the old cook stove...outside. My husband would go out and get poke salad, and greens...uhhh, wild greens. We'd cook them up...and anything out in the woods that used to be edible by the Indians, we would pick it and cook it. We made pies out of berries we would pick."

"When it rained or snowed, we couldn't get in or out with our pickup truck, so we had to leave the truck at the first cattle gate and walk in and out. We had to use the lanterns at night to see the snow drifts and the rocks that we had to step on, to get across the creek. Eventually, David and my brother-in-law built a bridge over the creek. And...we stayed there for a good while...until the snakes drove me away. I said, "I can't take this no more now. It was fun, but we got to go."

"There was this book...and I have em' in the other room...the two pages of the sketches and stories. A book called "Pioneers of the Ozarks" by Lennis Broadfoot. There were two men in it, John Counts and Pete Counts. One of them was a fiddler...he called him Fiddler Pete, and it showed a sketch of him...and his face is rugged, and a sketch of a cabin that he built...and a fiddle, a square fiddle that he made. In it, he said that he made the fiddle himself...and he would fiddle for folks at different things...for weddings or whatever, and would get together and fiddle all the time, and sing. And, he did that his whole life."

"John...the other one, fished all the time. He fished all the time...and he made his own fishin' thing. He fished with a bow and arrow. He would fish with this guy named Swiney who had a store and ran the post office...and Swiney would buy the fish from him, and sell to other folks. So...fishin'...to him...was his whole life. That's what he loved to do, and that's what he did."

"I know I've got it in my research...what kin they are to me...but I haven't been researchin'...going through my books lately...to know exactly how they are kin to me...but I think they may be brothers to my great-great grandmother. But, when I found out, I was so excited about it...and I thought, "Oh...I found some Counts." And, I copied those two pages."

"John Counts said in that book, "The Ozarks has been a wonderful home fer me." So...I agree with him on that. I want to go back and look at the cabin sometime, and look at what we had...how we lived our lives for a short time."

"My husband and I have been together for 39 years now...and a lot of our lifetime is something good to look back on...and think about, because we spent...we ummm...well, like my husband said...you know, we never had a lot of money...but we always...nothing was ever boring in our life. We was always moving…we was always on the go…always doing things. When we lived in Colorado, we went rock climbing with the kids…camping out. We was always doing something. We always had a very interesting life."

78   *Patty Armstrong*

"I was listening to the radio this morning and heard about Dick Cheney and the shooting...and that he sent the state of Texas the $7 fee for the license. He didn't have a license. Now...if *you* shot someone...*you* were hunting and shot someone...you would be in jail and have a big fine. I think he should not be above the law. He's our vice-president. That's just my opinion."

"One time I was hunting for a place to live...and I bought my own home when I was 51...and single. I bought a house...a $20,000 wreck. Then, I got a mortgage loan and rehabbed it. It's by the Spotted Cow in Peoria Heights. It's two blocks off of Grandview Drive...and it's wonderful. It was the worst house on the best street...and it was my lucky day."

"I took off all the cedar shingles with a johnny-bar, I took out carpeting...it all had to be re-plastered...bathroom gutted. It was a wreck. I can't believe I made the decision to do it...but once I did...it was all over. That was eight years ago. Aside from my sofa and chair...everything is an antique. One piece is a small hanging cupboard that came out of the Duryea Estate...the Charles Duryea Estate...the man who made the automobile."

"I love my house. I love every piece of furniture...every picture...everything. You cannot beat buying old, to furnish and decorate a home. I bought a brown mahogany table and chairs for $60...and had it refinished. My other house...everything was new. A dealer once said to me, "You go buy a new table and chairs and see how much you can get for it tomorrow. Nothing...nothing.""

79 *Steve Wallace*

"I'm from Oconomowoc, Wisconsin...and I was born in St. Paul."

"I'm the invisible man...nobody sees me. I take it for granted, even when you look right at me and make eye contact, that you don't really see me. So, I always assume, that they...other drivers...are gonna do something stupid, and I'm not going to be the victim. I try to be as defensive as I can be. It doesn't matter if I am in my Hummer or on this motorcycle. In one case, I've got 6500 pounds...and a bumper like you've never seen before. The other case, I've got 550 pounds...and no bumper. That philosophy has kept me alive. I'm 52 and I'm still breathing."

"I'm a University of Illinois graduate. When I was five, my dad got transferred to Indianapolis...so that's where I really grew up. That's where I got this Hoosier thing going...and that's where you turn into a gear head. You can't live in Speedway Town and not get into motors. That's where I was really...weaned in on gasoline. Then, just before my senior year in high school, my dad was transferred to Peoria. So, my senior year of high school, I went to Pekin High. It was in that next two or three years that I met my wife...and I been married now for 27 years. She is a Peoria girl. Her dad is a retired policeman...Peoria Police Department."

"So, the University of Illinois...went to college there. Then I moved to Texas...that's where my other accent comes from. I lived in Houston, then they shipped me to Chicago...than back to Houston. Then I got over to Austin, and then finally we said, "Where do we want to live?" We chose Wisconsin...because that's where we always went on vacation. We said, "Let's live where we always associate vacation. So, ever since, we have been in Wisconsin."

"I been coming here for this race since my senior year in high school. So, now, I find my best buddy, Curt Andrew...we hook up the bikes, take Friday and Monday off. We drive down on a Friday and go back on a Monday...and take the whole weekend to just enjoy the riverfront...the music...the people...and especially the Grand National TT races."

"I don't know if you're into motorcycle racing, but...there are super-bikes, like at Elkhart Lake...we go up there and they put these bikes with 600 horsepower around those curves at 220 mph...and that's a special kind of racing. But out here on this dirt track...that's racing like you'll never see. They'll take twenty guys...and put them into that *turn one* at the exact same time, going sideways at about a hundred miles an hour...and if one of them makes a mistake...it affects them all, because, one of them could clip the bottom out for the next twelve guys. And...no sooner do they take that turn, then they force them to jump off this hill...as far as a hundred feet in the air. Then, as soon as they land...they're forced into this "S" curve. That's what makes it a TT race."

"I think there are only two sanctioned TT races in the entire USA-AMA schedule. This race is the only race that is held at a private motorcycle club. The Peoria Motorcycle Club, I think...is the oldest established motorcycle club in the United States...and it's the only one with a sanctioned AMA race. It's a private fairgrounds...the motorcycle club owns that property...and they been doing this forever. I'm not old enough to tell you when it started."

"Out of all the motorcycle races you could ever attend, it is the most unique critter that you can ever see. When they talk about the missing link...you know, this race is the missing link. It bridges every other kind of motorcycle race you have ever seen. It has no equal...there is no similar race. It's like the duck-billed platypus. It's a mammal that lays eggs. It's the one that nobody can figure out where it came from...nobody can figure out what it does...it's just a unique critter all to itself. And now, and now...they've put this whole weekend around it. This is all just icing...the cake is out there in Bartonville. But, we have all this icing we're about to enjoy."

"I have a tarp company. I make all kinds of tarpaulins and protective covers. I sell to the military...been shipping a lot to Iraq. They make tents out of them, and truck covers...kind of an eclectic market. You know, every construction site, you see tarpaulins. Everybody needs a good tarp...I can tell you that. When I moved to Houston in 1976, the very first job I got out of college was for a plastics company that made all kinds of reinforced fabrics that were turned into tarps. I've been doing that ever since."

"My first motorcycle was a 1967 Harley Sportster. It was the only motorcycle, and the only year that they made it, that it had both a kick-start and an electric-start. The Sportster was sometimes called the XLH back then, if it was a kick-start...and an XLCH if it was an electric-start. Only one year, in 1967 did the bike come with both. I got that bike my senior year, right over here in

Pekin…and I rode that bike twelve months a year…right here in Peoria. Now, you haven't lived until the only form of transportation you have in a snowstorm…is a motorcycle. Everything after that is easy."

80   *M.K. Riddel*

"I'm M.K....and I'm 35. I was born here and was raised all around the area...Mackinaw, East Peoria, Germantown Hills. I work at Borders Bookstore. I'm the cafe supervisor. We just had a visit from the CEO, the president, and the vice president...just fifteen minutes ago."

"I had planned for these handouts, with all the executives at Borders...to give them ideas and things...and the G.M. was giving me the opportunity to speak, and explain all the things I am doing to help the cafe improve. While our sales aren't good, we're making more on the dollar...and things like that. I made this menu in full color, and then wrote all these ideas down. I was very nervous, but the fact that I got lots of congratulations...I got to talk to people that I wouldn't otherwise get to talk to...it made me feel pretty good that they listened, and they actually liked my ideas. That felt pretty good...that they were impressed. I'm still coming down from it. They were telling me they were impressed, so...it was nice."

"I have a masters in theatre, and would like to get back to doing that sometime. I got it at Bowling Green State University...Bowling Green, Ohio. The program there was different because they wanted you to be active in the theater program, directing, helping out backstage, and performing, any way that you could. Not every graduate program that is not a fine arts degree...and mine is not...if you work fine arts, they would be encouraging you to do that...but this is different. This is a lot more writing...a lot more scholarly, academia...they want you to go and teach somewhere...especially if you go on to get the PhD, which, I did the course work for, but didn't finish. I backed out shortly after that, but...it was a nice college, and I made a lot of friends. I do like a university environment. It seems there is a lot more open-mindedness. I really do like places that have universities. They are more liberal."

"The ACTF, American College Theater Festival...and there is a slash...Kennedy Center Theater Festival people...compete with each other. They do the show in their own place...and judges come and deem them worthy to move on. They take the whole show, or pick an actor or actress out of it...and they do that so that you get to see the best of the best. It's broken up into regions. Lately, our

region has been meeting at ISU...in January. In times past, they met in Columbus."

"It's really neat as a teacher, but especially neat as a student. You can see where
others, and their imaginations have taken them...what they do with the script,
and where...where they take the script. It's really a very good opportunity to
break barriers and think outside the box. So...it's not just that you follow what is
in the script, but if you can make it better by taking it a little further...to get
anachronistic...so that it's not just Shakespeare in Shakespeare's time."

"My orange hair...when I was three years old, the day of my birthday, I received
a...and this has to do with a trip...because, I've got this scab on my forehead,
and now I have a dent that you can see. I was three, and we lived on a very sharp
incline. I got a tricycle, and tried to keep it in the boundaries, but I went too
far...gravity took over, and I went "smack"...into a curb. We then went to the
Ozarks, and there are all these pictures of myself and my sister. We went to
Eureka Springs...and I've got this big...thing...on my forehead. The dent has
stayed with me forever more. It is actually the fascia that is broken. My skull is
fine, but...it might have a little to do with why I color my hair a bright orange. It
makes the dent less noticeable."

"I'm not one of those people that dyes their hair the bright blue or the green, or
anything. One time I tried blonde after having it red, and got something similar
to this...but only in the tips...and it didn't...didn't look good at all. This
was...Teri and I last night, coloring each others hair...sitting around her kitchen
table...her husband helped wipe us down and stuff. I hadn't seen myself, and
rinsed my hair, and she kept saying, "It sure is bright." I'm going, "Good." I've
always liked red, and the different shades...it just fits my skin tone. Then I went
into the bathroom and went, "OH MY GOD...I'M NEON!"

81   *David Morgan*

"I see that Alice cooper is coming in a couple of months. Alice Cooper was my first concert when I was like, seventeen. I was raised in a pretty conservative family. I was seventeen, and they were letting us loose…and it was Roberts Stadium in Evansville, and that was back when he had a pretty controversial image…1973 maybe? I think "Schools Out" was the album he was promoting. It was a real out-on-the-edge thing for me…a great concert…had a really good time. He plays golf now and seems like a regular kind of guy."

"I am originally from Evansville, Indiana…southern Indiana. I came here…opened a hotel, Signature Inn on Brandywine Drive. So, I came with the hotel in 1988. Dan was about five at the time, and my son Ryan was six months old."

"In Evansville, I spent a lot of time outdoors. My father had a small shop out in the country. We fished, and cut firewood to keep his fire going, in the wood-burning stove, out in his shop. We were halfway between the grade school and the high school…so, we walked both ways to and from school. I played a little sports…baseball and basketball. We did the typical things…running around the neighborhood playing tag and hide & seek…played with army men."

"Our family was always the family where my mom always had the treats…candy for kids. So, all the kids generally congregated at my house. Mom and Dad…older sister…younger brother James. James is an attorney for the Illinois EPA now. He's assistant attorney general. He moved to Springfield about a year before I moved to Peoria…so both of us are in Illinois now. My sister is still in Evansville taking care of my parents. They are older now, so they need somebody to watch over them. We still go to visit several times a year."

"When we first came to town, the first impression I got of Peoria…Mayor Maloof was being interviewed by Dan Rather on CBS news. It was right after I got the news that I was coming here that I happened to catch that interview. The "singing mayor" he was known as. It was when Peoria was kind of coming out of a downturn. In '88, the economy was just starting to spring back. Our hotel was the first that was being built in a long time. I was excited about the new opportunity."

"I went to school and got a degree in biology and chemistry. I was going to go off to medical school, and kind of got sidetracked. I have a good education, but not really making good use of it. I've always been in the hospitality industry…love talking to people…meeting new people. I'm great with faces and names, so that seems to pay off."

"I've always traveled my entire life. There are places I'd like to go back to. I've been to all 48 states…never been to Alaska or Hawaii. I think it's a great country. As far as international travel, there are a few places I'd like to go…Ireland, England. I've been to Italy, Mexico…Canada. My parents always took us every-where. Every year, we took two or three trips, and I just kind of picked up where they left off. The Tetons is my favorite place. It's just so majestic…so impressive. I think I would like my ashes spread out over the Tetons after I die."

82   *Valerie Louck*

"I'm 29. I grew up in Princeton and lived in Bloomington for quite awhile. I moved here for love. I moved over here and thought that I had totally found the love of my life. Things were going so well, and then two weeks ago, I was left. Everything that I believed was true in my life, ended up being false. Essentially, there was someone else involved and I had no idea this person meant anything…so it came as quite a shock when I discovered it was over…that there was someone else."

"I learned how to kiss at a Baptist church camp. I must have been eleven or twelve years old. I would go to church on Sunday…and church on Wednesday. I went to this co-ed Baptist camp, for a week during the summer…every year. We were all good kids…god-fearing good kids. But, they gave us a lot of free time at this camp…and so I found this little boy, and we kinda liked each other…holding hands down the path. Sitting there on a log, he just came over and gave me this huge kiss. Not just a little peck, but tongue and everything. I was so…I remember this sound…this popping sound when two lips come together when one isn't expecting it. So, I had this little crush at church camp. We wanted to think that God brought us together…but I think it was just hormones that brought us together…and the camp was just the place where it brought it out. I learned to be a wonderful kisser at a Baptist church camp."

"So, what I am discovering is just how difficult it is to find a decent apartment, something that is reasonably priced. There are so many places in town that look like they would be decent places to live. You get into the apartment and you can't even understand how they are able to rent a place like that, for the money they are charging for it. I was very fortunate to find a decent, safe place to live. I was unfortunate to pay more than I wanted to, but…I'm paying $545 for about 600 square feet. I can't believe how ungodly high it is to rent. It's cheaper here than in Bloomington, but still not cheap."

"I work at Methodist as an admissions manager in rehab. I go through the hospital and screen people to see if they meet certain criteria to come down for inpatient PT and OT, and maybe speech after their illness is over. So, I have a lot of ortho and neuro patients. A lot of people…they become so…so…ill…and you just can't walk away once you leave the hospital…their illness. So, what we do is improve their strength...get them walking better...work with them speaking better after a stroke. Everyone works very hard there at Methodist, and I am extremely proud to work...to work there. It is a wonderful, wonderful hospital with great people. It is the best place I have worked. Everyone is friendly, and they will go out of their way to help...help people. I have never worked in an organization where people give a hundred percent every day as if it's old hat."

"One time I had a friend that lived in Buffalo, New York. I decided to go up and see her...didn't want to drive. The train was high, and so was flying...so I took Greyhound. The bus left from Bloomington, and then it was supposed to go to Joliet and then Chicago...then eighteen million connections before you got to Buffalo. So, I get on the bus, and it's just me and one other woman...the bus is full of men...which was okay because nobody bothered us. But instead of stopping in Joliet, we stopped at Pontiac, right outside the maximum security prison, and a guy who had just been released after thirteen years in prison for "I don't know what" gets on the bus, and sits right behind this other woman and I."

"He gets to talking and says, "It's been thirteen years since I been this close to a woman...and you sure look good to me." I was...I was so scared. When we went to Joliet, I was so afraid we would stop there and pick up another prisoner, but we didn't. I made it to Chicago. We got on a bus and it broke down on the Chicago Skyway. Then the bus driver just left us. We had no clue where he went. So, maybe an hour later, somebody comes and they drive us to Gary, Indiana...and this was about 2:30 in the morning. The bus station in Gary is not the type of place you want to be...ever. We had a buddy system just to use the bathroom. Every drunk, prostitute, and homeless person was there. So, they finally got us another bus."

"I was almost accosted in Cleveland because I went out for a cigarette. I was so glad to be alive once I got to Buffalo. It is the worst way to travel. The trip back was uneventful, but I thought I was going to die on the way out."

83   *Evelyn Hutcheson*

"I'm Matt Hale's mother, and...I know the truth. Matt's father and I are 72 and 67. We need to see our son...and he needs to see us."

"The FBI had placed a mole in Matt's church...declared a church by the courts. Actually...the mole wore a wire and recorded many conversations with Matt. Matt repeatedly refused to have anything to do with killing anyone. There was never any evidence to convict Matt, yet...because Judge Moody allowed Ben Smith to come into Matt's trial and because Matt's attorney didn't present a defense...Matt was found guilty."

"So...because Matt was declared a terrorist, he was given forty years. He's now at ADMAX under the SAMs...in Florence, Colorado. He isn't allowed to have a radio. He won't have sunlight. He can't talk in a voice that...people can...understand. He has been under the SAMs for over two years. His father and I won't be allowed to see him or talk to him on the phone for one year, because Matt gave me a statement denouncing the murder of Judge Lefkow's husband and mother...and denied having anything to do with it. As you know, Bart Ross killed the husband and mother. Thank God he left a suicide note...they would have found a way to say Matt did it."

"Matt was sentenced to forty years on April 6th. For those that cheered because Matt received forty years for the solicitation of Judge Lefkow's murder...you just cheered the imprisonment of an innocent man. You just cheered the government, the FBI and the FBI mole that truly solicited the judge's murder."

"For those that wanted to believe my son was involved in the Ben Smith crimes, you have been duped. The FBI never had evidence linking Matt to the crimes...so, they found a way to punish someone for the terrible crimes Ben Smith committed."

"I wonder how many people have read the trial transcript? For those that have, they know Matt is innocent. They know the evidence just wasn't there for a conviction. How did it happen? Matt's attorney failed to put on a defense...afraid to fight the government. Did you know the government can do this to you and your family, if they decide they want to shut you up? You must never believe you have freedom of speech. Never say negative things about your government, they will find a way to stop you…if you say it enough times."

"It is sad that anyone never cared to know my son. Yes, he is a racist, he loves our white race. He has said some unkind things about other races. Is this reason to lock him in a hole for forty years? Seems to me, I have heard negative things about other races most of my life. I grew up to believe that everyone has a right to express their opinion."

"Matt went to law school so he could practice law…and was refused a law license because he is a racist. Yet, we have licensed attorneys that rob their clients. In Peoria, we have an attorney that was found guilty of sexually molesting a three year old girl and he was given fourteen years. The judge allowed him to remain out on the same bond he was out on before he was found guilty…so that he could close his practice and wrap up his personal business. Is this right? I don't think so. We have innocent people in prison because their attorney took money and slept through the trial. We have prosecutors that lie and put people in prison for twenty years…until a real attorney wins their freedom. We have the FBI in Chicago that put a man on death row for eight years by framing him. These men are still working for the FBI. I wonder if they worked on Matt's frame-up?"

"Do you care? Do you only care about those close to you? Well, I care about innocent people in prison…I care about my son. He is innocent and should be home on appeal if the appellate court judges were truly honorable."

"Ashcroft did this to my son and I have asked so many people to help him and everyone seems to be afraid of the government. We…we need to see our son…and he needs to see us."

84   *Han Zhang*

"I live in Brooklyn. I'm here on business…and checking out a couple of your restaurants. I was at Nathan's last year when Takeru Kobayashi ate 53.5 hot dogs in twelve minutes. He only ate 49 this year. The next closest guy was a guy named Joey Chestnut…but, he wasn't even close. I know that before the contest, Kobayashi meditates…and then eats the dogs in a style they call "japanesing", where he breaks the hot dog in half and eats both halves together, then eats the bun. It's a cool, cool thing to watch…until they start puking at the end."

"Joey Chestnut, he just won this other contest…I forgot what they were eating. I think it was waffles. He ate 65 hard-boiled eggs one time…in about six minutes. That was cool."

85   *Angela Ashburn*

"I'm from Creve Couer and I have lived in this area all my life…all 39 years of it. I am an accounts payable clerk at Pekin Hospital. Pekin is a small town…and they like to focus on their small-town status. They say that they don't like to focus on the other side of the river, and what's going on over there. But my job…it's a paycheck. That's all it is…a paycheck."

"This is a "girl's night out". We try and do something different each month…and last month was karaoke, and they're talking about roller-skating next month. We just try and get together…get away from the house, and the husbands and kids. We've just kind of collected a group of friends over the years…and we stick by each other for everything, probably thirteen or fourteen years now."

"Tracey's bachelorette party…Tracy and Val had their parties in the same year, and Val's was somewhat traditional…vulgar things on the veil, and we gave her a really raunchy list of things to do…and that's the way we spent the whole evening. Tracy's was a little different because she had to be stylish. We had to make her a stylish veil. We had stylish, raunchy toys that we gave out. We gave her a list of things to do…and this was downtown here. We bar-hopped all evening and gave out little things with her picture on it, so people would come up and ask her for a dance. She had to so things like…kiss a bald man on the head…and collect things."

"I will say that just recently, she was at a bachelorette party, and had a neat idea. For the bachelorette, she made her collect a bottle, a cork, a pen, and a napkin. At the end…and she didn't know what she was collecting these things for…but, she had her write a message to her future husband, put it in the bottle…and then throw it in the river. That was fun and creative."

"I didn't know I would have kids. I was a cancer survivor and never thought that far into the future. Having my son was great. I had Hodgkin's in my early 20's…and also had a relative who had Hodgkin's. His age was about my age when I first got it. It made him this…driven person. Me…I just wanted to go and party…because I never knew when it might be over. It was eight months of chemotherapy…and that was before I knew any of the friends I have now. That was a pretty tough period. But, the one thing that I have learned is…the relationships that I have built…and the friends I have had, that circle me…that is what always lifts me up. My son is the greatest thing that happened to me. He lifts me up. He makes me a better person. The cancer was one of the toughest…but I wouldn't say *the* toughest, because I have had other illnesses and stuff."

"I always try and look at the bright side. When I first found out I had cancer…I looked to my parents. They already knew…and they didn't break down…there was just concern. So, I looked at them and said, "Okay, what now?" That's been my attitude any time I have been sick or had some adversity in front of me. I ask myself, "What do I do to get out of it?" That is what drove me through that, and any other type of tough times in my life."

"A few years ago, I lost my job unexpectedly…and that was at a time when they said, "There are no other jobs out there." I worked at Affina as a trainer…in the call center. I had worked there for five years, and it was an unexpected thing. So, I decided that I was going to go back to school and go into radiography, and do something that I won't have to be…constantly at the same level…something that I can grow with, and make some money."

"I enrolled in school immediately. I was unemployed, but I was so excited I was going to do something…and then I suddenly started feeling sick. It was on the 4th of July that I found out I had…on my feet and legs…Vaculitis. It was a flesh-eating virus that I had only just heard about in the paper. So, I had to have part of my calf removed…and go to a wound care center every week from July to December, where they would cut out pieces of flesh."

"At the same time, I'm a single mom, trying to raise my son…keep a roof over our heads, still unemployed and trying to go to class. Meanwhile…I'm wrapped up and shuffling like an eighty year old person. I was on Prednisone, swelling up like I was back in chemo…and that was the lowest that I remember. Even more than the cancer, that was the lowest, because I had a child to take care of at the time."

"Every time I would go to the wound care center, I would say, "Oh, do you see a light at the end of the tunnel?" They would say, "No." They thought that the best that would happen to me is that I would only lose one of my legs. But…I didn't. I got through it…fought my way through it…and…the same week my unemployment ran out, I found a job at Pekin Hospital. So, that was a low point...but I had to take it and turn it into something positive."

"I'm hoping to work at the oncology/hematology place in Peoria. Those were the people that helped me, and that's where I would like to be...doing what they're doing. I'd like to do CAT scans or even just regular X-rays. I would like to be involved in that, and hopefully buy a house...so my son can have a back yard and a dog."

86   *Natalie Haurberg*

"I am Natalie. I go to Knox College and am studying physics as a major, and political science as a minor. I think physics is cool, and I enjoy learning about stuff…and I think it's fun, honestly. I want to go to grad school and I guess I'll just see from there…kinda depends…I want to work in astrophysics."

"My mom has a bachelors in dance from SMU and she choreographed shows. She choreographed, directed, and wrote shows for Six Flags for a long time, taught dance class…ummm…she did a lot of stuff like that. She's done a lot of writing and directing. She actually wrote the costume character show for several years at Six Flags. She wrote "Love at First Fright", which was the Halloween show that is still used at Six Flags. She now works with my dad in the office…and owns part of the company."

"My dad now runs a truss company…builds trusses. He got a masters in anthropology from SMU. He's an anthropologist."

"The first time I went to Belize, I was like…I think I was thirteen or fourteen. We went on this caving trip that I remember, that at the time…only less than 300 people had ever been in this cave, other than the original Mayans that had used the cave. We had gone…it was in National Geographic…they covered it…but I can't think of it…ummm…I think it was Tea Cup Village. Tea Kettle Village, I guess was the name of it. It is a little village in Belize. But we went to this place and they had advertised that this guide was around there and could take us there for a certain amount of money. We had to walk several miles back into the rainforest, I don't know how far it was. But, when we got to the mouth of the cave, there was like a river into it…so you gotta swim into it, and you had to swim, like, halfway through the cave, so you had to keep swimming, and ya know, climb through crap…and we went back a couple of miles in the cave."

"You kinda scale this set of rocks on the side…and then I'll tell you what you're going to find in there. There was this flat clearing…and he sits there and tells you he's going to show you something really cool and stuff, and then he has you turn off your lights on your hat-thing, so that you can see what real dark looks like. It's really creepy cause it's very, very dark. I had never seen pitch black in my life…and then you turn the lights back on…you walk around the corner, and this, like, this huge cavern opens up. It's full of Mayan pottery…like, this very special, ritual place. They don't know exactly what it was used for…but there was, like, pottery that was fully intact, and some of it…most of it was broken, because it was part of Mayan tradition that all pottery contained a spirit, and you had to break a hole in it when you were done using it…or you were gonna leave it or whatever…to release the spirit. So, most had a little hole in them. But, some were fully intact, which they think was weird, and these archeologists were investigating it and stuff…and all this was marked…you had to walk around it, and they showed you some really cool stuff, and there was a burial place, which is how they knew it was for rituals."

"The "Royals" used it, because in the Mayan tradition, the Royals had their heads flattened when they were kids. They took boards and put them on their foreheads…it was a sign of being a Royal. They also used these flat-headed dangle things to hang between their eyes to make them cross-eyed…because being cross-eyed was a sign of royalty…kinda like feet binding in China. Everybody back there in the cave had flattened foreheads, so it was obviously a royal burial ground."

"We left, and had lunch just outside the cave, and I didn't even have a sandwich because they brought tuna salad, and I hate tuna…I really hate tuna salad. I like fresh tuna. I don't like…I don't like tuna salad. And the other things they brought were like, turkey sandwiches covered in mayonnaise and onions…like, the two things I hate on a sandwich. I ate the bottom bread from the turkey sandwiches."

87   *Tom Nauman*

"I had a dream that happened…oh…mid-April of '90 or '91. It was a Saturday morning around 9 o'clock. I had been sleeping in after watching TV on Friday night. I'd been out looking for mushrooms earlier in the week, but hadn't found any. I could smell the coffee my wife was making…but I just couldn't get up. I fell back asleep…and I saw myself standing in a little area across the road from the house…crouched over, leaning on my hiking stick…looking for mushrooms."

"I heard "pop…pop"…and in my dream the sounds were accompanied by two grey morels bursting out of the ground. The sounds were loud enough that I sat straight up in bed and woke up from the dream."

"I got up, got dressed and headed across the road. As I passed the doorway to the kitchen, Vicky asked me where I was going. I told her that two mushrooms had just come up across the road and that the sound of them popping out of the ground had startled me awake…and that I was going to get them. "Yeah…right". She'd seen me do strange things before, but knew I was harmless."

"I went to the exact spot in the dream and…yes…yes…they were there. There were two grey morel mushrooms about an inch and a half tall each…and it didn't really surprise me. I'd have been more surprised if they hadn't been there at all, because the dream was that convincing."

"I looked around and didn't find any others. I figured these two were a gift from the mushroom gods, so I shouldn't be too greedy. I harvested the two and returned to the house. I placed the mushrooms on the newspaper that Vicky hadn't even looked up from. I don't remember her exact words, but I probably couldn't repeat them anyway. Every year, we usually have a competition to find the first 'shroom of the season…and I had just won for this season, because of that dream."

88   *Louie Dalton*

"I was born in Peoria and was here until the age of eight…moved to Arizona…several different towns. Stayed there until I was twelve, and then we moved back to Peoria. We moved out for my mom's health, and then after we were there…everybody missed the family, and wanted to come back to Illinois….everybody but me and my brother. I'm 61 and retired from CAT in '95…and then I was off work for a year and four months…had a heart attack and then recuperated…went back to work and then started riding motorcycles. I went back to work and started *paying* for motorcycles."

"I've got a Harley Davidson Road King Custom…it's a new one they came out with last year. And before that…two summers I rode the Harley Davidson V-Rod…a Porsche design Harley took credit for. They're not accepted by Harley riders…but probably the sweetest motorcycle on the road."

"I started off in my mid-twenties with dirt bikes…trail-riding…and crashed a lot of times. Then, I bought a road bike, went out on the road, and I didn't like it, so I gave it up. Then I started up again after I had the heart attack…thinking "Geez, I'd better have some fun". Then, I loved it…I loved being out on the road."

"I started out at Caterpillar in the shop and hated it, hated the environment, hated the work, so I got into…at that time they called it data processing…now who knows…they changed it to information systems, or whatever you want to call it. I got into supervision…I went into that and got into supervision…so I supervised for about twenty years. I got out of that and retired at 31 years and…uh…I been doing ok. I was doing ok until I started getting back into motorcycles. I've had at least ten since '96…in the last ten years I've probably had ten bikes…so…now I'm working paying for those."

"Way back when…they didn't have child abuse laws, so they could do pretty much whatever they wanted, and we got involved in things. At one point I remember, before I went to Arizona, we lived in Kankakee, and my aunt and uncle owned one of those cars with the running boards, and we would meet them down at the end of the lane when they were coming back, and we'd ride on the boards, and hang onto the posts. So I fell off and the car ran over both my legs…and it didn't break anything. It was like an old Model A sedan or something, or Model T or something. And then my dad...he had the big car with the full rounded fenders, with the headlights on the fenders...and you could sit on the fenders. He would let my brother and I ride, whenever we went any-where...and the wind was just my favorite thing...we would ride on the fenders and hang onto the headlights, and he would go down the roads...gravel roads...probably fifty or sixty miles an hour."

"Arizona has a really deep impact on my life, because, when we went out...I remember my dad bought a two and a half ton farm truck...a Ford farm truck...'35 Ford farm truck...and we loaded everything we had, including a dog, and headed for Arizona...I don't know how long it took us to get there. When we got there, he sold the truck, and couldn't find work...and I know that the first six to eight weeks, we moved into a trailer park...and back then a trailer park was just called a trailer park...across from a greyhound dog racing track...so...a pretty wild environment. Couldn't afford the trailer park, so the guy rented us a ten by fourteen foot woodshed...dirt floor...one light bulb...one outlet for where you screw in the electrical outlets. So, that's where we lived for about six to eight weeks. That has an impact upon you, I mean, even at age eight, you still remember all those things."

"One of the things we did in Arizona...they rotate crops out there...they irri-gated them then, I don't know about now. They would go through the fields and pick stuff and leave potatoes or whatever...well, they would let us scrounge through the fields and dig out whatever food we could find...potatoes or cabbage or whatever they were growing. Then, every Saturday and Sunday, when we weren't in school, we would go to the cotton fields and pick cotton, and that was age nine or ten, and the whole family did that. Then you get to go to the chuck-wagon and buy a soda and a bowl of chili...and that was your reward for working all day in the cotton fields...then the rest of the money went into the family kitty. Our family stayed poor...forever...forever."

"The reason I brought that up about the dirt floor...I went, "Never...never again.". My kids were raised...nice. They were raised with good housing, and when they turned sixteen, they got a car. I went the wrong direction with them...where we had nothing...we like, overcompensated with the kids. But that creates just as many problems."

"Probably the only bad problem I have is…I've always had addictions, and some of those I won't go into…but the addictions…you'll like…trade them off. To get one out of your mind, you'll trade it off for something that you get obsessed and compulsive with…like motorcycles…but I suppose that's really not that bad of a thing…to me anyway."

89   *Adonis Porch*

"I live here now. I am originally from Detroit, Michigan…and I am nineteen years of age. I moved down here in July of 2004. Growing up in Detroit was kinda hard because of the environment there, that I was raised in…but I was just a normal kid…doing normal kid things. But, yet there were some things I had to grow up and do at a young age. I had to baby-sit. I didn't get to do a lot of activities because I was home helping my mom while she worked three jobs. My mom worked for an energy company called Detroit Edison…she worked for UPS, and then she worked for a factory…and I can't remember the name of it."

"We had this thing called "safe night", that happened once a year…maybe two weeks after the school had started. A lot of kids that went to different schools…we would all get together, and instead of being out in the streets doing drugs and shooting…we would go and have a big party. One time, afterwards, all the schools came outside, and we didn't have nothing to do…so they actually went and ran into a gas station, took whatever they saw, and tried to run out before the door closed and locked them in…not exactly what they wanted you to do on "safe night"."

"My grandfather, Wesley Lee, is the comedian of our family. He has his ways…yet he makes sure we are taken care of. Last time I went fishing with him, I was maybe eight years old, and the reel was all tangled up, and I didn't know. He told me to stop pulling on it, and the boat started moving and got wrapped in the motor…and it broke. He got all excited and said, "You're never going fishing with me again. You just ruined my fishing boat…you're never going with me again." I said, "Okay…fine. Keep your fishing boat. I'll get my own boat.""

"I just found out that I am the big brother of a new sister…nineteen years difference. My new sister's name is Andria Singleton."

"My high school, Peoria Central High School, has the ROTC program. I am more active with that than I am, out in the streets getting into trouble and everything. The Junior ROTC program is a program within our high school where the different branches of service are. Ours happens to be the Air Force. We do parades. We compete against other ROTC programs…against Manual, Richwoods, and Woodruff. We're trying to raise money to go to Washington. We do community service. It also helps us get into colleges."

"One thing about me…I've always loved everybody, no matter who, or what they were. People with disabilities…I'm a real softee when I see someone with a disability."

90 *Lynn Niemeier*

"Last September...I saw my son finish his first half-marathon...not half-marathon...half-triathlon. He had been to Oregon, and this was eight months since he had been released from jail...for being a heroin addict. He's doing full triathlons and marathons now, and placing in the top ten. It's a way for him to stay healthy and focus his tremendous amount of energy to something more productive than what he did before. I am so proud."

91   *Nicholas Frain*

"Nick Frain, 38. We just came from a wedding...what was the name of the church...Holy Trinity Catholic Church? It's downtown Bloomington. A cousin of mine...she is originally from California...and...uh...her parents were originally from Chicago...she moved out to California...kind of a Sacramento girl who has some Chicago roots. So, she ended up going back here to school at Illinois State. So she met her...now husband, here at Illinois State, and that's where they're...we're kind of rendezvousing here...the family from California and Chicago...and I'm from Indianapolis. My family is from Indianapolis."

"I didn't know many people on the groom's side, just because I knew the bride's side. Like I said, she's my cousin, and I have five siblings...so all of my siblings are here with their kids. So, a lot of nieces and nephews are here, and I've got seven aunts and uncles on that particular side of the family. And so, six of them...five of them were here, so we got to see aunts and uncles that we don't get to see very often."

"The ceremony was pretty traditional...Catholic, which was kind of a traditional mass with a little bit of wedding thrown in on the side. So, we had...I actually got to do a reading...the second reading, which was from Corinthians. So that was kind of...love is patient...love is kind...yeah, let's not brag, let's not boast...the whole nine yards. So, we had that. We had...ummm...one thing that stood out. My wife and I were just talking about it. The groom was not Catholic, so in a traditional Catholic ceremony, when you've got both bride and groom that are Catholic...when you're Catholic, you know, you're both up there on the altar. Well, I didn't know this but, him not being Catholic...not being converted to Catholicism, they made them sit in two chairs to the side of the altar, and you know, when the priest brought down communion for her...you know, he just took the sign of the cross...took a blessing instead. So, it was a little...a little different."

"So, it was nice, and now we have a couple hours off between the ceremony and the reception. My brother...my brother right there was the best man at my wedding. You know, one of the traditional things that you try and do, like...hide the wedding ring and say you can't find the ring when they call for it...right in the middle of the ceremony? Well...he had put some tape on the bottom of my shoes…and so when I'm kneeling at the altar, at my wedding…he was going to put "Help Me" on the left and "Help Right Me" on the right…but he ended up just putting a couple of peace signs on the underside of my shoes. So, everybody kind of snickered at that."

"I thought this was interesting…one of the things the priest said. He said that when you get married, you lose your individuality…and I don't think he meant that. I was thinking, "Lose your individuality? You're still an individual." But then, he went on to explain that you lose those types of things that, like…things that you, like…go and do by yourself. That you should be considerate of the other person…consider the other person first in your life. Put them…put them first. I thought that was pretty good advice. Be respectful and considerate. Yes."

92   *Ron Stalter*

"My name is Ron Stalter, and I'm from Trivoli…I grew up in Trivoli."

"I used to spend a lot of time with my cousins…and one cousin had a cabin down by the river. Of course, that was a good place for underage kids to go and drink…right? So, we had parties down there all the time. The fun thing about the parties…well, there were a couple of fun things…and one of them was a mini-bike. We would drink and smoke cigars…and have wheelie contests on the mini-bike. We would be drunken, cigar-smoking, mini-bike riding kids…down by the river."

"By the cabin, there was an outhouse…and it had a really loud…super loud buzzer. There was a button that was in the cabin that you could use to set it off. So, one time we had this party…with girls…and this girl went in the outhouse…and after a minute, we set the buzzer off. The purpose of the buzzer was to surprise people, and see if they would come running out with their pants down. I mean…this buzzer was really, really loud. It was like, "WHAAAAAAAA!" The guy that built the place just had a good sense of humor…we didn't put it there. The outhouse was across this little bridge…went over a ravine and everything. He went to a lot of trouble to run the wire out there. We had people get real close to running out…pounding on the door, but nobody actually ran out with their pants down. Of course, it was still funny to us…the type of humor that only liquor and cigar smoke can create."

"I've done software development, networking, board repair…about everything associated with electronics or computers. In my past, I worked for WMBD…and a cash register place called ACME. I only worked at WMBD for five weeks, because after I started, I learned I wouldn't get weekends off…for like, ten years. I was a young kid, and I didn't want to ruin my weekends."

"I am currently rented to a business unit within Caterpillar…to help them with their IT strategies…for architectural choices. I help them to build relationships with the corporate office, and get them in line with software choices that are more corporate than business related. For example…this group that I'm working with picked software tools that they just felt like buying. So, I am there to get them to see the light on standardization…give them some processes that they didn't have before. They did development without any type of process before…so everybody was doing something different. So, I'm helping that group out right now."

"This year…just this year, I graduated from Bradley with a 4.0 GPA. It's challenging to work, go to school, and raise a family all at the same time. I had been going for eight years…part-time, while I worked. I finally got done…and it was thrilling to be done with that, and not have to go to class anymore. While I went to Bradley…and graduated from Bradley…I am not exactly a Bradley fan. I didn't feel like the school did me any favors, and I was happy to be done with them."

"When I worked for a previous company, my cousin was selling fake Rolexes…and getting them from some guy in Florida. He just bought one…and actually, he wasn't selling them…he was wearing one, and I said, "Hey that's cool…can you get me one?" He got me one, and I wore it to work. A couple people asked for them…and so I got them from my cousin and sold them. I didn't make any profit…I just sold them for whatever I paid for them. Pretty soon, everybody was wanting one…and I sold two or three dozen altogether."

"One day while I was at work, I got a call to come up to the foyer. I went up and there was a policeman there, who immediately handcuffed me, and said, "We know what's going on with the Rolex watches…we know everything." Well…the reason he knew everything is because I was set up. He knew all my contacts…he knew where the watches were coming from. He was a real cop, so I really thought it was legitimate. He said that if I didn't give him more details about my sources…he was going to take me downtown. He said, "Okay…I'm done with you…we're going downtown and we're going to book you." Well…I had never been to jail before. So, I started thinking…and said, "Well, I need to get my coat." I was planning on just taking off…I was going to go out the back, get in my car, and run off…seriously. About that time, the president of the company came out and surprised me…and I learned it was a setup. I was really, really glad it was a joke…and it was over. They hid a video camera in a rubber plant, out in the foyer…and for several years showed the tape to everyone in the company."

"As far as what's ahead for me…I'm more of a Forrest Gump…I just kinda float around…get bumped from here to there. I wish I could plan more…to figure out where I'm going to end up. Some people have some vision about where they want to end up, and I haven't gotten there yet…haven't figured it out…but maybe…that's the way it's supposed to be."

93   *Don Zessin*

"I live in Farmington. I am retired from Caterpillar. I have several businesses that I take care of...a music theater and a salvage yard...recycling yard really. I also have a few house rentals. I'm cooking potatoes for the rotary club today. We're selling "rotators". I think the Halley's came up with that...out at the Halley's sawmill. They made a machine where we can peel the potatoes, and it works out real well. You just take a drill at one end, and it's set on a platform...the drill goes forward. It's got springs on it...and you put a potato between a hard, little...oh...like a little pointed piece of metal. Then the potato just slides in between that piece of metal...a blade cuts it on the end...and the rotary...and as the drill turns, it moves that potato around and makes it curly. It works out real good."

"I grew up on a farm, just baling hay and doing farm work. I did it for my dad, and did it for money...not very long. I worked at a lumberyard...and then became a barber for about ten years. I got talked into being a barber by my aunt and my mother. I went to barber school down on Adams Street...Zach Monroe's. I worked as a barber from about '64 to '74, and one day I left the door open in the summertime, and looked down, and there is a skunk coming in my door. A live skunk, by golly...and it came right into my store. I held real still...and there was a customer in the chair, and I said, "Don't move." I didn't want to scare him. I didn't know if it was a pet or what. I didn't know if it was really wild. I still don't know...and I'll never know. He come in and looked around...circled around my barbershop...and then walked back out. Then, I watched it walk up the street."

"When I was a barber, I had a couple of pet alligators in an aquarium, and it was just an attention getter, you know? People liked to see 'em. I had to feed them minnows. One time, I was on Christmas vacation...and I took a couple days off. My meter quit working...my gas meter...and they both froze. They wasn't actually froze, but it was so cold, they died."

"The dinner theater...it used to be called Zellmer's Dinner Theater, and I've owned that building for thirty years. I rented it to Zellmer's, and we did various things with it. Well, Zellmer's is not there any more, and so we have a music theater there now, called Farmington Music Theater. Mostly, we have country music...mostly...a little bit of Elvis, a little bit of country, and so forth."

"I worked at a heat-treat furnace my entire life at Caterpillar...all my time. I worked in East Peoria...and those buildings aren't even there any more. I thought I would retire out of those buildings...and they tore them down. I finally retired out of HH. Probably the worst time there was when I got laid off for seven months...and in the seventh month, it started to worry me. It made me think about things. It made me realize that you can't take life too seriously...you just go on with life."

"I spend most of my time with my recycling yard. It's mostly a metal business...aluminum...and they bring cars in, and refrigerators. I pretty much just recycle metal. I don't get into cardboard and glass...just mostly metal. I also work in apartments...just kind of fixing them up."

"I always liked working with young people...always wanted to see them do good. I was working in Cub Scouts, and coached little league...coached boxing. A lot of people might not know that...but that's okay. I always wanted to see kids do good."

94   *Randy McCallister*

"I'm forty. I'm kind of semi-retired…I did well in a past life and saved my money, but I tend bar sometimes, and sometimes help my uncle in his lawn-care business. Also, I'm kinda lazy…don't want to get stuck in that 9 to 5 crap."

"I really…truly loved Underdog, although sometimes…some of the jokes escaped me until I got a little older. I remember at the beginning of each episode, a…a customer would always tip shoe-shine boy with a coin and say something like, "Thank you, shoe-shine boy. You are both humble and loveable", and then, shoe-shine boy would bite the coin to make sure it was real. It was very funny. I guess they probably still run Underdog on Nick at Night, or some other channel…is that still on…Nick at Night? I'll have to ask the kids. I think even when I was a kid, they were reruns."

"I don't remember any really bad violence other than Underdog plowing into criminals a lot with his…his…his fist extended, and that always happened after something happened to Sweet Polly Purebred…after her "I'm in trouble" song, "Oh where, oh where has my Underdog gone? Oh where, oh where could he be?" Simon Bar-Sinister was one of the bad guys…the best villain on the show."

"One episode, Underdog had destroyed a group of evil robots by singing a note high enough to break the glass brains in their heads…but it also broke all of the windows, street lights, mirrors, and even pickle jars in the town…even the pickle jars. That was the catch line…even the pickle jars. When all the people came to him to complain about the damage he just sort of waved them off and said, "I am the hero who never fails. I cannot be bothered with those details." Very funny…very memorable."

"When I was in the Navy, and I was going to school in Meridian…we had this football team that we formed…it was like, one barracks against another barracks…and we called ourselves "The Underdogs"…and we were. But, I remember one time, I found a twenty-dollar bill on the field where we played, and that was cool. I don't think we actually won a game…but I found twenty dollars. I used it to buy a ceramic Frankenstein statue out in town, which was broken a few weeks later when they brought the drug dogs through the barracks."

"They would bring these dogs through, and they would bark whenever they smelled pot...only I think there was probably so much pot in the barracks, that they couldn't ever really pinpoint it. They never looked where the pot was, because mostly it was hidden in cans of Duraglit, which masked the smell. The curtains reeked of pot, and the racks, and the...the...ummm...carpeting. The carpeting probably had pounds of marijuana ground into it over the years. Anyway, this drug dog they brought in was sniffing around the Frankenstein, and knocked it over...and broke it. The Navy was supposed to pay me for the damage, but never did...and I was getting too short...getting too close to leaving to complain about it. I didn't blame the dog...he was just doing his job."

95   *Don Gonyea*

"My earliest memory…and it's very vivid…I was three years old. I remember my oldest sister going off to kindergarten…first day of school. I remember the bus pulling up in front of the house…and my sister, Debbie, who is thirty months older than me, getting on that bus. It was a very exciting, and as I recall, traumatic day for her…which is probably why I remember it so well. These things stick with you. I remember sitting on the arm of the chair…looking out the front picture window…and watching her go off to the bus…crying. It's funny, I remember her first day of school better than mine."

"I remember September 11th. I was heading to the Metro when my cell phone rang, and it was my editor, telling me that a plane had hit the World Trade Center…and that I should get to the White House as quickly as I can…that we should probably get some reaction. We all thought it was an accident at that point. We thought it was a small plane…at least from the initial reports. Then, while I am still on the phone with him, the second plane hits. So, I flagged down a cab and headed for the White House. Somewhere in the back of my mind as I'm driving to the White House…I became aware that I may be going to a building that's a target. The Pentagon hadn't been hit yet, but it was clear that it was an attack."

"As I get to the White House, I'm going through the main security gate…and just as I'm passing through the gate, talking to the Secret Service guys that I see every day…somebody on the other side of the gate, that was already inside…right in that spot where all the TV networks do their stand-ups that you see every night, with the White House in the background…somebody from in there…I don't know who it was, yelled that the Pentagon had been hit. At that point, the White House emptied out…they evacuated the place. They told everybody to get out of there. I'm standing there, and I'm seeing women that work at the White House, running out…carrying their high heels…because they can't run in their high heels. They're kind of holding them and crying."

"The Secret Service guys…you kind of develop a rapport with the Secret Service guys when you're in the White House every day. They check you out, they know you're ok…you get to know them…it's almost like the relationship that reporters have with local cops in a small town. Suddenly, these friendly Secret Service guys…they've got machine guns…and Uzi's. They're not…they're not your pals any more. They're hustling your rear end out of there…because nobody knows what's going on."

"I knelt down in the middle of Pennsylvania Avenue, because you're always a reporter in the midst of something like this…even though you're potentially running for safety, or whatever. I knelt down and got my recorder out of my bag, so I could get the sounds of all of this stuff…Secret Service barking orders…people running by…sirens we were starting to hear, and everything else. And…at…at…at that point, there…there was a man from one of the TV networks standing next to me…and he had just talked to somebody on one of those big walkie-talkies on their hip, that they carry around. And…uh, he…he kinda looked at me…and his face was really white. I said, "What's up…what's going on?" And…he had just talked to one of their pre-positioned camera crews who were out at Andrews Air Force Base. They had been there since the president took off that morning…and they were waiting there until he came back, because there's always a camera shooting during the take-off and landing of the president. He…he said to me…and his face was just white…he said, "I just heard from these guys out at Andrews…and they said they just saw the 'Doomsday Plane' take off." It was just such a…surreal moment."

"I have worked for National Public Radio for twenty years now, starting out as a freelancer, and eventually becoming a staff reporter. It's a great place to work…and you always feel like you're doing worthwhile work in this profession…and in this organization. This is a very satisfying profession that I am in."

"I am a Midwesterner. I grew up in Southeast Michigan…Monroe, Michigan. It's about a half hour south of Detroit. It's becoming, kind of a bedroom community to both Detroit and Toledo…because it is literally only a half an hour from each. But, when I was growing up, it was literally a town of itself and had its own identity…then and now…mostly rural. We lived on an acre, a few miles outside of town. It's kind of…classic, small town America. My father ran a diner in town for a number of years…and then I-75 went through, in the 50's…and kind of took a lot of the traffic. It's happened to so many little places."

"I remember sitting down and interviewing Rosa Parks when I was in Detroit…ten or twelve years ago. At some point, she left Montgomery, and moved to Detroit. She was a fixture in that town. I identify myself as a Detroiter…even though I grew up in a small town, south of the city. It was really, just a nice reassuring thing…you'd just be walking around town, and you'd see…Rosa Parks. You'd see her in the grocery store…you'd see her just going about her life. When I interviewed her, it just confirmed what my suspicion was, based on seeing her around town. She was not someone who…went about her life, as a celebrity…as this icon that, she clearly was. She was as normal as normal could be…and humble as humble could be. When I sat down and talked to her…that all came through. She certainly recognized what she did…and understood why people wanted to ask her about it. She would talk about it, but didn't feel that she had earned any celebrity status…or…or…whatever you want to call it. It was something she did…something she believed in…and something she thought was important. She went on with her life…and, in this era where we encounter so many people who are trying to draw attention to themselves, it was fascinating to see someone who had truly participated in such a remarkable event in American history…and didn't want you to make a fuss out of it."

"I interviewed Johnny Cash…one day in 1980. That was very early on in my career…as someone…somebody working in this business. It was one of the…he was so…so nice. I was just a cub reporter from some local radio station. He didn't even need to give me the time of day…but spent a half an hour with me…and was thoughtful, polite…and answered my questions, no matter how stupid they might have been. I remember coming away from that, thinking, "This is kind of a fun profession". It was in 1980…so it was in one of those lulls in his career. His 1960's and 1970's "Folsom Prison Blues" era was in the past…and he hadn't had the resurgence he later had, the last decade of his life."

"I interviewed him backstage at a county fair…playing a county fair audience. It was really one of those moments that make you appreciate the kinds of situations you find yourself in…when you're in this business. I think it speaks to a core decency…all the well-publicized troubles and addictions, and everything else that a guy like Johnny Cash had…and we all know about them. But, all I know is…the half hour he spent with me, you know…I really wasn't anybody who was going to help him out or anything…given the small station I was working for, and all that. But, he was really…just a decent, decent guy. I still have a tiny picture on our refrigerator of me talking to Johnny Cash."

"Now, here I am going to the White House…doing things like…watching…watching a parade in Red Square, in May of this year, to mark the 60th anniversary of the…the fall of Nazi Germany. There are a lot of remark-able…remarkable things that this business has allowed me to see."

"Years ago, I was in a little town called Galena. Then I went down to this little farm community…Ursa, Illinois. Do you know where Ursa is? I think I have it right…U-r-s-a…but, look it up. I did a profile there…ten…ten or twelve years ago, of a farmer down there. His fields were just…I remember standing on the edge of his field, and it looked like we were looking across Lake Michigan. It just went forever…water to the horizon. He could kind of show me some telephone lines off in the distance, where the edge of his field would be. It was just…all water, from here to there. And that…those are pretty powerful stories when you're talking with people about what they're going through."

"Some of the flood stories were pretty emotional. I remember walking into a guy's house with him. In Grand Forks…North Dakota. Grand Forks was the town that flooded…and while there was six feet of water in the streets…the town caught fire, and burned down. There was water everywhere…but the fire trucks couldn't get through to put water on the fire…to put it out. That was such a dev-astating story to cover. It's just this little town on the edge of the prairie…and I remember going into this guy's house outside of town. He and his family…his wife and kids had, during the flood, gone to visit her parents in Minne-sota…yes…yes…Minnesota…or maybe Wisconsin. I think it was Wisconsin. I asked him if I could join him, when he went back to his house for the first time…and he said yes. I'm always…always appreciative, when somebody allows you to tag along…at such a moment. I don't know that I would…because you know it's going to be such a devastating thing…perhaps."

"We went into his house…and it so happened that he had kids the same age as my kids. The house…the water had gone down enough where we could go into the main floor of the house…but then, we opened the basement door. The water was like, three steps down. You could see…you could see…he was pulling stuff out of the water. Floating…was like, this little Disney video in a Cinderella video case…kids toys…school records…a college diploma, and things like that. That was a pretty…pretty, tough thing to watch with him."

"When I was a kid, I had a…and I still have it…a stuffed Quick Draw McGraw. Perhaps you were a fan? I had broken my leg when I was five years old…ice skat-ing. We had a little homemade pond in our back yard. I went to the hospital and got my leg set...and for whatever reason, other than it was a broken leg and I had to spend the night at the hospital...my dad bought it for me. I spent the night in the hospital in this kind of a full cast. My dad came the next morning and brought this stuffed Quick Draw McGraw. I still have it. It's now kind of tucked away on a shelf in a little corner of our house. My kids know that it's Quick Draw, even though most of his fur is worn off."

"I've never been a guy who has a five year career plan. I recognized early on that I had a knack for being on the radio...that my writing skills, and on-the-air skills are...are such that...this is something that I like to do...am comfortable doing. I've been doing it for 25 years, so...somebody must think I'm okay doing it. I like working for National Public Radio a lot...and when I got my very first radio job...and I found myself interviewing Johnny Cash, at a county fair...I had no grand designs that I thought would take me to the White House in 2001...following the president around the country. I won't cover the White House forever...I've been doing it now for five years, but after the next elections, do I look for something else to do? I'll look at what...what options are available. We'll see what presents itself."

"I think I have a lot of the important things that make a person happy...and feel like I'm pretty lucky in that regard. I've worked hard for it, as well. I've always worked hard, and focused on my craft...and every day, tried to learn something, and get a little better at what I do...and it's paid off. I am a pretty optimistic person...and I...tend to wake up thinking every day is going to be a good day...and most of them are."

96 *Frank Pignataro*

"The Pope is dead…long live the Pope. I'm sick of the Pope. Who cares what this new guy thinks? He's a joke…a goddamn joke. The Catholic Church keeps trying to turn back the clock. I'm waiting for the day when married priests bless third-trimester abortions…and give last rites to suicidal cancer patients. Why do they make a big deal out of this old-world eunuch?"

97   *Raj Mohan*

"I am an engineer, and not yet thirty. I am not a citizen here...and I will not stay here forever, as I miss my home. There are many things that I miss in India. I miss my father and my mother more than anything."

"When I was a child, my father worked in hospital...in Baharampur, and my mother stayed home with my brothers and sisters. We lived in a very tall building with many, many others, but we were on the first floor and had access to the garden. The building...the entire complex, was provided to us by the hospital. It was very crowded and unclean, except for the garden. The garden was immaculate...beautiful."

"The garden was right outside my window...and I would play in the garden and pretend I was in the jungle riding an elephant. While playing in the garden, I could smell the scent of my mother cooking fish in the kitchen...and I could hear the popping of mustard seeds in the hot oil as she placed the fish in the karais. There were many other scents, but...the smell that was the strongest was the smell of fresh fish frying in mustard oil."

"I would ride with my father to the fish market by bicycle. We had two very rusty and very old bicycles, and my father would let me ride with him to market as long as I stayed close by. We would ride over muddy gravel roads for several kilometers and talk about what happened that day. I remember the smell of the fish market...and the flies. You would not believe the flies. The flies covered everything. There was no refrigeration. Just like much of the world...no refrigeration."

"The market was always full of people buying and selling fish. My father would talk to the merchants and purchase the fish. He would talk to them in a very...animated fashion...waving his arms, and trying to purchase the fish for the lowest price. Then we would ride back home with the packet of fish tied to my father's bicycle. I could smell the fish as I was riding behind him."

"When I was very small, I would hold onto my mother's sari and watch her place the pieces of fish into the karais. My mother would sprinkle salt into the oil and I would watch it sizzle...and I would watch my brother as he would throw salt into the fire, creating these…bright blue sparks. The fire fascinated me then….and I am still fascinated by fire. It is like magic."

"As the fish would cook, she would flip it with khunti, which resembles a…a spatula, but it is narrower and…it is straight. My mother cooked other things, such as eggs, vegetables, and lentils, but fish was always the main food. We did not eat meat often. When we had meat, very often it was goat."

"I do not eat meat here in the United States…I mostly eat vegetables and fish. I have recently discovered tuna, which is a tasty fish. In India, we did not eat salt-water fish…we ate freshwater fish…at least from my region. But here, one night at a business dinner, I had the tuna at Jonah's, and I liked it very much. So now…often I buy fresh tuna and cook it myself."

"Sometimes…I will invite friends to my apartment. I will cut the tuna into thin strips and coat each piece with sesame seeds…and then slide the pieces into a shallow wok with a small amount of peanut oil. The sesame seeds pop…and it reminds me of home, and being with my mother…listening to the mustard seeds as they popped in the mustard oil."

98   *Paul McLaughlin*

"I had some little inexpensive binoculars that my folks had bought for me at one time...and I was always mislaying them. Mom would pick them up and put them aside...and then give them back to me every Christmas. I got those binoculars every Christmas for about five years. It was always a hoot...we laughed our heads off about it.
It was always a fun thing. It was the gift that kept coming back."

"My daughters have been gifts. It tears me up just to think about it...the days my daughters were born. I can't even watch a video of somebody else having a baby without tearing up. Honest to God...I'm getting soft in my old age. To see those little heads pop out...is just the most fantastic thing. My oldest girl, when she came out...she crowned...the doctor told my wife to stop pushing, and...Kate didn't wait...she didn't wait...and she's been in a hurry ever since."

99   *Fred Dirkse*

"My name is Fred Dirkse...Frederick Jason Dirkse to be exact. So, I have two big...you know, horror figures in my name...Freddy Krueger and Jason from "Friday the 13th". My current job is computer programmer...but really entrepreneur, which is really my main job. I own the OIC Group, and we mainly do custom software development, and a lot of websites...web hosting, and things of that nature. I also own a coffee shop...two completely different things, but that's generally the entrepreneurial part of things."

"I started my company mainly due to my inability to work for other people. Not necessarily because I think I can do it better...there isn't always a best way to do things. Very often, there are very few times where there is a single, right way to do it...there are different ways to do it. I have that mindset where I just don't particularly care working for other people."

"Starting the computer company, we have never had to borrow a dime...which is nice, especially in the technology industry. The coffee shop is another story. It was a fairly sizeable investment to get it going. Talking to Pat Sullivan about moving the computer company, we kind of, at the same time...Doug and myself and Pat...said the corner of the building would be a good location for a coffee shop, and a small café style restaurant. So being that it was something I wanted to do, and Pat said it would be great location for it...we just kept that process going...and so we did that...and in the process just kept asking as many people as we possibly could...general business owners, people who own a restaurant, or have owned a restaurant before...to get their input and opinion. Our whole objective in that process was to..."let's find a reason or reasons not to do it". That was the big thing. We couldn't find one, so we developed a business plan, and got things rolling with Pat. We applied for the loan, got approved, and just got it done."

"I am the last of the children, so to speak, in my family. My father was 59 years old when he had me. He's no longer with us, but...twenty year difference between he and my mom. I have five brothers and sisters...technically half brothers and sisters. My mom and my dad were married previously before that, and they were...well, my brother was twenty years old when I was born...so there was this huge gap. So, I had all these brothers and sisters, yet they were all old enough to be my parents. My dad was old enough to be my grandfather, easily. We were often mistaken...we would go out to eat, and the waitress would say something like, "You're here with your grandfather?" But then, "No...no, I'm here with my dad."

"My dad was a car dealer, and I've washed more cars in my life than I care to mention. I will never wash another car again. Went to a lot of car auctions...and wanted to be an auctioneer...attempted it many times as a child, but couldn't quite master it."

"We had a cottage on a small inland lake in Michigan, called Gun Lake. It was called Gun Lake because years back, there was some sort of treaty with the Indians where everybody decided to lay down all their weapons, and they had this big ceremony where all the Indians threw all their guns into the lake. I think shortly after that, they then killed off all the Indians in the area."

"There was one kid in the area...the association where the cottage was...you'd come around the corner...and that's where you could see all the houses. I was always excited, to see if their car was in the driveway...to see if I would have anybody to play with. He went by "Dickie" for a good part of his childhood, until he reached twelve or thirteen...then he decided to go by Richard."

"I grew up with almost all adult influences...there were no other kids...especially brothers and sisters around. Dickie and I got into mischief a few times with paint and turpentine. We lit the yard on fire once with fireworks, and almost burned down the garage. It was always fun."

100 *W.L. Yarosz*

"I'm Bill...Bill Yarosz. I'm 53. Right now, I live in Virginia. I was passing through...I'm driving a truck...just passing through, and I used to live around here...and I've got some friends here...so I just stopped in to say hi. Been driving a truck two years...and before that, worked at a nuclear power plant."

"I'll tell you a story about the time I got stopped in Decatur...by the cops. Oh my god! We were living in Decatur, Illinois at Christmas time...it was Christmas time, and it must have been, I don't know, maybe seven...eight years ago. Well, anyway, I had dropped my wife and daughter off at a friend's house, and my son and I went Christmas shopping up at the mall. So...when it was time to go pick them up...I went down to pick them up...and as I made this one turn to go to my friends house, I noticed there was a cop that was sitting in the median...and I didn't think anything of it, you know. So, I went and picked up my wife...came back out and the cop was still sitting there."

"When I went by, he pulled out behind me, and I thought, "Okay, he was running radar and he was done or whatever." So, I drive down the road and come to an intersection, and another cop pulls in behind. So now, I got two cops following me...and I thought, "Okay." So, I come to another intersection, and there's another cop at another intersection...at the crossroads...and he got there before I did...so I'm waiting for him to go, and he wouldn't go. He waved for me to go on. So I went through the intersection, and he pulled out behind me. So now I've got three cops following me."

"I'm looking at my wife and wondering, "What in the heck is going on here?" I'm not speeding or anything. So, we're driving down the road, and pretty soon a fourth cop comes behind, and now I've got four cops following me. All of a sudden, their lights go on. So, I pulled over...and the cops got out of their car and opened their doors...got behind their doors, pulled their guns on us, and then, "Put your hands up in the air where we can see you." My wife was just looking at me, like, "What did you do when you went to the mall?""

"Evidently, somebody had been robbed, down where I went to pick up my wife, and they were driving a...ummm...a Bronco. It just happened to be the same time OJ was being chased in his white Bronco...and I'm driving a Bronco. So, they see this Bronco with me and my son go by, and they thought we had pulled the robbery…so they pulled us over. Four cops pulling a gun on you…on a family. They…they came over and asked me for my driver's license, and he says, "Give me your drivers license." I go, "I'm going to reach into my pocket and get my drivers license." I didn't want them to think I was going to pull a gun. He took it back to the car…brought it back, and didn't apologize or anything…and said, "Okay, you can go." He didn't apologize or anything."

"I like driving a truck. I worked in nuclear power plants for twenty years, after I got out of the Navy…and I just got…burned out. I had to try something new. So, all my kids are gone…grown…nothing holding me back. So my wife and I decided to move and start a new career…and here we are."

101   ***Pastor Dan***

"I am a pastor, so there ain't a whole lot else my life has been about. Twenty years ago, before I came to Christ...and I was just hearin' what this young man here...we're just sitting at a picnic table, and brother I forget what your name was...Frank? I was just sittin' here drinkin' a lemonade and we're just sharing with Frank what God has done to my life and stuff. This life has been bad for me before I come over to Christ...drugs...alcohol...gangs. My gang leader and all...I shared with him about Jesus Christ saving my life and all, and just like I was sharing with Frank, my gang leader...he didn't care a whole lot about it. He didn't put me down...he said, "That's all right for you brother...you need it for you, but not for me." Three years later, he got it point blank in the back of the head with a 4-10."

"I got shafted by drug dealing friends. I remember sittin' in jail for three days, for a lousy three hundred dollars. I had friends that had all kinds of money, and my drugs, and they never come to get me out. So, when I started hearing about this Jesus, and how he cared for me and loved me, I think down inside, it was something I wanted to listen to. Nobody really cared, and I thought this...long story short...true...I gave my life to Jesus Christ sittin' on a couch. It was actually Jimmy Swaggert. It was sad, 'cuz when he fell, so many people wanted to hang him up to dry and everything. In my eyes, it was if I had fallen in a deep pit and Frank reached in and helped me out of that deep pit...and then a year later we found out Frank had shot and murdered some people. Even though we know Frank was wrong, my heart would have hurt for him...because that man was for me, and helped my life and stuff, and I would have been there to help him and stuff. This whole world seems to be about self, and what can we get for ourself and all."

"So, I started thinkin' about Jesus Christ, and his whole life was about helping people. So, when I decided to make that change and give my life to Christ, I didn't realize what was about to happen. But, when he came into my life...my heart...and came into my life, he imparted that into me...his desire for me to be there and help people. I thought that everything I have been through...and I was telling Frank...in 1978, I was looking at 60 to 120 years in prison. I ended up getting released, by the grace of God, with reduced charges and stuff. Now, I hold services in the prison. I have a street ministry and everything...previously

Friendship House…Trinity Temple down on Perry Street, and then we come out to places like this…sharing with this young man, Frank. This man doesn't know Christ, and stuff, and he's got a bad past, and we're hoping we can just get a handful of people to decide that maybe it's worth listenin' to the Bible…what God says."

"In my past, I believed in God and stuff, but I really didn't care, and then I got to thinkin'…if God is real, and I thought he was…I really believe that he created mankind. Well then, it almost makes sense to me that this thing called the Bible…if he was able to…to…write this book, through men…that…that would be the guy to listen to…if he really created men. I tell that to some people and they go, "You know…men, just men wrote the Bible." I say, "Who's smarter, God or men?" They say that God is smarter, so then I say that if man can develop a satellite and shoot it up into outer space, put it up there, and then simultaneously project a picture of me sitting here on the other side of the world…accurate picture…accurate words, and everything. If man…if man is smart enough to do that, don't you think this God we just admitted created mankind would be smart enough to work through man's minds and hands, and be able to write down in a book, words that was from him, and it wasn't tainted and stuff? You see, I'm from the streets, so I haven't been tainted by this over…over-religious stuff…this mindset, 'cuz I was never a part of that. It just makes sense and all. The Bible says there is one way to heaven…through Jesus Christ, and there are many ways to hell. So, what the devil does is try and deceive people like me and Frank…and the whole biker thing is…when you're dead, you're dead. That's fine, but what if there is the slightest chance the Bible is true? It's either all true or one big lie."

"Frank, before we get interrupted or anything, will you pray to receive Jesus Christ as your savior right here, right now? Would you do that with me? Would you receive Jesus Christ? Just pray with me Frank. A lot of people bow their heads and close their eyes, but you know what? I'm going to look you right in the eyes brother, because God has said everything he has done, he's done before the foundation of the world. In other words…and this just blows me away…he planned, millions of years ago…and I can't understand it…he planned for this old street guy…for me to sit here and meet with Frank. You know why? It's because he loves you man. All the crap that you went through, and the times you been burnt…you should walk with him Frank, and I'll tell you what…he's going to restore you life, gonna renew your life, and he's gonna bless you. Pray this with me…Father, I been runnin' a long time, and I'm done runnin'. I turn to you with all my heart, and I'm asking you to come into my heart. Forgive me for my sins and save me. Frank, right here and right now. I believe you died for me, and you paid my price. Come into my heart, and save me right now, in Jesus' name…and I'm saved, and ain't nobody gonna tell me any different. I'm heaven bound, in Jesus' name. I'm going to pray for you right now."

"Close your eyes, Frank. Father I pray right now in your name, Father God, that your love for Frank, Father God, is displayed right here and right now. I'm asking in your name, Father God, that you will open doors that need to be opened, and shut doors that need to be shut. I'm asking that you bless Frank, Lord God, and begin to give him a new hunger and desire for your word…the Bible. I pray that you protect him, and protect him by the blood of Jesus. I thank you that Frank is alive today, and I thank you for letting me meet him. He is now my brother in Christ…in Jesus name…Amen."

102   *April Rose Steffeck*

"I'm 25…originally from Killeen, Texas. My mother is a PhD, and a professor at Bradley, and when she finished her doctorate at the University of Texas, we moved here. I've been here since I was seventeen."

"Growing up on base, and my father is active military to this day…he's career…and I remember growing up on base and going to the 4th of July parades. Fort Hood is the largest military base in the world. The 4th of July and Veteran's Day parades were very extravagant. Growing up in the time that I did, which was over the Gulf War…I never heard one opinion that went against the government, and what the military was trying to accomplish there. I never really realized that people that disagreed with the government, would voice that opinion, knowing that it could hurt a military family…considering we were the ones giving people up to go over there…until I moved up to the north."

"Growing up on base, if you disagree with the military, and what the government is doing…you sit down, you close your mouth…and you don't say anything. It was either, be supportive, or don't say anything. It was *our* brothers. It was *my* dad…my friend's dads and moms that were over there…and you just didn't speak against it. It instilled such a deep sense of pride in what my father does, and who he works for…what he tries to accomplish every day…and a deep sense of pride in my government. If I might disagree with the president, I would never go so far as to say he was wrong, or he should not have done that. If I am an American…I should be a patriot. If I am an American, and if you are a patriot, you should go with what is going to be better for the whole…what is going to be better for the government. You don't disagree with that."

"My father is a lieutenant colonel in the Army. He is in logistics…what they call a "log dog". He plans everything. What's the name of the bureau that was created after 911? Homeland Security…he is working with them, between the military and them. Right now he has a deployment of troops going into Central America, and a deployment of troops going down to work with victims of Hurricane Katrina."

"My wedding reception is here tonight. We are setting it up. My wedding was three weeks ago, and it was a destination wedding on a little island in Lake Superior called Natalin Island. We got married in a church that was built in 1900. Because it was a small destination wedding with 27…27 people involved…we are now coming back here and having a big reception tonight for all of our friends and family. We have people flying up from Texas, and Washington state…driving down from Wisconsin, and all over Illinois."

"Three years ago, my dad was home for Christmas and Thanksgiving…which is a huge thing. I had an uncle come down from Wisconsin…had aunts fly in…and it was the first time I had actually ever experienced a big family holiday. Thanksgiving…the women cooked all day long…we had this amazing meal…and then, we all sat around and watched the University of Texas and A&M game. It was so memorable because it is so…all-American. I had never had all my family together before. We moved around so much, being in the military. It was wonderful."

"I'm a teacher in District 150. I'm head of debate, speech, and drama. My passion is…the children that I teach…seeing them change…seeing them grow…seeing how their points of view and opinions change throughout the time that I know them…and them watching them come back later, after they have graduated…hoping that I have somehow made an impact. I still feel like I have more work to do on this earth. The Lord put me here for a reason. I don't feel like I have accomplished that quite yet. If I have, it is of course part of his plan, and I so wouldn't know about it. I want to stay here as long as he has more work for me to do."

103   *Sebastian Fuksa*

"I am a chiropractor…Dr. Sebastian Fuksa, at Health Solutions. It's right over there, next to Buffalo Wild Wings. I am thirty years old. I got into this business when I was younger, right around twenty years old. I used to weight-lift a lot. I still do, but I do it smarter. When I was younger, I used to weight-lift…I hurt myself, and my lower back…to the point where I couldn't walk. I literally couldn't walk. I crawled everywhere, and the only places I crawled was from my bed to the bathroom and back. Ummm…I went to see medical doctors from…different types of medical doctors, from internists to an orthopedic surgeon, and I couldn't get any help. The only thing I was offered was drugs…muscle relaxants and anti-inflammatory drugs. So, that didn't help…I was still crawling."

"So, at the time I decided to seek chiropractic care…and at the time, I didn't know what chiropractic care was…but I took a chance. He examined me, took X-rays, and the next day gave me my first adjustment, where I was able to literally pick myself up from a crawling position to a straight-up position, with no pain. After several more visits, I got back to the point where I was able to do everything as before. I sought out more information on chiropractic, and that is how I got into the business."

"My whole goal as a chiropractor is to try and give people a different path to being healthy. I am not completely anti-medicine, but my opinion is that medication is way over-prescribed. There are too many people taking Ritalin…too many people taking too many medications. It really gets to me. I like to teach people the whole entire scope of health, not just the chiropractic aspect…the nutritional aspect…the exercise aspect."

"Originally, I am from Poland. I was born in Poland in 1975…in a city called Sonak, Poland. Living in Poland…my brother was then born three years later. So, when my family was about to leave, I was six years old, and my brother was three. We wanted to leave the country because of communism. It was very rampant. My dad was a very educated man…ummm…he was a professor at the University of Krakow…one of the biggest universities in Eastern Europe. He just wanted to get ahead…make a good living for the family, and not be under the communist regime. As a result, he…I'm going to take this back a little bit…he went to the United States by himself for about five months, to check out the country…to see if he wants to bring his family back. He decided he wanted to do that…came back for us, and then the whole family. In order to go to the United States and live there, we had to wait for a visa. So, we actually had to move to Austria as refugees."

"As refugees, we lived in a camp there, for about nine or ten months, through the winter, and through a little bit of the summer…and finally we got our visa. When we got our visa…ummm…we came over to the United States. We had one family here…distant cousin, like third cousins, that invited us into their home from the beginning. We didn't come with much…one suitcase, and that was about it. We lived with them for a few months, my father got a job, and after that we moved into an apartment that the third cousin actually owned. My father, being well educated, quickly learned the English language, and started moving up in his engineering. He is now the director of Mechanical Engineers in Skokie, Illinois."

"My grandma's house, where I was born, is very memorable. It was a very large…large house, and pretty old house too…probably 120 years old. It was very memorable as a child…running around that house. I will remember it fondly. My parents were here a month ago and we spoke about it. We went out, had some food, had some drinks…and relaxed talk. We sat outside on the riverfront and enjoyed each other…very much."

104 *Joe Slyman*

"I'm going to be extra sweet to my wife and family today...because it's Valentine's Day."

"I was in a bad accident in 1991...I'm lucky to be walking...and after that...my whole outlook on life changed. It was an accident where I broke my back. They weren't able to surgically go in and "pin and fuse", because it was too close to the spinal cord. I had to lay in St. Francis for 58 days in a traction bed. It gave me a lot of time to think about life."

"It made me realize that you need to...*try*...and realize that every day may be your last. One of these days, you're going to be right. My sense of charity from that point on has become very extended...and I don't look for rewards, other than my own satisfaction."

"You know, these people that come in off the street...my oldest brother who died two years ago of cancer...he kind of highlighted one statement, and it's stuck with me. "No one should go hungry as long as we're in this business." So...I'm living up to that."

"People...when they come in to my business...they're not just another turkey sandwich or a cold coke."

105   *Bill Kellerstrass*

"I got on the web and saw all of these "meet-up" groups. You go to this website and create these meet-up groups...at www.meetup.com. I think it's a great way to meet people with similar interests. I went to a few in the area, and then decided to create my own group...which was a pie-eating group. So...I created this group, and our first meeting was at "Baker's Square". That makes sense, doesn't it?"

"I go to Baker's Square and...nobody shows up. I guess they thought it was a joke or something. I'm sitting at this table for six by myself, eating a piece of French Silk pie, and sipping on a cup of coffee. I had already told the waitress that more pie-eaters would show up...but they never did. Pretty much...I looked like a dope."

"One time I went to confession at St. Boniface...walked into the confessional and started my routine, "Bless me father for I have sinned, it's been "blah blah" weeks since my last confession...these are my sins." Then I started rattling off my sins, and about half of them are made up anyway...I always felt obligated to have a few sins...and I can sort of see the priest in there moving around and I can hear him breathing...like he's a heavy smoker. I'm telling him my sins...and he starts laughing. But his laugh sounds just like Mike Lowry's, who lives a couple houses away from me."

"It's Mike Lowry in the confessional listening to my sins. So...I open my door as he's opening his door...and he runs out of the church...laughing. He goes over to the school and starts telling everybody in the class what my sins are...and one of them was that I stole a penlight flashlight from K-mart. So then, everybody starts calling me "K-mart." For a year and a half, kids would be calling me K-mart...and saying I wasn't very bright...you know, flashlight jokes like that."

"I didn't even steel the friggin' flashlight. I made it up just because I thought that's what the priest wanted to hear. So...I looked like a dope back then also."

106   *Bob Long*

"I was married almost ten years…but I'm divorced now. It's great. No more bitching, crying, or complaining."

107-108 Ryan Graham and Julie Habstritt

"I am Ryan Graham...I'm 27. I'm from a small town in southern Manitoba...Roland, Manitoba. It's the home of 4-H. Have you ever heard of 4-H? I got my degree up in Canada, and I was working for a company up there. Caterpillar had recruited a buddy of mine who had gone to the University of Minnesota. He told me to send my resume down...so I have been here five years now. I'm a product support specialist at Caterpillar. Both of us, we have just been to a wedding, and we're going upstairs for a dinner. Julie and I are just friends. She didn't know many people in the wedding...so she's my date for the night."

"Julie Habstritt...39. I grew up in the central part of Minnesota...I grew up in Little Falls. I've been in Peoria since 1995. I do market research, but I have an engineering degree. I was probably made to be an engineer. My mom always wanted me to play with dolls, but the only doll I played with was the one that came with a suitcase filled with clothes. I never played with the doll. I just played with the suitcase, and kept packing it...taking the clothes out, and then repacking it. I don't even know the name of the doll. It was one of those plastic dolls with short hair."

"In Minnesota, I remember going fishing with my dad a lot. My dad would just sit forever. I think he liked the peace and quiet. He would sit, and I would not. I got really sunburned one time. I learned that year that vinegar takes away the sting of sunburn. I learned that from my dad."

"One year I went to the boundary waters with my sister and brother-in law...and a friend of mine. Nobody could believe I could be that rugged. They plan it all out ahead of time...and it's planned so you don't see anyone else. You take certain trails...and you canoe for awhile. You portage your canoe on hiking trails, and about the time you're done canoeing...you're hiking. You're carrying your canoe, and backpack and stuff. One of the goals is not to see anyone else on the trip...and we didn't."

"You have to hang your food up in the tree at night, to keep the bears away. There are no outdoor bathrooms, or whatever. One trail...about halfway up, was underwater. I was walking on this trail with hiking boots...and it was too shallow to put the canoe in. So, I'm pulling the canoe with water up to my knees as I'm walking across it. It was a big adventure. Every day was a new campsite...something new."

"I never really fished much, but I remember one year, I think it was myself, my dad and my sister...and my mom...and the people that owned the canoes. I went to cast, and I like...cast...and the hook caught my dad's hat and sent it into the lake."

"I spent most of my days just helping out on the farm, ever since I was a little kid. It was a grain farm...at least that's how it started. The thing that's different, you know...is, Illinois is basically corn and beans. Up there, you've got wheat and barley, canola and flax...it's a lot more...well, one thing...June and July it's a lot more colorful because flax is purple and canola is yellow. So, you have all these...seas...of different colors. Then in 1990, we started planting saskatoons, which is a type of fruit that is native to the prairies. They're also called juneberries in northern Minnesota and North Dakota. They're similar to a blueberry, but more native to colder environments. They use them the same as blueber-ries...pies, jams. They just don't have as long a shelf life, so you've got to use them faster."

"For fifteen years, that's what they've been doing. We sold off our farm equip-ment...and rent the rest of our land. Then...we've got thirty...thirty acres or so of saskatoons. That's their full time thing. They've got a commercial kitchen on the farm now...and they produce preservatives. They do their own juicing...and all that kind of stuff. I've got some embarrassing pictures from when I was home in August helping out. I'm in the kitchen and I've got a hairnet on, and a rubber apron on. It's like...you know, there's this huge pot that you're mixing in...and I'm using a paddle to mix. It's just not too attractive...kind of embarrassing."

"Coming down here to Illinois was a little scary. I was in an environment where I knew everything that was going on...then I come down here, and I'm starting over again.
I completed a phase of my life, and then I...I kind of knew the structure that was coming up...but, moving 900 miles from home...that's...but then...my mom moved 800 miles from where she grew up...southern Alberta...so, I thought I could do it."

"I don't know much about the bride. She's an engineer at Caterpillar. The groom is also from Minnesota. That, I know from working here."

"I know he's a "wannabe" Canadian."

"I really like Minneapolis. I like rollerblading around all the lakes. The rollerblading trails are split…like, rollerblading and biking are split from the walking trails, so that you don't have slow moving vehicles with the fast moving vehicles, so to speak."

"There are small things that are different between the US and Canada. My friend Colin…from Canada…he's been down here a few more years. He's seen the cultural differences a little more. The one thing that he notices is…he has a pretty nice car. He would go for an oil change in Canada, and these guys are standing around going, "What's this young punk doing with this nice car?" Whereas, in the US, it's like, "Hey, did you check this feature out…did you check this feature out?" So, it's…I don't know how to quantify that exactly. It's like…jealousy happens a little more often of people that are successful in Canada. Whereas here…it's like…success is praised…almost."

"I'm hoping to become a citizen of the world. I've experienced Canada…been here for a few years. I got the opportunity to go to New Zealand for a month. I'd love to be able to…I've got a friend that lived in Geneva, and just moved to Amsterdam…I'd like to be able to do something like that. I'd like the opportunity to see different things, and meet other people."

"I once met an interesting famous person. It was Charles Lindbergh. When I was in, like, second grade…I met Charles Lindbergh…the guy that flew across the Atlantic. It was really a big deal at our school, because he was the guy our school was named after. We got out of class and followed this person outside…and then he basically just said hello to everybody. He used to spend his summers in Little Falls, when he was a kid…and you can still visit his home there. It's a blue house with white trim…two miles south of Little Falls. Lindbergh was an engineer also…he had to be."

109   *Perry Rice*

"My name is Perry Rice and I am 44. I was born in California...lived in California for about six years...lived in Seattle for about four years. I lived in the beautiful state of Michigan for ten years, went to college at Illinois State...that's how I got here. My dad worked for Whirlpool...he was in charge of commercial laundry at Whirlpool. I jumped off ship when he was transferred to Peoria to handle distributors."

"When I lived in Michigan, we used to shake cherries. My older brother got me a job...they took a lot of the high school kids in summertime...shaking cherries. Now, a lot of people don't know what that means, but it's a huge, huge, industry in Michigan. What happens is...they take this machine...it's basically a big tractor with an arm on it, and it shakes the heck out of the tree and all these cherries drop onto these mats...well, they call them tarps. Then they're pulled onto a conveyer belt and go into a tank. They have to do it at nighttime, because in the daytime, it's too hot, and when the cherries drop, they split. So, you start working about seven at night, till about six in the morning. It's very tiring and very hard work."

"One time, my brother...well, they bring donuts in the morning...about four o'clock, they put them out...and I ate his donut. He got pretty upset and started throwing cherries at me. About the third tree, I went tearing across the mat, went down the conveyer belt, squeezing all these cherries...jumped on top of him, and landed in the cherry tank and we started fighting. They let us fight for awhile...ten minutes, and after we got tired we just went back to work."

"I became a sales rep out of college, selling advertising solutions for a company out of Peoria called Multi-Ad. They instantly sent me up to the beautiful city of Detroit, where I worked for five years...then transferred back to Peoria to start up a new division. Worked in Peoria for five years, and then they offered me the opportunity to go over and manage a company they had just acquired in the United Kingdom."

"The biggest challenge I had, coming over running a UK company, were the cultural differences. Although we have a common language, there are different meanings. One of my first experiences was that I was faced with a lawsuit right away. The finance director came up to me and said we were being sued for wrongful dismissal. I said, "Why are we being sued?" He said, "We had to fire this person because he came to work pissed all the time." I said, "Well, pissed…we don't really let people go for being upset." He said, "No, no, no…he comes to work every morning pissed out of his mind." It finally dawned on me that he was talking about being drunk."

"Another time, we had decided to change the compensation program for the employees. When I….the day I changed the compensation programs, I put up on the wall, all of their times…and the very first person that I called in…an older person…she came into the office and I was waiting for her to show her the new program…to show her what the differences were going to be…what the new packages were going to be. Before I could say anything, she burst out crying. She said, "I just can't believe you're making us all redundant, you're letting us go." I said, "What are you talking about?" She was in tears and said, "Compensation is what you give us when you give us all the sack." So, then I realized they all thought I was letting them go, and giving them their severance packages. I then learned that I should have said remunerations instead of compensation."

"We became very comfortable over there, and it was a huge culture shock to come back to the US, after five years. The quality of time outside of work is highly valued in Europe. They immediately have four weeks vacation. Some may say that productivity levels are down because of that, but I don't know if that is true. It's just that they work a lot harder when they are at work. But, when they are done with work, they don't like to be bothered. Sundays, everyone sits in the park…maybe go to the pub and have a few pints. You have a lot of time to get to know your neighbors and friends."

110   *Frank Abagnale*

"I was raised north of New York City, in Westchester County, and I was actually one of four children in the family...a so-called middle child of the four. My parents, after 22 years of marriage, one day decided to get a divorce. Unlike most divorces, where the children are usually the first to know, my parents were good about keeping that a secret. I was in the tenth grade...just turning sixteen. I attended a private Catholic school run by the Christian Brothers of Ireland in a little town called New Rochelle. I had gone there from kindergarten to high school. About 2 o'clock one afternoon, the father walked into the classroom and asked the brother to excuse me from class. When I walked down the hallway, the father handed me my books and told me that one of the brothers would drive me to the county seat, where I would meet my parents, and they would explain what was going on."

"The brother drove me up to a big stone building, told me to go on up the steps, and inside my parents would be waiting for me. I collected my books, went up the steps, and noticed a sign on the building that said "Family Court"...but really didn't understand what that meant. When I arrived in the lobby, my parents were not there. After a moment or two, someone came out and escorted me into an immense courtroom, where I saw my parents standing before a judge. Eventually the judge saw me at the back of the room, and he motioned me to approach the bench...so I walked up in-between my parents. I distinctly remember that he never looked at me...didn't even acknowledge I was there...he simply read from his papers...that my parents were getting a divorce. Because I was sixteen, I would need to tell the court which parent I would live with. I started to cry...so I ran out of the courtroom. The judge called for a ten minute recess...and by the time my parents got outside, I was gone. My mother never saw me again for seven years...and contrary to the movie, my father never saw me or spoke to me again."

"I had very little to do with the making of the movie. I made no money from the movie. The rights to that film were sold more than thirty years ago when the book was sold and printed. About fifteen years ago, I read that Steven Spielberg had bought the movie rights...but then never heard a thing about it again. A few years ago, I read that Steven Spielberg was considering making a movie about the book...no one contacted me...I met no one...heard from no one at Dreamworks…never saw a script. My family and I went through a great deal of apprehension during the making of that movie…we had no idea how he would portray my life…we had no idea what the film was about…we were very concerned, having three sons in college, and on their way to college…about having a very unusual last name…what it would do to their life."

"We had no control, whatsoever…but in the end, my family and I were very pleased…I should say, very blessed, that it was Steven Spielberg that made that film. We feel he went out of his way, not to glorify the things I did…but to simply tell a story. As he told Barbara Walters one month before the release of the film, "I made this movie about Frank Abagnale, and immortalized him in film…not because of what he did forty years ago…but because of what he has done with his life these past thirty years." And in the end, my family and I were very pleased with the making of the movie, "Catch Me If You Can"."

"I make my home in Tulsa, Oklahoma. I live there with my wife of 28 years, and my three sons. My oldest boy is 26. He graduated from the Loyola School of Law in Chicago. He's a licensed lawyer here in the state of Chi…Illinois. I have a son that is 23 and a senior at the University of Nevada, and a son who is about to be a senior at the University of Kansas."

"I obviously receive a lot of emails, back at my offices in Washington, every week…from people as young as eight to people as old as eighty. People seeing the film for the first time…just as you think they're dying out, someone over in China is watching for the first time…someone is seeing it on HBO for the first time. Many of the emails people write, don't require an answer…they're just making a comment or a statement…they're just saying, "Well, you know you were a genius…you were absolutely brilliant." I was neither…I was just a sixteen year old boy. Had I truly been a genius…had I been brilliant…I don't think I would have found it necessary to break the law, in order to just simply…survive. There were many people who wrote and said, "You were certainly gifted." That I was. I was one of those few children that got to grow up in the world for "daddy". The world is full of fathers, but there are very few "daddies"…and any child who has grown up with a daddy…is an extremely gifted child. I had a daddy who loved his children more than life itself."

"My father was a man that told you every day of his life that he loved you…not only by the spoken word…but by sheer physical affection. Six foot three…every night...three boys...one girl...he was by your bed. He would drop down on a knee, pull the cover up...kiss you on the cheek...put his lips right up on your earlobe and whisper, "I love you. I love you very much". He never missed a night. As I grew older and fell asleep before he got home, I always woke up the next morning...and knew he had been by my bed. Years later my brother...six four, joined the Marines...played semi-pro for Buffalo...but when he came home on leave, my father would walk around to his bed...hug him, kiss him, and tell him he loved him."

"When I was sixteen years old, I was just a kid. All sixteen year-olds are just...children. Like all children, I needed my mother, and I needed my father. All children need their mother and their father. All children are entitled to their mother and their father...and though it's not popular to say so...divorce is a very devastating thing that unfortunately a child has to deal with, the rest of their natural life. A complete stranger...a judge...told me I had to choose one parent over another. I never made that choice. I would never make that choice. For me, it was a lot easier to turn and run...and so I did."

"How can I tell you my life was glamorous? I cried myself to sleep until I was nineteen years old. I spent every Christmas, birthday, Mother's Day, Father's Day, in a hotel room somewhere in the world...Japan, Hong Kong...by myself. Everyone that I associated with was at least fifteen years older than me. They believed me to be their peer. I never got to go to a prom...a high school football game...even share a relationship with someone my own age. I was always smart enough to know that I would get caught...only a fool would believe that you can continually break the law, and not get caught. The law sometimes sleeps...but the law never dies. It was just a matter of time when I was caught...and I went to some very bad places."

"My sons have grown up asking their mother, "Why is it that Dad wakes up and goes down to the TV room, and doesn't turn the TV on...he just sits there all night?" Because...there are things you can't forget...things you are not meant to forget. I entered a French prison at 198 pounds...and left the prison at 109 pounds. When I was sitting in that French cell...pitch black, blanket on a floor of stone...going to the bathroom in a hole in the floor...my father, 57, an extremely physically fit man, was running the subway steps like he used to do every morning on his way to work, and just happened to trip on one of them. Reached his arm out to break his fall...slipped again...hit his head, rolled to the bottom of the steps…he was dead. I didn't know he was dead…I was sitting in that cell. But, I was thinking about him…how much I missed him…how much I loved him…couldn't wait to see him…hold him…hug him…kiss him, but…I never got the opportunity to do that. However, I was fortunate because I was brought up in a country where everyone…everyone, gets a second chance."

"Everything that I have…everything that I have achieved…who I am today…is because of the love of a woman, and the respect that three boys have for their father. There comes a time, in all of our lifetimes…we grow older…we have children. And as every parent knows, whether your child is six months, or sixty years old, when a parent lays their head down at night…from the day they become a parent…to the day they die…the last thing they think about when they close their eyes…are their children. You still have your mother…you still have your father? Give them a hug…give them a kiss…and remember, no matter what kind of a relationship you had with your parents…you will miss them when they're gone…because…they are…you."

111   *Patty McMullen*

"I actually have my bills paid, and I have money in the bank…that happened two weeks ago. It's a wonderful feeling to be out of debt. You know how I got out of debt? I got married. I was unmarried for three years, and now I'm finally married again. It's taken me a long time to get out of debt…working full time at State Farm, and then working weekends at Bob Evans. To actually be out of debt is a wonderful feeling."

112 *Paul Stevens*

"I'm Paul Stevens, and I am 39 years old. I came into town today to pick up…get some lunch, and then pick up a new helmet. I've had this…ah…helmet for several years, and the lining is starting to wear away…and starting to smell bad. I met my brother at the Cracker Barrel for lunch…had a couple of eggs, hash browns…toast. I like their sourdough toast…although I wish they would put butter on it when it's warm…or not freeze their butter pads. Still, it's still pretty good."

"I like to ride on weekends…I don't ride much during the week, because I'm too busy. Sometimes, I will go out late at night and take a ride to Princeville and back…look at the stars…get the cool wind on my face…try and avoid rabbits and deer."

"When I was 23, I was in an accident with a Yamaha that I had back then. I was on my way to work…and at that time I worked for a guy who did drywall. I also had another job working for a…a…ummm…catering company, which is now out of business. Well…anyway…I was on my way to work, and…to get to the job site, I had to go down this one-lane country road…and it had this blind corner…hidden by trees and weeds. That's where I had my accident."

"I don't remember anything about that day…even now when I try and remember, there's just nothing…nothing there. I was in a coma for about three weeks. I remember flashes of light…strange people around me. I remember fighting with someone at one point…I guess it was a nurse. Then one day…my mom and dad were standing over me. I knew I was in a bed…didn't know where I was, when I was, or even who I was…not really. Everything seemed hazy…like a dream. I knew the left side of my body seemed strange…I knew I had a catheter in me. I didn't know that's what it was called then…but I remember that. Also…and this will seem real strange…I remember my hair…my hair felt very strange…felt dirty. I couldn't stop touching my hair, trying to get it to feel better. It seemed that if I could somehow make my hair feel better…then things would be alright."

"At some point, somebody…I don't know if it was my mom, or a nurse…somebody brought in this hair cleaner…the kind that you just comb in…I think it was called "Pssssst", or something like that. Anyway, I used some of it…used a lot of it…and felt much better. I can't explain it…don't think anyone can…not even a neurologist, but I think it may have something to do with the mind…focusing on one thing…may not matter what that one thing is…but the mind focuses on that, because it's trying to forget what happened, and it can't deal with the reality of what's going on."

"Later on, I learned that a truck came around the corner and hit me head-on. It happened to be another guy who was working the job site. It totaled his truck, and of course my bike….broke every spoke in the front tire…front fork was all smashed up. I later parted it out to my buddies."

"One thing about that accident…and I mean this…it's not just some story…it changed my life in a dramatic way. I was a bum…a hard working bum…but still, I was trapped in a predictable life. I was trapped in a lifestyle that all my buddies were in…going to work every day…doing something that doesn't inspire you, or…or, make you feel worthwhile. The accident, somehow gave me the ability to look inward…made me look at my life in a different way…made me look at the world in a different way. After my accident, I took some classes at ISU and Sangamon State and earned two degrees…both in communications. I'm working in a job that I love now. I really can't…really can't imagine doing anything else. I get to meet a lot of new people very day…and I'm learning…constantly learning."

"As you can see…I guess I wasn't smart enough to stay off the motorcycles…there is a certain power and freedom that I feel while riding…especially late at night with the cool wind in my face."

113   *Eric Roland*

"I'm only 22 years old…really. I'm still in school, and will be graduating very soon. I never wanted to be anything other than a writer…well, that's not true. Actually, I wanted to be a Ghostbuster when I was real little. I even knew what a parapsychologist was when I was like, four. I guess I'd still do that if I could get my hands on an unlicensed proton accelerator pack."

"I've really wanted to be a writer since I was in grade school, about third or fourth grade. I remember the first thing I ever wrote…I was in second grade, and they did this thing where the sixth graders would come to the second grade class and one of them would write a little book for one of us…and then we would write one, you know…for one of them. The kid who wrote a story about me…his name was Jim, wrote it about both of us battling aliens…and my rabbits turning into aliens."

"I wrote a sequel to that story for him…and mine was much better. The story ended with me sacrificing my life to save his. I was always a bit…melodramatic, even when I was just playing with my friends. I always wanted to be the hero who fell in battle…always"

"When I was in third grade, I wrote another little book called "The Knight". It was a comedy about this bumbling knight who tries to win the hand of a princess and save his kingdom from a vicious dragon, but it had a lot of jokes and funny illustrations thrown in there…a lot of Monty Python and the Holy Grail type stuff. Maybe it's just 'cause I wrote it, but I still think it's funny."

"Fourth grade, I think is when I really decided what I wanted to do with my life. I remember my teacher giving out this project that included all sorts of different assignments…some writing, some illustrating…you know, all sorts of artsy kinds of things. Anyway, you got to choose how many assignments you wanted to do. I don't remember how many there were, but depending on how many you did, that determined the highest grade you could get…and I was really ambitious and wanted to do everything on the list. It was a ridiculous undertaking for a fourth grader, but I was kind of showing off and trying to impress my teacher."

"I wrote this really cool story about me finding a magic lamp and getting a bunch of wishes. I think the first thing I wished for was like, ownership rights to Toys 'R' Us. Anyway, in her class, I wrote a bunch and I really liked it. I decided when I was in fourth grade that I was going to study journalism when I grew up, and that's exactly what I did."

"I had a brief interest in becoming a lawyer, for awhile. In high school, I became a punk rocker and got really interested in politics, so I thought the best way to get into politics was to study law…and when I first got into college…that's what I studied. I had a double major in political science and criminal justice so I could learn all sorts of law."

"Unfortunately, I didn't do that well in school, and I ended up transferring to ICC to try to figure out what I wanted to do with my life. I was still interested in politics…but didn't want to be a politician any more. I was taking some writing classes at school when it dawned on me that *this…this* is what I should be doing. If I were to become a journalist, I could write for a living and make the same…if not more of an impact, as I could in government."

"I got my associates degree and went on to ISU to study journalism…but I still minored in politics. I did a lot of growing up at ISU, and I learned a lot about the world that, you know, I wouldn't have otherwise. My views on life changed a lot…I think I became a much happier person. I got a job there working for a newspaper…and I'm learning a lot there…mostly about myself."

"So…I'm working for The Daily Vidette while I'm in school…you know, trying to prepare myself to get a regular job…writing for a living. Eventually, I want to be a novelist or a screenwriter. That's what I'd really, really love to do…write movies. I'm one of these sci-fi geeks inspired by Star Wars, and I'm full of useless entertainment trivia that I want to put to good use somehow…so I'll see if I can't do that. I'm excited about writing…it's really my passion….it's what I love."

114 *Elaine Mendez*

"I sold a New Mexico Big Top Peanut Butter song glass, for like...six dollars. It was Big Top before it was Jif...and it had the song "America" on the back...and it wasn't nicked up too bad. But, I mostly sell grape jars...Welch's grape jars...with Bugs Bunny and Cat in the Hat...Yogi Bear...Mickey Mouse...other cartoons like that."

"My son, Christian...he's twelve...and eats the Goober Jelly. We just throw those jars away."

115 *Sophia Salazar*

"I am originally from Trinidad. My name Sophia Salazar, and I am 39. It is such a beautiful place. I left Trinidad at the age of seventeen…and from seventeen until now, I have been in Florida…Hollywood, Florida. I just moved here two and a half weeks ago. My husband's job…he works for St. Francis Medical, which led us here."

"I am pregnant with baby number four. My oldest is sixteen. All of my pregnancies have been…a lot of people think it is so weird, but I have had no morning sickness with any of them. I just get up and go and continue my day until late at night…no bad feelings, no cravings. I don't know…I am a strange pregnant lady…I am. I work very hard every single day, dealing with the kids. My husband and I put together the new house, but my pregnancy, honestly, doesn't get in the way. I haven't even found a doctor up here. I am almost in my seventh month."

"I always tell my kids…you know, from how we grew up in Trinidad to how they grew up in Florida…and my husband is from Trinidad also…the lifestyle was so different. As I told my son…we would come home from school…and we needed to get our homework done…but first, we would go outside to play. We would play things like cricket, and marbles in the street, and climb a mango tree and eat fruit. It was just so different…and it's not that we miss anything, but that's just the way we grew up. And the neighbors…we all knew each other…everyone was there to help each other. It is not just like a "hi" and a "bye". If I came home from school and there was no one home, I could go to my neighbor's house and have dinner…take a shower…or just wait until my parents got home. It was just that family-oriented."

"I had a big family…the cousins were over every Sunday. We had a get-together every Sunday, where my mom would cook and there would be fourteen or fifteen cousins. You know what? I could call any of them at any single time. It was just so nice, and so different. I didn't miss a television…I didn't miss shopping. I told my son, I would not trade places with him today…I wouldn't. I would go out, and I really didn't have a curfew. There was just so much trust between my mom and myself. I could go out without having to worry about what time I came back. The trust was there. If I said I was going to Susan's house…she could call them at night, and that's where I would be. You know, we weren't allowed to smoke or drink, and it was just…it was just normal."

"I have never really seen snow…I have never seen snow. I was told the snow and the cold will be a big experience for me. What I can't wait for is the four seasons. See…in Florida, you just have solid heat…just like in the islands. This will be an experience for my children, who range from sixteen to six to two…and now my baby. But so far, I love it. I love the people. My husband was telling me how calm and quiet it was…and I have yet to meet a grouchy person. I have yet to meet someone who doesn't say hi…or have manners. In Florida, you see grouchy people everywhere you turn…but I have yet to see that here. So far, I like it…I think I will enjoy raising my kids here."

116 *Bob Hewiit*

"I'm buying water at the IGA in Farmington. I'm waiting to win the lottery. I inherited $100,000 a long time ago…but that's all gone now. I spent it. It just disappeared…poof. I work construction now…and it's either feast or famine…you either got a bunch of work or you ain't got none."

117 *Paul Baker*

"I'm here for Erin Feis. I am 41...today. Today is my birthday. I was born and raised in Cleveland, Ohio. It's just like any other town. Oh, we had a bit of a rough spell in the 70's with segregation...but for all intents and purposes...except for the bussing...it's just like any place else. I had a pretty normal childhood, with the exception that, when I was born, I had a lot of allergies. Basically, I was one step shy of being a boy in a bubble. There was a list of 47 things on the refrigerator that I could not come in contact with. I couldn't go outside and play...my mom had to keep the house immaculate, because dust was a big thing I was allergic to."

"My mom always wanted to play an instrument when she was growing up, but never did. Ummm...she used to do some singing and dancing...and things of that nature, but she never went into music as far as instruments go. She started taking me around to a bunch of different concerts and such...and took me to a Suzuki recital, where there were a bunch of little kids playing the violin. I was just shy of two and a half years old. I went to Overland Conservatory, which is by...where we were living...and they had a Suzuki program...first program in the state of Ohio. Dr. Suzuki had sent his prized pupil to open up a Suzuki program in Ohio."

"Now, I happen to be adopted...and my adopted parents...my mom is Japanese. She heard about the program, took me out to see the recital...and as she tells it, by the end of the recital, I said, "Where's my violin?" So, she went out and got me started on my third birthday. The rest is kind of history."

"My mother is Japanese, and my father is Pennsylvania Dutch. The only thing I found out about my natural birth parents is...my mother was Irish, and my father was Puerto-Rican. That's all I know. To me, it was always a taboo thing...because my parents are my mom and dad...and always will be. My dad passed about two years ago...and my mother is eighty years old. She's doing really well...knock wood. In the beginning of September, she will be going to Japan for the second time in twelve months. She was just there in April-May, and came home in June...to visit her sister, who is ten years younger. Her sister had a really bad stroke about a week ago...so my mom is going to take care of her. But, my mom is doing great...I hope she keeps going."

"When you go through enough tragedies, it kind of puts things in perspective...losing a friend...losing a loved one. There was a very tragic accident that happened five years ago...on the 19th of this month. This past weekend was the fifth anniversary. We were at the Milwaukee Irish Fest, and we were getting ready to do our show...and we got a phone call that there was a tragic accident back home...and, ummm...and I lost a son and a daughter in the accident. My oldest boy was ten...Alex...and my daughter, Alyssa was nine. Their grandmother...my ex-wife's mother...and my youngest son, Andy...who was eight at the time, were all in this...they got broad-sided by a dump truck that ran a red light. Somehow, miraculously...Andy survived. I lost Alex and Alyssa...and...and their grandmother also perished in the accident. The one thing that is not supposed to happen...you're not supposed to bury your kids. You're supposed to have your children. To see so much promise...so much future...and you know, I'm a proud father, so I'm going to say they were great kids. They were great kids."

"Alex was really blessed with sports, and Alyssa the most kind and caring person...to all animals...just everything. I was just so looking forward to watching them grow up. They were tragically taken from us...and it's just...just one of those things. Thankfully, Andy...he was...he was banged up a bit...he was...it's one of those funny lessons..."wear your seat belt...wear your seat belt...wear your seat belt." But, the fact that he didn't wear a seat belt saved his life. He got tossed from the car, and ended up surviving...and for the most part, he's healthy and happy and normal. He says he doesn't remember a lot about the accident, and I'm praying that's the way it stays. So far...knock wood...he's doing great. His 8th grade year, he's starting tailback on the football team...and just taking life by the horns and running with it."

"Brigid's Cross probably does about 200 shows a year. It's a lot of traveling...a lot of back and forth...in and out of town. We don't stay out of town for long periods of time...we'll go here and there, and that sort of a thing."

"The biggest thing I see is...with what we're doing, we've gotten a lot of comments like, "This is something that I can enjoy, and my kids can enjoy." We're getting a lot of thank-you's from people that way. It's like, "Oh, thank you so much for giving me something that I can enjoy with my kids." They can't agree on types of music or TV shows...yet somehow, someway...knock on wood...something that we're doing is relating to both adults and kids...and that's probably the most heart-warming thing, as far as that goes. To be associated with that type of thing...it's really a cool thing."

"I try to be a good person. I worry about the world being a good place for my son. There's a lot of scary stuff going on...I don't have to tell you that...with Iraq and everything. I am a guy who passionately loves my country. I'm not saying that we do the right thing all the time...but there is no other place where I would rather live. It sickens me to see people that can't seem to understand that you can support our troops and not support what's going on right now. It sickens me...that whole Vietnam thing, and how that went down...and I'm afraid we're about to repeat history...and it's just wrong to me."

"We start our show with a lot of patriotic stuff..."God Bless America". We may end the show with the "National Anthem"...and we always try to push that...thank the troops, and their families. It's a great sacrifice...and I'll admit I don't have the guts to be a soldier. I mean, there is no way in the world I would ever be able to do that. I wish I could...but not everybody is meant to be a soldier...but the least I can do, the least I can do, is support them, and show people how to support them...make them realize how lucky we are to have them. I couldn't imagine where we would be without them. The soldiers and their families...there's nothing we can do to repay them...but, the least we can do is try to rally support for them."

"We started, about three or four months after 911, doing "God Bless America"...and then I noticed that people were rolling their eyes because they were tired of hearing "God Bless America"...or "Proud to be an American". Four months...four months after we lost five thousand in the Trade Center...and it was, "Come on already." Come on already? Now, I'm not holier than thou...not trying to paint myself as being this great person above everybody else...but it's...it's sickening to me that people can't see how great we have it in this country."

"The coolest thing for me...and remember I said that this is a screwed up world we are in...people come out to listen and have a good time with us...and we can make them forget about what's going on out there for awhile...feel good about themselves...feel good about their country. I don't need anything else...that's good enough for me."

118   **Ed Kiesewetter**

"Eleven years ago…February 14ᵗʰ, which is coming up pretty soon…I had a massive stroke. I was working in the insurance business…and the doctor said I was supposed to croak. I was 61."

"I was in rehab for three months and came out of it…was able to go back to work for four or five years…and had a second stroke. I'm still recovering from that. That's why I'm in this wheelchair now. After the second stroke, things went downhill. Second stroke was in '95."

"The 27ᵗʰ of this month…I'll be here two years. I had three heart attacks since…and my kidneys failed once. I have sleep apnea and diabetes…and about a year ago, they told me to get ready for amputation…my feet. Being a stubborn German, I said, "Leave your hat in your office, Doc." I started taking care of my feet better…I decided if I wanted to keep my feet…I needed to start taking care of myself."

"Actually, I'll never get out of here. I had to do the Medicaid thing…sell down everything I owned to get down to what's called "spousal impoverishment". I have zero dollars…but I'm very lucky."

"I'm an old German that won't give up. You see that cane? My goal is to be able to walk without that cane."

119 *Anne Morris*

"I was born into art…and I have had to fight every man in my life to do it…my father, my ex-husband, my present husband. My father is a lawyer…was a lawyer, and actually I think he was a very frustrated artist, but thought that I should be a lawyer too. I said, "Dad, you come home every night from your work and have grumbled about your job. Why would you want that for me, your daughter?" Of course, the answer was to make a living. I said that I could make a living this way…and I have. I have done real well…and uh…my ex-husband thought I was obsessed…which I probably am."

"I create mixed media…collages…2D, on glass. It is my own invention. I work on glass…just a piece of glass. The way that it happened was…I just had all of this scrap glass around from framing and everything. I just hate to throw anything away, so I just thought, "Wow…I can just work on this…it won't warp…it feels cool." And, it just grew from there. So, what I do is…I take a piece of glass, and I work behind the glass and on top of the glass, and I wrap it in a very finely etched film that diffracts light…and I pour resin over it. I have been doing this for sixteen years. I am 48 now."

"My present husband thinks I should be helping him with his job. We own a 56 acre nature theme park in the quad cities. We have restored prairie…we do the high ropes course…the "outward bound" type thing. We do panning for gems. We get gems in from mines all over the world and bury them in the sand…and them the children get to find buried treasure and take their emeralds and sapphires, and rubies, and topazes with them.
We have a 56 acre haunted forest in October."

"My husband has been in the entertainment industry for years and years. He was a magician for seventeen years. He has the interactive inflatable games…and, uh, so he's just been doing company parties and things like that. So, we just decided that we need a place…ummm…where the parties come to us, instead of us going to the parties. So, we wrote a grant…and, ummm…and it took about six months. We got about a hundred thousand dollars to…uh…get it started…and, uh…it didn't go very far…not far at all."

"I told him the whole time that I would help him do this, and then I would go back to the art...and so, so...it works out. The business is growing, growing...phenomenally. We have a lot of youth groups...a lot of field trips. Kids like the prairie. We have six miles of wildflowers, and with the Monarch butterfly migration, you could make a haunted butterfly movie...you have to literally push them out of the way in late summer. It doesn't happen every year, but sometimes the Monarchs decide to land on our flowers...and so when it does happen, it's just fantastic. Really...you do...you have to push them out of the way, they are so thick."

120   ***Drew Hastings***

"I'm 51...just turned 51. Born in Casablanca, Morocco...1954...mother was English...ummm...looking for a way to get out of postwar England. Met an American G.I...it was a...we had a Navy base in Casablanca in the 50's. My dad was a small town, Ohio...from a long line of steel workers, from Wheeling Steel. He was in the Navy...met my mom...BOOM, they got married. She's seventeen years older than me...he's about nineteen years older than me. BOOM...had me, came over to Columbus, Ohio, two years later. So, I was raised in Ohio."

"My childhood was by no means a normal childhood. My dad left when I was seven. He left when I was seven...he immediately remarried. His name was also Drew Hastings...immediately remarried a woman...they had a baby boy. She said, "I want you to forget you ever had a wife and kids. We're going to name this baby Drew Hastings. This is the real Drew Hastings...not that other one." So, by the time I'm seven, there are three Drew Hastings...me...the one who left me...and the one that replaced me. So, I guess it's no wonder I try to make a name for myself."

"I got moved around a lot when I was a kid. I used to get my butt beat...'cause I was skinny...and they thought I was strange. I just think...you know, my mother was English...very proper English. I was in rural or suburban Ohio...and, you know, I think they just thought I talked funny. I would say, "Oh, I've soiled my trousers." Well, they don't say that in rural Ohio in the 50's. "Hey fellows, you want to go to the cinema?" You know, they didn't want to hear that. They'd say, "Faggot.""

"So, yeah...and when I was nine, my mother remarried into an Orthodox Jewish family. I was converted to Judaism for five years...and that was a fucking mess. So, basically that was me trying to fit in with a group of people that have spent five thousand years trying to fit in...and uh...that was a dysfunctional mess. I was basically raised Episcopalian...but I'm not really anything now...not really...not much of anything nowadays. Then...I kinda grew up in Columbus, Dayton, and Cincinnati. Never left Cincinnati...never moved out of Ohio 'til I was 38."

"I think what fucks up modern man and society...I don't think we were put on this earth to be happy. Everybody is concerned with being happy. "How am I deriving pleasure from this?" I don't think we were put on this earth to be happy. I think we were put on this earth to do what we do...to do what we gotta do. I think you should try to...leave a mark in some way. Ummm...and I think if you do what you're supposed to do, what you really like and enjoy doing...you'll be happy, inadvertently. But, I don't think the goal is, "Oh, what do I need to do to make me happy?" You know...I don't come from that school."

"Probably the thing that made me the happiest was buying a farm. I bought this farm, and I'm still not farming...uh...I'm not sure what I'm doing with it, but that probably made me happy. To buy that farm, and uh...you know, own a piece of land. I've wanted that for a long time."

"A couple of days ago, we lost twenty guys in one day...in Iraq...and they were all from Ohio, and I'm kind of a...you know...die-hard Ohioan. I mean, I'm like an Ohioan before I am an American...you know? I'm really kind of state oriented. That...that...that upset me. Seeing twenty guys and BOOM...just go like that in one day, and I was thinking about them, and they're all twenty-three year old kids, and...BOOM, they're just gone. For whatever reason...whether we should be over there or not...it doesn't matter...and thinking about it made me cry. I just...I just bit it."

"I was down in Peru in the early 80's. I was doing a trek. I'm really into archaeology...going up to Machu Picchu...trekking up there. One night we were trekking...and it was already dark. We hadn't got to a campsite to make yet. We finally got to this campsite and pitched our tents and everything, around all these kind of really weird rocks. You could hardly see them in the dark...and we went to bed. That night I had these really weird dreams...really realistic...of little children. I could see their outlines up against the tent. There was a light behind them, and they were like, clawing...trying to get into the tent...little kids. They were like, moving around outside the tent...little shapes of children. They were very real. I woke up the next morning, and there was light. A guy came down from the hill...a Peruvian peasant...comes down from the hill. He had seen us that morning...he had a little shack up there, and...he came down. He told us we had camped in a cemetery...a children's cemetery...and that four of them were his dead children. You know, they have a high mortality rate. We had camped on top of this children's cemetery, and that was very strange because I had…had this dream…and we had no idea we were camping on top of a ceme-tery. All these children were clawing…trying to get in the tent. Very odd."

"Before comedy, I played polo for six years, with two different polo teams. I owned a trucking business…trucking warehouse business in my mid to late 20's. I owned one of the first document shredding companies, before that was big…when that was kind of a really weird type business. I was in confidential document shredding, and I really never shredded the documents. I got paid to, and it got out of hand. I ended up with a huge warehouse full of confidential doc-uments that I'd been paid to shred, that were never shredded. Then after that…I went into stand-up comedy. I was about 32."

"I just wanted to do something…you know, by the late 80's, there was just too much government regulation…you know, how you're going to run your busi-ness, the color to paint the warehouse floor, who to hire, how many to hire. I just went, "Fuck this…I don't need this…nobody's gonna tell me how to run my business." So, I said I'm going to get out of business and do something creative. I had never really done anything creative in my life…so I followed comedy. I was always fascinated by comedy, since I was a little kid…watching on the Ed Sulli-van show…and Johnny Carson. Then one day, I was on the "Tonight Show" performing…and got a standing ovation."

"I just saw a clip on the news tonight about the movie coming out, "The Aristo-crats", on CNN. They talked about this movie, and it's a ton of comics, you know, all telling the same joke, and that all stand-up comics everywhere know this joke. I don't know that joke…and I been in this business twenty years…and I don't know that fucking joke. How I could have missed this joke…not heard it…I have no fucking idea. I never heard it. In fact, somebody told me a short-ened encapsulated version of it a month ago, when they were talking about that movie being made. Other than that, I never heard that joke, which tells you how removed I can be from stand-up. I do stand-up, and I do it very well…but, you know, I do my thing, and you know…I haven't heard that joke. Isn't that odd?"

"A typical day for me…I drink coffee, smoke cigarettes, try to write…run some errands, make some calls…try to write…answer emails…surf the web…putter around. I kind of have ADD, so I am always scattered. I answer all my emails myself. Sometimes I don't answer for two months, but I answer every email I ever get."

"If I should die soon, somebody please take responsibility for publishing my written works. I think they are really good and fascinating if you could piece them together in a memoir. Please get them published. Leave a legacy. Leave my legacy…tell my story."

121 Al Poling

"I was in Africa...Tunisia...several years ago...and had some spiced couscous. It's without a doubt...the best flavor I've ever had. I had it with fava beans and Chianti. Delicious. I think probably the worst food I've ever had...a Hardee's hamburger."

122   *Mike Hidden*

"I just heard that they found one of those miners in West Virginia…dead…one of them thirteen that got trapped. They haven's found the other twelve. I don't really understand why they can't get to 'em…they keep talking about the atmosphere not being good…carbon monoxide too high. Why don't they just put on air tanks and walk down there? They ain't even gotten to the point where the…explosion occurred."

"I know they drilled a couple of holes from the top and stuck a camera down there…then a robot…but from what I understand there's nothing from stopping them from going down the main shaft…I think it's a two and a half mile long shaft…'cept the air. I guess I don't understand. The only thing I can figure is they're afraid of another explosion."

"From the tests they took, the air…the parts per million…I don't think any of them can still be alive…unless they got to an area where they could block off the bad air…you know, barricaded themselves in somewhere."

"Every time I see a story like this, I think of that Bruce Willis movie, "Twelve Monkeys". In that movie, there's a story about a kid trapped in a well…and Bruce Willis knows that he's really hiding in a barn…you know, because he was a kid himself when it happened…before he traveled back in time. It's just a joke…the kid really isn't down there. It's all a big practical joke…but the whole country is praying for the kid."

"I keep thinking that maybe those twelve miners are hiding somewhere…that they're alright…but…not really. Even though the whole country is praying for them…I think they're most likely dead."

123   *Father Mike Driscoll*

"It just turned cold again. Now it feels like it's going to be Thanksgiving next week. When it was seventy degrees, it just didn't feel like it was going to be Thanksgiving."

"I just watched with my sister last night...have you ever seen the movie "Spinal Tap"? The movie? It's about this rock band...and it's totally goofy. They asked the lead singer, "What would you like on your gravestone...your epitaph? He said, "Here lies David St. Hubbins and why not?" They asked him, "Do you think that sums up your life?" He said, "No...that's all I could think of at the moment.""

"I think a lot of times I come across as pretty opinionated and certain. I think I would want people to know that...I know I was wrong a lot of those times. I think I would like to say something like that. When people said...all those times that people said, "Boy, he really thinks that he knows it all." No...I realize that I don't know it all, and that I wasn't certain all the time. I guess, as much as anything...that would be my epitaph..."He didn't know it all." It's what I can think of at the moment."

"I was born in this hospital, St. Francis...and now I am the new chaplain here. I was born in '61...December 28th of '61. My mom's dad came from Italy...but my Driscoll half is Irish. I went to St. Philomena's...and my parents still live just three blocks away from there. I've got two brothers and two sisters, and a couple of them stayed in the old neighborhood."

"Every day we played baseball at a field across from my house...all summer we would do that. In fact, we were all Cardinal and Cub fans...but my dad was a Sox fan...and my older brother. One of those guys that played in that field all summer, who my brother had not seen in twenty-some years...he emailed him after the White Sox won the Series this year, from California. I don't know how he tracked down my brother, but he said, "You were the only White Sox fan in the neighborhood, so I wanted to email and congratulate you.""

"The day I was ordained a priest, here at St. Mary's Cathedral...the night before...and there were twelve of us ordained that day...they had us spending the night, and I can't even remember…one of the buildings here…they had us spend the night so that we would all be here together…have prayer together at the Cathedral with Bishop Meyers. Spending the night…and there were some dorm rooms here that were free…maybe it was the College of Nursing dorm rooms that were free in the summer. We spent the night, and then went to the Cathedral in the morning for the…for the Ordination Mass."

"It is a Catholic Mass, but then right in the middle is another ceremony that takes place…with the Bishop anointing with oil. Reading through the Bible, when something is consecrated, they pour oil on it…dedicating it to God…whether it be an altar, or you sometimes see in the Old Testament, they pour oil on a stone. Now, it's no longer a stone…it's an altar…dedicated to God. King David, how did he go from being David to King David? This anointing of oil…the prophet anointing him with oil. So, it is a sign of being dedicated to God. There is an anointing of oil in the sacrament of baptism too, so that every person who is baptized is dedicated to God in a certain way, too…and in a different way with holy orders, as we say…the sacrament of holy orders, which is when you are ordained a priest."

"We just finished the seminary, and so we had two weeks off. Then we went to our assignments. My first assignment was St. Paul's in Danville, Illinois. I've had a few different assignments in the Peoria Diocese, which stretches from the Quad Cities area to Danville. It goes all the way across the middle of the state, and goes as far north as Mendota…and the northeast corner…I guess there's not much out there…and then down to Lincoln…all the way through the middle of the state."

"I didn't really think about the priesthood until my junior and senior year of college. I went to the U of I and majored in economics. I had plans on going to law school. I would go to mass on Sunday, and sometimes during the week as well. I think it was those quiet masses…not so many people there…it was just quiet…and the idea just kept coming back to me. I found myself daydreaming during mass…not paying attention, and daydreaming of becoming a priest."

"The beginning of my senior year…the summer between my junior and senior year, I took the LSAT test, the law school entrance test. I took that test, and at the same time talked to a few priests and visited a few seminaries. I decided to go to the seminary."

"The seminary…it's five years. I did two years, and then left after two years…and didn't plan on going back. But, three years out, the idea still wouldn't leave me. I went back and thought, "Okay, I'm going to know very quickly whether this is it, one way or the other." And…I did. I thought I would either be there a couple weeks and say, "This is the end of it."…or I would say, "This is what I'm going to do." And…I never had any doubts after that. There really wasn't one moment where I knew I was going to be a priest…but over a stretch of years, the thought…the idea…would not leave me. Sometimes I've wondered *why*…but I never wonder *if*. I sometimes look back and say, "God, why did you want me to do this?" But…I never look back and wonder *if* I was supposed to. That question doesn't enter my mind."

"In Catholic school…years ago, kids talked about becoming priests or nuns. That was when there were more nuns in the school. In China, they could have had a person who might have been a great basketball player…but if he was never around basketball, he would never know it…even if he had the talent. I think…that is what we are going through in the church, to a degree. I think we have young women…girls out there, that are called to be sisters…but if they're not around them, to see them…they won't know it. It's the same with the priesthood. So, once you're in a cycle with reducing numbers…we have to break that cycle. Then, once it builds, it keeps building on its own, I think."

"I think that it's cultural…and it's just not the Catholic Church. People say we have a shortage of priests because priests can't marry. Really? Well, there were a lot of priests fifty years ago, and five hundred years ago…and they weren't marrying then either. So, that can't be the reason. I know Protestant ministers in the different towns I have been in…they are facing a shortage as well. That's why I say it is more of a cultural thing…I think. The shortage of priests and ministers and orthodox priests, the ones that can marry…they are facing a shortage too."

"The whole Carl Sagan thing…the Atheist's famous line, "Well, I'll believe in God when you can show him to me under a microscope."…you know, hard and fast proof. My response to that is, "You say that there is no god…the universe just came to be as it is? Can you prove that to me? Can you prove the universe just came out of nowhere? No…of course he can't prove that…and I can't prove to him that there is a god. So…we just have to make a choice."

"When I see sickness and death…do I believe this was all an accident…or do I believe that this is all the plan of someone who knows what is going on? What am I going to believe? Well…I'm not going to believe the first one. What a way to go through life. So, death and sickness…that reinforces my beliefs. Every time, which is frequently here…doctors and priests, we all see suffering and death. Which am I going to believe, that there's no sense to the world…or that there is not only meaning to it, but there is an all-knowing and all-loving god, that has allowed this to happen for reasons that I just cannot understand? I'm going to go with that one every time. That reinforces my faith. The alternative is to believe that there is…no meaning to any of this."

"It's impossible to reconcile the idea of evil, with a good god. All the world's religions and philosophies deal with that question of evil. I give the analogy that…a two or three year old has to get a needle stick with a shot…maybe an IV or something. What can mom and dad say? To a two year old, a word like "anesthetic" doesn't mean anything. What do you say? "Trust me. This is good. This will make you better. I know it hurts right now…but you have to trust me.""

"There is more of a gap between God's knowledge and ours, than ours and a two-year old's. If we don't explain it to the two-year old because we know he couldn't possibly understand it…and we just have to say, "I love you. Trust me."…that…is what God is trying to say to us all the time. "You cannot understand it…not now…but you just have to trust that I know what I'm doing." If we get to heaven, it will all be made clear. Until then, we are just that two-year old."

"Personally, that is how I get through it every time…I keep reminding myself that God knows what he is doing here. It doesn't look like it sometimes. If he's good, why does he allow it? I have to think either he doesn't exist, or he's not good, or…he knows a lot more than me, and this will be made right…somehow."

"Shortly after I was ordained, and for a variety of reasons, I became interested in the old Latin mass. It changed when I was four or five years old, so I just missed remembering it. That is a growing thing. John Paul II brought it back to a certain degree. In 1988, he told the bishops to be wide and generous in allowing Latin mass again, for those that have the rightful desire for it. So, I say it when I can…which is pretty frequently. I say private mass here. Pope John Paul II gave it a push…and Cardinal Ratzinger, when he was cardinal for twenty years, wrote about the importance of tradition of things in the mass."

"Mass today, and if you went to twenty masses today…picked them at random…you would say, "That's not as sacred as that old Latin mysterious mass." There is now handholding and hugging…and it just doesn't look as sacred as the old mass. It's not. It is more focused on people than it is directed toward God. The way the mass is said…I look at you and speak to you in your own language. If I turned around and started speaking in Latin, you would go, "Wow, this is not geared toward me…it is geared towards God.""

"This would have been a controversial thing to say when I was in the seminary, except that Cardinal Ratzinger has been writing these things for twenty years now…and now he's Pope. Now…I can say these things with no fear. I can just say, "You've got to read some of the Pope's writings on this." There are Internet rumors that anytime he may say, "All priests can do the old mass again." There is speculation he may do something like that. *That…that* would be a big thing in my life. Most of the people attracted to it are my age and younger."

"If I stay at this hospital until I retire, I would be happy with that. Not everyone gets to do that. Some people have to do jobs they don't like. Thank God I love what I'm doing. I don't like every moment…I don't like it when something bad is happening, but still, I should be here during those times. I have no other goals in this life, other than I think I would like to be Bishop or Pope…for just one day…and then pass it on. Just one day"

124   *Steve Bilbrey*

"I am from Anaheim, California. I was ten when I left Anaheim. I'm 41 now. My family moved and we ended up...up north in the Chicago area. We're here at Tanner's Orchard just visiting, and we're staying at Lake Wildwood with friends. This is my daughter...Sara...and this is Molly."

"In Anaheim, my dad would take us out fishing almost every weekend...and the weird thing about it...we used to go out, my brother and me, and Dad...we used to go out in a twelve foot boat, with a thirty...thirty year old motor on the back of it. We used to go miles and miles out...and now it just seems so dangerous, and I would never do that with my kids. Also, in Anaheim, they had these rain rivulets that were pretty amazing. The rain would wash out these rivulets...and to us they were canyons. They would be eight or ten feet deep, and we would walk down the middle of them, barefoot. It was nice being barefoot in southern California...having such a beautiful place to grow up in."

"One Christmas, my cousins stayed with us...there were four of them, and four of us...and all the adults. When we came downstairs on Christmas morning, everyone got brand new bicycles. It was pretty magical. That day in southern California...it was just about like this...so, we all went outside and rode these brand new bicycles. I couldn't figure out the gears, but that was a pretty magical day. Everybody had a new bike...sissy bars, banana seats...all the old stuff."

"We just bought this scrumptious caramel, apple-pecan pie. It weighs about eight pounds, and it's still hot on the bottom. It's wonderful. We were petting some goats, and this big one...the brown and white one with the big horns...he walked up to the top of the fence and leaned way over. I was petting him on the nose...and he got the tip of the bag, and started pulling it close to him...as strong as you could pull. I crushed the side of the pie trying to hold it back, and I finally had to grab the plastic bag and yank it out of his mouth. It came out with a snap...you know? So, any opportunity these guys have...these goats...they'll take advantage."

"The kids went through the corn maze today...and that was great. I'm spending some time with my college roommate, my best friend Sergio, and his family...wife Liz. It's nice to see old friends, and our kids are having a good time together...playing and feeding the goats."

125   *Jay Wright*

"I'm Jay Wright. I'm 22. I turned 22 a couple of weeks ago, so I'm fresh...fresh, freshly aged, you know. I live on a farm about fifteen miles outside of town. It's a pretty cool spot. We've got horses and a mule and a donkey, and a bunch of cattle and stuff. I grew up at a myriad of places...ummm...I grew up in Evanston and moved here when I was about four."

"Me and my mom had a falling out my freshman year. I went to a Catholic high school, and they instituted a drug test and all sorts of stuff like that...and that's...I'm not really about that."

"I work at Jakes pizza...a delivery job, and I like to think I am pretty good at it. I make minimum wage...about four bucks an hour after taxes during the summer, but during the school year, I make about ten."

"I'm sort of a spiritual person, but I don't follow any guidelines. I'm really anti...organized religion. I know they have many good uses, but I mean the whole Christianity thing...like I don't know. The only thing good thing is that they have good morals. I mean generally every religion has a set of morals, and they're all generally the same. I don't understand why people are always killing each other over religious thoughts, like Jihad...and us killing other people...I don't know. I think Bush is an evil, evil person. He's just out to make his buddies money. I think he's an idiot as well...a puppet on a string."

"My dad was really cool and my mom was really strict....like...I have always been rebellious, and my dad has known that 'cuz he was a similar way. So, obviously he has been there as a figure and doesn't like, come in and say "No...You can't do this", unless you're doing something like, really "bad" bad. Like, as far as smoking pot goes...he busted me right when I got into smoking pot. He didn't bust me, but called me out and said, "I know you're smoking pot. I know there's nothing I can do about it."...which is the truth..."but if I catch you smoking pot...blah, blah, blah, blah, blah" And then I've just been like, "Fuck you.", and "Whatever." That's pretty much what I did to my mom. I've always been rebellious and don't like authority of any type."

"I think they should legalize pot. It's not a bad drug. Alcohol is a more affecting drug than pot. It's like…smoking a joint, what are you gonna do…hang out and be like "alright" and maybe laugh a little and whatever? You're not going to get up and start punching people just because you're stoned on weed. But, if you get drunk, you know, fights tend to happen. I mean, some drugs, people tend to get up and…on shit, and do crazy weird shit. Naw, I don't have anything against drugs at all. I think they should legalize every drug, so that they could better inform us about them. Better drugs would completely remove the drug under-world, which is the way it is now. Somebody gets ripped off of crappy drugs, you know, and people will get pissed, and there will be some sort of retribution. People are getting robbed, shot…all over this money that's caused by the drugs being illegal. I don't really do too much myself. I don't even really smoke pot anymore because I'm on probation."

"I do have a sort of dream. I'm trying to throw this festival. We're trying to get all the local bands around here to have a festival at my house. That would be an awesome experience…it would be like…"Look what I did…I made this awesome party…the coolest party ever…and it just happened because I worked really, really hard and helped the cause of it happening.""

126   *Peggy Wilson*

"I work in a candy shop in downtown Bloomington. I'm originally from Colorado...the Denver area. I went to Dinosaur National Park when I lived there. You sit on this big raft with fifteen other people. It's a real serene place with these flat cliffs...and you go through there and it's real calm...and then you go through these rapids. Then...you know, not so calm. That's why I like it."

127 *Bill Greene*

"I am proud to be an American and be able to fly in the United States. There are other countries...and most Americans do not understand...the privileges we have as compared to overseas. People take for granted what we have here in America."

"My name is Bill Greene. I came upon my aircraft from a good friend of mine that I grew up with in high school. He was an aviation buff also, and admired the P-6 Warbird. He did all the restoration on the aircraft, and I acquired the aircraft from him about five years ago, and uh, it took maybe two years of uh...telling him that I could take care of the aircraft, and keep it in great condition...just like he has...and uh, overall...and...he knew how meticulous I was, and how much...how much of a perfectionist I was. In doing so, he finally agreed, after two years of talking him into it...he sold it to me. I was very fortunate to purchase it from him and finish out the restoration, putting on the lettering, and uh, and doing the highly polished...ummm...finish on the aircraft, and ummm...bringing it up to military specifications...the way it was when it came off the flight line at North American."

"Some of the requirements, judging requirements...some of the technical things...they want the lettering to look original, and the...the...all the way down to the wax rope. It used to have nylon ties on it. They gig you on those nylon ties being there. We had to put the wax rope back on the wires. These would tie-wrap the electrical wires on there...to keep things from hanging down there and everything."

"I started flying back in early 1975, when I got out of the service. I was in the Army...always enjoyed aircraft, and had an interest in aircraft, even as a child. My mother always knew where I was, because...where there would be remote-controlled airfields, about half a mile from our house. If she couldn't find me, she knew I was at the airfield watching them fly remote-controlled airplanes. Ever since then, I was always curious about aircraft...always enjoyed aircraft...and so, when I got out of the Army, I started taking lessons, started flying...and over the years, I purchased my first aircraft, and finished up getting my pilot's license. In doing so, I just tear-stepped my way up into the larger aircraft...faster aircraft...more complex aircraft. Once I saw this aircraft, I just had to have it."

"I traveled all over the country, different air shows…thought about it…inquired about it…and found out some things about the aircraft…what to look out for when you purchase one…and stuff like that. So, after two years of looking at it, and negotiating, the gentleman who owned this aircraft…the dream finally came true…I purchased it and finished out the restoration."

"I have over 1250 hours of flight time. When you fly…you have to learn one thing about flying…flying is that particular something…that you can't think of anything else but…flying. I work a lot, I work all the time. But, when I get in that aircraft, I forget about everything that I have done for the day…as stressful as the day was…when I get in that aircraft…start it up and walk around it…my mind is focused on flying…flying that aircraft. It is a release, in my lifestyle, to relax. When I go up, I tend to enjoy and just relax…flying the aircraft. There is nothing more peaceful."

128   *Melissa Rives*

"I've always been a big fan of the library and reading when I was a kid. I grew up in Deer Creek, and I started early with Stephen King. I live out by London Mills now. I write poetry...had a few published...been in a few books. I'm kind of a dark poet. Want to hear one?"

"In it comes, like an icicle to the heart,
a moment when the air is crushed from the lungs
until reason is left shivering without a blanket.
Cold winter wind shifts through veins
turning the blood into muddy slush.

Cryptic thoughts murmuring in vague voices
breathing frost upon the soul, begin to spread
their patterns upon the windows looking out...
while popsicle fingers grab your throat.

Confusion setting in as eyes glaze over
like an old mirror, or
the blinding light of winter's white.

With every heart-beat comes the sound
of breaking glass or avalanche,
wherein the spirit must prevail
or shatter and become
the sound of fear."

129   *Daniel Hartmann*

"I am originally from Bavaria...just south of Bavaria...just to the border to the Alps...near to Austria. It is about two hours south of Munich. We are here for fun. We come from a small village called Stein. We are here with 24 people, and we make music at the Oktoberfest. We have a big brass band and we make music...three guys, called the Hartmann Trio...the village band of Stein and the Hartmann Trio. We are here to have fun and drink some beers with the guys here...sing a little bit of songs and just be here. We are here the fourth time...in 1997, 1998, and 1999...and now we are back and looking forward to the Oktoberfest."

"Stein is a small village, about two thousand...two thousand people. At home there are a lot of mountains...we live between the mountains, in a valley that is a border to the Alps. It is about forty kilometers to Austria...it is about one hundred forty kilometers to Munich. There, we are the village band. There is always much fun...much beer and much fun."

"I have had a lot of fun in my life. I make very, very much music...about one hundred to one hundred twenty times a year. I also...I also go to work, but music...that is my life. We come to America four times. We been to the USSR...we been to Japan. We just like it. Because of this, there have been a lot of good days in my life."

"I have a girlfriend back home, but the family thing doesn't work. Because of the music that we play...such more time...if I have children, I want to be there for the children. I have parents back in Stein...and my two brothers, they are here with me. We three are the Hartmann Trio, and we...we make music together."

"Three years ago, we were in USSR and made music on the USSR tour...and there was a marriage...a girl that came from our town...and she married a guy from USSR. She wanted her music, and the guy from USSR...he wanted his music. So, we came there...the first time we played, and then the other guys played...and then we played together. They had never seen us, and it was so much fun. This was one of the most greatest things in our tour...to play with other musicians we had never seen before...and we played all night. It is wonderful making new friends and playing music."

"We play at home, we play at the Oktoberfest in Munich. But in another four or five years, I will have a family...and then have another part of life. In Bavaria, I like it. The people are friendly...and the town of my birth is where my family is. One day I will stay in Stein and have a family and children...but until then, I will make music, drink beer, and have fun."

130   *Carrol Van Velkinburgh*

"I'm eating a yam with brown sugar and butter on it. It's good…would you like a bite? Would you like one? They taste more like pumpkin pie."

"I am 73. I'm from Quincy…still live there. They always said I came from the wrong side of the tracks. I lived in the poor part of Quincy, but I loved it because people were more friendly, closer together, and more family-orientated. You didn't pick on anybody. You were a group of people…not a single person. Like today…they will pick on one individual. We just…we didn't do that. We were a group of happy people."

"I worked at the Pentagon with Secretary of Defense Charles E. Wilson. I was his receptionist. Every time you're in the military you just work with ordinary people. You wear a uniform…and I got to work at the Pentagon as a receptionist."

"My brother talked me into it. I wanted to join the Navy, but he said, "No…the Marine Corps is the best outfit." Now, don't call me a BAM…'cuz I will call back at you. Marines have called me a BAM before, which is Big-Ass Marine…but I just call them the other…Half-Ass Marine. That's what you call men Marines that call women, BAMs."

"I met Mr. Nixon, and Patricia Nixon, his wife. He was just another person…and I'm not somebody that gets all blowed up just because they meet somebody with a big name. They're just people. They were at a party, the night before Thanksgiving in 1953…at the Secretary of Defense office. I always liked being in the service and meeting all those nice people. The one person that I met…one day we were having lunch with Mr. Wilson…Arthur Godfrey was there. They were talking…arguing over a big bull that Mr. Wilson owned, but Arthur wanted it. I thought, "Here we are sitting in the Pentagon…and they're arguing over a bull?" I couldn't understand that. But, they were friends…and that's what they wanted to talk about."

"For two years I was in the Marine Corps, and then I was in the National Guard for seventeen and a half years. I took my training at Parris Island. That's where they take all the women in…to get their Mickey Mouse shoes. I remember those black shoes that we called Mickey Mouse shoes…black shoes."

"You know, I always wanted to go around the world...like on a slow boat to China. I don't think that's going to happen now, but I'd like to do that. But...every day, I come up out of my bed thanking God that I am alive...and I go to bed the same way. I don't have any bad days...ever. I have a lot of friends, a good family...a nice family. I wish them happiness, and health, and contentment. You know...I wish the world was more at peace...you know, that we wouldn't be fighting other people's battles over in Iraq and Afghanistan...that they could just came back here in the States, and everybody would be happy and content."

131   *Wayne F. McDaniels*

"I went to grade school in Peoria, but I can't remember the name of it."

"My name is Wayne McDaniels. I'm 28 and from Chicago and I got stranded. I really need $30 to get to my friend Richard's house. He's got all my shit. I don't want anybody rippin' all my shit off...so he's got it. I can take a bus right down there if I had $30. Richard's got work right now. He works at Methodist...he works in the office."

"One time I wuz' workin' in an office puttin' paperwork together and that...for people to fill out and that. I wuz never real good at it, and so when I dropped out of school I lost that job. It was a school program, and they didn't want me working for them after that. I've been a dishwasher, janitor...and that's about it."

"I wuz workin' for the Steamboat carnival down the road there and they fired me. I just walked up to 'em a couple days ago and asked 'em to hire me...and they did. I fell off a ride, backwards, and hit my head on a light and broke it. I ended up falling onto one of them lights they put on 'em, and I busted it. The boss then said, "I can't have you doing that." They're strict. He was being a real asshole when I was puttin' the rides together. He was being a real dick. It all started from breakin' the light bulb and all that. I got hurt bad...my back...but I didn't have to go to the hospital or that."

"They give you money for tearin' the rides down and all that, but I couldn't get the money 'cuz I got fired. I really need $30 to buy me a bus ticket...it's right down there."

"I wuz sleeping down there where that parkin' lot...that parkin' deck covers them other people sleepin'. It's hard on yer back." I got this blanket and pillow, but they don't help much."

"I got kicked out of high school 'cuz I'm handicapped. I got me a chemical imbalance. I used to take medication, but not no more...until I found out the medication can kill ya. They took it off the market and all that. I took it over and over and then said, "Nope, I ain't takin' that no more.""

"I'm gonna get me a job up there in Chicago and take martial arts. I'm trying to make it up the highest grade I can. I take…kinda…three different kinds…I try to learn it all. I like it alright, but it kinda hurts when ya get kicked the wrong way. My parents said to find me a job and take martial arts, and so that's what I did. I already got kicked in the shoulder last year. I'm gonna fill me out some applications and get me a job in Chicago and take martial arts."

"One of my brothers…he's traveling around with a different carnival right now. I don't know how he's doing. I lost his number and everything. I lost all my brother's numbers. I got two brothers and two sisters. My dad…he works for a trucking company, and I live with him sometimes."

"I wuz' at a party once and got a ride from a couple guys goin' back home, and they pushed me right out of the truck. I was all banged up. That's kinda how I feel now. I could use $30 and something to eat. I'm hungry…do they have pizza at them carts over there?"

132   *Sara Schwarzentraub*

"I got into the Illinois Math & Science Academy up in Aurora. It's a really good school...like, it's really hard to get into. Like, they only accept the top ten percent...pretty much. The best thing about it is, like..."Membership and Inquiry"...where you, like...go around and talk to scientists and work with them. I'm working in a project at Argonne. I'm working on the Minos Star Detector data, which is like...neutrinos. It's pretty far out there...even though I've never really been out of the state."

133   *Edgar Winter*

"You know...my very first memory of music was being nestled in my mothers lap...ah, as she played piano...and I was so young...I don't know how old I was, but...I finally realized that she was creating this music. I was hearing this beautiful music flowing over me and I was just able to sort of...peak up over the keyboard and able to associate it...you know, with the motion of her hands. I realized, "Wow, she's really...she's making...she's really making that music." The reason I bring it up is because someone once asked me, "What was your first memory of music?" I really had to cast my mind back to try to remember what it was. And I...I think that's significant...because a lot of people, the first thing they remember is maybe...something mechanical like records that they heard. And in my case, I think...for that reason I really associate music with...with...with family, and with deep emotions, and with love, and that...that type of security. I have always thought of...thought of music as a very spiritual thing that...that goes far beyond any secondary reward. I always loved music just for itself...or for the beauty of harmony and rhythm."

"I was born in Beaumont, Texas, which is a...a great musical environment, to grow up in, first of all. It's not at all what...ah, some people would expect. It's right on the Louisiana border, so there is a lot of French-Cajun influence. There is music called swamp music...but ah...it's referred to as zydeco...all New Orleans stuff. It's close to the Mexican border, so there is...hot Latin rhythm players. There is real country, real authentic country."

"There was a...there was a...blues station called KJET, that was right down the street from my grandma's...we used to go over there for fried chicken every Thursday night...and there was a DJ...Clarence Garlow, who was a famous blues guy. Johnny and I would go over to the radio station...ah, and jam on the radio when I was around probably seven or eight."

"Johnny and I started...ah, when I was four years old. We started playing ukuleles and singing Everly Brothers songs, "Wake up little Susie, I want to go home...kink a kink a chink." We were little kids, and I don't...I don't actually...I remember going on this TV show...a local TV show called "The Don Mahoney Show". Don would ride in on this big white horse...and the ranch...it looked like a Roy Rogers you know, kind of deal. And they would have kids on, tap dancing and stuff, ah…like that…and Johnny…Johnny and I played our "ukes" and sang. That was when I was six, but my mother tells me that actually I went on a radio show called "The Uncle Willie Show" when I was four years old. That's…that's pretty young."

"You know…my musical background…our…our family was all musical. My mother played classical piano. My father played a little guitar and banjo…played alto sax in a swing band in his youth, and he had a barber shop quartette that would come over to the house and ah…sing. I sang in the choir…so I sang in the choir when I was six or seven. And to me, music was just such a common place every day thing. I…I didn't realize that there was anything unusual or…or out of the ordinary about it, until I started trying to put bands together with some of my friends around the neighborhood and…they couldn't play. I said, "What's going on?" I said, "Your daddy didn't show you any chords?" I mean…I just thought it was like…people learned how to read, and learned to talk, and learned how to add and subtract and I figured everybody learned music…which is a household thing. I mean…even my grandfather, great grandfather, everybody played something. So ah…I was really shocked, you know, when I found out that…that some people just didn't have that…that natural aptitude or…or ability."

"I never had any desire to be famous…at all, but my brother Johnny, made up for that. He was…you know, he watched "Bandstand" and read all the magazines. You know…he was Johnny "Cool-Daddy" Winter, with the shades and the pompadour, and you know…like, rock and roll."

"Johnny and I…we did all kinds of ah…we did all kinds of stuff growing up. We played for the…like, we played for Assembly, you know, at school and after the…you know, after the football games and sock hops…you know, that kind of stuff. We used to go out to the…we used to go out to the clubs. There was a…there was a black club called "The Raven", where all the artists like Ray Charles and Bobby "Blue" Bland and B.B. King…ah, this was when Johnny was about fifteen, I would say…and there were, you know, like 5000 black people. We were like, the only white people there. B.B. was so…he was such a gentleman. He was so gracious, you know. He invited Johnny up to play and then on his inter…on his intermission, he came over and a sat at our table and, I know that meant a lot to Johnny. First of all, you know, he did not have to do that but he's a…he's really…you know…I think B.B. is really a great…a great person."

"We played with B.B....the last time I saw him was about four years ago...at the Montreal Jazz Festival. You know, they have a lot of blues players on it as...as well, and we jammed on stage with a whole host of great guitar players. Gary Moore...I remember was there...and there were a lot of...just a lot of great guitarists. Actually, George Duke, the jazz pianist was there. That was really a fun...really a fun jam."

"We used to do...you know I think one of the things that people think...have the conception that there...that there was a lot of racial tension, of the South being segregated. I grew up playing with...with black kids. I...I had, you know...bands. I played in bands...and it is true that some clubs wouldn't hire...you know, they wouldn't hire a band if it was mixed, racially. There was like...there was...there was a club I remember, called "The Derrick", and they had "Big Sambo and The House Wreckers", a great black band...but...and then they had white bands, but they wouldn't hire mixed bands, and they wouldn't let me sit in. This was in the early 60's, it would have been. But, we used to also...there was a jazz club called "The Tahiti", that we used to go to all the time, and we also used to sneak into the...the tent revivals. If you think rock & roll has energy...it pales in comparison to like a, Pentecostal tent revival. It's like, one of the most amazing experiences. And that was when I...I really first realized the...just the amazing spiritual quality, you know, that music has. I was sort of a serious musician...and it was just my own private world that I could escape into."

"When I played Woodstock, it really changed my life. It was in a time when...against the social backdrops of civil rights and peace movements, people sang songs that they really believed in. I said, "Wow, you can...you can really...the power that music has to get a message across, is something I never really considered." It was just a fun thing for me and it was like my own private world that I could escape into. As a kid, you know...I couldn't see well enough to play sports and stuff. I couldn't play football and basketball, so I...I had a natural affinity for music, so that sort of became my thing."

"The type of music that can bring tears to my eyes and moves me is mostly gospel and blues...stuff like Ray Charles. I'll hear Ray Charles sing "Georgia"...and he was my first influence...and he had such emotion and intensity...realism, and ah, his voice....just ah, ah, it really took you somewhere else. I think that...I think that he has just, has become so much a part of the...the universal consciousness of all things. There is even now, you know…people that ah, don't necessarily make any attempt to copy Ray in any kind of way. It's just that, every body wants to sing with that type of sincerity and that…that intensity that he…that he had."

"Certain songs affect me. "Yesterday" by The Beatles is one. Songs that I remember in relation to something specific…you know…to a time in my life. Certainly, I think everybody has an….ah, emotional impact…and sometimes you know, it's not the song itself, but it's what occurred in your life at that time…that causes you to feel that way about it. But I think every music…every music has like its own…ah, sort of soul. You know, regardless of, if it's country or jazz, or even if it's something like polka music…you know…there is going to be somebody that plays that stuff, you know, with such mastery, and that is so much a part of it, that it's going to make you…feel that. To me that's all music is about; it's an emotional bridge. It brings people together. To me, that's…that's what I always listen for in music…the magic. Either it affects you or it doesn't. It takes you somewhere, or it doesn't…and that…to me is, what I think of as, you know…music being good or not. It's not the technical facility of it, or the structure of it. It really is the emotion."

"I am absolutely at a good point in my life…living in Beverly Hills with my wife Monique. It truly is the best point of my life. We have been married 26 years. We get remarried every year on our anniversary. We moved out to LA in 1990, and we have been there since then. We had lived together in New York for about twelve years, you know, prior to that. And ah, you know, I got my digital studio at home and…I can wake up at four in the morning with a musical idea and…you know, go in and create something, and you know, have it together in…you know, in a hour or so…and that…that gives me a great sense of musical freedom."

"The only thing I miss in terms of the way music was made, like back in the 70's…and I, you know…everybody has the tendency to think that they grew up in some kind of a special era…and certainly like the 40's and 50's with you know, the swing and jazz era, that was really special. I think the 70's, if you look at it objectively, was a lot of great music, you know. There was a lot of musical freedom. It was before…before ah, music got so commercial, and record companies started to intervene…to the extent that it made it difficult for artists to simply embrace the music that they learned to play…and ah…and do it."

"Back then, it was very common for groups to have two and three songs and go into the studio and actually write and create an album in the studio. That no longer happens because record companies want to hear demos of every song because of all this pre-production. And...I remember when that change came about. I knew guys that would record a whole album and then have it, you know, have it rejected...not approved by the record company...and then have to start all over again. So, ah you know...it can be discouraging, you know, to say the least. Now, with all the technological revolution, the digital revolution...every body has a studio. Everybody is pretty much free to record, you know, to write and record what they want now. It's just a question of selling it, you know, to a company. But at least you can get it into the physical universe now, where as before, you were reliant on studios to do that, which was like, you know...could cost you...$100,000, you know, to get a decent...even a decent demo recorded."

"I would like people to ah...think of me as...as someone who really cared, and hopefully that I have left some good memories along the way and...you know, things that were important to me were...really trying to...trying to give back something that makes the world a little better and you know...a brighter place to be. I think that's the most we can all hope for."

134   ***Chris Sollenberger***

"High school was fun. I got to play sports all the time. I played left field...played regionals on my birthday. A lot of my life revolved around sports. Of course, I didn't become a professional baseball player...but went into construction."

"It's my dad's business...and he didn't want me in that profession. But, I used to go to job sites with him when I was younger...and regardless of, if it was winter or not...I always liked being outside. I always liked being around construction."

"I think the accomplishment...after everything is said and done...the accomplishment is what does it for me. My dad started showing me stuff when I was fourteen...cutting wood and stuff like that. Building houses and then seeing what you accomplish...and some of them are $300,000, $400,000 houses...and I'll never live in a house like that, but it makes you feel good...being able to build something like that."

135   *Donna Robinson*

"I'm kind of a Marshall County girl. I'm from Winona, lived in Toluca...but live in Lake Wildwood now. I am 45."

"I've worked at Tanner's Orchard for six years. I've worked every year at "U-Pick". I bag caramel apples in boxes, and clean...work the cash register, and sell apples and pumpkins. They do this "all you can carry" thing here. It's how many pumpkins you can carry for twenty feet...and there's been all kinds of methods that people have used. One guy used his coat and tied the arms around his waist...and then held the other end and carried the pumpkins. Another guy loaded up his girlfriend with pumpkins and then carried her. It costs $25...and you get to keep all the pumpkins you can carry. Mostly, it's a good way to *break* pumpkins."

136   *M.J. Dunn*

"Dogs are kind of my thing. I really love dogs...and I have had many, many dogs in my life. I think probably the strangest dog story I have, took place at my aunt's house one Thanksgiving, about fifteen years ago."

"We got there early in the afternoon and had dinner...all the traditional food. She always had turkey and ham...although ham is not my favorite...ummm...so I always have the turkey. She had the stuffing and mashed potatoes, gravy...you know, turkey gravy, corn...green beans...rolls...some kind of Jell-O thing...olives. I really like the black olives. I kind of do the thing where I fill up my plate with turkey, stuffing, mashed potatoes, corn, and black olives. Then, I take the gravy and pour it over everything. Now...my uncle, he does the same thing, but then he'll stir up his plate...so that everything is mixed together. I don't go that far because it looks kind of gross. I still do the thing where you put an olive on each finger, and then eat them one by one. My own kids do that now."

"After dinner, we all sat around their fireplace and had coffee and...and hot chocolate. So, we sat there for awhile and talked...mostly about my dad's toenails. My uncle tried to play his Irish pipes that he got that year...and my sister threw up in the kitchen garbage can. So...that was kind of gross. Then my aunt started talking about Roger...who was this black Labrador, that was...I think he was thirteen or fourteen years old. He mostly just layed around because he had bad hips...but, they gave him these arthritis pills a couple times a day. He could barely make it out the back door to go and take a leak by this tree...one that was only a few feet away. He couldn't hike his leg anymore, so he did the girlie thing. Then, after he got done, he would need help sometimes...getting up the two steps to come back in the house."

"So, my aunt is talking about Roger, who is lying under a card table in the side porch...and starts crying about him. You know, they've had this dog a long time, and it's pretty sad when a dog who's been this lively animal, you know, gets old. So, she's talking to my uncle...Uncle Floyd, and he's a veterinarian. They're talking about Roger...and at some point, Roger comes in and lies at my aunt's feet. Have you ever seen the look in a dog's eyes when they're just so sad that you can...feel their pain...you know what I mean? Roger had that look, that look of helplessness...of quiet helplessness."

"My sister and I went outside for awhile. We actually went into the woods a little bit and smoked a cigarette…my parents still didn't know I smoked at that time…and I wish I had never started. We went back into the house, and there on the kitchen table…was Roger. There was this old grey wool blanket on the table…and there was Roger lying on his side…on the table. My uncle, the veterinarian, had just given Roger some kind of muscle relaxant…or some type of medication to sedate him. Then, after my sister and I came in, and my mother explained what was going on…he took a bottle out of his bag…filled a hypodermic needle, and injected it into Roger's leg."

"After maybe ten seconds or so…you could see that final long breath…and then he was dead. My aunt and my uncle…tears were streaming down their faces. And, because they were crying…everybody else was crying. After a few more minutes, my mom said that it was for the best, and everyone agreed…then told my sister and me to go into the living room."

"That kitchen table…where the turkey platter sat, just a couple of hours before…now there was a dead dog lying there. The whole house was very quiet. Then…my uncle folded the blanket over and wrapped Roger up, and took him outside. He buried him out by a storage shed…just on the edge of one of their corn fields. I don't think they farmed, but they leased their land to another farmer. My mom wouldn't let us go outside to watch, but we saw where he had been buried later on, when my sister and I went outside to sneak a cigarette. The shovel was still stuck in the dirt mound."

"Later that day…and it was dark by then…my aunt was serving pumpkin pie from that table. It was the kind of table…do you know what "cracked ice" is? It's a pattern, usually grey, or yellow, or red…that you see on those tables that they made in the 50's and 60's. The chairs also have that same pattern…chrome chairs covered in that vinyl cracked ice pattern."

"So here she is cutting pumpkin pie on the same table where Roger died….and she sort of had that same look of sadness that Roger had…that same look of helplessness. Since that day…when somebody in our family gets that look, we always say you have "roger eyes." "Jackie, what's wrong with you? You've got "roger eyes" today."

137   *Charles Ash*

"I'm 67...from Farmington. Years ago, I was invited to Wisconsin...at a ceremony to read the role from the state of Illinois. I done that for a number of
years...in conjunction with a POW-WOW. Last year, when we was done with
our POW-MIA recognition ceremony, during the first ceremony...or during the
first part of the POW-WOW, the individual who had been sponsoring what was
going on up there...made the statement that he wasn't going to allow us to come
up there any more...or not allowed to have that ceremony. So, I came down
here, crying around about not being able to go back up there...and I was over at
the American Legion headquarters in Bloomington one day, and one of the guys
there told me to shut my mouth and bring it here. So, that's what I'm trying to
do. For the first time, for what we had...I think we're doing...alright."

"I retired from Keystone five years ago...thank God. I was a millwright for about
25 years, and then I got allergic to the lime out there...and they forced me out
and made me go into the Engineering Department. So, the last ten years I was
there, I worked out of Engineering. Things kinda went downhill there for a long
time."

"The Marine Corps kinda made me grow up. In that day and age, it was either
that or go to jail...that's why I joined. I got into a little bit of trouble, and figured
it was best to get out of state for awhile. San Diego, I think anybody will tell you
that it was hard...but well worth it by the time that it was over with. Went to
Pendleton for ITR...then after that I went to 2nd Battalion, 5th Marines as a 106
recoilless rifleman. At the time, I didn't have a high school education, and
decided to go ahead and get one...a GED. They made me take an aptitude test
first...and I done pretty good on the aptitude test, so I would imagine. Within
three months after I took that, I was in Fort Huachuca, which was the Army
Intelligence School...cross training. From there, Okinawa to Vietnam...to Okinawa...back to Vietnam...back to Okinawa...then home. I was then in the Air
Wing the last few months I was in. I don't talk about what I did in Vietnam...not at all."

"I don't know if you know what the story is on Jane Fonda or not. When she
went to Hanoi...the prison camp there...all the prisoners were lined up, and had
a piece of paper with their social security number on it...thinking that when they

shook hands, they would hand her that piece of paper, so that she could bring it back to the states…and then find out who was there. It didn't turn out that way. She shook hands with all those guys…took those pieces of paper…and when she got to the end of the line, she handed every one of those pieces of paper to the camp commander. One guy died from being beaten…two others are still crippled today, where they can't hardly walk."

"Jane Fonda is not one of my favorite people…no sir."

138   *Taru Sharma*

"I was contracted as a lead software engineer and then became hired as a lead systems engineer at Caterpillar. I am from India originally."

"In India...most places are at walking distance, and so was the bazaar. I used to go with my brothers when they were young and could not run errands themselves. It was fun to show them how to transact and get the money back...from the shopkeeper. It was always fun to go to bazaar with Papa. He would get us candies, which were a rarity in my house. He would also take us to visit my uncle's family once in awhile. My brother would ride in front seat of the bicycle and I would be at the back seat. He used to make us tell stories while returning back in the evening, to ensure that we have not fallen asleep...and fallen from the bicycle. My uncle's children were around the same age as us and made good company for games and having fun."

"I learnt how to make perfect round chapattis from Mom. I remember the garden full of roses, chrysanthemums, dahlias and all sorts of vegetables...the prayer room, which always was bathed in the fragrance of incense...and the small room which was solely used by children when they were studying. There were three of us...me and my two younger brothers. Somehow, there was an unwritten agreement amongst us siblings...I would do the household work and my brothers would run errands."

"While I am looking back...I cannot forget the school...a place I enjoyed most, and according to Mom, unlike other children who used to cry to stay home and not go to school, I used to cry for going to school."

"Initially the school wouldn't admit me because of my age...less than four years old. To appease me, Mom had to sew a school uniform for me, get me a school bag and watch me put on the act of going to school."

"She used to invent creative ways to teach us...sing poems with us, while bathing us...ask questions while making chapattis...make us repeat math tables while she was ironing clothes. It was one seamless life for all of us. One of her significant contributions was to pursue Papa to get library subscription...and the world opened up to us. All sorts of books started pouring into the house and our horizons broadened. We learnt about places we had never visited, food we had never eaten…and ways of life we had never seen."

"Now that I am thirty, I understand the challenges of adult life and I have to appreciate my parents for doing such a good job of raising us in spite of all the challenges they had to face."

"I do not have children as of now…but I hope someday I would have them and we would do all these things together…cook, shop, tell stories and maybe some day they would look back at these, the same way I am doing now."

139   *Elsie Hallman*

"I'm 52 and proud of it. I come from Bowling Green, Kentucky. I'm livin' in Creve Coeur now. I don't really like anything about it. I don't get out much...just stay inside. I have some activities...and friends. I don't really know a lot about Creve Coeur. I have a couple of roommates...and I just take care of the house. I try to take care of the two guys that live there. It was kind of an accident that I came here. I just met a friend, and I decided to make a move. My girls grew up...grandchildren and everything. I just decided to move north. I lived here when I was twelve years old...and I graduated from Newman High School...in Newman, Illinois. So, I been here about two and a half years."

"I always liked school. I was always interested in journalism...English. So, I got a scholarship to go to Eastern Illinois University. I went there for awhile, and then decided to get married. I wanted to be a journalist like...oh God help me...I can't even think of her name now...ummm...Barbara Walters. Yes...my favorite. Yeah, you know...but since I was a woman...you know."

"But, I've been writing. I've kept a journal since I was like, twelve. The scholarship was great. It was only like, fifteen hundred dollars...but it was great. I graduated fourth in my high school class. It was exciting. Now, I didn't graduate from college...I didn't get to finish...but, I got the scholarship and pursued the journalism. I've wrote poems...I had one published in the Western World of...ummm...a portrait book. Then...I wrote several and sent them off, and got money for 'em. So, I write, and keep stories and stuff...interesting things like that. That's, you know...a hobby."

"I was adopted...and my father was my best friend. He was a construction worker, and he died in 1994. He drove a bulldozer, and then became a foreman."

"I'm really a big fan of Willy Nelson. I saw him here at the Peoria Civic Center when he was here. I would like to be able to meet him...to meet him in person, because he is...he's so smart. He's a good guy."

140   **Michael K. Medlen**

"I am here in Peoria for the air show."

"It was New Years Eve...1969. I was contacted by the S-2 for the 9th Infantry Division Artillery, that intelligence was received from military advisors that approximately 300 VC were moving supplies across the Mekong River. I departed Dong Tam in my L-19 Bird Dog and went to the location were the suspected VC were conducting their movement. I contacted Spookie, a C-130 gunship that was flying in the Saigon area. They came down to my location where I briefed then on the target and where they could shoot. The intelligence was good and we caught a large number of VC in the area. After Spookie expended all of his ammunition, I called in an artillery mission where I conducted some troops in the open mission. As the artillery was impacting the area, I called for attack helicopters from Dong Tam for additional support. The mission ended with no more ground fire being received. I landed back at Dong Tam around 3 in the morning. For this mission, I was awarded the Air Medal with "V" device."

"I'm 64 years old....raised in Montgomery, Alabama. I started out my career as an aircraft mechanic in the Air Force. I then joined the Army as a rifleman in an infantry unit. I became an officer and deployed the 39th Infantry Platoon...scout dogs, to the Republic of Vietnam in 1966. During that time, not one of my soldiers was lost to combat operations. I returned to Vietnam in August of 1969 flying L-19 Bird Dogs."

"If I had it to do it over again, I wouldn't change a thing."

141   *Leslie Emery*

"I was born in London. My parents are British, and my relatives are British, and I'm British. I don't sound British…but when I want to, I can. I can sound British. We moved here when I was little. So…so…so…but they still…until you…if you live in a place until your teens, but then you live somewhere else the rest of your life, you will always have an accent. But, if you move before your teens, you will lose that accent. Does that make sense? So, if I had moved here when I was sixteen, I would still have a little bit of an accent. But, since I moved here earlier…in my young, youthful life…I don't."

"I live in Madison, Wisconsin…and I am here selling my artwork. I went to an artist's party last night. The people that put the artist's party on, are the people that run the show. They have a party every year for all of us. It is a fabulous event, and we get an awards presentation and a dinner. It's a chance for all the artists to get together and say hello. This time, they did this fabulous presentation of "Proud Mary ala' Peoria". The director and her two cohorts are dressed up. She is dressed as Tina Turner. The two cohorts are Tina Turner sidekicks…and then they have the Riverfront Queens that…what do you call it? They are the back…background singers. Have you heard of the Riverfront Queens? They are five guys in drag. I think they are husbands or something. They did this fabulous rendition…and the gal that's dressed as Tina Turner has this fabulous silver wig. She is a scream, to begin with. She is so funny."

"They do this song…and the song is about Peoria. They do the singing and dancing…and it was just a very unusual event for an art fair dinner. They put a lot of time and energy in it…and they were all dressed in costumes. They all had fabulous wigs, and the men…the men looked like "tanks in dresses". They were fabulous, and some of them still had their mustaches on. It was just great. It's kind of…one of those things where you had to be there."

"My paintings are abstract, just about my own personal aesthetic…mark-making, and vocabulary of colors and symbols. Not really symbols, but…a way of moving the paint and color around. Colored pencils I use, in different resists, to hopefully…emote a feeling of a…of a really beautiful peace. They're not representational. They're all about color and line and form…design and movement. They are beautiful colors…beautiful pieces. If you can imagine a room, and you went in and saw this in the room, wouldn't you think it was a beautiful room? These are not paintings where you go, "Ooooh, what's going on here?" These are paintings that are interesting, and they make you want to look at them. They create a personality to the room."

"That's what I do...and I've done it for a long, long time. My mom was an artist, and I had teachers who were artists that did this. I've just always done it...and always done well...even in the rain. It's like, "Why are we staying here in the rain?" People come and you get to meet them, and they buy directly from you. It is so direct and straightforward.
It's not like somebody is being paid to sell these. It's not like somebody is buying a used car or you're in a store and somebody is working on a commission. They are made by me, you buy them from me...and they are part of your life."

"Some people have trouble spending $3800 on a painting...but they can go spend $38,000 on a car. Okay, let's just say $28,000...that's about a new car. In five years, that car...that new car, will have needed gas and oil and tires and mainte-nance...and maybe a few big items...maybe. Then you have a car that has maybe a hundred thousand miles on it after five years. Then...you sell it for maybe $5000...or $10,000. But, if you have this painting...after five years, you have this painting that you didn't have to fix, or maintain...or...or...pay a whole lot for...and it's worth the same or more. It's in the same pristine condition even though it was used every day for its purpose...and you didn't have to do anything to it. So in the end...artwork...and especially paintings, because they "make a room"...are the best...the best...the best value you could ever spend your money on."

"Let's say you have this $3800 painting for twenty years. It has cost you $190 a year, or about $4 a week, for this painting...and you still have it. It's like...it's like...it's nothing. This...this becomes a bargain...this becomes...tinted windows or a sun-roof."

"This makes your room beautiful...and becomes part of you."

142   *Steve Cigolle*

"Basically...I'm photographing the B&SF railroad. I come down from Naperville to photograph this spot right here. Actually, this area is pretty well known. It's Edelstein Hill...which between Edelstein and Chillicothe is the steepest grade between Chicago and Kansas City for the railroad, climbing out of the valley."

"I develop software for a commodities exchange in Chicago. This is my hobby...for fun. I'm just trying to get different exposures...but, it's a little bit dangerous being this close, with a train lined up. I really want to stand between the tracks, but I'm a little nervous with the two trains being lined up. This is a...a control interlocking...so the dispatcher, who's in Texas, lines up these signals to tell the train whether they can keep going east or west. Then, there's a set of crossovers, so a train can go from one track to the other track...and they have these crossovers every ten to fifteen miles. So, the trains can run around other trains. That way, trains can go either way on either track."

"I actually grew up between Peoria and Dunlap...but we moved away in 1975. My dad wanted to experience warm weather in Florida. He worked for Caterpillar...then we went to Florida for a few years...then we ended up moving to Ohio. That's where his family is from. But, for me, Illinois has always been my home. All these other places just aren't the same. I guess that's partly why I like coming down here. It's neat to photograph it as an adult, because I remember it as a little kid."

"My parents told me they used to go dancing right over there, at "The Hub". They would go dancing on the weekends when we lived in Dunlap. But, my father passed away about eight years ago. I got a call about two in the morning that he had passed away...and it was very sudden. He died of a heart attack in his sleep, and it was a total shock to find that out. He was only 67...so, relatively young. For us, he was the first one in our family that passed away that was that close...so, you realize that your family isn't going to last forever. When you're younger...you feel like your family is going to last forever...but that brings it home...that there are limits to how long your family is going to be around."

"One time I rode the train from Chillicothe to Chicago, for a day...in 1971...and we went to the Museum of Science and Industry for the day...then took the train back to Chillicothe. That was an exciting day…and liking trains as much as I did…it was hard to sleep the night before."

143   *Don Shoemaker*

"There's this big yellow monolith in town. It scares the hell out of me some-times...but I think it means well."

144   *Sue Parrott*

"The last time I checked…I was 39 years old. I'm pretty sure…but I wouldn't swear on it. You know how women lie about their age. Sometimes people just call me "Mom". I tend to be a…a mom to all the kids in the neighborhood. I got one boy who is in Iraq right now…well, not in Iraq, in that country next to it…ummm…Kuwait. He helps out the helicopters and things. He's been in the Army…uh…a couple…a couple of years."

"When I go up to the restaurant, everybody always says, "Hi Mom."…even the old guys who sit round the big table and smoke and drink coffee all day. I'm everybody's mom."

"These kids around here are sorta strange…well…more dumb I guess, than strange. Last winter, I watched out my window at the kids down the road…they was sleddin' down the hill right by my house…sorta on the other side of the gulley. Well anyway, I could see they wuz riding down the hill on some weird contraption they had built. I watched 'em for awhile before I went out to see what they wuz doin'…uh…'cuz I heard one of 'em crying about something. Well…anyway I looked at the thing they was sleddin' on. It was a bunch of glass milk bottles that one of 'em had put together with hay twine. They wuz riding down the hill, going over rocks and stumps, with their little butts sittin' on glass. I woulda been takin' one of 'em to the hospital if one of them bottles broke. Try explaining that to the hospital…to the doctors at the hospital, "Kid was sleddin' down the hill on milk bottles…milk bottle broke, and cut up his ass.""

"Two summers ago, a bunch of kids was runnin' through the corn field…chasing each other, and three of 'em got to the end of a corn row and smacked right into a barbed wire fence. One kid cut open his lip…another got a big gash cross his cheek, and the last one put out his hands to stop himself…got all wrapped up in the fence and had to be cut out."

"I like to sit out in the yard on my swing and talk to the neighbors and watch the kids. When it's hot like this, we sit around and maybe cut up…cut up a watermelon and drink iced tea. They got some pretty good watermelons up there at the Jack & Jill in Roseville. My brother's son used to work there, and every once in awhile he'd bring back watermelons that they wuz gonna throw out. I always like free stuff, specially if they wuz just gonna throw it out anyway. COF-FEE...GET OVER HERE...COME HERE...COME ON...now sit down and shut up."

"My dogs, they tend to bark a lot...mostly at nothin' at all...the big one, we call him Coffee, first off cause he's brown, but also when he wuz little, he was lickin' up some bacon grease out of a old coffee can that he dug outta the garbage, and he got his head stuck...so after that we called him Coffee. Before that we called him...I 'm pretty sure we called him, after his dad...Smokey...or ummm...Little Smokey. That's right. The mangy lookin' one, we call him Sonny...and I don't remember where we got that name from. He's only got three legs 'cuz he got too close to the tractor one day...ummm...them disk things...I forgot what you call 'em. He favored it for a long time, and then we could see it might kill him, so we took him to have it cut off...and it didn't cost...it didn't cost that much...we know the man that cut it off."

"My mom died this year. She was in the hospital for a time and then she kinda went out of her head with blood poisonin' and all...and then she died. My dad is livin' alone now...doesn't know what to do with himself. I told him that he needs a friend...I told him to take Sonny, but he says he don't want no gimp dog that barks all the time."

145   *Teri Huss*

"Right now, I'm working at The Dress Barn. I'm a…ummm…sales girl. I'm Teri…I'll be 55. I was born in Lincoln. My father, back from the war, worked at Caterpillar…he met my mother in Lincoln…and end of story. I mean…not exactly the end…but that's how I ended up in this area. He worked right under the cupola in the old foundry in East Peoria. He would pick up the engine blocks…they weighed about four hundred pounds…and that's what he did. He's deceased…been gone about sixteen years now."

"Two years ago, I had what they call a gastric bypass…surgery. I've lost about 135 pounds. In the meantime, I developed what they call a ventral hernia. I knew that it had to be repaired, and I kept going, "Oh God, I want this other…I want this other, extra fat and stuff to be removed…because it's not going anywhere otherwise. So, back in March, I had the hernia repair, and then we had the plastic surgeon come in and do the rest of it. It has made a big difference in how I feel about myself."

"Just a couple little stories my father loved to tell. My father never let me forget…something that I did. When I was two years old…Smokey Mountains…the bear…the bears…oh yes. Dad said when they would allow them down into the lower end of the park…which is no more, 'cause they shoo them way up high…they got rather obnoxious about tearing car doors open, and things like that. But…at that particular time, they were still loose. I became rather mesmerized by a cub, and Dad said that I just kinda froze…and the cub stood up on his hind legs…sniffing the air. My dad is watching, because he knows "momma" is not too far away. This cub kept coming towards me…and finally got nose-to-nose with me, and Dad said, and I'm quoting my father, "She let out a war whoop that sent the cub tearing back up the mountain." It scared the hell out of him. About the time I did that, Dad grabbed me and ran for the car, 'cuz he knew…momma wouldn't be that far behind."

"Another time, there were skunks under the bed, and I thought they were kitty cats. I was underneath calling, "Kitty…kitty…kitty.", with a family of skunks under there. It's amazing my mother didn't scream, and I didn't get sprayed."

"Speaking of kittens...Petey died. He's been gone...what, five or six years now? He was a cat that I hand-raised. I have six cats. I am a cat lady...I love my cats. I hand-raised Petey. He didn't even have his eyes opened, and I bottle fed him, and was up with him around the clock. He lived for about seventeen years. It was rough. Sometimes, even now when I think about it, I get angry...because I still want him around. He was a very good cat. I've got other cats in my life, for heaven's sake...and I've had others in the past...but Petey was special. He was like one of my kids...and was in fact, the dog that my youngest son never had. He followed him around, and was crazy about my youngest son, Danny. It was amazing to see how he reacted to a four year old. They were inseparable. He could be in my lap, sound asleep, and Danny would come in the door, and that would be it. He would be gone...he was after his kid."

"It was really rough on my son, too. He was 21, and he brought him out of his bedroom...and Petey was arching his back and paddling, and I said, "Danny...he's trying to die...you need to say goodbye...we need to put him down ." I'm not sure what was wrong with him, but I think it was some form of cancer. I said, "He's trying to die." Danny said, "But, we don't put people to sleep." I thought, "That's one you're gonna have to learn, because...yes, and no." We went through my father-in-law's death. With the medication, and the things that you give them, it can...it has a tendency to stop their breathing. So, yes and no. It's not something you strive to do...but...it's just hard...hard losing family members, and...animals are like family members. Some people don't have any use for an animal, or get close to an animal...and I have a hard time understanding what they're thinking...you know?"

146   *Matt Jones*

"I got to meet my favorite band…L.A. Guns. I hung out with them for a whole weekend in Ohio. There's not much to do here in Canton…make fun of people…make meth…that's about it."

147   *Anna Jacobson*

"I have seen a lot of beautiful women, and I think I am average. Quite frankly, I have gained twenty pounds in the last two years…so I am not nearly as confident as I used to be. I own a business, and I am single. I want to create enough money so that I can live in a safe environment. I have been married to three liars before I was 26…and now I'm 38."

"I go to bars and eat because I don't like to sit in a restaurant by myself…so I go to bars and sit with a book. Usually, when you read a book, that tells everyone else that you are by yourself and you want to be left alone…usually. Unfortunately, sometimes I run into people that are already drunk and are looking to pick me up. Usually, they are all married. They don't say it…but I can see a ring on their finger. They have a ring on their finger, and are usually from out of town. They are usually salespeople. Sometimes it's better to just go along with things, rather than causing trouble, and everybody not having a good time at all."

"I don't think that most of them would go through with anything…most of them are probably committed to their wives. They're showing off for each other. They're all in sales…all big-minded…they're "OOH-HOO, I'm in charge" type people…A-type personalities. The fact of the matter is, even A-type personalities know when to call it quits. So, I don't think that many of them would actually take me back to their hotel and do anything…but they want to look like they would in front of their friends."

"I usually go to the same bar about three times a week, it just depends on what is going on. I lead an abstinent lifestyle…now. I have never gone to anyone's hotel room. Although, I can say that a lot of wives are worried about that type of thing…and I can say that, honestly, I have been approached by them. I have lost a lot of my friends because they think their husbands might be interested in me…because of the openness that society has now…and that the fact that husbands want best friends instead of wives. They treat some women as best friends, so they feel open to say any sexual remark that they want to, which has made wives incredibly insecure…and so now the men can't talk to anybody. Many wives tell their husbands to not talk to any woman, no matter what the conversation is about. It's definitely a problem with society being so open."

"Most friends that I had that were single, I'm not friends with them any-more...within a year of them being married. I just had an experience this week-end, where a couple...where a woman got upset, because I was totally interested in another gentleman who I feel is afraid to ask me out. He's been with me several times, and I feel he is interested in me...but I'm not gonna ask him out...so...I'm waiting for him. This woman, who was my friend, got totally upset when I was talking to her husband about a way to create an environment where this *other* gentleman would ask me out. She was upset...and was crying and everything. Now...now, she's not my friend"

"I know that there are codependent women who cannot be on their own...because they don't want to. They hook up with people...and give to peo-ple...just to be with them, and they are insecure in their relationship because they really didn't like the guy to begin with. I think that's a big problem...I see it a lot. Women just don't want to be alone...and they're not willing to wait for the proper one. They go from relationship to relationship to relationship...and they never want to break up with anybody, because they don't want to be alone."

"There is a big societal issue. Recently, I took someone to court and I was asked, "Were you wearing a shirt the night that you were assaulted, as tight as the shirt you are wearing today?" So, I said, "Excuse me...is your client unable to control his urges when he sees someone with a tight shirt? That is a societal issue...not mine." If you wear a loose fitting shirt, guys are looking for opportunities to look down your shirt...down your cleavage as the shirt falls open. What are you gonna do...wear a turtleneck in a hundred degree heat?"

"I was involved in a court case not that long ago...and as part of the settlement, I agreed not to talk about it. It was a big case at Mitsubishi...a big sexual harass-ment case. Do you know anything about it? I don't want to say what my real name is...I can't. But, you wouldn't believe what happened there. You wouldn't believe what I put up with...and I can't talk about it. What happened there changed my life...some bad and some good. I can say this...after the settlement, after we were all done...I now have a nice house, a boat...and my own business. I have a franchise business that is doing well, even better than expected for my location."

"The one thing about owning a business is...you can't go anywhere. I have a lot of turnover and have to be there a lot. My employees are...unpredictable. I had one guy cut his finger this morning, so I'll have to cover for him tonight. I'll also have to pay for his stitches…a little cut that only took three stitches…but it will probably cost me $700. You wouldn't believe all the costs and government regulations that are involved when someone gets hurt. It makes it difficult and costly for business owners."

148 *Janette Smith*

"I'm now retired from Lucent Technologies. I sold communications equipment for thirty years. I am 55, and from Groveland. I grew up in Centralia, which is a small town about an hour east of St. Louis. It is a rural area, and has just about 13,000 people. I was eighteen when I left. I grew up on a farm, and probably one of the things that I still…that I think the country is missing…when you grow up on a farm, there is more of a community. We were small farmers…not everybody had a combine, not everybody had a corn picker, a baler…and things like that. So, in the fall especially, it was a real community, because the farmers went from farm to farm and "combined" everybody's fields, and baled everybody's hay. It was a neat time, and a great place for a kid to grow up. I am not so sure it is like that so much. Back then, in a small rural area…it was very much like that."

"We had a small family, and we pretty much stayed home every holiday. In my family, I had two brothers…and it was just the five of us. We had the usual Christmas Eve festivities…dinner, and things like that. We didn't travel to other family members…we had a very small family, not many living relatives…even back then."

"In the summertime, my brothers and I worked in the fields in the day, and then we would go out on our bikes…might be gone the rest of the day…just riding and having races. Our parents usually didn't know where we were. We walked bean rows in the fields. I don't know if back then, my dad couldn't afford chemicals, or they didn't have them. Our method of weed control was "kids walking bean rows"…chopping weeds, and things like that out of the bean rows. That's what we did in the summer."

"My friend Bill, owns a plane. I met him, and we been together about five years. He bought the plane right after I met him. We both love to fly. I took lessons in the 80's, and love aviation. It's just a great time. He has a beautiful plane…we take it all over the country and show it. It has been completely restored and wins awards just about every place we go. We meet a lot of people, and it's neat to see people interested. Aviation in general…I think is a wonderful sport."

"We just got back from a two week European trip. We went to Italy and France. I love to travel, and we just had a great time. We arrived in Rome, saw the Vatican Museum and the Sistine Chapel, and went to the ruins…then we went to Assisi, and then Florence. I got to see things I have never seen before…just amazing to me. We went to Paris…after we left Florence, we toured the southern part of France, and then we spent the end of the vacation in Paris. It wasn't my first trip…I'm pretty familiar with Paris, and I love it. I don't have to do anything there…I'm happy just walking the sidewalks and having coffee."

"For the first time, this trip…I'm an avid gardener and have a huge garden…and I had not been to their gardens before….in Versailles. I guess they don't have their fountains on…they only turn them on once every two weeks. When we were there, they had the fountains on, and there was classical music playing. We would walk down the little walk areas. It was just a beautiful misty day."

149   *Heywood Banks*

"I'm from Michigan…and I live north of Ann Arbor, in Howell, Michigan. I've been married almost thirty years. I traveled around when I was younger…we lived in Vermont for awhile…and then moved back…but, I've lived in Michigan almost all my life."

"When I was younger, I cleaned cages at a veterinary hospital. I did some house painting, and things like that. I was a bus driver in Detroit…but pretty much…I've been a performer for over thirty years."

"When I was six, we moved out of a neighborhood with a whole bunch of kids in it, where we played Peter Pan…pirates. I always had a sword made out of a yardstick or something…and, you know…a towel for a cape. We moved to this neighborhood where there were no kids, whatsoever. It was like…houses on two acres…and all old people. So, I spent a lot of time…and you can tell by listening to me…I spent a lot of time by myself. I had a tree house, and I worked on this tree house for ten years…well, eight or nine years, until I was about fifteen. I had some buddies that would come over…and that's what we would do on a Saturday…just work on the tree house."

"I started out as…I mean…in…in high school, when I was a kid…I started writing songs when I was fourteen. I got a guitar and started writing songs…and the first songs I wrote were funny songs. A friend of mine…a friend of my parents, gave me a Tom Lear CD…well, not a CD, but a 33…a small 33 of "An Evening Wasted with Tom Lear." He was kind of a…he was a fantastic…a fantastic writer. He…you know, he was a great pianist…and he would write really weird songs to beautiful melodies. That was kind of the template I took. You're humming along to something, and you realize that you're singing about dust mites, or the pancreas…or some…some weird thing. So, I started writing songs…started learning the craft of songwriting…and applied it to writing funny songs."

"In high school, I had a trio…and we sang Peter, Paul, and Mary songs. I had an exchange student from Australia…he and I…and a girl…her name was Chris Lahti. She has gone on to win an Academy Award. Christine Lahti…she was the one in the bathroom when they called her up for the Oscar."

"One day, I was going...I was already married, and I was going...my kids were little, and we were living in a little house...and I was going to a gig...and I was packing up to go. I was getting in the car, and it just struck me as being a fantastic day...this...being able to do this...to support my family. It was a struggle...a real struggle for a long, long time...to try and get somewhere. I've tried every possible venue. I was a folk singer for a time. I've played in bars and stuff...Mountain Jack's restaurants. There's like, a bar that's a holding tank for people going in to eat...and I would be in there. I tried...I tried writing country songs...tried just being a regular songwriter...but it turned out, being funny was just right for me."

"These odd coincidences happen to me...like, every time I would look at the clock...there was an eleven or something. I would hear something on the radio...and I would turn, and there it would be, written on a truck. It's...it's almost kind of like, your brain...and I think that's where some of my songs come from. I'm driving...and my brain keeps disconnecting...and these weird things kind of come together."

"I've had people that will dress up...make entire Heywood costumes, with lettering all over the jacket. I used to have real long hair, and slick it over. This one guy got a wig and you know...it was kind of like a "Rocky Horror" thing. Like...in South Bend, Indiana...for some reason in that town...people started treating me like the Rocky Horror Picture Show. They throw toast on stage...gummy worms...marshmallows. They really get into it...they get *too* into it. In fact, I just played South Bend...and I got a new guitar...and these little kids come up front. They just wad those gummy worms up and throw them...they throw them hard and try to hit me in the face. That's why I have to put a shield over my face. They really try to wad up...wad up the bread, and throw it at me. So...I'm standing there thinking, "Okay, this is how I make a living. There's a check coming.""

"I won this Johnny Walker comedy search thing back in `88. I went out to Los Angeles and won the final against...Tim Wilson was one of the people...and a couple others. It was one of those things where it was like, "And the winner is"...there are cameras there from CNN, and all this other stuff. "And the winner is...Heywood Banks...and you win...this door." Then, you walk out the door...and you're outside. "What...what just happened here?" So...when I was out there in California, I was on "Evening at the Improv", and MTV..."Half Hour Comedy Hour", and quite a few other things."

"What I aspire to do by writing these goofy songs…is maybe put a little bit of education in there. Some kids may be listening to a song…and they hear the word *colostomy* and ask, "What does that mean?" I have a song "Smokey the Bear", about cartoon animals coming to life…and there is a word in there…*anthropomorphic.* It sounds corny as hell…but by doing that, I feel like I move civilization forward…just a little bit…in my own little way of trying to do some good."

"I'm not really religious. But…and this sounds kind of weird…but, I will literally…when I get up in the morning, I will say, "Okay angels…I need some funny jokes. I need some funny songs here." I'll be walking around, and something will pop into my head…and there it is. If I don't do that…I can go for a year or two years and not write anything. But, if I start saying that, over and over again…and I don't know if it focuses me or whatever, but I will write something."

"I think I may be just a big…a big *unknown* to a lot of people. I think one day, the bubble is just going to burst, and I'm going to be everywhere with "Wiper Blades"…and "Toast"…and mattress companies with "Dust Mites"…and the Diabetes Foundation with the 'Pancreas Song.'"

"I think to be really famous…would be a horrible existence. You totally trade your life for money. I grew up in Birmingham, Michigan, and I've known Tim Allen since high school. In fact, his first cousins live across the street from me…these people I have known since I was two. Tim always said, "Is your mom like, an aunt or something?" We were always kind of confused with the relationship. But, I wouldn't want…and he's an extremely talented guy and deserves all of his success…but I would hate to…be him. He may have a hundred million dollars, but can't go anywhere. You can't walk into a restaurant…can't walk into a WalMart…can't do anything. You've traded your life for…that."

"Last year…it was at Christmas and I was at WalMart…and there was a truck parked out front. People were handing out sheets…collecting stuff. They would hand you a list if you wanted to buy poor people something for Christmas. Here's a list if you want to buy somebody some size 48 stretchy pink, stretch pants…or a doll…or a toaster. So…I thought, "Well, why doesn't WalMart just give them a truck full of stuff?" Why should I have to buy…buy something at retail…to bring out and give away. Why don't we just give them some money and then they buy stuff from WalMart at half-price or something? I just had this vision of buying something…giving it to them…they drive around the back of WalMart and unload it…and bring the empty truck around again."

"I can say without equivocation that people in this country are passionate about their toast. Toast is the reason I have been able to perform for 25 years. It built my house. I think…I think I need to have a Heywood brand toaster. I sent stuff to Toastmaster…and a few other places, and they just didn't want to do it. But…we'll see what happens next."

150   *David Flites*

"I know that I was created to live a life of abundance...so that I could give and contribute to this world. My wife and children are...a gift to me. The realization...the self-realization about my own human dignity, has allowed me to see the dignity in others, and translate that through my medium...of portraiture. The dignity...having discovered the dignity of the individual, through Jesus...has to be the...best thing that has happened to me."

151   **Mike White**

"Let's just say I'm in my 50's. I am a construction laborer...and right now I'm a laid off construction worker, which is good 'cuz my back wasn't gonna take too much more this year. I almost walked off the job about three weeks ago 'cuz that asshole I was working for was bitchin' at me for not doing enough work. Hell...I was doin' the work of three guys...and this asshole starts bitchin' at me...and so I walk off. He says, "Where you goin'?" I said, "I'm leavin'...I'm not listenin' to that." So, then he says, "Alright...alright then...just forget what I said. You come back and I won't bug you any more. Go have yourself some coffee and a donut, and then come back up here and help these guys out." So, then I said, "Well...okay...but I'm not gonna listen to that shit anymore...I'm doing my job." What an asshole...what a fuckin' asshole."

"When I was a kid...and this was when we lived down there on Laramie...I always liked it when my mom took us to Mr. Donut...that one up there on Western. Most of the time we got us a box of *day-old* that they had there sittin' on the counter. We'd all sit at the counter eatin' them donuts...all five of us, including my fat cousin Roland, who lived with us quite a bit...and we all shared a chocolate milk. And every time I'd go...I'd see them donuts that was all dressed up like clowns. I'd always ask my mom for one of them clown donuts. The whole donut was pretty much covered with icing...you know, making up the clown costume, and it's face...and everything. I'd ask my mom for it every time we'd go...and she never did buy it for me."

"When I got old enough to earn my own money...which was from a paper route, a Journal Star paper route...and I was making about nine dollars a week...I would have me one of them donuts, every Friday. I'd meet the Journal Star guy at Mr. Donut...I forgot his name, but he had these dark yellow teeth...I remember that. I'd give him the money for the papers. Well, it was a check I'd give him, 'cuz I put the collectin' money in the Madison Park Bank. Then after I paid him...I'd order me a clown donut and a chocolate milk...and I was by myself...and sit at the counter and eat it, dipping the clown into my milk. This was at 6 o'clock at night...and I'd be sittin' there by myself eatin' and drinkin' with adults. Sometimes I would be in there alone. But...I always liked doin' that...going to Mr. Donut."

"I only had the paper route for about a year and a half...and then I mowed lawns and did other stuff to earn money...but I kept going to Mr. Donut on most Fridays and gettin' me a clown donut. From the first time I seen them donuts...I just got it in my head that I had to have 'em. I still like donuts...and now I go to Dunkin' Donuts...but they don't have them clown donuts no more. I like them double chocolate ones, though."

"So then...my brother was readin' in the paper about these clowns robbing a donut store...damn clowns, can you believe it? White faces, red noses...and these big wide grins...and I had to laugh. He said these two clowns walked into a place called Henry's Donut Shop...I can't remember what city it was in...Seattle? But, it was owned by a couple of Vietnamese folks. They made the Vietnamese lady open the safe that was in the back, and they took about four hundred dollars. I guess donut shops are good for robbers, 'cuz they're a cash business...don't take credit cards or checks or whatnot. They also took some donuts with 'em when they left. It didn't say what donuts they took...but it makes sense to me that if you're gonna rob a donut shop...hell, take some donuts. I would."

152   *Sam Wright*

"It's not enough to complain that business is not good…so, I'd say it's okay. I sell hip-hop types of shirts for a living. I sell sorority and fraternity. I sell a Negro League shirt…there's a Kansas City Monarch…a shirt that Josh Gibson wore. I sell other ethnic types of shirts like Dr. King, Malcolm X…Richard Pryor."

"I travel all over the Midwest…and I do pretty good here. I sell quite a few of the Richard Pryor shirts, being that…this is his hometown. I'm 62…so I'm about the same age as Richard…and his aunt was my next-door neighbor in St. Louis. One Saturday I was out cutting my grass and saw a lot of kids running to this limousine…and out popped Richard Pryor. I got a chance to meet him, and…he was a funny man…a funny man."

153-154 Mallory Williams and Amanda Douglas

"Today, we're out buying some pumpkins, wooden pumpkins...for a birthday gift...and we both went to the pound and got a dog. We went over to TAPS in Pekin and got a dog. It's a Jack Russell Terrier. He's my baby...and his name is Guss. He was already named. The pound had already named him...and it's Guss with two *s*'s. I don't know why, but that's what they had him named...with two *s*'s."

"I'm 22...from Canton. I'm an assistant activity director at Sunset Rehabilitation & Healthcare. It's a nursing home...and I arrange for people to come in...and I take them down for the activities...go out in public...to play bingo, and go out to eat...stuff like that. We have one resident there who worked for NASA and helped pick out the monkeys that went up to the moon. He met Robert Kennedy, and he had a real interesting life...the resident, not Robert Kennedy."

"I'm Amanda Douglas, and I'm 22. I've known Mallory for fifteen years. We were in second grade...and I sat in front of her. We couldn't talk in the class...so she would be like, "Throw something away, and I'll meet you at the trash can." We would throw Kleenex's away, because at that time everybody had a box of Kleenex. Our Kleenex didn't last long."

"I work for the Peoria Zoo Society...and I'm the development coordinator. I raise money...or, help raise money to expand the Glen Oak Zoo. You should come to the zoo. We're going to triple the size of our zoo...going to bring the "Heart of Africa" to the "Heart of Illinois". We need 32 million dollars...we're at 19.5...we need 25 to go on the ground...and 32 to finish. The plans are in place, we're just waiting on the funds...so we hope to go on the ground in the spring."

"I was down at Lake of the Ozarks, where my parents live. I've always gone down there for the summer. In the summer, it's one of my favorite places in the world. They have a dock because we're right on the lake...and my boyfriend asked me, "Do you want to go watch the sunset?" We went down there early because it looked like it was gonna rain. He got down on one knee and proposed to me. My whole family knew...they were up at the house watching through the window. He was nervous...he kept fiddling with his pocket. I thought, "Oh, it's probably with the new pants he's got on." Then, he got down on one knee. I was very surprised. I cried...and then went

back up to the house to tell everybody…but they knew. They were watching and taking pictures. We've actually been together six years, and we're still engaged."

"There aren't any marriages in the nursing home…just death. Death usually comes in threes at the nursing home. So, when we have one person die, usually two more die, in like…the week near it. It happens about once a month. Sometimes you go in spurts where people die…but they're not constantly dying every day. My own father died six years ago…and my mother died five years ago. My father had a massive heart attack…and we found out after my mother died, that she had cancer. We didn't know what killed her when she died. Cancer is a nasty, nasty disease."

"One day, I hope to finish nursing school…and move out into the country and have lots and lots of kids. I want four…at least four. You have to have an even number…so, if you ever go to Disney World, everybody has somebody to ride with. You have to have even numbers…and I just want a big family."

"I just want to have a fulfilling life…do what I want to do…just be happy…nothing too deep…just be happy."

155 *J.T.*

"Folks always comin' round wantin' to know how the shit works. Fuck that shit. All anybody need to know is…we keepin' the fuckin' peace. You want to know what we all about…you want to come down and want to know what the fuck we all about? This is what we all about…hanging on the corner…keepin' the peace. You want to know what it's all about? Respect. It's all about respect…mother-fucker."

156   *Ken Ferino*

"My name is Ken Ferino. I am 56. I am co-owner of a local steel company. We, uh fabricate and erect structural steel. Oddly enough, I went to school to work in construction and I ended up actually working…in construction. I went to Bradley University and got a part-time job when I was going to Bradley, and it turned into a full-time job, and eventually ownership of the company. I came to Bradley, planned to leave in four years…and here I am."

"In Peoria, we did a lot of these strip centers…a lot of Kroger's stores, Barnes & Noble. Looking across the street…that Target store, the Cub store…ummm…the Lowe's store, ummm…Home Depot…a lot of those kinds of things…Walgreen stores, CVS stores…a lot of retail stores."

"I'm from Chicago. I love Chicago…love the ethnicity of it…and ummm…my family…I was the first generation to marry out of the Italian heritage. Not that they're old world and all, but I just happened to be the oldest of the grandchildren, so I was the first to get married, and kinda broke the mold. I love Chicago…the ethnicity of it…the food of it…the excitement of it. I don't go back as much as I used to, not with the business. I have a son here who's getting ready to go to NYU, and sorta keeping busy with that. This year my son graduated valedictorian from high school. He's going to NYU, and God help us, he wants to be a filmmaker."

"But…we do go up there, and probably will do more once he is away…you know, will travel a little more. One thing I tend to do when I go is…I bring a cooler up and go to a lot of…uh…Italian deli's, Italian grocery stores, ethnic grocery stores…and bring back ingredients and products that I can't get down here…products I can't buy down here."

"I like the size of Peoria. I like the values, and generally the morals. It just needs a little more pizzazz…a little more…ummm…entertainment…a little more culture, but not necessarily high-end culture. It needs a little more street life…just something to make it a little more interesting. Some ethnic restaurants would be nice. Now, we go to Rizzi's…we go to Jalapeno's quite a bit…there, mostly because of the waiters. The food is good, but the waiters sort of make that place for us. We go to Pannera's quite a bit, just 'cause it's close."

"This business is all-encompassing, I put family first, and the few times I get to relax, I go to the golf course. I kinda stay to myself pretty much. I just don't join a lot of clubs, and things like that. I golf on weekends…strictly weekends…just hack around and get aggravated."

"My first job was mowing grass. I must have been around fifteen, 'cause I was try-ing to save up and buy a motorbike…a little Honda 50. Not the one with the scoop…the one with the real tank…not the girl's bike. I was fifteen or sixteen, and just mowing grass in the neighborhood. It was my first job, and I took it pretty seriously. I take the work ethic seriously. First of all, I was involved with Boy Scouts. I was also very involved with sports…and I just started working. Where I came from, you just worked."

"I had relatives that owned businesses, and I had the grass mowing thing in the neighborhood. Had an uncle and a grandfather that owned a huge gas station in Chicago…gas station and car wash…and ummm…I worked there. It was seven in the morning 'til seven at night. During the summer, I worked construction, and uh…had a life guarding job. All these jobs entailed early morning hours…getting up early. The construction…I had to drive to Indiana, and had to get up at 5 o'clock to be at work at seven. It was a lot of hours. If I wasn't dedi-cated to that, I was dedicated to sports…early morning workouts, and that sort of thing. It all just lent itself to the work ethic."

"I think the younger people are, the less of a work ethic they tend to have. In my office and out in the shop, that's a different situation. We hire…and that is only three full-time people…I have to say the work ethic is fairly good there…and in some cases, very good. In general, in the general population…and in the kids…the work ethic is horrible…it's horrible, and getting worse."

"The people at work probably think I am more of an ass than I probably am, but when they hire me to do a job, they get someone that is very driven, and ummm…just working for them as hard as I can. They probably have the wrong impression…especially the ones I don't work with day to day. The people that do work with us day to day, know I have a company that is driven, that pays atten-tion to a lot of details. I just work well with people who want to do it right."

157-158   *Sean and Amanda Fitts*

"My name is Sean, and I'm forty. I'm from Maine...Waterville. It's in central Maine...in the middle of the state. It's about a half hour...45 minutes south of Bangor...home of Stephen King. Waterville is a town of about 5000 peo- ple...and I actually lived outside of Waterville, in a suburb called Pittsfield. Radar is a big thing there...protecting the east coast. There's a company that builds fire alarms, there are shoe stores and factories, and stuff. Then I moved out to L.A. for fifteen years and met her...met my wife in L.A., and then we moved here."

"I guess the way we got here...I was a chemistry teacher, and we were paying $2000 a month in rent. So I guess, around the time, our jobs were getting to us...and the lifestyle in L.A. was getting to us...and her grandfather passed away, and so that opened up a house for us here. We just kind of moved here to have a new start...do something different."

"My name is Amanda Fitts...I am thirty. I am from Peoria...and I spent seven years in Los Angeles. He's a teacher, as he said, and I am a teacher too...but when we met, I was just kind of working in the school, doing administrative stuff. So, we met that way. We both started meeting with a group on Saturdays, eating sushi. We're both vegans. We weren't vegans to start...but we are now."

"We were both meat eaters when we met. He had actually been a vegetarian years before, but went back to eating meat. A year after we were together, we just gradually stopped eating meat. We would still eat dairy and eggs...and things. I don't really know how we started cutting out the meat."

"I had a couple of friends who passed away from heart attacks...and I was only like, 37. So, that kind of woke me up to the fact that I should watch my diet. Where I am from in Maine, people eat *fried everything*. Everything is loaded with fat. My dad had a heart attack too, and I started thinking about my health. So, we started cutting back on the red meat...and then chicken, because we learned that chicken has the same cholesterol as red meat. It has the lower fat, but the same cholesterol. Then we cut out...we were on fish for awhile...but then found out the fish was loaded with mercury and toxins, so we decided to cut the fish out."

"It was pretty easy in California. There are a lot of options there…a lot of veggie restaurants. There aren't so many here. We went out last night here to the Flat Top Grill. They have a lot of vegan options. We also go to One World…Tanh Linh, the Vietnamese restaurant…and Sizzling India."

"We became vegan in California because we met this person, kind of a celebrity in L.A., and her name is Sky Valencia. She does a lot of things for animals, and for dogs especially. So, she asked us to come to a party she was having at the mayor's mansion in L.A., so…we thought we would go and see, and it turned out there were a lot of vegan options there. We tried them…we tried Silk, which is a milk…a milk substitute. We tried it, and it was really good, and so that became our milk substitute. And we found all these other meat substitutes. So, I eat burgers and things like that, but it's all vegan stuff."

"He really likes the salmon substitute. It looks like salmon and tastes like salmon."

"Yeah, it tastes just like it…and I grew up eating salmon. The thing is…when you start eating the stuff, the meats and stuff…after awhile, it almost starts tasting just like the real stuff."

"The Morningstar Farms buffalo wings are great…the corn dogs…and the sausage is good too."

"We do a loop around…I don't really know the names of the streets…but we do a loop around this neighborhood and back. It's probably a mile and a half or two miles. We do it every other day in the mornings, to just kind of wake up…get going. It's helped me a lot…I've lost about ten pounds. Of course we eat light anyway…because we're vegans, we don't end up eating a lot of heavy foods…so, that helps."

"I'm also a cycler. I started cycling, because in L.A., I hated the traffic so much. I started cycling to work, and ended up doing about seventy miles a day. I haven't competed, but I keep thinking about it. I have the endurance, I just need to pick up the speed a little. I used to play a lot of sports in college, but…it's been awhile."

"I probably started running about eight years ago...but I do a lot of different things. I like to bike also. We also have a gym at home that I use. Running is just something I like to do when the weather is good for it."

"I was really the only person in my family to go to college...and I finished grad school...went to Scripps Institution of Oceanography in La Hoya, California. I didn't know if I would ever make it through...but the day that I finished...I had my own personal celebration that day."

"Just recently, I finally figured out what I want to do with my life. I was a teacher before, but I just wasn't happy at the school. It really got to me...there was just a lot of pressure there. So right now, I'm in a school-counseling program at Bradley. I'm really enjoying that a lot. So, this is something that I finally really enjoy doing. It makes my life a lot better."

159-160 *Tom and Shawn Armbruster*

"We went in front of Judge Vespa and got married today...on Valentine's Day. It just kind of struck us as a good day to do it. We didn't have a lot of money to spend...and we just loved each other so much...we didn't want to wait."

"She was getting ready to move to Peoria from Sterling...and I came home from work and found an *offline*...on Yahoo Messenger. It said, "I'm moving to Peoria, can you tell me what it's like?" I sent her a message back, and she happened to be online...and we talked for two hours before I said, "I gotta go to bed." I got up in the afternoon and she was still online. We chatted until I had to go to work...and it took off from there."

"So now we're married and...we're going to Ming's for sushi."

161   *Nancy Richards*

"I'm on my way to the grocery store to buy some ice cream…Edy's ice cream…Double Fudge Brownie. I'm also getting the slow-churned French Silk. I like to buy the light kind…it has chocolate chips in it. It's crunchy and creamy all at the same time. I don't eat the soft-serve kind anymore because it's…too sweet or something."

"I work for CISA Case Management as a case manager…for people with brain injuries. We provide home services for people who have acquired brain injuries, so they won't have to go to the nursing home. I've been there for about thirteen years. Before that I was a substitute teacher."

"I had a guy…a client who was talking about committing suicide because…he had been in a car wreck and his wife left him. He had a house, but he had several mortgages on it and they were threatening to take it away. He had a lot of problems. I got him some help…so that he could stay with his cousin, and she helped him…straightened him out."

"He'd been driving to Bloomington and was drunk…and knocked over two telephone poles. I don't even know how he survived. He was going so fast, he knocked over two poles. After that, he was getting bills from the telephone company. They wanted him to pay for the telephone poles that he knocked over. They were like $650 apiece. So…I wrote to them and told them, "This guy is pretty destitute. He has physical and cognitive problems…not to mention his financial problems. He just can't pay it." They quit sending the bills after that. So, I helped him with that. I also help people get wheelchairs and ramps for their vans. They're always very grateful to get those things."

"My mom and dad owned the Tastee-Freez here in Elmwood. They had that business for ten or twelve years. They bought it when I was eight or nine…I think. I started out there washing windows and hosing sidewalks. I worked for my dad…and they paid me $45 a week. I started out…before we opened up, we had to clean everything…so, I started out doing the opening…the opening cleaning."

"We'd open up in March…the end of March, and we'd close down in August. Probably the best thing about working there was we got to eat chili-dogs whenever we wanted…and ice cream. Our busiest night was Sunday, after, you know…if there was a game or something going on at the school. If there was a band concert, we'd get lines on a Sunday night…in the summer."

"The hardest part…we lost a lot of ice cream in the chocolate when we made the dipped cones….and then we'd end up having to eat it….somebody would have to eat it, or we'd just throw it away. If you dip it, you know, you'd have to turn it over in the container…and a lot of times it would just fall in. Also, the milk shake things…you know, the mixer would go through the bottom of the cups. It would cut the cup and start leaking. That happened a lot. I had a lot of vanilla shakes, and chili-dogs when I worked there. I liked the soft-serve back then and had a lot of that…a lot of ice cream."

"Before we had the Tastee-Freez, we lived over on Maple. We were all pretty close…everybody was a friend…all about the same age…and we'd have these big card games. We sometimes had three or four picnic tables lined up…and we'd play Nutsy. It was called Nutsy. It was a solitaire, kind of a solitaire game…but you also put cards out in the middle. It was a game of speed."

"Richard Griswold that lived next to us…he was kind of the town kook. He would watch us out of his back yard…and we were all scared of him. When mom took out the garbage, he would stand in the back yard and pretend he was shooting at her. He was just a weird…a weird man."

"My dad died in 1996…and ever since then, until September of this year, I took care of my mom. She had Alzheimer's…but she wasn't that hard to take care of. She could stay by herself some. She just had vision problems…and she had a stroke a couple of years ago…then she couldn't walk, so she required more care. She couldn't get up and go to the bathroom by herself…she'd topple over. She passed away in September."

"So, I just applied for a job with St. Francis doing the same type of work…case management. People that get out of the hospital…get them services…whatever they need…so they don't have to go to some type of institutional facility. I think that's important."

162   *Marlene Allen*

"I had a surprise birthday party when I was age six. I was born on June 6th...and my mother had a birthday party for me...and it was such a surprise. Nowadays, I'm not one to like too many surprises. I live in Sandwich, Illinois...and there aren't too many surprises there in Sandwich. It's just this pretty small *white bread* kind of town."

163-164   *Jane and Tim Johnson*

"I'm 42. Forget about him…focus on me. Forget about him."

"I'm Tim…forty years old. I have a fencing company in Jacksonville…about 140 miles south…thirty miles west of Springfield. I grew up working on farms and that. I was doing some survey work…and people started asking about fencing…so I just started doing that on the side, and it just kind of took off."

"Jacksonville is small…simple…and still somewhat safe. I've lived a lot of places…and Jacksonville never changes. You know, you can just kind of hide in Jacksonville. Springfield's not that far if you want to do something more exciting."

"We actually just got married this morning. We did a courthouse deal. We've both been married before. I went to school at ISU, and I came over this way quite a bit. We just wanted to get away for the weekend…so here we are. She just started a new job, and all of that…and we didn't have time to really go anywhere. But…I actually enjoy coming over here."

"We went to Richard's and had a terrible meal. We first went to Sully's, but couldn't get waited on…so we left. But, I still enjoy Sully's. Tomorrow I plan on…you ever eat at Jonah's? I enjoy that place too."

"I had the filet at Richard's, which was about a quarter of an inch thick…which was really sirloin…and not a filet. The service was bad. I ordered it medium, and it came out well. It was also expensive…for what we got. It wasn't expensive if we would have got what we ordered. So now…we're down here at the river passing the time of day."

"I thought it would be nice to bring her down here. I was hoping for some entertainment, but with it being November…I guess there aren't any bands here. There doesn't seem to be anything going on down here…and no concerts in town."

"A couple of years ago, he asked me to go out with him…and I didn't. About a year later, I needed a fence removed, so I called him. We'd both been single for about ten years. It was a huge learning experience for me, personally. I learned that even though you might be a victim, you have a responsibility in what you choose to do. I found

peace over those ten years. I gave up relationships...I gave up dating...I gave up all of it. I had to focus on myself...unlearning bad behaviors, and learning more appropriate behavior."

"I was kidnapped by my ex-husband. He broke into my house at 2 o'clock in the morning...stark naked. He kidnapped me and my child. He took us for a ride...and this was about eleven years ago. He didn't really do anything. He was just kind of...nuts. I had a shotgun loaded, underneath my bed...and was ready to shoot him...if I had to. He didn't have a gun...would never bring a gun...he was just too much of a pussy to do that. At one time I felt...actually prayed that, I could shoot him without my daughter present. Isn't that nice?"

"That first night we went out to dinner...I took her down to the shop. She didn't know where I lived...and I told her I lived in my shop. We got cozy on the futon we had down there. That was probably the most interesting and fun time we had. I won't go into the details...but we had a pretty wild time."

"So, later on...we're probably going to go and have sex. We did get married today. We're going to try and duplicate the futon night. Then tomorrow, we're going to go to church and pray for our souls."

165   *Cecil Brown*

"I been coming over this way for about a year now. It's because of my third bout with cancer. My salivary gland...my face...they took surgeries there already. Been six months since they first found the tumor. Delay, delay, delay...misdiagnosis, misdiagnosis. Had a lump on my face...told two doctors about it...both said they thought it was a lymph node. First surgery, wasn't expecting to find cancer...found cancer...didn't know what to do with it, so they just sewed my face up. I think 'cuz I'm old and got some other things working against me, they just didn't worry about it. I'm 79."

"Before I retired I worked in cost accounting...worked in TT with the engineers. They tore down that building a few years ago. But, I worked there 22 years, then went out to Oregon for five years...that's where my first wife had cancer...out there, back in '69. She died of cancer...started with pancreatic cancer and then it spread to her liver. She was only 39 years old...only 39. I married a doctor's widow after that, who...he himself had died from brain cancer. Matter of fact, today woulda been her 76th birthday. Went out to the cemetery this morning with my daughters."

"I came from Tennessee, up there in the northeast corner. I was born and raised on an island...a so-called island. The river split and carved out an island...an island about eight miles long. So, I spent most of my time there fishing and swimming. Had a paper route...delivered the Kingsport Times."

"I joined the Navy when I was seventeen, because back then, everybody got drafted. 1944 and 1945, I spent time on an aircraft carrier. Believe it or not, I was in the fire control division...that's not firefighters...it's in fire control, you know, 40mm guns. Bon Homme Richard was the ship....just like John Paul Jones ship. We brought down a few kamikazes. Our fighter squadrons participated. We had planes up all the time, and we were in the center of the fleet...destroyers and all...all around us. Every once in awhile one of 'em...the kamikazes, would get through...most of 'em got shot down before they even got to the fleet though. At Okinawa and Iwo Jima, we took quite a beating there...but I wasn't there...got there just after that was over. We spent most of our time running bombing raids up and down the coast of Japan."

"I was a plank owner on my ship...the Bon Homme Richard...Essex class, they called it. The Hornet, Wasp, Yorktown...all wooden decks. I worked in the navy yard. I didn't question it. I worked there on my first assignment...first assignment at sea, after boot camp and training. About half of my tour was spent after the war...built bunks on the flight-deck, and carried troops back...back to San Francisco. They called it the magic carpet."

"I was in Hawaii when they pulled the Franklin in. It was a horrible sight. It was an aircraft carrier like mine, but it had a bomb go down the after elevator...went right into the bomb magazine. It just burned to a crisp. Out of a crew of about 3000, they had about 700 survivors. It was horrible...just horrible."

"After the Navy, I went to college...fact is, I went to high school first, before college. Well, not really...I took my GED test. Back in 1944, I was going to be eighteen in August and school didn't start 'til September...and I didn't want to be drafted. If you're not in school when you're eighteen, they draft you. So, I volunteered for the Navy...my parents signed for me...thought it would be better than getting drafted. Little selfish too...I'd rather somebody be shooting at my ship instead of me...better than being in the cross-hairs of an infantryman in an open field. They'd be trying to kill me on my ship, but they wouldn't be trying to kill me personally. I guess it was a good decision, 'cuz...I'm still alive."

166 *Paul Steffeck*

"I'm from Stevens Point, Wisconsin. It's a small city by most standards…25,000 people. It has the University of Wisconsin…and Stevens Point is actually one of the bigger cities. There are only four million people in Wisconsin. There are about that many deer also…so it makes for an interesting population. Stevens Point is probably known more for the college than its natural resources. It's probably known more for the college because the director of the forest service went there…and Terry Porter, who played for the NBA for a bunch of years, also went there. There are a lot of paper mills in the area. It's mostly a blue collar community by most standards."

"My dad grew up in Wausau which is about 35 miles north of Stevens Point. On one occasion…there was an old lady that lived down the road, and she was kind of a nasty old lady. One day…the day they come and pick up all the Christmas trees, he went all around the neighborhood and picked up all the trees…set them up in her back yard, and planted them. So, she then had a forest in her back yard. It was mildly entertaining for him. I remember he enjoyed telling me that story. Then, when I was sixteen years old, just before I turned seventeen, my brother and I were working on his pickup truck, out at my parent's house, and a police car pulled in to tell me that…my father died. He passed away."

"In my senior year in college, I had all the NFL scouts come in and work me out. I had a really bad ankle sprain, playing football. I didn't miss any games, but I was very limited. A lot of the scouts just thought I wasn't playing well. So, most of them…just let me go. I fell through the cracks. That was a turning point in my life. It humbled me. I was definitely arrogant…I thought I was better than other people…and I wasn't."

"After college, I played arena football out in California. In '02, I was released by the Firebirds…and so Coach Caudry called me…picked up my rights, and said if I wanted to play arena football, I'd better show up and play with the Pirates. I'm not playing any more…I've had five knee surgeries. I have now basically given up playing football. I am the receiving manager at Dick's Sporting Goods. Some days, it's a lot of fun and some days, it's just kind of a pain in the neck. Like any job…you have good days and bad days."

"Once, when I was playing for Bakersfield, in California...and that was Arena-2...we went to the Quad-Cities to play a game, and when I came back to my hotel room...ummm...there was a college girl waiting in my room for me. I actually walked back out. I was shocked. That was something I thought would never happen. I walk in...this girl is sitting in the corner, and I thought I messed up...wrong room. Then, I found out from the other guys that they also had visitors."

"I learned that if you want to find out if you're a good guy or not...look yourself in the mirror, and if you can say, "I'm happy with who I am.", you're doing okay. If you look in the mirror and you have any doubt that you're doing something you shouldn't...then you need to change."

"It's the highlight of my day when I know I'm going home to see April. I just...I can't wait. I'm at work, and I can't wait to go home and see my wife. It's little stuff...going for walks with her...good quality time where it's just us. Until I met April, I didn't realize it, but I was miserable. I would go out to enjoy the nightlife in town...go to the bars three or four days a week. Now, I haven't been to a bar since July...and probably three months before that."

"I feel *complete* being married. My life means something."

167 *Fay Opper*

"I'm 73. I'm selling Premier Design Jewelry. I've been doing this for a year and a half. It's high quality, good jewelry. The company is located in Texas. I don't make it myself...nope. I had been thinking about it for three or four years, and I wanted to do something...I think, because I was bored. I never, in the world, liked the idea of retiring and doing nothing. I have always been a busy person...all my life. I feel like if I am doing something of a positive nature...that...that...that...I would have a better perspective of myself."

"The last 25 years that I worked, I took care of the elderly, until I became one myself. The thirty years before that, I raised nine children. My children are all over the country. I have one in Hawaii...a daughter in Arizona...I have three children in Colorado, one in Boulder, one in Littleton, and one in Aurora. I have four that live in the state here...one in Gridley...one in Washington, but she's getting ready to go live in China for three or four years. She's going with her husband who is an engineer. I have another son who works for CILCO and lives in Spring Bay, and another in Mackinaw."

"My family got together a lot, because my mom and dad oriented it that way. My mother and dad was married for 68 years before they died. They were a very family-oriented family. We would have picnics and gatherings for holidays...in the summertime. They were my inspiration, I'll tell you, they really were. They were something you don't see very often. They were from around here, but then after they retired, spent a lot of time in Arizona. I lived in Arizona twenty years myself. That's where I took care of the elderly. There should have been six of me so many times, 'cause I had so many jobs. They all wanted me, and they didn't have enough people to care of all of them. Of course, it was a city of nothing but seniors."

"Last year, in August...for the first week in August, we were in Snow Mountain Ranch...in Colorado. I had all nine of my children with me, for one whole week. My children go on vacations every four years together. They plan...they plan the trips themselves, and that one there was a memorable time. It was the first time I had them together in fourteen years. It's easy to start crying when I'm talking about my kids, 'cause I dearly love them, and they all think I'm absolutely crazy, because they don't know why...why I had all of them. I've got pictures of them on my front wall...of my kids and I, in the middle...my grandkids over here...and all of them that was there...over here. That was spectacular to me, 'cause it might be another fifteen years before it happens again. I dearly love my kids."

168   *Dan Uphof*

"Dan Uphof, 47. I'm offering bottled water to family homes and commercial businesses. I work for Oasis Water. I'm originally from Benson. Born and raised in Benson, 'til I was twenty years old. Went to work for Caterpillar, went to ICC and got my degree, and...ended up here."

"Benson is on Route 116, about 25 miles east of here. The population is probably about five hundred. There are two bars, a bank...a little gift shop. I haven't been there in a long time. Most of the guys I hung around with...some of them are still there...most have moved out and are gone. As a teenager, we never stayed in Benson. We would drive to Peoria...went to the movies. There was a lot of drag racing...that's kinda what we did. Went to the Steak & Shake in Peoria. Went to the Palace Theater, Madison Theater, Star-Lite Drive-In. My buddy and I used to sneak in...about three or four guys...and we would take our girlfriends in. Just for the heck of it, we would throw them in the trunk and go to the Star-Lite Drive-In. It was neat...nobody checked the trunk or anything."

"I was sixteen when I got my car and started dating. Blonde hair, blue-eyes...I dated her for about five or six months. She found somebody else, newer and better...but we had a good time. It was puppy love. Now, when I met my wife, we went through a dating service. Not an online dating service. This was before them...and I don't recommend them. I can't even remember the name of it, but you pay for it. They tell about your likes and dislikes...same thing...then you meet them."

"This might sound stupid...but, in the winter...in Benson, my dad would take us kids, and we'd tie a rope around a car, and take a car hood or sleds...and he'd pull us around town. Back then the cops...there were no cops, because it was just a small hometown, like Mayberry. He would drive us around town and take us sledding in the winter. In the summer, we played baseball. Everybody would kinda get together, and we just played a lot of baseball. That's what we did as kids. There was no computers, you made your own fun back then...not like today."

"I worked at Caterpillar for about six years. Actually, I worked there for about four and a half years. I uh, graduated from high...what was weird is the exact day

I started, was the day my dad retired. He had 35 years in. His health was deteriorating, and he worked there pretty much all his life. He was an operator...operated the heavy equipment out at the Proving Grounds. October 2nd, 1978 was the day he retired...'cuz that was the day I hired in. I was in the assembly line out in Mossville. Like everybody else that was hired in '78...got laid off in '82."

"Man, it's a little warm today...would you like some water?"

169-170 *Arlo and Annie Guthrie*

"Hurricane Katrina...I was watching the TV, and about the third or fourth day into this horrific event, I saw a little scroll on the bottom of the screen saying Amtrak was resuming service on the "City of New Orleans". They were headed into town...into Crescent City, and I thought that there would be an opportunity for me to do something."

"When I saw that scroll come across the screen, I sent out a little email to my family and a few friends. They forwarded it along to other people...without telling me. Within twenty minutes, and I'm not making this up, I got an email from Jennifer and Richard Pryor, who said, "If there's anything we can do to help, let us know." And I thought, "This might actually go somewhere." Twenty-four hours later, I got a call from Willie Nelson saying, "If there's anything I can do, let me know.""

"Yes, my dad had sent my sisters and the whole family, an email. He...he sent me an email and shared with me...his ideas about New Orleans, and a tour. I loved the idea myself...so I forwarded it along, and called my sister Cathy...and we forwarded it along to our friends. The next thing I knew, we were getting responses from people. The first people to respond were Jennifer and Richard Pryor. They wrote an email saying, "How can we help?" We went on from there...and at some point when I was getting hundreds of emails...I realized, we have to do it...it has to happen. So, it started with an email that basically, everybody thought it was a great idea...and we went from there."

"The Pryors helped to financially support the show in Chicago. They also let people know about the event. They had information available on their website...and have just been supporting us the whole time. We were chatting back and forth with emails, and ideas...and that kind of thing. Just hearing from them was great. It was like, "Okay, let's do this, it's a good idea...and we're not the only ones who think so.""

"So, Richard and Jennifer sponsored the first show we did in Chicago...and I just found out, just a few minutes ago, that Richard Pryor passed away. I just wrote him a long note yesterday, telling him about all the stuff that he helped put together. So, I was wiping the tears away...this was a guy I had never met, but who had been loved dearly in life by millions of people. It was so nice to work with people like that...who, out of the blue, have just come forward and helped to put this thing together. This is not an easy task. We just did Farm Aid last year up in Chicago. It takes a whole year for all of those folks to put together one show. My daughters...and my family, have worked their butts off to put all seven...all eight of these shows together, in about three to four weeks."

"We are literally on the "City of New Orleans" train. We're not on it constantly, because we have to do gigs...but it is our main means of transportation. So, right now, we're all in Champaign, getting ready to head over to the Canopy Club to do the production for the day...get the show rolling. Myself...I did a bar gig in Kankakee the other night. I played with my sister, Sarah Lee. I'll probably do a couple of songs tonight, but not a set. I'll be doing the organizing all the way down to New Orleans."

"Rising Son Records is a company my dad started in the eighties. He realized the music business was changing...the music industry was changing. The people that were running the record companies in the early days were retiring...and the people that were taking over, weren't the same type of people. In his heart...and he worked with some real industry guys that were there because they loved the music...the change over to people who knew how to make money, started happening in those days. My dad went to Warner Brothers, and the people that he worked with were getting ready to leave...and he asked if he could have his catalogue back...and to his surprise, they said yes. So, he started Rising Son Records in the early eighties...1985. He has been putting out his own records as well as licensing his original CD's, and has been manufacturing them since his Warner Brothers days."

"About ten years ago, he asked my sister Cathy and myself to come in and take over...to work for him. He was in business for ten years, and we were all finally out of high school...and we all sat down...and it all kind fell into place, working for him. We've been in the industry our whole lives. We grew up in it. We understood it. So, we took over and have been running the record company together...my sister Cathy and I. That's been ten years now."

"We all grew up on the road together. We all work together now. I think that says a lot for our family. We still all get along...we still like each other. We've been doing this our whole lives...although it's different, because now it's us kids running the show. We're having a great time on the road. We just spent three days in Kankakee before coming down to Champaign."

"The last time I was here was about 25 years ago."

"I used to sing with my dad…my sister Sarah Lee, and Cathy, when we were teenagers. We would go on the road and sing backup here and there. For the first time in ten years, we sang the song "City of New Orleans" together…at a radio station in the Berkshires, just before we took off. During the song, I realized how it had…changed. Because of the events that took place…that are taking place…because we're on the train…because we're going to New Orleans…and none of us had ever ridden on the train "City of New Orleans" before…and it's not about the train. It's not about the train anymore…it's about the people. That in itself…being on the train and being together…people that we grew up with…family…we've got my brother's band here, my sister Sarah Lee's band…they're playing. This is…this is the first time that, that has happened. We're all playing together, and we're all on the train. For us, that is pretty cool. It's an amazing thing."

"The "City Of New Orleans", my dad has been singing…and we've been listening to that since we were born…and here we are…we're actually on it…really cool. My mom, my dad…my sister Sarah Lee and her husband Johnny Irion, and their daughter Olivia, who is three. I've got my two kids with me…and so, we're having fun. The whole family is here."

"We're trying…we're trying to target all the, sort of…nameless musicians who play in the bars and the clubs…and out on the streets in New Orleans. Without them, the culture begins to fade away. There wasn't much I could do about the food, which was the other great thing, but…I thought as far as music goes, I thought we could do something."

"My dad, Woody Guthrie, wrote a lot of songs about his adventures during the dust bowl…during those times. It's disasters like that…that form the heart of the nation's experience in history. If you do the right thing…then, well, you've just got a better nation in the long run…and you get a better world almost immediately. He lived in a time when there was a lot of division on social issues…political ones…and all kinds of stuff going on. But every once in awhile, something happens when you just have to put all that stuff aside…because the nature and the size of the disaster somewhere just takes over. You have to go out and help people of all persuasions and political opinions…and I wish they would do a little more of that in Washington…and other places around the country."

"My dad wrote about 3500 songs. He only recorded a couple hundred of them, and the rest are just sort of sitting there on scraps of paper. I mean…if he came to visit you in your house…there wouldn't be anything safe. He would be writing on every piece of paper. As he ran out of that, he'd be starting on your linens…or sheets…pillow cases. He just kept writing…just kept writing. He only recorded a couple of hundred…so the rest of that stuff is just…clumps of paper that people pulled out of the trash and sent to the family. For the past fifteen or twenty years, my sister Nora, has been getting those lyrics out to different bands, different artists from around the world…not just here…and making new songs with the old lyrics. Frankly, my dad is doing better now than he has in a long, long time."

"Christmas is coming up and we have no idea what we're going to do this Christmas. We're usually all over the country, and we have kids ourselves. Christmas is still up in the air…not really planned. We'll just have to figure it out. But, on a normal Christmas morning when we are all together…just like everybody else…we wake up on Christmas and the kids are all excited. They open presents under the tree…and we stay in our pajamas all day…just hang out…have a peaceful day…just like everybody else."

"One of the last songs my dad wrote is a peace song…but not the big *wide world* peace that you can march to…it's the little peace inside yourself that makes everybody happy to be around you…that puts a smile on your face. I think if more people worried about the little peace…the big peace would take care of itself."

171-172 *Tracy Hillyer and Khloe*

"I'm Tracy Hillyer and I will be 27 in a month. I work in the parts department. I process orders for Indonesia and Columbia and I run all kinds of marketing programs, reports, sales reports...miscellaneous stuff...and that's about it, really. I live towards Spring Bay. I grew up in the same house that I'm in right now. Ummm, my parents lived there for...for, well...for 27 years. I lived there 'til I was eighteen, and I moved out on my own. I've lived in several apartments, and when I finally got settled...that's when I bought that house. My parents now live across the street, and my brother lives next door to them. So, I live in the house that I was pretty much born in."

"I am Khloe and I am four. I watch movies. I have Sponge Bob....and Patrick is a starfish."

"We just got back from a vacation. We went out to Colorado. Drove out to Colorado, went through the Rocky Mountains, San Juan Mountains...Utah, Arizona, Las Vegas. The San Juan Mountains are in the southern part of Colorado. They are absolutely beautiful, but I was scared to death. It's awful going up the mountain because it's a two lane road, and there's like...a foot of gravel alongside the two lane road, and then it drops off to, like, thousands and thousands of feet. It was beautiful, but it was really scary. In fact, I got out at the top of the mountain and cried. I was still alive...I didn't die. We drove through the mountains and went to the four corners, Utah, Arizona, New Mexico, and Colorado. We went to the Grand Canyon. It was awesome. We didn't go to the bottom. We had Khloe with us and that was about all she could take."

"I like...I like to play on my swing set. I have two swings, one monkey bar, and I have a slide."

"We went to Las Vegas, and it was really, really cool, and we're probably going back this year without Khloe, because we took her, and we weren't able to do some things we wanted to do. But, she enjoyed it. We went to see the white lions and Siegfried and Roy's Secret Garden. We went down to Freemont Street. We were only there for about a day and a half. We swam in the pool, and that was about it."

"What about all the statues, Mom?"

"On the way home, in a small town in Oklahoma, we got stopped...'bout 11:30 at night. The cop came up to the door and said, "Can I see license and registration?...blah, blah, blah." We explained that we rented the car, so we didn't have registration. So the guy ran the plates...came back with a pistol in his hand and said, "This is a stolen vehicle." Another cop comes speeding around and pulls up...so now he's got backup, and tells us to get out of the car. So, we explain again, "This is a rental car...this is not a stolen car." So, Kris had to get in the back to get the papers he had signed...the rental agreement. So, he started digging through the trunk and they freaked out...thought he was looking for a gun, and ummm...they started looking...told him to get out of the trunk. So anyway...they finally found it and we got everything straightened around. But for awhile, I was afraid I was going to have to bail my husband out of jail while we were on vacation."

"My cat...one time...he climbed up on the roof. You know how he got up there? He climbed up there...he climbed up the gate. My dad got him down with a ladder."

"I've always enjoy learning things...taking classes, going to school. If I could be a full-time student, I would do it. I take anything...anything and everything. Well, everything except for math."

"I have a cat....Jack. He's black, and he has a white spot on his neck, and he catched two mice one time...two big ones...and then he ate 'em. He eats grasshoppers too."

173   *Luke Curtis*

"I am Luke Curtis…next month I'll be 34. I work for ISU…and I also sell art-work that I get from a business associate in California. I've sold artwork to several big businesses in the area. I just sold a large format "Dogs Playing Poker" to a riverfront casino…no kidding…I swear."

"I'm sort of lost right now. I was divorced several months ago…not really by choice. It's very odd…I still love her very much…but I also feel a dozen other emotions that I can't quite describe. I can tell you that divorce, in my opinion, is worse than having your spouse die. I can tell you that because my first wife died. There is a bigger story there, which is not uncomplicated…and I won't go into…but there is a certain finality in death that you can never get in a divorce. Neither experience is by any means good…in any way…in fact, quite the opposite. They are both so bad, that you just want to die…you just want to die. I went through months and months of being so depressed that I came close to just "doing it" a couple of times. I used to work with this guy…who…he was divorced from his wife…he lived in Bartonville and hung himself. His son found him…and it is that picture…that picture in my head, of his son finding him, that kept me from doing something stupid."

"After an argument with my wife, she made the decision to move out. She packed her bags…literally, and went to live with her mother. She took everything that she could. Of course, her mother never did care for me…I think I was a little too strange for her taste. Her mother is…very conservative. Actually the whole family is very conservative…very tribal…and strange in their own way. I never fit in with the rest of her family…so that was always sitting there in the background. I think that was a big factor. Of course, you can never really know what is in someone's head…and my wife was always very, very close with her feelings…very careful on what she revealed to me…and her family. That's another story in itself. Of course, I had my own problems…at one time or another, I'm sure I was a real jerk, at least through her eyes."

"The day that she left was devastating to me, and even more so in the next few months. She called her mother to come over and help her pack…and later called her sister. I had to leave the house for awhile and let them do what they were there to do. I got in the car, not really knowing where I was going. I just drove around…I can't remember where I went. But, at some point, I came back home and they were all still there. I went into the bathroom and took a shower…I'm not sure why. I asked my wife to tell her sister to get out of my house…we never got along…and I didn't want any trouble. That pissed off her sister and she went outside and called the police. The police came and talked with everyone…and I agreed to let her sister in the house, as long as she didn't speak to me…and she didn't, so that worked out all right. After a few more minutes…she was gone."

"My wife left and didn't come back. She never came back. I think once she was with her family, there was no more thought of trying to reconcile with me. I think she made the decision long before the argument, anyway. There were a couple months of crazy…and what turned out to be, unrealistic attempts on my part, to try and get her to talk to me…which had the opposite affect. I said and did some strange things. But throughout the whole thing…it eventually became obvious that she had no desire to stay married. Of course, I fooled myself…and she helped also. She would throw me a bone when she wanted something from me…and it worked. I was desperate to have her back…but it never lasted for long."

"We were divorced in Pekin, which was quite an experience. We both agreed to go lawyer-less, and so I downloaded some free forms off the web. We agreed on a settlement, and met at the courthouse. We exchanged neutral pleasantries and waited for our turn with the judge. She was teary-eyed, and I was strung out on an overdose of Xanax that I ordered from an overseas website…you know, to help with my depression. The wait was longer than we expected…we didn't get into the courtroom until almost closing time. The judge was in a really bad mood…she didn't like the way I filled out the forms…and she was very rude. Of course, if I had to sit in a courtroom and deal with divorces all day long, I suppose it would get to me also. After sitting on the stand and answering some very basic questions, the judge signed the papers and…that was it."

"When we left the courtroom, we both went across the street to the County Clerk's to sign some papers, and the weather had turned…it was raining like crazy…coming in sideways, cold and windy. Neither one of us had raincoats or umbrellas. We ran across the street and signed the papers…and then ran across the courtyard and stopped at the entrance of a coffee shop."

"I asked her in for some coffee. She said, "No, I'm too upset right now." We stood there for a few moments...both at a loss for words. I think we said good-bye...and I walked through the rain to my car, opened the door...and started crying. I couldn't stop. I tried driving home...but the rain and the tears made it almost impossible. I drove towards East Peoria, and finally pulled into a cemetery parking lot. I sat there until it got dark...and then I drove home to an empty house."

174   *Michael White*

"I saw an opportunity here on the corner…and I took it. My goal as an artist is to make the world a better place. I don't want to be just another dead artist some-day. I want to change the world and make it a better place…with my artwork. I feel…you know…I definitely have spiritual values on everything. I have learned that when you paint from your spirit…things mean more. When you paint from the inside, you're generating originality from your spirit…when you paint that way. So, all of my paintings were birthed that way."

"This one…this one right here…with the eagle head and the circle, I had no idea where I was going with that painting…and that started out…that started out with a 911 picture. Ummm…I just started painting, and it unfolded into that picture. As you can see, at the bottom…there is a cross in the water…it forms the cross of Christ. We shed…and you see, the meaning behind it is…we shed our blood for good reasons and good causes. But, as you can see, the red turns into blood…because his blood runs deeper. So, there is that spiritual element."

"This eagle…this eagle is over at Wildlife Prairie Park. I got into his cage. He never moved from his perch…stood there and defied me…hissed at me. He has a clipped wing and can't fly, but…it doesn't mean he's not an eagle. I thought…"America". It's not how high you fly…but how well you take your stand. It was just profound to me. "I'm an eagle…and I'm not moving.""

"This one over here, I call "Higher". The interesting thing about it is…I knew for six months while I was painting a bigger picture, I was going to paint this one…and I knew I would call it "Higher". The day that I started it…and of course, you're painting out of your spirit…and the day I started it, two hours into it, the space shuttle blew up. Later, I was watching the movie that one of the astronauts made before, and he said, "If everything goes fine, I'll be back…but if not, I'm just going higher." And that was the name of the painting…"Higher". The day that I finished the painting, my mother called me unannounced…and said, "Grandma just died." So…she went higher."

"So, my thing is…and I've had many people come and ask, "Can you do skulls…can you do this or that?" I say, "No…there's enough of that." I want to bring more peace, more joy, more happiness and contentment to the world…so,

I'm going to paint on this side, you know? I'm not knocking anybody that does...they can do what they want...but my goal is to bring more life and truth out of my spirit."

"I grew up custom painting vans, and I owned a sign shop. At one time I had eleven employees. My dad is an airbrush artist too, and I'm raising the next generation of airbrush artists. I have six children."

"I used to travel all over the country painting motor homes for companies. I used to do Harley Davidson shows...Goldwing shows. One of my big projects that I have done is the Grande Prairie Mall. I did a 45 foot mural in the mall over there. It's in the food court, and has a "Route 66" theme. I did a big project for Walter Brothers there also....Peoria Speedway...Riverside Church."

"There's a certain amount of talent that is required. There's a lot to be said for...just plain sticking with it...and a determination that, you know, in yourself that you can do it...and you do...do it. I think some of it is part of a call. I've always been one where, I'm not after the easy road...I'm after the right road. So, I feel like I am on the right road. My goal is to...somehow...use my talent to glorify God. Also, to make the world a better place...somehow."

175   *Frankie See*

"I live in Chillicothe…but I'm originally from Dallas City. It's a little town on the Mississippi River. I can't remember how many miles from here. The next biggest town is Niota, which is famous some years back for being flooded out…the dike broke. It's right across the river from Fort Madison, Iowa. Dallas City has four of five thousand people, I would guess."

"I was in the sixth grade when I left…my parents left for work. My father worked for Standard Oil Company, better know as "the pipeline". We moved to Laura, which is on Route 78. I'm 64…so that was a long time ago."

"Before we left town, I was riding my bike down by the river and fell into a ditch…and had a real bad cut. My mother took care of it…she shaved the back of my head…put lots of tape on it…and I never went to the doctor. We had a few doctors, but I didn't go. Still don't. It's a good idea to stay away from doctors."

"My dad was always inviting people to our house…and he'd forget to tell my mother. They left on vacation, and when they came back, Dad had invited some people for dinner one night…and when they came, nobody was home. He always asked everybody, everybody to come over for dinner…but he just didn't communicate that to my mother."

"I'm a retired manager of an insurance company. I like a little gardening…I like to cook, and fool around with antiques. We used to sell antiques at flea markets…but we don't do flea markets any more. We're in the Illinois Antique Center…and it's an interesting place."

"My husband used to like to hunt. So, we started going to gun shows…and his parents liked antiques…so, he always grew up with antiques. In the process of buying and selling, we just accumulated more and more things…and that led to occasionally selling something…trading. He loves to trade, so this…what we do now, is an outgrowth of that. Before that, my husband was an agent for State Farm Insurance…just what a person that majored in geology would be."

"We're going to keep doing this as long as we can. He is sort of a Type-A...doesn't know how to relax...so, he's always doing something. I'm kind of ready to just sit back in the porch swing and swing for awhile, but I'll do what he wants to."

176   *Robert Branan*

"Today...I woke up. I have a chance to do anything I want to do...and make amends for anything I've done wrong. It's another day for me to start new...fresh. Every day, I kind of look at my life that way."

177   *Adeletraud Smith*

"Adeletraud Smith…it is German. My nickname is Trudy. I come from Bad Hersfeld in Germany. I live here now…married to my husband, Al Smith. He works for the State Farm Insurance, and he is a security systems…ummm…he works with all the computers. I am a housewife right now."

"My husband lived in Germany. He worked at Spotz & Troller…by the computers. So do I. We met…fall in love…and got married over there. Later on, we moved here, in 1981. We moved to Texas, Austin Texas…and then came here. We came here in 1999."

"In Germany, I had lots of friends, between boys and girls. There were a lot of boys where I lived in Germany before we moved somewhere else…then there were more girls. We played baseball and hide & seek…things like that."

"My family went to lots of vacations together and lots of Oktoberfests. Even the town where I am from, we have Oktoberfest in October…for about a week. We had many other family things to go to…different family reunions. I spent a lot of time with my family."

"Before I was eighteen, nobody wants to let me in a disco. They all thought I wasn't even sixteen yet. I don't want to say how old I am now…but let's say I'm old enough to go to a disco. But, I don't do that stuff anymore. The German-American Society has many things going on, and I am involved with them. Mostly I am with my friends."

"The last two years…my dad passed away, then my mother passed away…May 31st. This year, my brother passed away, June 29th. I am the only one left from that family. But, I have my cousins and aunts…and stuff like that. I hope to go back and visit. I hope the next time I go back will be a nice situation…not like it was the last two years. My brother's death was worse than all of them, and I went back to Germany this year when he passed away."

"I do not have any children. I wish…but it didn't turn out. So, I have three poodles, and a bird, and a husband. He is drinking a beer right now. You can't miss him...he is a little bit heavier...and has a beard...and has on a hat that looks like this."

"We now live in Mapleton, close to Bartonville...but the address is Mapleton. We like the cold and the snow here. If you live for eighteen years in Texas...it's hot constantly...and we get tired of that. I think I love the four seasons here...it's almost like in Germany. The only difference...where I lived in Germany, it's not that hot as over here, and it's not that cold. The hot I don't mind, but the cold...I hate that."

"The people here, they are pretty much the same. You have good people and bad people. Everyone has their own heritage, and some are from Germany...their mother and father came from there. So, it is important to remember that even though you live here in America...remember where you came from."

178   *Kay Price*

"Kay spelled backwards is "yak". Not the animal, but someone who talks a lot. That's me."

"I was born in Liberty, Nebraska on the 4th of July…a long time ago. I married a man that was riding a yellow Caterpillar tractor, and he brought me to this wonderful place. I had never heard of it before, never saw it before in my life…but, I will never move back to Nebraska. It's very dry and hot there. I like it here."

"When I was thin, and I wore high-heels and panty hose, my husband and I went to the Hub Ballroom…and it was Christmas time. It was Christmas, and all these important CAT people are there…and these are the people you have to impress, because your husband works for them, see. All of a sudden they started playing the Beer Barrel Polka. If you are from the part of Nebraska where I am from, you hafta' know how to "polka"…and you have to have a large area to polka in, because I kick high, and because I cover a lot of territory. So, I'm out there and we're *polka-ing* around and we're smiling and looking at each other and having a great time at this Christmas party…when something grabs my spiked heel. Now, because the message has to go all the way up your leg, through your spinal cord, and into your brain, and then back to the other leg…to tell it that the first leg hasn't got to the floor yet. Well, the other leg went up before the first leg came down, so that both legs were off the floor at the same time…and I fell down."

"I looked behind me and wondered what was it…that grabbed my heel. And, as I looked behind me, there on the floor was this woman's half slip. My heel had gone under her dress and caught the lace on her half slip and ripped it right down to her ankles. I thought, "Oh my, I wish I could dig a whole right here in the Hub Ballroom and crawl in it." But that little lady…and she was probably in her 50's…she just bent over, wriggled that thing back up…pulled her skirt back down, and went right on dancing. She didn't even say anything to me."

"I'm a champion chicken-caller and I have trophies to prove it. One day, it was very, very hot, and I had these two little boys who have since grown up and talk in deep voices…like this. They used to really love me. We went to the Heart of Illinois Fair and they ate watermelon and rode rides, and then they threw up. But, we had a really fun day. Then we went to the Ag Barn, and the chickens were there. They were having a chicken calling contest. They said, "Mom, you should sign up because, we raise chickens." So, I signed up and then asked, "What is a chicken calling contest?" The man said, "Well, we're going to put the chicken in this little pen here, with all these people sitting around it. You have to go in and get the chicken to eat out of your hand." So, I went around and got the apron with the doughboy on it, and I got the farmer's hat from the Farm Bureau and I went in there and talked to the owner of the chicken, but I didn't want anyone to know that I had talked to him."

"There were these city girls that ran around and chased the chicken like it was a dog, and some tried to call the chicken like a dog, and some tried to pet the chicken like it was a cat. But, I knew better. I put oats in my little apron skirt and a little bread in my hand...and I walked very carefully. Little Henny Penny came right up...ate out of my hand...and I won the trophy."

179 *Lori Hadley*

"I lived in Chicago a few years ago. I don't know if you've ever bought White Castle burgers and brought them home in your car…but the smell stays in the car for days…even weeks. I've always tried to find out what it is about them that…stays. I never have, but I know that same ingredient must be in Velvet Freeze Wonder Dogs. I got a bag of six of them four days ago…and I think I'm going to have to sell my car."

180   *Sue Hughes*

"I was born in French Morocco, actually…North Africa. My dad was in the Air Force, and he was stationed there. So my mom had been there three years…and I was born and lived there for a year. I haven't been back, but I'd like to. I turned fifty this summer."

"My 50th birthday was the longest birthday…it lasted forever. I got a trip to Maine from one of my friends. So, I will die and be tossed off a lighthouse somewhere in Maine…if I don't retire there first. I will leave from Maine one way or another. I got to go four-wheeling with another friend…and I had never done that before. My daughter had a big 50th party for me at a Chief's game. I had a lot of friends come. It was better than I could have asked for."

"My mom was very much…as I was being raised…she almost raised me as being African-American. We lived in Peoria, and actually I tell my kid's friends that I am more African-American than they are…because I actually was born there. They get a big kick out of that…they think that's pretty funny…that Mrs. Hughes was born in Africa. That was very much a part of my life. Even though both my parents are American, and they are white…I just always had African things in my room. The things we brought back…I got. You know, the furniture and stuff we brought back…I ended up with it, and stuff like that. Even way back…race never played an issue in our family."

"This is my grandson here. His name is Gabriel…as you can see, he is truly African-American, and this is my granddaughter Lauren. They have different parents, but they are both my grandkids…wonderful grandkids."

"I am the service tool hotline at Caterpillar…worldwide. I have the tools that actually repair the machines and the engines. Not a work tool that goes onto the end of something, like a hammer on an excavator. I actually have the tools that repair the machines. I get calls from around the world…or emails…and I tell them which tools to use…sometimes procedures…and things like that. I've actually emailed every continent, including Antarctica."

"I used to work at Methodist. I left Caterpillar in '82…had my family…went into the medical field, and then came back in '97. I wanted to be home, and I was pregnant when I quit. I stayed home and had four kids. My friends that stayed at Caterpillar…none of them had children. They wanted to, later in life, but found out they couldn't. I feel like that was a blessing to me…that I had children. My friends are all retiring now, they've got their thirty years in…but, I've got a beautiful family."

"I am at that point again, where I know that I have to stay to pay the bills…but I've hit fifty and know there is much more to this…much more to life than this. I like to think my friends know where I am going. I'd like to be able to do things…go overseas…help people. I have a "save-the-world" syndrome, and that's kind of why I left Caterpillar years ago…because I didn't think I was doing anything to help anybody."

"Quite honestly, I'm going back to nursing school in the spring. My goal is…I hope to get all my preliminary classes out of the way and start nursing school in three years…and in five years, I hope to graduate…leave Caterpillar, and then take it wherever the Lord wants me to take it. Perhaps that will be Africa."

181   *Lisa Neal*

"About ten years ago my grandpa gave me a great piece of advice. He told me if I wanted to stay alive, I should never...ever...under any circumstances...change the channel on his TV when he leaves the room. He has the CNN logo actually burned into the screen. You can turn the TV off, and it still shows the CNN logo. He doesn't even use the remote. It's...weird."

182 *Ellen Johnson*

"I'm from New Jersey...Bergen County...a little town called Midland Park. My father worked for the telephone company in New York City. My mother was mostly in the retail business, in various department stores...yes, mostly department stores as I remember. I didn't go into New York myself, very much. I never had the desire. I still don't. The plays, shows...they are so expensive. They are so incredibly expensive...plus, you know, the parking. It's just incredible. I don't think it used to be that way. Just like...going to a concert these days...it used to be affordable. It's $130 a ticket, and you still don't get good seats."

"We were not a religious family. My parents were just not interested...but the friends I grew up with were strict Lutherans...one family...and the other family was strict Catholics. We were like...what were we? I didn't know. We didn't have all those rituals and...and I have to admit I was happy. It was nothing I really desired. I liked what we were...and what were we? I really didn't know. I didn't know how...I didn't know how to fit in with all of that, but that was all okay."

"My mother was always very...my mother *is* always very progressive-minded. She is a progressive person, always talking about social issues. She's very liberal and progressive-minded. So, I was always thinking about those kinds of issues. She would be cr...she would...one of the things that she would do...she used to work two jobs, when we were growing up. On Sundays, she would work in the local Presbyterian Church nursery...to take care of the babies while the parents were going to services. My father would stay home and work in the garden. My mother would go to the church to work in the nursery...and sometimes she would take us along, and watch us. Somebody had to watch us. So, we would go along and play in the nursery."

"We would walk around the church and see what was going on...and I didn't understand any of that. I would hear her sometimes...and I remember one story she told. The minister made fun of her, in front of everybody...a very derogatory remark about her in front of people, about a personal affect of hers. It was very insulting...just not very nice. I remember her cr...discussing religion with people...and I didn't understand what was being said...but she would question things, and not be afraid to ask questions."

"In 1978, I was channel-surfing…and on a Sunday, I saw a news program, and it was Madalyn Murray O'Hair on this local talk show. Sitting on a chair…on a raised platform…surrounded by all members of various clergies…priests, gurus, ministers…all there in the audience…sitting there, ready to refute, live on the air…anything she had to say. It was qui…it was really stacked against her…however, everything that she had to say was absolutely true. They couldn't refute what she had to say…but you know, you know…it was a stacked deck. I remember saying, "Ahhh…that's what I am. That's who we are. There is somebody talking about a family like mine….somebody who is an Atheist. I want to…I want to find out more.""

"So, I wrote away to the organization and said, "Oh, please send me more information. I just saw Madalyn Murray O'Hair. Oh…how interesting." And, I found that letter ten years ago. You know when the Murray O'Hair's disappeared? I don't know if you know about that. But, we went through the building…went through everything…and I found that letter, that original letter I wrote. I took it of course. They saved everything. They saved everything, including that letter. I still have that letter that I sent to them.""

"Then I joined. It was really quite nice to…I guess it's kind of like, during that time, being…a homosexual. No one ever talked about that. You didn't hear the word. You didn't hear the word…what you were. You didn't fit in. You didn't know how to describe yourself…anything about yourself. I think it's analogous to that…learning about being…who you are.""

"I have read Robert Green Ingersoll…from Peoria. I am a great admirer of Thomas Edison. Thomas Jefferson, John Adams…Abigail Adams, George Washington…I admire those people. I am very interested in American Revolutionary War history. I admire the founding fathers. I admire the scientists of today, the physicians of today…teachers, physicians…scientists. I can't think of more noble professions. They truly improve our lives and work to help everybody. It's all based on science and logic and reason. They are the people that really improve our lives. There are just so many people in the Atheist scientific world who I admire…there are just so many. You know, there are roughly thirty million non-believers in the United States…defined as not affiliated with any religious organization. They don't ascribe to any religion.""

"You can't really get a religious person to listen. They have to come to you. You can't really go out to them. If somebody is not interested in questioning or just exploring subjects...don't bother. I don't just simply go out and try to challenge people's beliefs...people that I meet. But, people that come to us...that want more information...that's when you give them the information, and let them do with it what they want."

"The truth hurts. People don't want to know it. Like, when televangelists are exposed. Does that hurt their following? No. People don't want to know the truth. They want to believe this. I lot of people know these things are baloney...but they don't care. I have seen this on television. They will expose Benny Hinn...or Popoff...or one of those...those nuts who just blow on people and they fall over and everything. They do these great exposes by these incredible news organizations. They walk up to these people and say, "Now, what do you think? We've just exposed this guy." Then the lady says, "I don't care." They want...they want to believe it's true. And, if that's what people want...that's fine. Ignorance is bliss. But, there are a lot of young people who do want to know, who do want to question...and a lot of them are crazed when they first start talking to you, because you're everything that they have been told to despise...you're just a horrible person. But then, you talk to them, and they calm down. The bottom line is that we have more in common than we have differences."

"Remember those thirty million people that are not affiliated with any religious organization...those are the people you want to talk to. The rest of them...and I'm not making any comparisons as far as ideology...but, but...when it comes to talking...our government...for those people that you can't reason with, the analogy is like racism. The American public had to be forced to treat black people as equals. You couldn't reason with all the people to do it. So, the people that you can't reason with to obey the law when it comes to state/church separation...you just have to apply the law, because they are not going to listen. They are going to break the law any way that they can...just like racists of the past. They had to be forced to allow black people to sit anywhere on the bus that they wanted to. Many will have to be forced to obey separation of church and state."

"I am the president of American Atheists, and a leading spokesperson for Atheist civil liberties. I have two kids. My daughter is twelve and my son is sixteen. Having my two children...of course being a mother...is the best thing that has happened to me."

183   *Mary Koonce*

"I get a ton of jokes about my name, especially working in a bar. I work at JT's in Tremont. I'm originally from Delevan, which is about twenty miles south. I'm 23. I'm also a bank teller…in addition to tending bar. I originally started going to JT's because one of my girlfriend's ex-boyfriends was there a lot…sorta hanging out there. We'd be there, and I started talking to one of the managers, whose name was Gary…and he talked me into getting a position there. It paid more than I was making at Applebee's. We joked about it for awhile, and then I came in one night in *sweats*. Well…KT was sitting down at the end of the bar…and Gary said, "This is the girl I want to hire." Then KT said, "I don't think she's got the guts for it." He said, "Sweetheart, let your hair down." So, I took my hair out of a ponytail…and he goes, "She's hired." That's all I had to do, take my hair down…he never talked to me before or anything. That was it."

"I remember everything about the night my boyfriend committed suicide. It was parent's weekend. My parents came down, and he didn't want to meet them. He was scared…because we had gotten into a fight about a week prior to that. He had broken his hand, because he hit a wall. He was really embarrassed because he knew my parents knew the story. So, he refused to meet them."

"So, I came into a bar, and he was there. I gave him a hug and said, "They're not there any more." He looked at me and said, "Ummm…that's great…I'll be back in a little bit. I'm going to go talk with somebody's parents, somebody else's parents…and I'll come back and see you." I was dancing with his guy friends out on the dance floor when he came back…and, you know, being in college you think, "Oh, I'll see him in a little bit." I looked up at him…and that was the last time I remember seeing him. I never saw him again. I went to a couple of parties trying to get in touch with him. The cops raided one of the parties I was at, and I was underage at that point…I was twenty. The cops got a call…there was something else they had to go to, so they left the party. They didn't bust anybody. I looked at my guy friend and said, "That was too close of a call. I'm out of here…and I'm going to Todd's place.""

"He lived across from the police station, and there was probably ten cop cars out front when I got there. There was an ambulance out there, and I remember thinking, "Just keep it under control…it's parents weekend, they're probably not raiding parties anymore. Just walk upstairs, just act real calm like you're going to your boyfriend's apartment, and nobody will question you or anything."

"I got up to his apartment, and I just remember this light pouring out of his apartment onto this stretcher. It was like…butter colored. It's really weird that I remember that. So, I'm always a person who thinks the worst of everything…and all his roommates were gone. They were right outside this apartment, and the door was open, so I ran down the steps and went back to the party…and begged my guy friend to go back with me. He was telling me the whole entire time, "You're making this up, there's nothing to be worried about." So, he gets upstairs to Todd's apartment…and sees the light, the butter colored light…and neither one of us could go in."

"We walked around back, and he had a balcony outside. I begged the cops to tell me what was going on. None of them had any authority to tell me what was going on…but I could see them doing CPR on somebody. I couldn't see his face or anything. I just kind of stood there freaking out…and they moved the person, and my friend went to look. Doug went to look…and he came back and said it was Todd. I just remember…everything was just a blur. They did the whole entire movie scene…like, "Why do you think he did this?" I was like, "Well, You have to tell me what he did, because…I don't know." They said, "Could you sit down on the steps…we have something to tell you." They continued asking me questions…and then they wanted me to call his parents. I had met his dad one time. I never met his mother. So…I refused to do that. I didn't do that."

"The day of the funeral we got lost…not on the way…coming home. I'm sorry I'm getting all confused. We were leaving the funeral home to go to the cemetery…and this is like, a comic thing. I rode with one of his guy friends…one of the guys that was there…and his twin brother was following us. My mom and dad were in front of us. The cops didn't do a very good job of closing off the lights so that everybody could get through, and he was a young kid that passed away in college…and a ton of people were down there. We were driving, and they turned the traffic lights back on. The cops got out of the way and let traffic through."

"So, we got lost…all of us. My parents walked up on the wrong funeral…some other cemetery…and there were four cemeteries. The twins were calling back and forth to each other. Thank God we had cell phones, and we finally ended up there...but thinking back on it now...it was funny...kind of like you would see in a movie. "Where are you?" "Well, where are you?" "Well, we're at this cemetery." "That's not the right cemetery." "Where are you?" I don't know." "I don't know where I am either. We're lost."

184 *Charlie Kear*

"I'm forty. We've got a mechanical bull here tonight…something different for The Hub. We normally don't do anything other than live entertainment when it comes to dance entertainment…or bands. Other than that, we were trying an alternative…something different…something The Hub has never done. Anything to make…to get people interested in something different…that's what we're doing. The Hub has never done it before and we're always game for something new to do. If you take something like a ballroom floor, like this one…most of the people who danced here were from the 1930's and 40's. This place was packed back then, anywhere from 800 to 1200 people."

"Nowadays, most of those people are gone…and there are really only three ballrooms in the state of Illinois left. This here is the second oldest ballroom in the state of Illinois. It's the…out of the three still here, this is the only one running."

"I ran several nightclubs…ever since I was 21, mostly small bars and taverns, but never a ballroom. This one here, we re-opened about five years ago. How I got into it was…I work at International Supply Company, which is across the street. They build generator sets for electrical backup…just like down in New Orleans when the floods came through. We provided the electrical backup for them…the giant ones that almost provide enough electricity for one town. Fortunately, they bought the Hub Ballroom after Ray Hanlon had passed away. The company bought this property and building…bought it for storage…and that was one of the reasons this building was bought. This used to be a double-decked ballroom, but now the bottom part is used for storage."

"They knew that I had ran dance establishments, and stuff like that before…and said, "If you want to run it…we'll lease it to you." And as far as a ballroom goes…I had no idea what I was getting into. As far as entertainment otherwise…yes. I knew my old time Rock & Roll, Country…but I'd never worked with Big Band orchestras…and we still have a lot of the bigger orchestras play here, like Jack Morgan, Bill Hardesty…Ken Polson…I've got a whole list over there on the wall. They're going to be here tomorrow…Ken Polson. So, this is going to change from a big rodeo tonight, to a ballroom tomorrow. Most of the bands are not local, which makes them more expensive."

"That's how this place is working. To keep the ballroom going, we have to have stuff like the mechanical bull...karaoke...anything that is different, that's never been a part of The Hub in the past. We put in game rooms...just stuff to help make money...you know. Back then...that was just never a part of a ballroom. When you went to a ballroom, it was suits and ties and dresses...and you know, really nice clothing. It's not that way any more."

"Now we get anywhere from 75 to 100 people, and the place seats 650. It used to seat more with the double ballroom...but not anymore. We like to keep it as nostalgic as we can...so we keep things looking the same."

"These days, the older generation goes to bed by eight or nine at night, so the younger folks are keeping us in business. The older folks aren't going to wait and go out at nine at night to be entertained. So, when we do our big bands on Sundays...we do them at three in the afternoon. That way, they're over by 6:30...and everyone can be in bed by 9 o'clock. But, big bands are starting to draw a younger crowd. There is a show on TLC, "Ballroom Bootcamp"...which is starting to bring back stuff like this nostalgic style of dance...ballroom dancing."

"You know, Conway Twitty played here once...and this was before there were any motels close by, so he stayed down there at the Rocket Motel...down there on Route 29. You know where that is? They're still in business...just like us."

"There was talk that this building may be sold again, and then someone else may take over the business. But, this is getting way too much for me. It's got the biggest overhead that I could ever imagine...you know, as far as a business. It takes someone that has a lot of money, and a lot of time to keep a place like this going. The count goes up and down of course and we don't take anything out of the business...it all goes right back in. We build up the count with an activity like the mechanical bull."

"We never dreamed that would be one of our biggest activities that we do here. It don't have anything to do with dancing...it's just something that the younger generation goes for. It's not like it was, so we gotta do things that will attract the younger people...whatever that is."

185 *Pat Crouch*

"I was the oldest one of four...my brother was the youngest, and the rest of us were girls. I always went out and drove the tractor and worked right along with my dad. I worked on a farm with my dad, between Brimfield and Princeville...Monica. At one time they had a post office in Monica, but they've done away with that."

"I'm a checker at the IGA, and I just celebrated my 50th wedding anniversary. The kids planned it...we had two hundred people. It was so good to see all of our friends. We were just overjoyed. It was wonderful to see people from prior years. We're still talking about it."

186   *Susan Lawson*

"My name is Susan. I am 47. I have lived here all my life…never left town. I work at Caterpillar, and I take care of the VP's…do presentations, computers…make 'em look good. I love my job. Right now I am working on…I'm a move coordinator for the whole building. I'm moving everybody in the building…moving people from other buildings, over to our building. So, I'm coordinating, maybe 300 people, to be done by the end of the year."

"I've got a big family, and we have a lot of fun. Ummm…ummm…got four kids…ummm…I have two older boys. It's very funny, 'cuz right now they are comparing *who* in the family…likes *who* better. You know, my one son…everybody likes him better than the other kids."

"Right now, I have a son that is 22 years old son that is on the list for a pancreas transplant. It's a big thing. He's got diabetes, and he's real bad. He has a lot of seizures, and passes out. They're pretty bad…so, we've just been working on that. We just found out, this month, he's going to be on a list in Chicago to get a transplant. Curing the diabetes is really an important thing right now. He got diagnosed when he was sixteen. So, he's insulin dependent. My mom, my sister, and brother…all have the older kind, you know…they just have to watch their diet, take pills."

"My son also has Crohn's, which has been real tough. Crohn's affects the digestive system…and two years ago, he was just in horrible pain. We took him to the hospital and found he had a perforated small bowel…out of the blue. I really cried that day, 'cuz they said it was Crohn's, and I knew what a life with that would be. So, he's had a rough life…came within six hours of dying. They had to do emergency surgery. His diabetes has been real bad…so, hopefully this will give him a new outlook on life…actually give him a life. When we were there in March, there were a hundred people on the list, and they say it goes pretty fast. Hopefully, four or five months, we should get it."

"My daughter is a big dancer. We just got back from Myrtle Beach. She's a good dancer. Myrtle Beach is great. We drove down and I think she danced on Monday and Tuesday. She did a duet, and got third overall, out of forty groups…for twelve and under. There were a lot of people, and we had fun. We went to Dick's

Restaurant, which is real fun. It's like Ed Debevic's where they are really bad. They make hats out of condoms…pretty funny stuff. We had a good time. We also went to Marguarittaville, the Jimmy Buffet thing. We went out on the beach and lost the dance-owner's daughter…she was with us and wandered off. That wasn't a good thing. She just went with some other people. It wasn't a major thing, it was kind of a funny thing afterwards."

"I'm a good mom…and also the life of the party. Once, there was this big manager at CAT…he was always kind of this, sexist kind of guy. I had been there about six months, and came back…I had been married and divorced…so, I was dating this other guy. One day he said, "You know, that Tom is a pretty good looking guy. How did you ever get him?" I said, "Well…the blow job helped."

187   *Daniel Bronski*

"I climbed Castleton Tower last March. It's a 500 foot free-standing tower in the middle of the desert…in Utah. It's one of the fifteen most classic climbs in the United States. It's this 500 foot tower with this big crack going up one side. The whole way up, you look down…and you can see 1000 feet down. These mountains are everywhere. It's this big, huge valley with this tower in the middle, and mountains everywhere."

I just moved here six months ago from Iowa. You'd think that there isn't much climbing there…but, there's more climbing in Iowa than there is in Illinois. But around here, there's a place over here in an old grain silo…Upper Limits. It's not Castleton, but…it's something."

"I go to ISU and work at a health food store. It's not Whole Foods, but…it's something."

188   *Sandy French*

"I am 57. I'm proud of it, because every birthday I celebrate is alright with me. I was born in Dallas, but my family moved a lot…so I don't know what to call my hometown…Cincinnati, Indianapolis, New Orleans, Springfield. My father was an insurance adjuster. I guess I am a native Texan, but you'd never know it by the accent. I work at Converse on Main Street."

"From kindergarten to freshman year…first semester, I lived in Cincinnati, Ohio…in Price Hill, on a place called Belvor Lane. We had a really close-knit group of kids. We would play with each other at night. Our subdivision actually backed up on a cemetery, and in those days…in Cincinnati at least, the cemeteries were segregated. This was a black cemetery, an African-American cemetery. We used to play "ghosts in the graveyard", and games like that. We were never really worried about the ghosts because we figured they were black, and you couldn't see them. They had a trash heap where they would take the really, really ugly…old plastic flowers…and put them there to be burned. We would take those and play "bride" and things like that, with those flowers. Then my sister, she was the terror of the neighborhood…she would chase people with dog poop on a stick. It was a really ghoulish kind of childhood…but anyway, I don't think I'm too weird now for all of it."

"The day before Mothers Day this year…we had an accident with the first new car we bought since 1980. We bought a PT Chrysler convertible…PT Cruiser convertible. We love the car. We were sitting at a red light at Sterling and Nebraska, waiting to turn right on red, and a lady turning left onto Nebraska, turned left in front of a young lady driving a Sebring convertible. She was seventeen. The lady that turned in front, spun around and went into the side of our car. Perry was driving and we had the top down. The whole car was just mashed. I was looking the other way, so I didn't see it…and I feel guilty about this to this day. The lady who caused the accident by turning in front of the other one, she was severely injured, and her mother was killed…in the accident. We didn't know it at the time."

"The rear end of her car ended up in our car, and Perry looks over, and we could only see one lady. We didn't know there was a lady dying, or dead in the back seat. I feel so guilty to this day. Perry looks over and says, "You stupid woman." I then said, "Oh shit, this was a new car." We picked it up on May 7th of 2004, so it was a year old when it was hit…exactly a year old. We then heard that the woman driving the car was severely injured, and that she lost her mother…and that she is now in a nursing home, and she's even younger than I am."

"What was lucky is…I think God put a bubble over us…the lady's rearview mirror flew through her rear window, hit Perry on the hand, and when they opened the car and got me out, it was laying next to me. It missed me. It shredded the seats, but I only had one little cut. Perry had a cut. We didn't even have to go to the hospital. We should have been hurt…just looking at the pictures afterwards…but we were not. So now, every time we go through that intersection, we say a little prayer for Betty Calloway's soul…and for Shelia Grimes, her daughter."

189   *Jeremiah Schaub*

"My name is Jeremiah Schaub and I am 26 years old. I work at Hot Topic in Northwood's Mall. I am a keyholder, which is partial management...main focus is to get customers exactly what they want. I walked into the store one day, just talking to one of the girls that worked there and said, "Hey, you guys hiring?", and they said "Yeah, as a matter of fact, we are...here's an application." I filled it out and got the job immediately."

"My first tattoo right here, is a Slipknot tribal "S". It's a band symbol, and it was my first tattoo. I didn't really know not to get something that everybody else was gonna have...but I got this here, so that in case I ever grow out of the band, my last name starts with an "S" also...so I can say it stands for my last name. However, now that I'm friends with the band, I doubt if I'm going to grow out of them."

"This next tattoo was my nickname, *Monster*. It's got the monster tattooed, and it's got 513 in there, which also happens to be my anniversary. I think it's cool that it helps to spell out *Monster*."

"This next one is a portrait of Marilyn Manson. All three of his symbols in there...shock symbol, the omega, and the mercury. This one...to me...I've been a big Marilyn Manson fan for awhile, but the reason I got Marilyn Manson tattooed on my body is because he is the reason I met my wife...in high school. She was...and this was in a time before Marilyn Manson was popular...you know, scaring parents and everything...nobody knew who he was, and I was just starting to get into him. I saw a girl walking through the hall with a Marilyn Manson shirt...and it's like, "That's very odd, I've got to meet this girl." So, I went up to her and said, "Hey, nice shirt." She just kinda kept walking and didn't know who I was. The next day I saw her and she was wearing a "Nine Inch Nails" shirt, which was also kinda rare at the time. I'm like, "Hey...cool shirt." She just kept walking. The third day I saw her, she had a KMFDM shirt, which was unheard of at the time. KMFDM stand for "Kein Mehrheit Fur Die Mitleid", roughly translated means "Nobody For The Majority". So, she like...I went, "Oh my God, she's wearing a KMFDM shirt...it's awesome...I've gotta meet her. So, I went up to her again, "Nice shirt."...and...nothing."

"So, the day I finally got to catch up to her, she was wearing a Manson shirt again, and happened to be talking to a group of friends. I knew one of the girls she was talking to, so I went up to 'em and said, "Hey, how are you doing?...and then looked at the girl and said, "Hey, nice shirt." She looked up at me and said...and I was wearing a Manson shirt too..."Yea, you too." We started talking...hit it off...and we been married for six years and been together for nine...and it's very wonderful. If I ever meet Manson, I'll have to thank him, because he is the reason we met."

"The next tattoo I got was my lucky rocker hand...no, I got a cartoon monster...it's got the Frankenstein, and bride of Frankenstein behind a castle, and I'm really, really big into monsters...I eventually want to have a monster sleeve. I might do it different and have all white kitty monsters and stuff...at least the top half of my arm."

"This guy right here is the lucky rocker hand, a big symbol with concertgoers...it used to be the number one, then it was peace, and now it's the lucky rocker hand. It's not like a lucky rabbit's foot. It's a lucky rocker hand."

"These guys right here...I wanted to keep the idea of traditional swallows, but change them up a little bit. So, we changed them into horror movies. Remember Freddy Krueger and stuff...and Pinhead? So, I've got the inferno behind Freddy and the box behind Pinhead."

"This is my newest one...which is a mummy pinup girl. All of these, I've gotten at Nick's Tattoos. I've pretty much gone in and let the artist do what they want, and you see the amazing work you get when you just let them go on their own. I think the pain of getting a tattoo is worth it...for the art. One thing...people always stare at me as I'm walking along...and my name might be Monster, but looks can be deceiving...I'm a nice guy."

190   *Dave Stovall*

"I'm a UPS driver by trade. My name is Dave Stovall...and I'm 46. I've been with UPS for 27 years, and I drive over the road at night...up to Rockford...the airport, and then on the weekends, I am an entertainer. I do an Elvis Presley tribute show, and perform quite a bit. I play at Graceland every year during tribute week. I've got a huge show coming up at the dome...August...play there in August."

"I've done a lot of neat things. I've done a lot of different parties, started off at a lot of, you know...little hole-in-the-wall taverns, then just kept trying to improve the show, making it better. I've got to do some really neat things. I've had as many as seven shows in one weekend...a couple were just appearance-type of things...so, not too bad. A couple were like, two or three hour gigs...so I was pretty wore out by time I got through. Sometimes I don't play for a couple weeks...like, this week I'm off."

"I always liked Elvis and then when that show was on TV back in the eighties...ummm..."Puttin' on the Hits", and a buddy of mine said...and I wasn't even aware I had hair like his, I just kind of parted it and it wasn't this thick and you know...black...he was like, "Why don't you enter that contest at the Holiday Inn on Brandywine?" So, I thought about it, and studied for almost like a....well, I always been interested in Elvis...I studied for like, a week, real heavy, and then went out there and lip synced to "Burning Love" and got second place...you know. The Blues Brothers were big around here at that time, so they got first. I just kind of took it from there and developed it into an act...and ummm...when the karaoke stuff came around, I started singing more, and working on that. Now, it's a full blown show...I have fifty something lights I hook up."

"The whole bit...yep it's pretty neat. I get to be Elvis."

191   *Bryan Thomas*

"I was born in Galveston, Texas...but I live here now. I am 23. I was three years old when we moved here. My parents got divorced...so I moved up here with my mom. I don't keep in touch me my dad at all. He's a jackass."

"I'm a body modification artist at Mojo Studios...primarily with body piercings, and sometimes large gauge work...and stuff like that. Working at a tattoo shop, I just stick with the piercing. I work on a walk-in basis and do navels, eyebrows, nostrils...basic stuff, but occasionally do more. I do some intense modification work also. That would be surface piercing...back of the neck...center of the chest...and a lot of large gauge stuff. The gauge size is actually the size of the piercing itself...a large diameter around. Normally you do a small little hole, but these are large holes that are big enough to stick your finger through."

"I've gotten a few people that have come in and gotten piercings on the head of their penis. Nothing is strange to me anymore. They make some great sounds when they're getting that done. It's fairly intense...there's a lot of pain involved. There are a lot of places where certain piercings just won't work out. A lot of it is just anatomy dependent...where it is, where the muscles flex, and stuff like that. A lot of people want stuff that I can do, but won't heal...so from a professional standpoint, I advise them against doing that."

"My mom is sitting right over there, so I can't really talk about some things, but the best time I ever had in my life was the first time I got laid. It was awesome. I won't say how old I was...I was a little bit of a late-bloomer. My mother is sitting right over there...but, the whole event really didn't last that long. It lasted maybe three minutes...and there's really not a lot to divulge in those three minutes. That's a joke."

"The first time I had a marker when I was a kid, I didn't draw on paper...I had the natural reaction to draw on my skin. I had a desire to modify myself...and I never really fit in with the "norm" of society, so to speak. I started reading on the Internet about piercings...and why people got heavily into it. I found a lot of meaning in the whole tribal culture aspect of it...people using piercings, scarification, tattoos, and stuff like that, as a right of passage. You know, not just going into a place and saying, "Wow, this looks cute.", but putting some meaning into it. Obviously it all hurts, all leaves a mark…and the jewelry is just a reward, and you get scared each time. I've had hundreds of piercings, and each time that I do it, I still get anxious…I still get nervous. Every time I do it, I am that much stronger by one thing. I have earned that right…by experiencing that little bit of pain. I've earned that and moved on. I find a lot of strength in myself and become a better person because of it."

"Unfortunately society pretty much judges a book by its cover. It's hard to kind of look beyond the ink or the piercings and try and see why that person does it…and that's where the true beauty lies."

"I went out on the bridge today…they had this thing called "Meet Me in The Middle" where people from both sides of the river met at the reopening of the McCluggage Bridge. I listened to the mayors…and LaHood, and others. I pretty much don't care what they say. Our representative is too much a pain in my ass…as far as the tattoo industry. They keep enacting harder laws and make it more difficult for us to stay in business…make a living for ourselves…when it's really, none of their business. It's too much of "upper white class suburbia" trying to decide what is best for all of us…when they don't take the time to research anything. They just decide, "Well, I don't want my child having a tattoo…so, in the state of Illinois, the age limit needs to be 21." But, if I'm eighteen, I can go out and vote…go in the Army. But in Illinois, the age of consent is 21 for a tattoo. They're in the process of trying to change it, but our representative just vetoed the bill going through…like four or five times now. It just pushes the law back…and he was actually trying to make the law stricter…to where no one is allowed in our shop whatsoever if they are eighteen. So, I did not pay attention to what they were saying because I could give a rat's ass about their opinions."

"I would like people to be more open-minded and discover who they really are. I want them to not be so biased, and have an open mind…quit worrying about what the other guy thinks, because in the end…none of it matters…you either leave this life a happy person or you don't."

192   ***Roxy Whitmore***

"We're pissing away $177 million dollars a day in Iraq and Afghanistan...for both of these goddamn disasters. Billions and billions of dollars. We're getting our guys killed and injured...for what? You know, to put this in perspective a little...I just read this...a billion seconds ago, you know what year it was? It was 1959. A billion days ago, humans weren't even around...but a billion dollars was only about eight hours ago, at the rate we're spending money. Iran and Korea are on the horizon...and where are we gonna get the money to do them?"

193   *Lori Fleming*

"I was born in Washington, DC, raised outside of Detroit, lived in Kalama-zoo...and now I'm staying right around the corner...you can see the roof if you stand right here."

"I was young enough when we left Washington, that I don't remember it at all. Both of my parents were working for the State Department. My father at one point worked for the CIA...but it never appeared on his resume, and my mother was working for Southeast Asian Affairs at the time they wrote the China White-paper. My anecdotal information on that, is that it was the paper on why a war in Southeast Asia could not be won. I think that was 1951. My mother then became a housewife, and my father became an automobile executive."

"I had a really good day last week...I found out that a legal suit I had won, after two years...I'm actually going to get a check. Also that same day, I found out a major corporation wants to interview me...and they actually scheduled the inter-view for next week."

"I was...*was*...a marketing and sales representative for an industrial company, and right before 911, we went into a recession. The headquarters of the business I was working for decided to sell off the business. So, I was laid off and spent a year and a half going to interviews. The jobs that I interviewed for...they were just all put on hold. So, I opened my own business, which has certainly been full of its own challenges. Occasionally, I will throw out a resume, because it will help me financially. I always wanted to open my own business...but really, not for another five years."

"I owned a store that had 2500 feet of this kind of stuff. I had a little money...and so decided to start a business. I originally started the business in a town where the major employer was Pfizer...basically a recession-proof business. Stryker was the other major employer...along with two universities. Pfizer bought another business and ended up moving a lot of employees out of town. So, I had this business...and when they moved, all the white collar jobs, all the peripheral businesses moved a year later. So, the first movement was white-collar R&D jobs...and then the supplier base that supported those. As there are certain down-periods in my business, as in any business…I decided to hit the road and promote my business. That's why I'm here. I'm plugging the holes."

"I actually enjoy selling this stuff…Tupperware, because it really is an excellent product…not just a good product…an excellent product. People think it is expensive, and it can be a little pricey, but the lifetime warranty more than makes up for it. They've come out with so many new things…and the microwave dishes are probably the best."

"These here are called "Rock 'N Serves" They do not stain…spaghetti and things like that…they don't stain. They don't pit when they go in the microwave. They go in with the seal on, and all you do is you rock this tip to vent it. You know, steam moves a locomotive…so you know what it's going to do to your seal if you don't let the air out. When you take it out, the handles stay cool, and you don't have to get the hot pads out…like you would with corning ware, or something that's, you know…glass. They've got little feet on the bottom, and the rounded corners. It's got a fill line…this frosted line here, so that you know how full to fill it. This little thing pops off so you can clean it, if you do get some boil-over. It's just like a little teeter-totter. Of all the Tupperware…I think I love the Rock 'N Serve the best. It goes in the dishwasher…freezer, microwave, and this goes in my lunch all the time. The frosted bottom is great, because you can cut in it…and you can't see the cut marks…or scratches. You know how sometimes you will scrape in a bowl, and get scratches? You won't see that. They came out with other colors…clear with a black seal. They even have them with NASCAR logos on them. There is a set with the large divided dish…the large deep dish…two medium shallows, and then a medium deep. Now, when you buy one set for $69.50, you get a second set free."

"Today I watched the news about the hurricane damage in New Orleans, and Mobile…from Katrina, Hurricane Katrina. I don't mean to make light of the situation down there…I know how devastating it is…but, there was a shot on CNN…it showed Lafayette Street…and floating on the water, amid all kinds of debris…were some Tupperware containers with bread inside. It looked like bread. Do you know Lafayette Street? That's the street where Lee Harvey Oswald would hand out leaflets that talked about supporting Castro. That street…that area…including Camp Street, was a hotbed of activity in the late 50's and early 60's. Now, it's just gone."

194   *Laura Picker*

"Occasionally, I have students that come up to me and say, "That was a really good class, and we really got something out of today." I get that occasionally…not every day. That makes it more valuable when you get that, occasionally. Like…just this summer I saw this complete…full, double rainbow, right over my mom's house…right as she was getting married…there was this beautiful double rainbow above us."

195   *Bill Staines*

"I'm 58, and I grew up in Massachusetts...and I've lived in New Hampshire for thirty or forty years...thirty years. I'm from Lexington. Lexington is Lexington of "Lexington and Concord", and Paul Revere. When I was growing up, at least musically, Boston was my hometown. The Boston music scene...it was just a wonderful time to grow up. It seemed like there were a lot of musicians in my class...and it seemed like folk music was...it was a pop music...even before James Taylor. I would go to high school concerts and see people like Joan Baez and Buffy St. Marie...the Kingston Trio. It was just a great time. I got to know a lot of people that later went on to become legends in the music scene. Lexington is a suburb of Boston, and it was just great growing up there."

"It would have been 1964...I believe it was, it was that civil rights summer, and I was just out of high school. The Folklore Center in Harvard Square used to do a weekend marathon hootenanny, and anybody could sign up if they wanted to. They would pass the hat all weekend. It ran from about noon on Friday...and continued until about midnight on Sunday. They would pass the hat to people standing on the street. People would stand in front of the Folklore Center...and all the money went to some sort of charity that they named beforehand, which was how they got the permits to close down the streets and stuff."

"One weekend that I was playing there, was the weekend that they discovered the bodies of the three civil rights workers. The money, instead of going to the local charity was going to SNICK...Student Non-Violent Coordinating Committee. So...the city cancelled the permit...and they had to hold it in a church...on the second floor...in Kenmore Square in Boston. I spent three days there with people like Tom Rush and Jim Queskin and Tim Hardin...just a whole slew of people that were coming in at 2 o'clock in the morning. I remember one time, Jim Queskin sweeping up the floor...and I just stayed there those three days. I was seventeen...and I remember when there wasn't anyone to play, I would get up on stage. It was just a great...great musical time to grow up."

"The person to give me my first gig was Jerry Corbett...and he was singing with Jessie Collin Young at the time...Jessie and Jerry...and they became The Youngbloods. So, all of these people came out of Boston and went on to become legendary people of the 60's...folk groups and folk rockers. I remember that weekend distinctly because I stayed up for three days without sleeping. Maybe I caught a nap here and there, but I just met so many people coming through…and it was just a wonderful time. Aside from the politics and everything that was going on in the country…it was just amazing to hear the music…all these people together in one place, in one weekend."

"The Sunday afternoon concert at the 1965 Newport Folk Festival…I was there with some friends of mine, just out of high school, and the Sunday afternoon concert was billed as what they called "The New Folks Concert"…although the people in the concert weren't necessarily new in folk music, they hadn't had the festival in years because of some problems with the town…and when they started it again…they called it "The New Folks Concert". Gordon Lightfoot…Kathy and Carol…The Chambers Brothers…The Farinas…just a whole load of people…. and after I had listened to Lightfoot and heard the type of music he had done, I really walked away from that festival knowing who I was as a musician. From that one particular concert…I knew the type of music I wanted to play. That concert literally changed my life…it was just a really important event for me. That whole weekend, Ian and Sylvia…Pete Seeger…Odetta…all these people had an effect on me. It was just a real special time."

"*This* is the only thing I know. I got out of school and started singing in the coffee houses, and I'm still doing the same thing forty years later. I've been doing this full time sine 1969. It's really all I know. I live in New England…and work three nights a week, east of Buffalo and north of Washington. I'll be in Philadelphia one night, and the next I'll be in Syracuse…then a little town in Vermont. Then, I do three month-long tours a year. This is the 26th year I have done this fall tour. I wrote a song called "Child of Mine" that I think is as good as any song I have written. I guess "River" is what would be considered my signature song. I usually finish the show with it."

"My dad left home when I was about twelve years old. You know, we saw each other…but he and my mom were separated. The thing I remember most about him was that he was a violin player…not an exceptional player, but he played in quartets and things like that. My first instrument was a clarinet, and when I was in fourth…fourth through seventh grade…he would sit down and sort of lead me through these practices, you know…and it got to the point where I really looked forward to it, because I would do my scales, and he would do these harmony parts to them…and I really…it really gave me a sense of how beautiful music can be. It was fun to sit down and play…and he also played the mandolin…and I would sit in his lap while he played "Red Wing", and other fiddle tunes. So, later on in life I realized what I had missed after he left…but that's the way it is for a lot of people."

"When I started writing songs in 1965, whenever I would write a song…I would record it. At the time, it was rumored that if you recorded a song, and mailed it to yourself with the date on it, and didn't open it up…that was sort of the poor man's way of copyrighting it, because it had a government stamp on it, and the date. It doesn't really hold up now…but, the point is that all through my life, my musical life…whenever I have recorded something, I have kept two copies of it. I have kept a journal since 1978…so there are volumes of that. I've got all that…still have the tapes of me singing when I was seventeen…and it's probably sludge at this point…but, songs that I couldn't even remember, that I had written…are in a cabinet in my house. It's like a bookcase…and the bottom part of it is filled up with songs from music I was doing for Burlington Northern Railroad…and all the stuff that you'll never…nobody will ever hear that stuff. There are like…thirty second pieces of music. All that stuff is there."

"If I suddenly have two hours left to live, I could put a ribbon around that cabinet and say, "I am out of here…and there I am." Not a lot of people can do that. They are very successful, but what they have done with their lives has been like…creating clouds. They've invented marketing schemes and things like that. They've made a lot of money…but the marketing schemes are now out of date, because something else has taken their place. Some people go to work everyday completing a process, and then they come to work the next day…and it needs to be done over again."

"There's nothing wrong with that, except at the end of your life, you say, "What have I done?" You can say, "Well, I've got a nice house, I've got a nice family…I've put the kids through school…I've done it all, lived the dream…but…who am I? I know who I am. I can wrap a ribbon around my bookcase and say, "There I am."

196   *Ruth Mitchell*

"I think it's always best to tell the truth, because…and I know this from experience…it gets hard to remember what you said. That's just me…but, I know some people who have really good memories, and they are pretty good liars. In that case, it might be best to tell a lie."

197   *Candy Werneburg*

"I am 37...and I live in Princeville. I am working in the yard today."

"Princeville is a nice small town. We have everything that you need here, as you would in a big town...except for crime. You see people walking and riding their bikes. They are out all day long, and also at night. There are more and more people building these big houses just outside the community...but we still have a hard time keeping businesses alive here."

"I used to own a business in Princeville...a video store. I was working at Alcoa and got hurt...an injury. I was a packer and got hurt on a piece of equipment that they failed to...change the way they were doing things...so, I decided to quit because I was going to get re-injured. My husband also worked there...and since we still had the one income...I decided to start my own business. It lasted for four years, and when the economy fell, I decided to close the business, instead of losing what I owned. I walked out of my building, went across the alley, and into the back door of my home."

"In town, we have three restaurants now, two taverns...a funeral home, a pharmacy, a hardware store, a Casey's...an ice-cream shop, several churches...and a monastery that is further out. There are three banks in the area...ummm...a pallet plant. There is a canning factory...Seneca Food Canning Factory. Can you smell the pumpkin? There are a lot of Mexicans that work here and live here. They come in...and a lot of them are from Texas. They come in and stay for the summer, and then they go. The school system is set up to provide for them. The kids go year-round. At the canning factory, they used to have little huts...little houses where they would live. I think...they don't do that anymore. I think a lot of them rent places now, and live in trailers, and also live with family that is already here."

"My dog's name is Toby. He's a fox terrier, and he's our baby. I had a big cockatoo when I owned the video store...and when I closed that...we chose to find a new home for the bird. It was difficult on me because I had owned her for two and a half years...raised her. So, we decided...my husband and me...decided to get another pet. We love our pets...we love all pets. We shopped at all the humane societies, and couldn't find anything. We looked in the paper and drove an hour away to look at him. He was the last of the litter…and he was waiting for us. He fits in our little family now, just perfectly."

"My husband…him and my brother-in-law…because me and my sister are married to brothers…were out trimming trees over in Chillicothe. My brother-in-law was up in the tree cutting a limb, and my husband was down on the ground with a rope in his hand…coiled around his arm. Now, when my brother-in-law cut the limb, the limb weighed more than my husband…and he shot up in the air with…with the rope on his arm. He had to literally run up the tree or smack into the tree. When the limb fell and hit the ground, the rope released…and he came down. It would have been nice to have a video camera…and sent it to "America's Funniest Home Videos". It was…you know, a Three Stooges moment."

"As you can see, I am picking grape tomatoes…lots of them. There are two bushes here, and they have taken over my yard. My husband…he eats them like candy."

198-199   *Pam and Michael Parks*

"Ummm...how old do I want to be? Okay, I'm 53. I'm from Champaign...and I'm retired. I was an administrative secretary at the U of I."

"I'm Mike Parks. I'm 56. We basically...we basically rode up here from Champaign to get something to eat. We rode up on our motorcycle...in November...cold November, to eat at Joe's. It's pretty cold, and that's why we're not gonna ride back tonight."

"I'm from Alabama originally...Selma, Alabama. That's the place where Martin Luther King had the second most famous march...from Selma to Montgomery. I left there in 1967...joined the Air Force, and then got stationed at Chanute in Rantoul. I'm now retired from the University of Illinois, where I was a sheet metal worker."

"We been married 32 years. We met in Washington D.C....at a party, after some demonstrations about the Vietnam War. That was in 1971."

"I went back to Alabama after we first met...and I didn't take her with me. I thought about her all the way down there, and all the way back."

"We got married and ran around for four years...then we had three kids. We have five grandkids...well, we'll have five grandkids. One is due in January...so, we have four now."

"We spent our honeymoon in Seattle. We both took off a month. We towed our motorcycle there, took a week to get there...stayed two weeks...and then took a week to get back."

"We did a lot of motorcycle riding...a lot of traveling. We been to the Bahamas, Aruba, St. Thomas...ummm...Guadeloupe...all over the United States. We've met Hillary Clinton, James Brady...and just met the university president and the chancellor of the university. We also met a guy who just donated $17,000,000 to the university. We also met Bonnie Blair...we met her."

"In fact...our daughter used to speed skate with Bonnie Blair. Our daughter set a record in the 777...a 777 meter race...short track speed skating. Bonnie Blair has thighs like this, and so does our daughter. Our daughter is very impressive."

"We're thinking about going up the street here to the Rhythm Kitchen. They got this guitar player named Freddie Jenkins that we heard was pretty good. Rosa Parks died...and I'm not related to her...just have the same last name...and we heard they was playing some 70's soul music at the Rhythm Kitchen...and doing something for Rosa Parks...you know, a tribute or something."

"Rosa Parks, you know...back in 1955...she was like, the...the mother of the civil rights movement...but one thing you might not know is...she worked with the NAACP for a long time. She was part of a whole movement at the time. In other words, she didn't do it alone...there were a lot of brave folks that was behind her. But...she was a hero for doing what she did, because nobody knew what was gonna happen."

"I think people like Rosa Parks are sometimes looked at like they were saints, that they're somehow better...more noble than the rest if us...by the media. It kinda gives people the impression that, you know, that from the moment they were born...they were called to do what they did. A lot of people don't think about, you know, ordinary people...people like us, that fought for civil rights."

"You know, sometimes people don't get things done...like some of the earlier things that Rosa Parks did...and people, you know...like her. Sometimes they succeeded, even if it was just a little bit...and sometimes they triggered something from the heart...like what happened after she was arrested. But, history was changed by that woman...because even with all the...the uncertainties of what would happen...she did it. She was the one."

"We been married 32 years. That might not have been possible before Rosa Parks...and people like her. People like us...we all changed the world."

200   *Cynthia Bond*

"I log into my email account and I get this pop-up for classmates.com…every time. There's a reason why I haven't talked to any of my classmates in twenty years. I don't particularly like them. Not only that, but even at my age…I read in the paper about all these people I went to high school with…dying, of one thing or another. It's very depressing."

201   *Latisha Jackson*

"My name is Latisha Jackson...and I am 23...23 years old."

"Well, one thing...I found out why I been so bitchy, moody, and needy lately. Yep...you got it...I'm pregnant. I went to the doctor last week. Took a test at Walmart two weeks ago...don't ask. It was positive. I took another one when I got home. Damn thing read positive before it was all the way through the friggin control window."

"I been so damn tired lately...tired beyond belief. I been sleeping ten to twelve hours a night. I been told that it's like this in the first trimester. I didn't know that I was in my first trimester...with my first boy...so I missed this part. But lemme tell you...a day at work just physically takes me out...to the point that it's everything I can do to even drive to the friggin daycare to pick up my boy. This is crazy...nuts. This shit is ridiculous. I barely have the energy to open my mail. Thank God Jimmy was home to deal with Michael...'cuz I went to bed at 7 last night and slept till 6:30 this morning...except for the three or four times I had to get up and pee."

"Everybody pretty much knows how much it sucks ass being fat and overweight. But try being fat and overweight when you're pregnant. It pretty much sucks ass. Do you have any clue how expensive them damn plus-size maternity clothes are? Again...it sucks ass. And of course, no place around here carries plus-size maternity. The closest is across town. I know there's tons of stores on the Internet...but I ain't got no credit card. So there goes that option. I'm gonna need work clothes. I have a pair of maternity pants, some blue-jean bibs, and one decent shirt left from my first one...but that's it. Now...I won't be showing for at least a couple more months...but still...I like to be prepared as I can...and so far...it ain't gonna happen."

"There has been one good thing about this pregnancy...I quit smoking. I ain't had no cigarette since three days ago."

"With my boy...when I was pregnant with him...I was at the mall and was drinking a damn coke...and this woman come up to me, "You do know that drinking soda is bad for your baby". I was so pissed...who made her God? It's not like I was sitting there smokin' a joint and guzzling down a beer. So I drank me a coke...big friggin deal. I told the woman to mind her own damn business. I still get mad thinking about that."

"Another time...I was on the escalator and this woman starts rubbing my belly and telling me that I should talk to it all the time so that the baby will know my voice. Since when has my body become public friggin property? Did I say you can touch me? Just 'cause I'm pregnant don't give everybody the right to touch me and tell me what I should and shouldn't be doing. When you see a pregnant woman...try to keep from touching and telling us what we should be doing."

"Oh yeah...and if you ever get pregnant and your OB puts you on prenatals with stool softeners...it's a lie. There's no friggin stool softener in those damn things...trust me."

202   *Amy Sielaff*

"My sister writes…my mother writes…I write. I have a couple of books started. I have one started about my future mother-in-law that I kind of need to wait on. I used to do poetry…a lot of poetry. But, I probably would not be ready to publish anything for another two years to be honest. I'm one of those people who needs their space…you know what I mean? I have a lot of short essays…just about general things. I am interested in anything having to do with literature. I don't know that I have a favorite author. I have a least favorite genre…I don't like romance novels. I like mostly…I like many crime novels. I like a lot of the sappy…um…underdog-type novels. I like mysteries. Edgar Allen Poe, yes…I like Edgar Allen Poe."

"I've read some things by famous authors, and I can't stand them because…like, one of the things about Steven King…he's a huge author…everybody loves him…but, he just drags on and on. You can get to the middle of one of his books and realize there were a hundred pages you could probably skip. So, my personal opinion is…I don't particularly care for him. But, other people love him."

"There's a book that I like…it's called "The Bitch in the House". It's a compilation of short stories, and they're by everyday normal people talking about…like, a mother talking about everyday life as a housewife. Another is women talking about why they never got married…but, same concept. I think people like that type because it shows them that people are not that different."

"I think a common denominator…at least with me, is that most people that are talented at writing are very…off-kilter. They have some type of mental instability that I can…I can relate to. I think that most are…I don't want to say loners, but they are a little bit more introverted. My friends…they know that I am a little more insecure than the people at work think that I am. People perceive me as being confident and a little bitchier than I really am. There is a different persona at work than at home."

"I was born and raised Catholic, and I consider myself a Christian. What you need to realize about religion…I believe in God, and all that…but, what I choose to believe, isn't what Christians say the Bible tells them. I always get involved in these types of discussions, and sometimes I take the other side. I got into a huge discussion with someone I am close to, a few years back...because they were all, "Well being gay is against, you know, God's wishes." As far as I'm concerned, my opinion on gay people...number one...it's not my business...if it's against God's will, and if there is a god...that's between them. Number two...in the Bible...one of the main things is, you don't judge other people. And number three...if there is a god, there is scientific evidence that shows there is something different in the pituitary gland, and all kinds of things which can determine this. It can be blamed on stress that the mothers were going through...like during the depression and so on. But, what if God put gay people on this earth to teach us acceptance...you know...if there is a god, and all that?"

"I think people need the security blanket...people need to believe, to get through the day, without having to be on Prozac. People need to believe there is a reason for everything. I don't believe in the Bible...verbatim. To me, I think the Bible is like folklore...people sitting around the campfire, telling stories, from generation to generation. Have you ever played the game "Operator", where one person says something, and by the time it gets to the end of the line...it's been distorted? That's how I see the Bible. I don't necessarily believe the prophets when they said they saw all of these things. I believe that the values are good, but not the events. I consider myself a warped Christian."

203   *Deb Johnston*

"I'm dealing with cancer right now...with my mom. Most food doesn't taste right to her...and she isn't that thrilled about going out in public those three days in the week that, you know...she has to wear the chemo drip. For five years my mom has been living with cancer....but no matter how I choose to say it...I know time is running out. I think her bravery is the most incredible thing I've ever seen in my life. She doesn't complain...and her doctor is amazed when she tells him she is not in a lot of pain...even though we know that can change. Mom says she's a bit more tired than she used to be...and she did come to my house on Thanksgiving. She said it wasn't that bad."

"Right before the holidays...Chuck and I parted ways after five years. Mom called him "the chameleon"...which was a well deserved nick-name. So, we decided to have a quiet Christmas Eve...just me, Mom, and her friend Glen. Mom thought it would be aright if she had a Tom & Jerry, so I brought the brandy and the mix. She baked the lutefisk for the first time this year...and we loved it. To non-lutefisk eaters it looks like a massive block of fish Jell-O....and smells like you would imagine fish Jell-O smells. Lutefisk eaters drown it in the best creamery butter with a few good sprinkles of salt and pepper. Mom and I are members of Sons of Norway, Nordland Lodge #544...and we take lutefisk eating seriously. Glen makes a lot of jokes about it that Mom doesn't particularly appreciate."

"When my brother John arrived, he scanned hundreds of Mom's old and new photos for the virtual picture frame that was his gift to her. He set the display to random and we watched it for...hours. A stoic picture of my great grandparents and the log cabin....Mom laughing last Christmas Eve....my dad, Albin, who passed away long ago....the babies...the birthdays....random memories mixed with the present."

204   *Christine Engel*

"I am from here. I have three jobs…I am a mom…I work at a fabric store…and I work at a residential facility for adults with disabilities."

"My best memory wasn't when I was a kid…it was when I became a mom. I was scared to death, but ecstatic at the same time. How can I describe that? I don't know that I can. It was…the best. I was married to a guy who was in the military…he was a Marine. My husband and I are divorced now…he's living in Pekin, not in the military any more. My first son was born in Beaufort, South Carolina, and then my second son was born in Yuma, Arizona…opposite ends of the country."

"We lived on Lady's Island in an apartment…a little strip of apartments behind a strip mall, where the "Upper Crust Pizza" was. Have you ever had that? There's one there and one in Hilton Head. It's awesome…amazing…the best pizza I've had in my entire life. I wasn't impressed with Hilton Head…very touristy…very expensive…not my thing. I wasn't impressed…only went for the day, then turned around and came back. It was nice living on Lady's Island, because my brother was living in Savannah…so we were really close. When family would come down to visit, they would get to see both of us…so that worked out really well. But, being a mom, becoming a mom…that's my very best memory."

"My grandparents aren't alive anymore…they all died before I was eighteen. I am the oldest of seventeen grandchildren. I'm 31…and for twelve years, there was one of us born each year…for a straight twelve year period, out of…ummm…five kids. My dad has four sisters. There are no cousins on my mom's side of the family…and I'm the only one that remembers Grandpa. He died when I was five. Most of my memories of him involve food…sitting and eating donuts with him. He worked at Caterpillar…his brother worked at Caterpillar…and my dad works at Caterpillar."

"If I had to pick a role model, it would have to be my parents, not just one of them…it would be both of them, for different reasons. They've been on welfare…been jobless…been laid off…laid off and on strike. They became students in their 40's. My mom went and got her masters with three kids at home. Good role models."

"This...this is my youngest son, Gavin. I always wanted my kids to know how much I love them...because I don't...I don't get to spend every day with them. They spend half the time with their dad. I met their dad in high school...actually I met a friend of ours at the mall...and started dating a friend of his, and was then introduced to him through that friend. I fixed him up with a girl-friend...they dated for a little while, then broke up. My boyfriend and I dated for a while...and then we broke up. So, we started dating, and I got married at nine-teen, right after high school. We moved away...right away. Two years...two and a half years later, we had two kids, and got divorced after almost five years of mar-riage. Young love...two kids living on Lady's Island."

"My whole family...we get together at Christmas...the extended family, and usu-ally do a pot-lunch type of thing. Sometimes it's just snacks, sometimes it's a full course meal. Every year...every year we have stuffed animals of the "Rudolph the Red Nosed Reindeer" characters, from the cartoon. My mom...that's like, her favorite movie...so, she has all the stuffed animals. I think they sold them at CVS a few years back. It's been at least four years that we do this. Every year, we do a play. My dad reads the story, and the rest of us act it out. We videotape it and send it to our relatives out of state. We do it every year...and it's getting better and better...every year. We're getting better and better every year."

205   *Tony Johnson*

"Me and my girlfriend…I got her down here working with me. I'm trying to be discreet about it…sneaking a present in on her. Now that she down here working with me…I got to be sneakier. I'm running from store to store…and I work three stores down at Roly Poly. I'm running from one store to another store on my own block that I work on…trying to be sneaky. She there now…and I'm on the clock. I got to go. I got to go."

206 *Pam Witzig*

"My name is Pam...Pam Witzig. I'm 52, and I don't know when that happened. I still haven't gotten over my 30th birthday. I was four or five when I left Fairfield...I hardly remember it. I spent most of my childhood in the Decatur area...and when I was very young, we lived in Booty. Have you heard of Booty? There were two or three homes there and no school. Then we moved to Decatur."

"We were in an old neighborhood with a cinder alley...and a neighbor boy, who was a lot like Dennis the Menace, got us into trouble. He threw a dart in my knee one time...so I ran into the house with a dart in my knee...a really sharp dart. Boy, that sucker really hurt. He also hit my sister with an arrow...the kind with a steel point on it. The worst was the time he was using a hammer. My younger sister was looking away...and the claw of the hammer came up into her forehead. There was blood everywhere...blood in the sink. The funny thing about it was, I remember a second grade story I wrote when we were making little books. The teacher was amazed at my writing. I ended the story with, "She came home with stitches in her head and a sucker in her mouth." My second grade teacher was impressed with that."

"I remember playing jacks on the porch with Staley balls. They came from the Staley plant...I don't remember what they were, but they were a byproduct of some kind. We lost lots and lots of Staley balls in the shrubs."

"Daisy was a big-headed black woman who looked after us when Mom was working...my mom she sold real estate. I had never seen a black person before...and she kinda scared me. She was introduced to us...and she stayed with us for a year. She was really sweet...Daisy. Mom would go way out of her way every morning, because Daisy didn't have transportation. There was a bus, but she didn't use it. Daisy had this wig...and she'd take it off and scratch her head.... pretty gross...but she was really sweet."

"I do a lot of things...but mostly, I'm a headhunter. That is my first love. I have an executive search firm that I started in 1986...and we recruit advertising professionals...for advertising agencies...primarily, all over the country. Although, we do a broader blanket, like, marketing communications. It's mostly ad agencies all over the country."

"When no one would hire me, I had a life as a realtor…and interest rates got so high in the early 80's…like fifteen percent…that's when I decided to go to school. I had one semester of a full load at ISU when I was 31. We had five kids at home, and my husband was laid off…and suddenly it was a luxury to be a full-time student when there was no income for seven people. So, I finished that semester, then went to work at an employment agency. Everything needed a four-year degree…even if I were to sell Nabisco in a territory…or pharmaceuticals…they wouldn't talk to me without a four-year degree. I thought it was absurd. I can do anything I put my mind to. They decided to make me an employment counselor…and while I was there…not too long…I decided that I wanted to recruit, and I wanted to work in PR. So, they said, "Yeah, you can create your own desk and work in PR…and advertising." I was there for two and a half years before I decided to go on my own…to do it my way."

"I built a successful company. I have said many times that I am a "Nightingale-Conant" student. Do you know what that is? They are a publisher of audiotapes. Earl Nightingale was really big as a motivational speaker, and was a radio voice in the early years. One of his big books was "Leave the Field"…on tape. The bottom line was…I just believed in myself…and it's what I wanted to do. But, I really did get a lot of confidence in listening to those tapes. It's all about attitude and what you believe you can do. Whatever the mind can believe and perceive it can achieve. So, if you are not capable of a thing, you can't conceive it. If you can conceive it…you're capable of it. If you're capable of it…go do it."

"I know some guys…very simple minds, and they are dishwashers. They are very proud of their jobs. They might work at a grocery store bagging groceries…mentally challenged…but so proud to be making their own way. They ride across town on their bikes with their radios…their prized possession, and…but they just can't perceive of a bigger life than that. I can. I did it because I believed I could."

"I remember leaving Decatur when I went into the "Milwaukee Brace". I have curvature of the spine. I had a bad case of bronchitis when I was nine or ten…and it wouldn't go away…wouldn't go away. That's when they took X-rays and saw the curvature. Even at that age when the nurse said, "Oh, looks like someone wasn't standing straight."…I knew I couldn't possibly stand that way if I wanted to. I actually got the brace after several fittings, on my tenth birthday. It had this leather girdle and these two steel bars in the front, with pads…. one steel bar in the front, and two in the back…crude-looking."

"The summer I got the brace, I moved from Decatur to Lincoln…so I moved…and these kids didn't know me, or knew me only as this…this freak. The only way they knew me was as this kid that came in the classroom with this brace. I wore that brace until I was fourteen. And you know…I think it is true that what they say, "What doesn't kill you makes you stronger." Kids are cruel…and it does build character when you have challenges. I had my challenges…still do…and I *definitely* have character."

207   *Ed "Too Tall" Freeman*

"I'm now 77. I was invited here by the people that put the air show on. They invited myself, the Sergeant Major, Matt Dillon, and Bruce Crandall…who is the CO of the 229…the 229 was involved in the Battle of Landing Zone X-ray"

"I'm originally from Boise, and when I was seventeen years old, my brother got…my brother who was older than me, and was on Luzon…he got a grenade in the face. It took one eye out, and his voice box. I tried to get my momma…my mother, to let me go into the Army…and she said, "Huh-uh". I had a brother in the Philippines that was in Air-Sea Rescue…and she decided the Navy was a safe place to be. She signed for me to go in the Navy, and I went in for two years, and I hated every minute of it. I was on a tanker…a young boy off the farm don't do well at sea…I didn't. It was a miserable time…all we got to do was chip the damn paint off the deck and repaint it. There was no challenge, at all. So, I served my time and got out, came back, and went back to school, and then immediately joined the military…the Army."

"I went to Germany for four years and trained hard 'cuz we thought the Russians was coming…somebody told us that. In four years and seven months, I was a master sergeant…the highest enlisted rank you could be. The Korean War broke out, and I volunteered to go to Korea, because I had missed the other wars. That was me…I was a professional soldier. I had no more said that, and they had me moving out to go to Korea. They were eager to get me there."

"I was assigned to an engineer organization…combat outfit. But, we did not do engineering work…we was committed as infantry because everything was chaos. The whole damn thing was a chaos operation…so we were assigned as infantry and given certain fronts to hold. On the 9th day of April, 1953…cease-fire talks had been going on for over a year. Somebody in the organization decided we should take a hill called "Pork Chop". I went up there with 257 men and I come off with fourteen. I was met, when the battle was over by General Van Fleet…he was the general in charge of the battles, the Army there…and he decided to make me a second lieutenant…gave me a battlefield commission. I had welcomed that because, just before that, I had been injured…and they summoned a helicopter to come pick me up…life-flight…you know, a medivac. They took me out to the helicopter, and I look at this guy. He's got a leather jacket…he's clean-shaven…looked like he'd been fed pretty good, and I said, "Shit, I gotta be one of them…I can't keep this up…I'm running out of green stamps."

"It took me two years to get there because I'm six foot four, and the Army turned me down when I requested flight school. They turned me down and said, "You're too tall." That's where I got this name…"Too Tall"…it just stuck. After two years the Army decided they needed more applicants, so they lowered the height requirement, accepted me, and I flew for the next 36 years. I was in the…I taught in the Huey line at Fort Rucker for a two year period of time. After I retired, I was 39 years old…retired as a Major…and went to work for the U.S. Department of Interior, and flew for another twenty years. I had 16,000 hours just in helicopters, and 8,500 plus in airplanes."

"In Vietnam, this guy indicated…this operations officer, caused us to lift a battalion of people into a little small area, about half the size of a football field. They suspected there were enemy there. Little did they know, there was three regiments. But, we lifted this battalion in there, about 375 men. On the fifth clip…we went four times in there and nobody shot a round at us, and we thought it was a cake walk…on the fifth clip, them son-of-a-bitches came out of that hill, and out of the bunkers, and ate our lunch. I mean, shit, they just shot us up big time…ruined a lot of helicopters."

"Well, we staggered back to the pickup zone, which was about a thirteen-minute flight away…a Special Forces camp. We was reloading and trying to figure out what helicopters would fly and which ones wouldn't. Got it all squared away…and knew we had to go back in there, because these people only had basic food and ammunition, and about a hundred rounds apiece…and that don't last long with an M-16. So, the ground commander, Colonel Moore…he called and said, "No more helicopters can come in…you can't survive." Well, by then, he's engaged three regiments at about twelve to one odds…against him. By the way, this is the same organization that General Custer had…1st and 7th Cavalry."

"A little later, my boss says, "I need a volunteer to go back into Landing Zone X-ray and take ammunition, food, water, and haul out the wounded. I said, "I got it." I was the oldest man in the organization…I was the only man who had been in combat, and I felt the responsibility of leadership among all these young boys…helicopter pilots. So, I got out to my helicopter and fired it up, and the commander followed me out. He's standing there with a gray-headed guy with a dunce cap on…and he followed me out. I said, "What the hell are you doing?" He said, "I'm going too." I said, "What happens if you get zapped, you son of a bitch…who's gonna command the company?" He said, "We'll worry about that when it happens."

"He and I fired up, and we shuttled in and out of that place for fourteen and a half hours. The last flight was at 10:30 at night…hauling loads of wounded out as we came back, and hauling food and medical supplies as we went in. Everything went fine…not so fine…got the shit shot out of us a lot of times. The battle turned, and we had enough ammunition to push them back…eventually, a couple hundred yards away from the zone, and then we could go in fairly loose. Three days of battle was over, and we lost 308 men, and they lost a few thousand."

"It turned out to be the first time we had ever seen a uniformed soldier from North Vietnam. They were all in uniform, and they were well-disciplined, and fighting sons a bitches, 'cuz they didn't give a damn. You'd have to kill every one of them. It was that type of an operation."

"So, basically, they made a movie out of it, "We Were Soldiers", and made a book out of it called, "We Were Soldiers Once and Young". Mel Gibson played the part of the commander. I was played in it as "Too Tall". I was eventually awarded the Congressional Medal of Honor for that day in November of 1965."

"That was our job every day…hauling people into the battle zone, supplying them with their needs…it was the only way we traveled…by helicopter. We had, not quite a thousand helicopters…and 23,000 men, with the 1st Cavalry…Air Division they called us. It was the first organization in the military to operate like that. We took helicopters right to the battle. We would find the enemy with *search and destroy*, they called it. We'd find them and go out and land the troops."

"One thing that I would want people to say about me when I'm dead…"He was a hell of a good soldier.""

208   *Anetta Strawn*

"I work at Cracker Barrel in Bloomington…and it's so much fun. I meet people from all over the world. I get to enjoy, and talk to…and meet all sorts of people. We've had bicyclists through here from France. I've talked to people from Australia and New Zealand. I talk to people from all over…we get a lot of people traveling through…tour busses and so forth. It's a great place for breakfast, but I think the best thing to eat here is the chicken strips. That's what I eat."

209   *Dawn Stewart*

"I'm 31 years old. I lived outside Hanna City for a good part of my life…right off of Murphy Road with my…my grandma, and my dog. Grandpa died before I was born, so I didn't know him at all. He was a farmer…and he sold seed corn…worked for FS, and that's about all I know about him. My grandma was the one who raised me…and she was my best friend. I still keep in contact with my mom, but we don't have a close relationship…at all…she's kind of a meth-head and lives with this…pardon my French…this asshole, in Bartonville. Grandma was really, always my mom…my real mom. She always cried when she talked about my birth mom…she's been in jail several times, and Grandma felt responsible for, you know…how my mom turned out."

"We used to play this game called "exquisite corpse". We would play it when my cousins came over. The idea of the game was to write down the beginning of a sentence, then fold the paper so that the next person could only see the last word you wrote. Based on that word, the next person would add some more to the sentence, then fold the paper again…so that the next person could only see one word. Does that make sense? When the paper had gone through five or six people, then the paper was unfolded and the sentence was read…always by Grandma. The sentences were always strange…you know, something like "The blue…dog sat…in a rainbow…of color, tastes good…like a cigarette should.""

"We also played a version of the game where each person would draw part of a picture, and then do the same type of thing…fold the paper where the next person could only see a few lines…then, based on those lines, the next person would draw another part of the picture. We always had a theme for the picture, like animal or person or machine…you know, something like that. So, we had some interesting pictures…some really surreal looking drawings."

"What I didn't know then…I always thought Grandma came up with the game…but, it was originally played as a…a parlor game by some of the early surreal artists, back in the 20's. Man Ray was one of them, and Miro was another…I don't know who else…whatever surreal artists were alive back then. They would play the same game, and how the game got its name was from the first time they played. I think the sentence they came up with was "The exquisite corpse will drink the young wine.""

"I didn't know any of this until recently when I went to the Art Institute in Chicago. In the section where they have artists like Picasso and Dali...Miro...you know, the surreal artists...they tell the story about how the game was played, and they have drawings that they created from the game. Most of them are much stranger than anything we created when we were kids...but I could see that there were a lot of similarities in how each individual piece, kind of fit together in a surreal sort of way. It said that when the game is played that there is a...sort of...an unconscious reality in the...personality of the group."

"I'm not sure I can explain this properly...but, you know when a group of people get together...they kind of become like-minded...and it's an unconscious type of thing. You know, sort of like when the Nazis got together, they became like-minded...just like any organization...Boy Scouts...Methodists...doctors...they become like-minded. Women, working together go on the same menstrual cycle. I think it's an interesting idea...an interesting concept. It's an unconscious type of thing."

"I always liked Marc Chagall. He is without a doubt my favorite artist. He did a painting called "White Crucifixion" which is...the body of Christ as a Jewish person, surrounded by Jews...Russian Jews...being persecuted by groups of other people. Jesus Christ is wearing a prayer shawl around his waist...with a stream of light shining on him. I think it is supposed to represent the crucifixion from the Jewish point of view...but I could be wrong."

210   *Rizzo*

"My name is Rizzo. I'm 26 years old...from Chicago. I tour with rock bands, doing merchandise...tour manager. We're here today putting on a show, down at the riverfront. I was actually born in Indiana, but grew up in Naperville. I got kicked out at seventeen, and so had to go back to Indiana and live with my mom. I just had your typical teenage disagreements with my dad and my step-mom. It pretty much sucked having to start my senior year at a new high school, but that's what happened. My folks and I had a disagreement about who I was dating, and of course when you're sevent...and there were many underlying problems as well...and of course, when you're seventeen, you're always right."

"This band I'm with is a rock band out of Chicago..."Lucky Boys Confusion". They were previously on Elektra Records...basically, been touring the country...Japan and whatnot for...God...five or six years now. Elektra has a big following in Japan, and they really like to promote bands out there. That was before my time...I've only been with these guys about two and a half years."

"There are so many stories with the band. I don't really know where to begin. Every day with the band is a different story...a lot of them you don't even remember. But, one time, with my very first show...and I was just talking about this in the van on the way home, actually...we used to have this old roadie, and he had a pretty violent temper. We stopped at a gas station...this was my very first show, so I didn't know the guys too well.
The guys went into the gas station, and Willy, our roadie, was looking for a pack of cigarettes that he had, and he thought that somebody stole them...and he just went ape-shit in the van...and started punching the ceiling...screaming...and scaring the hell out of me really. I didn't know what to do. I'm stuck in the van with this guy...and I don't know what to do...so, that was kinda like my introduction. He got fired about a year later for being psycho."

"I took a really cool trip to the Grand Canyon with my girlfriend a couple of years ago. It was our first road-trip together...and we were only together about a year...and it was our first road trip out there, and seeing all the sites and stuff...just doing something different than this. I mean...you see stuff with the band...but it's nice to actually see something else, you know? I took a few days to go to the Grand Canyon, explore it, do some hiking. We tried to make it down to the bottom, but we got to the five-mile point…and by then the sun was so hot, and we were so exhausted, we had to go back up. Luckily we didn't go to the bottom, because we barely made it back up."

"When I am home, I run my own business. I sell business machinery and heavy machinery for companies on Ebay. I am the only one in the Chicago area that concentrates on heavy machinery and business equipment on Ebay. It's pretty cool. When I am home, I make sales calls…I dress up like a big boy…get out there in my shirt and tie, and I've sold everything from, like…anything related to business. I've sold everything from copy machines to forklifts. There's nothing too big. I just sold a milling machine two weeks ago. The thing was 25,000 pounds. People…people just buy anything on Ebay…it's great."

"Our singer's name is Stubhy…his real name is Kastube, but Stubhy was just easier when he was growing up. Guitarist…Adam…another guitarist named Joe. The bass player is Jason…and the drummer is Ryan. My name is Ryan too, but it got too confusing…so they call me Rizzo."

"My family really disagrees with what I do, and I only talk to them a few times a year. It's too bad, but what are you gonna do?"

211   *Laura Kosko*

"I was born in Peoria...my name is Laura Kosko, and I am 23, and I have been here my entire life...never moved away from Peoria. I am currently working at "Just Bead It", and I have worked there two and a half years. We sell beads, links, purses, shoes...kind of a fun little shop...kiosk. I went to Limestone High School and graduated in the year 2000. I am doing more schooling...I just graduated in '03 from Western Illinois University in Macomb with my undergraduate degree in history and political science...and then I just went back to school this last semester...and I'll be going back for my masters, working in secondary education...for history, and I hope to eventually teach high-school history."

"This job that I have at Just Bead It is part-time...I eventually want to get into teaching, and then go on further and work toward a doctorate. So...I am thinking about getting a job here or maybe going further north...depending upon where I want to go to get my doctorate."

"I like the fact that we have all the stores, and everything you could possibly need in Peoria...so you don't have to go to really too many...anywhere else...like up in the Chicago area...but I like it that you're still able to get around. When you drive up to the suburbs of Chicago, you can take twenty minutes on the same road, from stoplight to stoplight. Here you can get to where you need to go. I mean...I live pretty much right in the middle of Peoria, and can get anywhere within fifteen minutes."

"I know a couple of guys in...over in Iraq, from college. Serving from the Peoria area...they are in Company "C"...ummm...Marines. I'm not real happy with that situation. I don't think we need to be there. I think we have some major issues going on...politics-wise...what our reasoning is for going over there. We all know that the general underlying reason is...weapons of mass destruction...and you know...we want to democratize the east. My question is, "Who are we to say we should democratize the east?" We are throwing a lot of money...we are putting a lot of men and women's lives in danger...and...and it's at what cost to democratize the east?"

"I am not a President Bush fan. I look at myself as a 23 year old trying to make it and be able to live on my own...and have insurance and that kind of thing...and the economy hasn't been good. It hasn't been good for people who have even graduated before me, and people that are graduating now. We can find service jobs for eight, ten, twelve bucks an hour…that's not a problem…but let's try to get a job where we can have a career and afford to live decently…modestly. You know, you need insurance and those types of things…and we're worried about whether we're going to have social security or not. So…I'm looking at Bush's policies through the eyes of a 23 year old."

"I would love to see Hillary Clinton run for president."

212   *Greg Funk*

"I'm Greg Funk…I'm 44 years old. We're here for a family photo. We had a family reunion yesterday…and they came from Florida, and all over…and…uh…wanted to get together on a nice day and get a picture to kinda…kinda…you know, cement a moment in time. We have almost thirty people. My…my parents live in Florida, and all the rest of us are here…here in Central Illinois…and…uh…they come up usually once a year, and we haven't had a family photo done in awhile. It's a good opportunity to get together. They got grandkids now…quite a few…old and young. Germantown Hills is where we all kinda grew up…and we all went, to some extent…all went our separate ways, for the purpose of education."

"I'm a mechanical engineer. I've got an engineering consulting company. Our office is in Germantown Hills. My brother Randy and his wife are from Oklahoma, and, uh, they were able to get up and spend a couple days together. We just been over…I have a home over on White Oak Lake. It's a fifty acre lake in Germantown Hills. It was a good setting for the reunion…it was a fun day. It was a hot day…99 degrees. We were all gonna cool off in the water and kinda just play around and eat a lot of food…relax."

"We moved from Dunlap when I was in high school, and I am six years older than the next oldest in our family. We moved while I was in high school, and ummm…we built a small cabin on the six acres that my parents bought, out of leftover lumber from some houses that were going up in the area. We basically spent the summer in this cabin. We had a loft where all of us kids kinda slept. My parents had a bed underneath the loft. We had an old…uh, chest-type soda cooler…that was our refrigerator. We had a grill for cooking. We had an acre and a half pond…and, uh, that's where we took our baths. We went down with a towel and a bar of soap."

"We started in the summer when school got out, and I think it was about October when we finally got the house done and were ready to move in. It was an interesting experience. Erecting an outhouse was a…was a…interesting thing to go through. It was interesting to note how swiftly we could give up the sophistication and technology of modern life. You adapt quickly, when you…when you need to. We adapted, you know…pretty quickly. The variety of foods that we ate, shrunk dramatically, to what was convenient to keep, and easy to prepare. On the occasional sweltering night, we would seek shelter at a local motel. But, that summer was pretty much working on the house. We provided most of the grunt work...the labor...hauling buckets of mortar and stacks of bricks, and lumber. We did all the painting...all the staining. It was a great family bonding experience...making your own place to live."

213   *Jerry Bratcher*

"My mother and father separated when I was very young. It wasn't until thirty years later that I got to meet him. My wife and I flew to California from here...and walking up to see him at that airport was probably the best day of my life. It was 1981, and I was 33 years old. I can't really describe the feeling."

214 *Mary Knobloch*

"I'm a retired teacher and a farmer's...a farmer's wife. My name is Mary Knob-loch. I taught grade school. I taught on a Navajo Indian reservation. "Ya 'at 'eeh...Hah-neh t'eh bin'yeh, doo'non't 'tlahdah. This was in Winslow, Arizona. I only taught there three years, and then I come home and married a farmer from Wyoming, Illinois. I went out there...it's interesting out there...everybody should do it. I went for the first year...you know just to practice...and I'm getting ready to leave and he says, "You want the job or don't you?" I said, "I've got my senior year left." And then he said, "We're not worried about that or about about your age...you've done fine." He said, "So, if you leave, you'll never know." And I said, "You're right, if I leave, I'll never come back out." So I signed a contract, graduated my last year, and went back out there and taught."

"Out there, the kids don't have to come to school. The only ones that come are the ones that wanna come...the parents want 'em to come. They have no discipli...no discipline problems at all. If they did have discipline problems, you just sat one of them out and went out and talked to the parents. So the parents would come to school, and you would just go out and talk to them with an interpreter...and you know...we had to go to training...to speak the language...their customs and so forth...and live with a family for a while."

"Bob Manygoats...he was just a little cute kid. He was intelligent...we had him IQ tested...he had, like, a 170 IQ. His mother wouldn't let him go to school for the gifted because she didn't want him to leave home. Smart...very smart."

"But you know, they had all the different customs...and you had to abide by 'em. They had witches out there. The men are the witches...not the women. First night I was there, I didn't even know what an Indian looked like. Teachers had housing...right across there...on the campus compound. Across the fence they were having a pow-wow for the night...and they danced all night long, and then come sunrise I thought...westward ho...circle round the wagons...they were going to attack me. Of course, I was the only teacher there...none of the rest of them had arrived yet."

"It was interesting out there...everybody should do it."

215   *Matt Coker*

"I'm Matt Coker. I'm…52. I couldn't remember if I'm 50 or 52. I'm an illustra-
tor by day and a musician by night. I draw product illustration on the computer.
I uh…sit on my butt and draw pictures all day. It's boring as hell, but I really
enjoy it…but I also really enjoy this. I love getting out…away from the desk, and
playing music. I get all welled up about music. Sometimes a song will just grab
me. It's amazing. I listen to headphones at work when I'm drawing…and I think
it was yesterday…the music just started getting to me. I swear to God, it's like
you get welled up inside, and I don't want anybody to see me…there's like, tears
in my eyes. I wear glasses, and I make sure I keep them on and my head down.
My desk faces the wall…and I don't even remember what the song was…but it
got to me."

"My most interesting job was as a potato peeler in a potato salad factory. I had
gone to school at Western Illinois University…dropped out after my first year,
and I needed a job. I had really long hair…and got this job at Danner's Salads.
We would stand around this trough, and somebody would dump the potatoes in
this thing…and it would spin them around and peel them. They would all come
out, and we'd have to take the eyes out with a paring knife. So, I stood around
this trough of water and potatoes, with these little old ladies…and these loser
guys…myself included, and…I'd have to wear a hair net, taking eyes out of potatoes all day. I would get little cuts in my thumb. The real highlight was when I
got promoted…to cole slaw maker…where I then got to work with big cabbages
instead of little potatoes. It was horrid…just horrid."

"I recently met my girlfriend on the Internet. It was fantastic…I…uh…was
divorced five years ago, and I had a girlfriend who, in fact, played in the band. It
fell apart…and so…it's hard…hard to meet a woman. You know, it's hard to
meet someone today. But, for the heck of it, I went and got on this chat line, and
found this americansingles web site. I thought, "What the heck, I'll try it." I
started talking to these women…and I met this one. It turned out she only lived
four blocks from me. So, we been together ever since. That was a year and a half
ago. I met a few others, but this one really clicked…she's amazing. Americansin-
gles.com…try it. You can usually tell if you're going to click or not."

"Actually, I didn't get that many hits…from my bio. You post a bio and a picture. I didn't get that many responses, so I thought…maybe I'm a…I'm a loser. My brother did it too, and he didn't get any hits…so I felt better about that. You gotta…you gotta post a picture. I didn't for awhile, and didn't get any response…and I don't know…if you've ever looked on there and seen the ones without any picture, you gotta wonder what they're trying to hide. But, I think it's a great way to meet people. I know it's kind of embarrassing to admit that's how you met, but once you get past the stigma…it's okay."

"They say that hanging out at bars is way down the list…that you typically meet someone through your friends, church…or parties, I guess. Bars…it's hard to meet people. I'm glad I met her. She's a nurse…working now, or otherwise she'd be with me. She's a nursing supervisor, who is on a twelve day stint right now…twelve in a row. We just went on a vacation and she has to make up some time."

"Probably the hardest piece that we play, are the instrumentals…the jigs…reels. When I sing, I can just belt them out, but the instrumentals…I have to really concentrate on getting the keys right, and the chords right. The best that we do is probably "Old Hag Ye Have Killed Me"."

"I have been doing this for about twenty years. I've been with this guy here, about twenty minutes…it is his first night. He's doing a heck of a job, though. We play in Chicago and St. Louis, but mostly in this area. We have this one song called, "The Waxies Dargle" that we learned from a band called "The Pogues". There is a part in there where I say, "Whaddaya have?", and the crowd is supposed to answer, "I'll have a pint." Well, one time we were playing in this bar that had ceiling fans, and one of the guys raised his pint up…and the pint went right into the ceiling fan…and broke…shattered…glass and Guinness everywhere. Of course, we tried not getting glass splinters on our tongues as we lapped up the beer off the floor."

216   *Jill Grube*

"I am 28, and I was born and raised in Peoria. I have recently moved back…I should say, about three years ago. I have been away to learn the art of cooking…and learn the restaurant life…the restaurant world. I have wanted my own restaurant since I was about eight years old. I have always had this passion for cooking, you know. I still have my first cut from the first knife I used when I was that young…you know, my scar. But I just…I love seeing people smile. Happiness in others makes me happy, and what better way to feed you…than through my own passion. So, I've just always been fascinated with cooking food. It's just so…*ever changing*, that you can't…you can never be bored by it."

"My mom is a great cook, but hates the cleanup…so we always traded out. So, if I got to cook, she would clean up. When she cooked…well, we kinda still walked away. I'm just fascinated with it. I have over a thousand cookbooks. I always tell people…wherever they go, to bring me back a cookbook, because I like to see what the other locals are doing. I had a friend just go to Texas, and I just want to see what they're doing…pickled venison and stewed armadillo…things like that."

"But…I just really, really enjoy this life…and it's kinda crazy because, everyday…twelve plus hours a day…on your feet, you rarely get the appreciation, but you get…you can sense it from others. Usually, when you are in the back cooking…you know, cooks don't get tipped out, the servers do…so, it's a tough life to be back there twelve hours a day, doing what you love…and not hearing the appreciation…someone being appreciative of something you have done. So, I guess, what better way than to open a restaurant…and then I can walk around and have a good time. I can see it…can see it on peoples faces…I'm passing on my happiness to them."

"When I was a kid, I had the Eazy-Bake Oven…and you know, the blueberry batter, cake mixes, muffins…things like that. I had this kitchen made from cardboard, you know, that looked like…I think Fischer Price did a lot of cooking stuff. I had the Eazy-Bake and I…just had it all. I still have my first cookbook…The Care Bear Cookbook. I just was always, always into reading about food. I almost have a photographic memory, where I can read it very quick…and I can duplicate it. I can also eat a dish…and just by seeing the components, and tasting it, I can pull it out…duplicate it"

"It's just been fun over the years to learn. I traveled a ton...been to Maui...I went to college at Purdue, to get my restaurant management degree...lived in Missouri...had to do an internship...banquet internship. I went to culinary school in Vermont...New England Culinary Institute. I lived in Maui and Boston, because in culinary school, you have to have internships there. You have to go where the food is...you can't stay in one place like Peoria or Cape Cod...because there are different types of cuisines around. Every single job I did was to learn a different type of cuisine."

"I worked in Boston, and kind of moved down the coast. I worked in Boston at a fine dining restaurant...L'Espalier...my dad still can't pronounce it. It was a great restaurant. You know I learned so much from each restaurant...you learn how to use all food. You get in a whole side of lamb...and you can make a sauce, a soup, and a stock out of the scrap, or the waste, or the bones. You just learn so much...and I just continued to move down the coast. I worked in a place in Cambridge called Salamander, which is...Asian fine dining. Really...kinda crazy food, but really, really nice food...lobster tails with like, tempura...just different kinds of spices...just different ways of doing sushi...sushi rice...a real Asian touch."

"I worked at The Catered Affair. It was a gourmet catering company. We did parties for the Kennedys. Fifteen million dollar homes...I mean, you went in there, and you might do dinner for three people...but they paid a $150 per person...and you just did it for them. So, you learned the art of putting a personal touch on everything. You think of everything, and what they want out of it...and then you try and put more into it. We did hors d'oeuvres parties...big, big dinners for 1500 to 2000, where they paid $10,000 a table. So, you learn the high end...and you never think a catering company can be high end...'til you see that. So, I learned the art of doing banquets, and making sure the first plate and the last plate are similar...which is what we like to do here. If we serve twenty salmons tonight...the first and the twentieth should be the same...consistent."

"I continued down the coast and lived in Hyannis...Cape Cod, Massachusetts, and worked at Red Jacket Beach Resorts, where I was executive chef of the summer resort. There, I truly learned management, and realizing that...when you are up at a certain level...sometimes *you...you* are all that you have. If you fire someone, or someone has to leave…you have to pick up their job. The job pool, where you can pick from people, is just not there."

"I moved back after Cape Cod. I was burnt out…worked seven days a week…breakfast, lunch, and dinner for about three months straight. There comes some point in your life when you want to know why you're doing this. So, I moved back home to regenerate. I worked here for a couple years…drove by the Galena Road property and…everything happens for a reason…I just decided to buy the building and knock it down. Whenever you do a restaurant…financially, it's going to take a toll. I'm lucky that I have the support of a lot of special people. I don't have investors…it's all through my company, however, my parents are definitely very supportive."

"I've always believed if you're going to do it, you should go all out. Now, you have to have a budget, but you can't skimp on anything if you want to be the best. This vision has been the same since I was eight years old…that I am going to be up there as the best in the country…with all the big hitters out of New York and Chicago…California. So, you just can't build something going, "I *hope* I can pay for this later." Instead, "Let's do it because we *will* pay for it later." The first year or so, you don't make money. We're doing great now…doing great numbers…we're in line with where we need to be. However, the heat is killing us somewhat…it's a hundred degrees out, and who wants to go out and eat when it's a hundred degrees?"

"I have been lucky enough, that my family…we just always get along. Even with my cousins…I have cousins in Ohio…and my grandparents that are here…we just all have such a great time together. I was always made fun of, I guess…because I would rather go out and do something with my folks, and my brother than go out with my friends sometimes. When I lived in Hawaii, everyone came out to Hawaii…my family did. When I lived in Boston, they always came out. They loved it…they were like, "Where else do you want to go, because we'll go there too."

"My parents played quite a role in the restaurant…kind of watching over my shoulder, and making sure everything is going okay. Even though it's mine…I own it and it's my show…they are still there to help. My mom…she's probably around here somewhere. We put up a sign, and I need some paint, and she runs a lot of errands for me…takes care of a lot of things for me. I really love my family."

"This restaurant…I didn't do this just for me…I want everyone to experience it. I think people deserve this kind of dining…this type of food…this type of experience. Of course, you do it for yourself, but when you can walk up to a table, and they're saying, "This is amazing."…*that*…*that* is enough for me…*that* is enough pleasure for me."

217   *Ngoc Minh*

"I'm sixteen years old and go to school. I have three blogs...and I'm thinking about making a multilingual blog...for Vietnamese and English. I want to make money from blogs...designing blog themes for my friends and other people. It's better than stacking groceries on shelves, which is what I do now. My brother said that I am a "shelf technician" because I am very careful that the groceries line up."

218   *Jay Navin*

"I am forty this year...thirty-nine now, but forty in just a few weeks. If I tell when my birthday is, I will expect a gift. I suppose I should feel bad about turning forty, but I really don't see the big deal. I didn't freak when I turned thirty...why should I now? However, when I turn fifty, I think that will affect me...I will probably cry and look back at my life...up to that point...and realize that I haven't accomplished much. I know so far, I haven't really contributed anything to the human race...haven't even tried. I think the human race is screwing things up enough without me poking my nose in things. Who knows, maybe by then I will have discovered how to...turn Cheerio's into an alternate energy source. Of course, being in retail sales, I am probably not going to do that."

"I used to be a runner...a long distance runner. I ran a few marathons several years ago...and I've been thinking about...about running again. I always enjoyed just going out on weekends and running for ten, fifteen, or twenty miles. You know what felt really good about running? Stopping. I'm not kidding...I really liked the feeling after the run. I felt like I accomplished something each and every time I went out on a long run, and completed it. I was never a fast runner...I probably never went any faster than seven-minute miles...and more often than not, would do eight-minute miles. I never really liked running with anyone, because it would always throw my pace off...and I wouldn't enjoy it. Running was always something I did alone. I owned it. I felt powerful. I was God."

"One time I went out and ran on the Rock Island Trail. It used to be a train track, but was converted into a running and biking trail. It was a brisk day in the fall. All the leaves were already off the trees, and the trail was moist...not muddy, just moist...soft. It was exactly the type of weather that I liked...cold and overcast. I got on the trail and I ran to Princeville...and just a little further. I planned it so that it would be a twenty mile round-trip. I ran out, and then on the way back...at about sixteen miles...I stopped at a little grocery store right off the trail, to get some water. I walked through the store and got some very strange looks by a couple of customers and by the cashier. I thought it might have something to do with my bright pink running shorts...but that wasn't it."

"When I got home, I walked into the main bathroom and caught myself in the mirror. First...you have to understand when you...when you run in cold weather...there isn't a lot of sweat. When you sweat, it provides needed lubrication. I actually had to stop at a dumpster behind a donut shop and take a handful of donut grease to lubricate my thighs on a previous run. A lot of the big races provide globs of Vaseline out on boards once you get out quite a ways on the course. But...anyway, to get back to my trail run...I looked in the mirror and saw two big bloody blobs where my nipples rubbed against my shirt. They had bled quite a bit, and left a trail of blood down the front of my shirt. The cold, lack of lubrication, and the type of material that I wore that day...and the constant movement...rubbing...irritated my nipples...so that they bled. After that day, I learned to wear little band-aids on my nipples when it was cold."

219   *Kelly White*

"I am Kelly White. I am 35, and I am from Mount Pleasant, Iowa. I'm here for the Midwest League all-star game. We're about thirty miles from Burlington, and Burlington has the Burlington Bees, which are an affiliate of the Royals. We go to a lot of their games, but we also go to several different places where the Midwest league plays, and we've actually come here…this is probably our fourth or fifth time already. My husband…he's a big baseball fan and he likes to get autographs, and that. So, I guess the kids and I have kinda become…become big fans, because we go all the time, We also go to…the last couple of years we went to Kansas City, to quite a few of the Royals games."

"We actually just drove from Chicago today…here…so, we were in Chicago and did stuff. Probably, we don't do a lot of big-time traveling…you know, like five hours away, and stuff. I guess my husband and me…before we had the kids…we went to Chicago…ummm…over the weekends and stuff. But now, there are just millions of people there…and that was pretty fun, just walking around watching the people, and stuff. We park the car at a hotel and just walk around. The first year or two we went to the museums and to the ballgames…and now we just walk around. We're not big shoppers. We just walk around and watch the people. It's fun."

"My dad watches the kids when we work, and stuff, and he likes golf. He just hits balls out in the yard all the time, and he's taken…er…my son has taken that up, and ummm…like, we were at the bank one time, waiting…ummm…for my mom, and my son saw his golf clubs in the back of the truck, and he was like, "Hey, I need to take a couple of swings here…while we're waiting.""

"I am a cosmetologist, and I work three days a week. I like it. I think working three days, I don't get real burned-out on it…whereas if I worked, you know, five or six days a week, I would probably get burnt out about it."

"One thing that I remember…it was our first day out on the floor cutting when I was going to cosmetology school…actually cutting the public's hair, and you know…you're new at this, you know, just kinda practicing really. The first customer I had was a guy, and he was in a big hurry to get home and watch the Iowa football game. So there I am, you know, a twenty minute haircut…and it's going to take me an hour to do...you know, 'cause it's my first time out there. I remember that. Not fun...no...not fun at all. That was a lot of pressure."

220   *Connie Schwarzentraub*

"When I was a kid, we had a horse. We'd just jump on it and ride all around. One night it stormed and lightening hit the trough…and killed the horse. I went out the next day to ride, and…no horse. I was ten. You're riding it one day, and then a storm comes up, and then…no more horse. I learned then that you never know what's going to happen next."

221   *Jared Brown*

"I am not a crier...but, I can remember a time I cried. When Bobby Kennedy was shot, it seemed like the country was just going to hell...and I remember watching a documentary on that, several months afterward, and I thought I was pretty much inured to it. I was watching with my daughter, who was five or six...and I remember I started crying...and I just couldn't stop it. I knew it was not a good example for her...but I just couldn't stop."

"I am originally from New York. I was born in New York City, and grew up in Los Angeles. My parents moved there when I was about five. I went back to New York to go back to college...then moved all over from there. In San Francisco I got my masters degree. In Minnesota, I got my doctorate...then we moved to Illinois after that. I now live in Bloomington."

"Tonight will be a showing of "All the President's Men", at the Normal The-ater...which is a film directed by Alan J. Pakula. I have written a book about Alan J Pakula. It has just been released, and is called, "Alan J. Pakula, His Films and His Life". So, I'm going to introduce the picture, and then talk about it after-wards, and take some questions...and then...ummm...have a book signing."

"I wrote a book about Alfred Lunt and Lynn Fontanne. They were two of the greatest actors in the twentieth century in America...probably the greatest acting team ever, called the "Fabulous Lunts". I wrote a book called "Zero Mostel, A Biography", a history called, "The Theater in America During the Revolution", and then this book about Alan J. Pakula...and next year, I am coming out with another one called, "Moss Hart", tentative title, "Moss Hart, a Prince of the The-ater"."

"For this book, I did many interviews...more than sixty, actu-ally...ummm...with different people. That was a means...a means of getting to know Alan Pakula. So, I was using that for research...and you know, you use published sources for research...but there wasn't much published on Alan Pakula. There were no books...there were articles, but...they didn't fill in every-thing, certainly. So, I wanted to talk with his family, his friends, and people he worked with...and those were what those sixty interviews constituted."

"The people I interviewed…foremost was his wife, Hannah Pakula…his widow, Hannah Pakula, and she helped me a lot in locating other people by giving me their phone numbers or their addresses…and I would write to them, or called, to get in touch with them. I spoke to people like Meryl Streep, Harrison Ford, Robert Redford, and Jane Fonda. I got the interviews by partly going through Hannah, because she knew these people…or most of them. Also, because…when you speak to one person, they will say, "Well, have you spoken to Jill Clayburgh about this?" I would say, "No." Then they would say, "Well, here's how you get in touch with her." So, one interview tends to lead to another interview. Ummm…she did not put me in touch with Redford or Fonda…but, I knew they were going to be very important sources…and I was able to track them down myself…and people like Kevin Klein…and the same is true of Meryl Streep. Hannah provided me mostly with the names of family and friends, and some…some of his co-workers…but basically, not performers."

"I have worked with actors all my life. I have been a professor of theater, and directed about a hundred plays…and I find actors in general to be very articulate, very bright…and usually very forthcoming. That certainly characterizes the people I spoke to. They were extremely articulate. They had interesting things to say. They were willing to share it. All the people I mentioned, I thought were fascinating. I got a great deal from Robert Redford. He was an especially good interview because he was able to answer questions for a long, long time. He told me information that he has apparently never given to anyone else. So, some things in my book about "All the Presidents Men" are new. I don't think anyone else knows about them. I have to say Kevin Klein was a good interview. He loved the experience of working with Pakula in "Sophie's Choice", and never had another experience like it. The directors he has worked with have always been *wanting*, in comparison to Pakula. He has been waiting all his life to find another director like Pakula…and never has. Meryl Streep was very good. Candice Bergen was good…I would have a hard time picking anyone who didn't match the description I mentioned."

"I think I have a marriage that I am very, very happy with. My wife does a project called, "The Discovery Walk" at Evergreen Cemetery every year. It's based on history. They take people that have been buried in the cemetery, usually for more than fifty years…and essentially bring those people to life. People, actors of course…come up from behind the headstones and talk to the audience briefly…and there are usually eight of them in the presentation. The audience moves…the actors don't. They remain behind the headstones, and the audience moves from one location to the next location in the cemetery, by a guide."

"I am 68. I can't imagine having done anything else with my life. I have enjoyed teaching a lot…I have a family that I love a lot…books that I'm proud of…plays I've directed. You know what a mensch is? It's a Yiddish word, which means, essentially, a good human being. I hope I have been a mensch."

222-223   *Jeannie and Ken Hupp*

"I'm Jeannie Hupp and I'm 47."

"I'm Ken Hupp, and I'm 47 as well."

"We have three boys. Thaddeus is 22, in the Navy. Julian is twenty…yes, twenty…in the Air Force. Gideon is fifteen, and at home. He's a freshman in high school."

"Thaddeus was on a plane in Atlanta when 911 hit…when they blew up the Twin Towers…when the planes went through the buildings. He called from the plane and said, "What's going on? There are security people running all over…people in the airplane…they won't let us off…they won't tell us what's going on." He was just freaking out. Ken was watching the television…talking to him, as the Towers were falling. He said, "You don't want to know.""

"Thaddeus is now in Virginia Beach…he's at the Naval Station in Oceana. He's a petty officer first class. He's an ejection seat mechanic on F-18's. He…well actually he's shop supervisor…and head of his…there, they call them AME's. I don't know what that stands for, but they call them ejection seat mechanics. They have titanium shells and they're rocket-launched…that's all I know. He's certified for explosives…and all that fun stuff. He made petty officer after three years, so he's doing pretty good…having the time of his life. He's been on one Mediterranean cruise…the George Washington…and he was bitching about not being able to secure his bunk, because the latches didn't latch tight. He said, within a week of being there, he smuggled a power screwdriver, a hasp, and a padlock out of the shop…screwed it onto the bunk, and locked it up."

"On the cruise, they got sidetracked and spent some time in the Gulf…a show of force. He sent pictures, but didn't tell us where they were from. It was a guessing game. "Do you know where this is?" You could never tell where they were."

"He sent a picture of the Vatican to Caitlin, his fiancée, and said, "If you can tell me where I'm at, I'll talk to you." She said, "That kind of looks like the Vatican," I said, "Oh, it can't be." It became a game. He would email us about where he had been. Sometimes he could tell us where he actually was...sometimes he couldn't."

"When he went through the Suez Canal...we got pictures of it as it was happening. He took the pictures, then immediately downloaded them, and emailed them...the same day."

"When he was over in the Iran-Iraq area, he couldn't do that. He did say, "Mom, there are oil wells on fire, and they're just letting them burn. I can't tell you where I am, but you might be able to figure it out from that." I could figure it out, but I didn't want to. He thought he was going on another cruise...he thought it would be February or March, but now it's going to be June."

"The squadron he's in is based out of Virginia Beach. It's not a boat-based squadron. They're flying Super Hornets and use that squadron for training. When the Hornets first came in, Virginia Beach didn't want them there, because they're bigger and louder...faster. We've discovered that Virginia Beach doesn't really want the Navy there...which is ironic because there wouldn't be a Virginia Beach without the Navy. Every time the city council brings something up...they're anti-Navy. They don't get it."

"Our other son is in Georgia...Robbins, Georgia, which is a suburb of Macon. He's what they call a "drop-monkey". He's a network coordinator...he's the guy who moves or gets a new computer, he installs the network, and makes sure everything works. He's on call on the weekends, which is a bummer, because he can't drink...doesn't know if he'll get called in. Of course, he's underage anyway...not supposed to be drinking. His wife is 22, and so she makes sure there is alcohol in the house. They're living on base and liking it. She works at the pizza shop there on base...most of the time she likes it."

"The three kids we have...they were such a joy when we had them. Every stage of their lives, they've had their trials...that I sometimes would have liked to kill them for...but overall, they just bring the biggest joy to me."

"All three boys...I've done everything with them, from being Cub Scout leader to coaching baseball...to going to football games. I tried to be a dad versus a father whenever I could. Teaching Thaddeus how to work on cars...what little I knew...helping Julian debug computers...and with Gideon, he has brought me back to a love I forgot I had. I used to work behind the scenes in high school, and when he

got involved in "Corn Stock", it brought all that back. I volunteered to build sets for Corn Stock Theater."

"Gideon was in his first production this summer…"Over the Tavern". He played a thirteen year old retarded boy, which was a challenge because he didn't have a lot of speaking parts. His favorite word was…"shit". But, he had a lot of acting…and interacting with his onstage siblings was quite a challenge."

"Aside from helping at Corn Stock, I work third shift in the heat treat department. I maintain the furnaces and try and keep things from blowing up at night. It's a real dirty place. The only time you can see clear through the building is on Sunday night, beginning of third shift. The only time the air is clear enough is then."

224   *Jerry Thomas*

"Throughout my life, I've made a lot of mistakes...I've shot myself in the foot many times. However, this last one was pretty big. I blew my whole leg off. I'm still trying to recover from that one...but meanwhile...I guess I'll just keep limping."

225 *Earl Vittitoe*

"I was born in Bloomington...my name is Earl Vittitoe, and I am 49. I moved all over the country because my father was in the military. I ended up spending my high school years in Hawaii...and from there...I, ah...I also went in the military. I went in as a technician, working on nuclear missiles in Europe. So...I spent eight years doing that...having a lot of fun. It was a very interesting job."

"My last year, I was no longer repairing the missiles...I was engaged in actually targeting the different cities in Eastern Europe. So, we have these sites in Germany where we actually had heads "mated" and ready to launch...part of the cold war. A lot of interesting things happened up there...getting a little strange up on the site. It appears that "shooting the moon" was a form of greeting back then, to just about anybody, sometimes inadvertently to visiting dignitaries...so, sometimes they got to see our best side."

"Not wanting to spend my entire life in Germany, since there was no other place in the system, I...ah...decided to get out after eight years and started working in the computer industry. Started off teaching computer systems and electronics...software, at a computer company in Alabama. Five years of that, got a little...got a little boring. I ended up getting recruited by RCA to take a job in Europe. So, I worked for a non-existent Air Force unit for a couple of years....basically doing intelligence throughout Europe."

"Had a lot of interesting and strange people...got to see Ellie Wessel get his Nobel Prize...his Nobel Prize, in Norway. He was the Nazi hunter. He got his Nobel Prize in 1987, and I was in Oslo when he got his...I actually ran into the guy on the street...right as he was leaving the theater, right down from the congress hall. I didn't really know who he was until the Norwegian police pulled me back as I was running into him...didn't even know what was going on. They awarded him a prize that day, and I just happened to be there."

"There was this Air Force major, an intelligence officer, and one day we were talking about secure communications...talking to him about upgrading the secure communications local area network to a fiber-optic link, for obvious reasons. These folks had never heard of fiber-optics...this was about 1986...1987. So this major questions me, really pretty directly for about 45 minutes about all the aspects of fiber-optics communications and how we would implement it. The next day, I meet him down in one of the…one of the secure rooms, and he asked me if I knew about the communi…communications meeting the day before. And I said, "Yeah…I know about it." He said, "Did you go to it?" This guy is an *intelligence* officer and he has no idea he talked to me for 45 minutes the day before."

"When I was running a nuclear fire platoon, we had a brand-new platoon leader come in, and he didn't know that a lot of…a lot of the troops took speed when they went into the field…since you're up for a couple days, and you need a lot of energy. So, he goes out to the field with us…and I know that the troops have speed. I know they're taking it…they buy it legally from the Germans and pour it into their Cokes. So, the lieutenant goes over to one of these privates…underneath one of the launchers…and it's really hot that day, and he asks him for a drink of his soda. The guy looks over at me, and he knows that I know he has speed in his soda. I just give him this look…like, "Do what you think is right." So…he hands the lieutenant his Coke and the lieutenant drinks from it. So, this lieutenant is crawling through the mud for the next twelve hours, humping cables and helping the guys out…and then he crashes for about eighteen hours, and has no clue what happened to him."

"What I'm going to end up doing, is…is going back to Hawaii and teaching…so the plan is to get my masters, do some part-time teaching, and then retire early and go back to Hawaii…teach at the University of Hawaii. That reminds me…do you want to hear my sheep story?"

226   *Elaine Lucas*

"I am actually a great-great-great granddaughter of the founder of Washington…William Holland. That's why we have Holland's Mercantile…the candy store you were just in."

"I always wanted to have an old-fashioned candy store on the square. And since there wasn't anything like that…and when I was a kid we used to go to this place called "Johnny's Bakery"…they had penny candy and stuff. We'd buy donuts for a nickel…and stuff like that. This building was originally Law Holland's Barbershop and Pool Hall. We went down to the wood floor…and there are still a lot of cigarette burns there…where they would be playing pool and flip their cigarettes out."

"My granddaughter is the eighth generation descended from William Holland that has never left Washington. Generations of us have stayed right here in Washington. At the time I opened up the store…1987…baseball cards…sports cards were real popular. There's a picture right over here of me with Muhammad Ali. We used to go to Chicago, to the sports show up there. All these people would be there…sports stars. We would meet people there and have memorabilia signed."

"You see all these things along the side…all these marks? Those are cigarette burns from many years back. This big seed counter here, which is the longest one…this eighteen footer, was from a grocery store down in Southern Illinois. We had to bring it up on a semi. It was so heavy. It was just a deserted grocery store and we bought that out of it. All the seed counters…all the counters are originals from other stores."

"We started out with 24 jars of candy…and now we have about 200. People still just love to come in and get a sack. We try really hard to carry the stuff that nobody has anymore…Niconips…Horehounds…Chuckles…all the old stuff that people can't find anymore."

"There was this little boy in third grade…and they had a school tour around the square…and they were telling him about the history. His grandmother came in and said, "You should see what he wrote about this." He wrote a three page letter and said in there, "If anything ever happened to Holland's, my life would be over." I had my picture taken with him, and I'm going to frame the letter."

"I was just thinking about those miners in Virginia. In my mind...I think everything is all part of a bigger picture...that none of us are ever able to understand. The accident that just happened...and the confusion over whether they were alive or dead...that was human error. God didn't give people hope or despair. That wasn't divine error...that was human error. And...if you notice the notes that they wrote...they weren't despairing notes...they were at peace. They said, "I love you...I'm at peace"...things like that. They weren't, "Why did this happen to me...what's going on here?"

"I remember...a long time ago...and my mother was a great person as far as seeing the big picture. She said, "None of us can see the big picture. Why does this baby die, but that person, an absolutely horrible person can live to be 85?" She said, "If you take any piece of a huge ship...a nut or a bolt, or a piece of tin...anything...and you throw it in the ocean...it can't float. But, when those pieces are all put together...that ship will float." I think that was her philosophy...that all these things will make sense someday, to those that believe."

227   *Juana Lucio*

"I'm 28. I didn't like high-school, but I'm very proud that I graduated. I do healthcare work in Bloomington....and live in Normal. People are always mistaking me for a high-schooler. It's like, "I need to see your I.D...I need to see it." Mostly...I lead a very boring life. I don't do a whole lot. I really...don't do a lot. It's boring...but you know, it's not bad."

228   *Joe Lowry*

"My name is Joe Lowry. I'm a deacon here. I am 66 years old. I'm proud I've got this far. My dad was 63 when he passed away. My mom was 82. Originally, my family…our family was from Missouri. My dad moved up here in '50…1950 to work at Caterpillar. He was a farmer in Missouri…and what possessed him to do this, I really don't know…but we been here ever since. He's since retired from Caterpillar and passed away."

"I too am retired from Caterpillar. I seen…got my thirty years in, and I seen the door open in 1994…when things weren't real well, at that time. There was a lot of hate and discontent and the Lord opened the door for me…and I went through it…and I've never been sorry since. I was raised Protestant…and I don't know how I ended up marrying a Catholic girl, but I did…and we was married sixteen years before I decided to take up instructions to learn more about the Catholic faith. Some friends of ours encouraged us to go on a marriage-encounter weekend. We did, and that's when I decided I needed to learn more about the Catholic faith…and get God back in my life."

"One man…you know…we see movies on television about prisons, and gangs and all that…and that's not far from the truth. I went on one particular prison weekend, and a man came up to me and said he'd been thinking about accepting God in his life, and I said "Well, you know that decision is yours." Then he said, "I'm not able to do that." Then I said, "What…what do you mean?" He says, "I'd have to get released from the gang to…before I could accept God into my life." I said, "Well, I guess I don't understand. How has this gang got to owning you this much?" He said, "The gang is the reason I'm in here…to work for the gang inside these walls." I said, "You've gotta be kidding me." He said, "No." Well…by the end of the weekend he told me that regardless of what the gang told him, he was ready to accept God in his life. I went back later for visits…and he had a smile on his face from ear to ear…he was very happy. So, I feel that as long as we keep God in our lives, and I don't mean to sound like a fanatic, but we need God in our lives…and I don't care who you are. We need God in our country. There are people out there trying to take God out of our country. It's sad…very sad."

"After high school, I went in the Army…well got married, and then went in the Army. I was a mechanic…truck mechanic…worked on personnel carriers. I was with the 11th Cavalry over in Vietnam. You know…a lot of things happen, and you wonder why. My wife…she said she prayed for me every day when I was in Vietnam. I come home without a scratch…and there was times I didn't know how that had happened…but it did. So, the Lord had a plan for me, and at that time, I wasn't knowing what that plan was."

"We was married in October…October the 9th, 1965, and I was…I knew I was going to get drafted, but didn't know it was going to be so soon…but I ended up being drafted the first week in November, 1965…so it was only three weeks. In that three weeks, my wife got pregnant with our first daughter, and she was…well, I got to come home before I went to Vietnam, and luckily it was right after she had the baby…or, right at the same time she had the baby…'cuz they arranged my leave according to…you know…whenever I got the call she was going to have the baby. Well, I got to go home, but…so I got to see my oldest daughter. She was like two or three weeks when I left, and thirteen months when I come back home."

"It's a big adjustment. I really didn't have God in my life…not that I didn't believe in him, but whether I did or not…it will be…anytime you're separated from somebody…for any length of time…you gotta get reacquainted, no matter how much you loved the person. I know I changed…and she probably did too. You follow what I'm saying? Being in…fighting in Vietnam for a year…there's no way you're going to come home the same person. God was looking out for me…and like I say, I guess I didn't realize it at the time. I can look back on a lot of things and feel he was there to help me."

"With people from the Vietnam…just not people from Vietnam, but every war we ever had…we've had people that dodged the military…to keep from going in to serve. It's really sad when a person doesn't have enough patriotism to serve his country. If a person can't serve his country…or his god…he certainly doesn't serve himself. I seen a lot of people go to Canada…hide in colleges. I'm not saying I'm a hero or anything like that. I was scared to death…but I'd rather take my chances than to run. My grandsons, today, really have a lot of appreciation for their grandfather, because he is a veteran."

"I went over with the 11th Cavalry...went over as a whole unit. Took all our own equipment...had our staging area at Bien Hoa...and later become the 90th Replacement, which was just outside of Bien Hoa. Bien Hoa...I was trying to think of how far it was from Saigon. We set up our staging area there...as our equipment got over there. We did everything at night. We went over and picked up our equipment at night...drove it back...cleaned areas...ya know, cleaned brush out. Everything was jungle. Then later, we went down to Xuan Loc, which was down south. They had taken a bulldozer and bulldozed a road around our base camp...the rest of it was just a dense jungle...like trying to look through that wall...you couldn't do it. I spent...lemee see...I guess it was three months...probably four, in Chu Lai...just down from Danang. Then we went back to our base camp after that long...and I couldn't believe the changes...what the Corps of Engineers had done to our base camp while we were gone. Beautiful...beautiful. Had streets...and when we went down there, it was monsoon season...everything was muddy."

"Marine Corps had a big base in Chu Lai. I know when we went to Chu Lai, we boarded our personnel carriers and then on LST boats...and then on up by water. Why they did it that way, I don't know. Well, we get up there, and we couldn't believe it. There's all these Marines out there swimming in the ocean...and we ain't had a bath for three days. It was a luxury we weren't used to."

229   *Harriet Sue Glidewell Stiles*

"I go by Suzy, and I'm 55 years old. I live in Mapleton, and have lived there for 23 years."

"One thing that I have noticed…my mother and father were ministers…pastors of little country churches. They never owned a home, never owned a new car…uhhh…lived on public aid the last 22 years of their lives…and I scrimped and saved and had enough money to bury them and buy them a tombstone…and they're buried in the Pekin Cemetery. What amazes me is that every time we put something nice on their graves…within 48 hours, it's stolen. I wondered what was going on, but then I have a friend who has an infant daughter and a brother that's buried on the other side of the cemetery…and she said they had stuff disappear off the graves all the time."

"You know, what has society come to? People are willing to go to the cemetery and steal from the dead? I know there was a woman up north somewhere that was prosecuted. They said that they found $1200 worth of stolen cemetery artifacts in her yard. She had decorated her yard with stuff from the cemeteries. What has society come to?"

"I grew up as a preacher's kid in Kentucky. I was born in Hickman…my father went into the ministry when I was two, and from then until high school, we moved about every two years. Had I moved the last time my dad moved, I would have attended four high schools."

"My younger daughter cleans houses, my son drives for Pepsi-Cola, and my oldest daughter followed in her grandfather's footsteps, and she is a minister. Her and her husband are ministers in Southern Illinois."

"My husband and I…we are beekeepers. When he retired from the city, we got involved in bees. Different ones take a turn staying here…selling honey, and that's how we get to keep selling our product. We sell honey and tell people about the bees. We've got 25 hives. With each hive…when a hive is really strong, it can have as many as 50,000 bees. We have a lot of them in our yard. Honey bees take a bad knock…people think honey bees are mean, but the only time a honey bee is aggressive, is when you open its hive and mess with it."

"They don't want to be bothered. If society was like the honey bees, we'd be a lot better off. They have a queen. She takes care of laying the eggs and making sure there's the young to reproduce and keep the hive going. There are those that when they hatch, they know they are the workers. They'll keep the hive clean, and in their later years, they'll go out and be the foragers…they'll go out and in the later weeks, they'll go out and gather the pollen and bring it back into the hive. It's a constant working…they all get along, within and without. They fend for each other. Society would be better off if we were all bees."

230   *Joyce Mitchell*

"I am soon to be 58. We've been in this area for twelve years. I come from the Ottawa area. My husband was a school superintendent, and there was an opening in this area…a lot of his family is from this area…so, we moved back here just because of that, basically."

"Growing up as I child, I lived in Marseilles…like I said, we grew up near Ottawa, but we lived just below the bluff…the Illinois River Valley bluff. I must be like a cat with nine lives, because I fell off those bluffs many times. I always enjoyed doing things outside. We moved to the country when I was going in fifth grade, I guess. That developed my love of nature. We played outside until it was dark every day. Then, we came in…and we only got two channels on our TV, and it was black and white. We didn't have the choice of DVD's or video games…all that stuff. So, I guess I just grew up with more of an appreciation of nature. We would get animals to keep…raccoons and possums, and flying squirrels and such. We only had the flying squirrel for two hours because it got in bed with my grandma…so we had to turn him loose."

"One of the reasons I'm out here is…I'm helping people with nature. I am a retired schoolteacher, and one of the big things I taught, when I was teaching third grade…we did native Illinois animals, and then we would bring kids to Wildlife Prairie Park for a field trip. I know about most of the animals there…and I work with the hawks and eagles…the owls, and the raptors. I work with the raptors…giving programs. I go out there and teach…and not have to do any papers, or any report cards, or homework, or anything. I just show up and help people, which is a lot of fun to do. I taught at Illini-Bluffs. I taught third grade there for nine years, and one year of second grade."

"At Wildlife they have a raptor program at 1:45…a raptor program every day during the summertime, and then on the weekends when summer is over. Probably starting next week, we'll go to weekends. You'll see a barn owl fly…they have it trained to fly to different stations. That's actually when it eats, during the day…in that program. It's actually a working bird…it flies for its food. Depending on what birds are out, you'll either see a barn owl, or the…ummm…turkey vulture. Once in awhile, they'll bring the eagle up. They also have a red-shouldered hawk…a red-tailed hawk…a peregrine falcon, and a kestrel. I lot of people call the kestrel a sparrow hawk. It's the smallest raptor we have...about the size of a fat robin...almost dove-sized. The males are real pretty...kind of a slate-gray color. The females are a speckled, tannish...beige color. They are very pretty. This time of year, you will see a lot of doves on wires, but some are likely to be a kestrel. Sometimes you will see one holding a mouse...as it takes it back to its perch. They do not usually eat on the ground."

"Having grandkids...it's just a wonderful opportunity to start over again. We did a lot of things with our own children...and being able to do those same things with the grandkids...and they live a little over two hours away from us...we'll bring them down for a week, or two, or three...and spend the entire day at Wild-life. We have one that is almost three and he spent from nine to four out there, and didn't want to go home. They'll go out on the trails with me...and help with the animal programs. They get to hold the snakes...play with the turtles...and things like that. They also get to go up and get closer to the raptors, because I get to go into the cages and handle them."

"If you can start kids out with nature, when they're little like that, they'll develop a love and appreciation of nature...and hopefully that will carry through and keep them conservation-minded as they grow older. I am definitely an advocate for nature and children."

231   *Shelly Hines*

"I have a store in Washington called "Sentimental Journey". I'm not going to make a million there, but I do alright. My mom owned it before me. She had it for ten years"

"My mom is a character. She...when she was growing up, she was always the prankster in the group. She would play jokes on people. She took a whole group of women through a car wash...in the Jeep. She got a group of women together and said, "Let's go out for a drive." She got all these ladies in the car and drove up to a car wash, and the women said, "What are you doing, Karen...what are you doing?" She then asked the guy at the car wash, "Can you turn off the brushes for us?" Then...she drove through the car wash."

"She and my dad were in AMBUCS...and at one of the conventions, one of the guys was getting relatively intoxicated...and for some reason, she got hold of a razor and shaved his leg. The next morning she said, "We had fun with you, Charlie...we shaved your leg last night." "Oh...you did not." "Oh yeah, pull up your pant leg.""

"She's retired now, in California. She was the first woman in town to join the rescue squad. She did that for ten years. She got her real estate license...did that for ten years. She owned the store in Washington for about ten years, and then went off to California."

"Everybody doesn't always like to be like their mom in many ways, but I like to look for the good in things, just like her. She speaks her mind...and I speak my mind. I try not to ever really beat around the bush. I try and tell people what I think, in a tactful way. My mom probably doesn't have as much tact as I try to have...but maybe I really don't."

"My sister had a miracle in her life a couple of years ago. She had a hysterectomy, and they told her afterwards that she had complications, and had to go in for another major surgery. It couldn't be done here...had to go to Mayo and find out who does this the best. This thing never fixes itself...it's call a fistula. This happens less than two percent of the time, and of those cases, they don't...fix themselves."

"We started praying…and she went to see "The Passion of the Christ" before her next surgery. She said that during the movie…she saw this guy being healed…and she said, "That could happen to me. He can do that if he chooses to." She said the following week, she went to the doctor and said, "I'm doing better." He said, "You can't be…but let me go ahead and examine you." He then said, "Oh my gosh…there's a film here." A fistula is like a hole between your bladder, and it allows you to leak urine. He said, "There's a film here…do you believe in the power of prayer?" She goes, "Yeah…I've been working on it." He said, "There's a film forming here…I've never seen anything like this. Can I call my nurses in to look?"

"It healed itself. That is a really, really, really, minute chance. It maybe could happen…maybe one in a million…but…oh, and…and my mom was told that she couldn't have any more kids. She had both ovaries removed…and there was like a millionth of an ovary in there. They said…that's not possible. Lo and behold…I was born 42 years ago."

232   *Andrew Young*

"We knew we were under constant surveillance. We never quarreled with surveillance. We never complained about it. We wanted the government to know what we were doing. I remember one time when we found a microphone under a pool table...we didn't destroy it...we put it up on top of the pool table. We wanted them to get accurately, what we were saying. We felt that Hoover was our enemy in many ways...and the FBI was there...we thought that if the record was complete...we had a friendly Justice Department that would judge us fairly."

"I started working with Dr. King in 1961...and I was with him until his death in 1968. I really believed that every minute of it was wonderful...whether we were traveling together to Europe, when he received the Nobel Prize...or walking the streets of Chicago on a cold winter's day...ummm...or on the hot roads of Mississippi and Alabama, trying to get the right to vote. It was my total life throughout that time."

"People know Martin Luther King only as the great orator...from his "I Have a Dream" speech. But...he really was just a regular guy who laughed and joked a lot...loved to eat soul food...and a pretty good athlete. I like to tell kids that, even though he wasn't very tall...he was a good basketball player...because, he could shoot equally well with either hand. He was actually, only about five feet seven inches tall."

"The real thing about him, that we don't remember enough is...he devoted his life trying to teach us that we can solve our problems without...killing people...without violence...without hatred. He believed that you overcome hatred with love. He used to say, "I admire the good samaritan...ummm...but I don't want to be a good samaritan. I don't want to pick up the people on the Jericho Road after they have been beaten up. I want to change the Jericho Road so that people don't get beaten up.""

"I was here in Peoria just a few months ago. One of the things that I've tried to do is help people to understand that...today is not a black holiday for Martin Luther King because he's a black leader...this is a holiday that celebrates the willingness and ability to solve problems without violence. That was Martin Luther King's dream. Now, when I talk about Dr King's message...I want to be sure and get through to Richard Pryor's people. Richard Pryor put Peoria on the map."

"Atlanta Metropolitan College was a college in the heart of the ghetto...and they asked me if I would do an orientation of all the new faculty. I said that I'd be glad to try. I started thinking, "How are you going to shake people up and help them to understand that they had moved from one world to another...and how are they going to understand and appreciate that world?" I finally told them...I said, "You're going to have to listen to a record...and you're going to have to listen to it three times. The first time, all of you will realize that...it's nasty. The second time you listen to it, you'll realize that it's funny, and you'll laugh. The third time you listen to it...and most of these are people with PhD's...I said, "You will begin to understand the depth of sociology...and the depth of the life of 4000 young people that you will be attempting to teach." I used your homeboy...Richard Pryor to educate a whole lot of very smart white folks."

"Another person that put Peoria on the map was Richard Nixon. Richard Nixon used to have an expression. Whenever you brought him an idea, his question was, "Will it play in Peoria?" The reason he said that was...Peoria...he saw...was right in the middle of this nation. You are the heart of the nation. You are not a big city, but neither are you a little country town. You are the essence of Middle America...and that's really where all of our leadership comes from. So...don't knock your hometown."

"I'm from New Orleans. I felt that this could have been the finest hour of this country...and it still can. Our economy needs a big boost. If we took Katrina reconstruction seriously, we could put everybody at Caterpillar back to work...everybody in the automobile industry back to work...it would be about a hundred billion dollar infusion of new money into the reconstruction and redevelopment of the levies...barrier islands, and housing and businesses. All of the manufactured goods out of Peoria goes down the Mississippi River on barges...all of the agriculture from here...and Iowa and Minnesota...goes down the Mississippi. You have to have a good working port in New Orleans for the economy in the Midwest to function. We can't let New Orleans flounder."

"I was a boy when Franklin Roosevelt built those levies with the Civilian Conservation Corps...and I played on those levies. Nobody has done much with them since…and you got to have…you got to contain that river. You got to manage the flood waters…and if a country can't do that…it has no business existing."

"I think we could have solved some of the problems with Iraq without going to war…but I understand the wake of 911…and I kind of disagree with the president. He says it's not about oil. I relay think it is…but…I think oil is something you have to fight about. I mean…as cold as it is, if we didn't have a regular supply of oil in the world…our economy wouldn't work. To me, the notion…oil is valuable to our national security…and I don't criticize him for wanting to protect the oil fields. When Iraq invaded Kuwait…Kuwait is closer to the Saudi oilfields than you are to Chicago…or even Springfield. The American people understand that…they like to heat their homes, drive their cars…have air conditioning…they like lights. I'm willing to fight for my lights…and gasoline and heating oil. That's America's national security that you have to protect and defend. I think Iraq is different than Vietnam. Sadaam Hussein has been around a long time doing bad things…the two million people he killed were all Muslims. When he made threats of "weapons of mass destruction"…you had to take him seriously."

"I'm just saying…yes, we could have done this a better way…but, it's not Bush's war…it's our war…and we have to fight it as a united nation. If we don't find a way to make peace there, then we have to turn it over to the most senseless and ruthless terrorists I've ever seen or heard of. People driving cars filled with bombs…driving them into funeral processions…bombing hospitals…worship services…Sunni's blowing up Shiites…this is the kind of savagery we have to stop. It's like the police in the city. When a city gets out of hand, you have to enforce the law. There are times you have to use force to make peace…and Dr. King agreed with that as well."

"I always like to remind myself…I'm 74, next month…but…I got me a girlfriend that is 104 years old. I stay with her, because she still looks good, she still wears high heels…she can still get out and do the "electric slide". She tells my wife, "Don't worry baby, I'm not gonna steal your husband…I'm just gonna borrow him every now and then." I like that spirit. I hope I'm like that when I get to that age…if I get to that age."

233   *Stella Cieslinski*

"I took a trip with my son to Key West, Florida. We rented a red Mustang convertible. It was...days of doing nothing...nowhere to go...just driving in the sun and the wind. He drove most of the time...so, I had nothing to do. It was wonderful. You should try it."

234   *Christina Cherry*

"I'm 27. I started my real life after college...after I got a degree in accounting. I just recently got married and moved away from home...moved from Texas. I try hard not to sound like I'm from Texas...you know, "you all" and all that. I couldn't find a job in accounting, so I stayed home and learned soap making, and I do accounting for my husband's business. He's incorporated...and a telecom engineer...has a consulting contact with Synergy."

"Soap making is not hard to do if you have a little bit of information. Soap is the result of combining fats with some sort of caustic agent, such as lye...using water as a catalyst. You can make soap from things that you buy at the grocery store."

"My mom told me a story of something that happened before I was born. She said that she belonged to this church...and one of the ladies that didn't belong was always saying, "If I had as much money as the rest of you...I could join your church and be just like you." She said that nobody really had any money at their church...everybody dressed in shabby clothes. So, one day after listening to the woman again...my mom called her over to her car and pulled out a box of home-made soap from the back seat. She gave her the box and said, "If you really want to be like the rest of us...take this home and use it.""

235-236   *Mary and Dick Van Norman*

"I was born May 11th, 1944…during the war. My dad was in the service…in the Army. I think I was about six months old when he first saw me. I was the first girl of seven kids."

"My parents bought a tavern…well, first of all, my father was an only child…and his parents owned a construction company where Hamm's Marina is…up Galena Road. They put in all of the roads in Detweiller…Detweiller Park. My dad bought this tavern at Spring and Adams…the PepsiCola Bottling Company was right next door. It was a mixed ethnic neighborhood then…Belgians, Irish, and Germans…and Dutch. It was like a family…people that came in there…it was like your family."

"I went to Catholic grade school and high school…St Mary's Cathedral…The Academy and Spalding. When I was five, we moved from over the tavern to Galena Road…to the country. The lane that we lived on…on both sides, there was nothing but fields…corn fields. Growing up was so fantastic. Our days were so…carefree. My father wasn't very active with us, but my mother did everything with us. She was a living saint. She would take us to Glen Oak Lagoon…and we ice-skated. My mom was very athletic when she was growing up…she took us to a lot of things…did a lot with us. Her parents emigrated from Ireland."

"Her father died when she was three months old. He worked with the street-cars…and went to work one morning…and one of his best friends, that he worked with…played a practical joke and took the streetcar off the track. How that was done, I don't know, but he was putting it back on, and another streetcar came around the corner and crushed him between the two. He died three days later. My grandmother never remarried, and raised five kids by herself. My mother said they never felt poor because…they lived across the street from Proctor Hospital…and had every activity they could ever want. They swam…she was a great swimmer and diver…basketball…tennis. Girl's sports weren't like they are today. I mean, girl's basketball at the Academy…where you could only dribble three times…that was just stupid."

"When I was a freshman at the Academy, I was somewhat of a contradiction…shy in class, but bound and determined to go out for cheerleading. I was scared to death, being only a freshman…but I did. You had to go through so many tryouts, and then some were picked…and they dwindled it down. It was a…ummm…what do you call…it was an *assembly*, for the Academy and Spalding over in the Spalding gymnasium. The whole school was there, from both schools, and they announced who was picked to be the cheerleaders…and I was one of the six."

"My name is Dick Van Norman…and I'm 69…born in 1936. I'm retired from Caterpillar, and retired from the Air Guard. I worked as a timekeeper at Caterpillar when I was going to Bradley…worked in accounting, foreign finance, and retired out of security."

"Mary and I do in-home daycare…so we take care of up to twelve kids a day. I can change diapers just as fast as the guys who flip burgers at McDonald's. We got into daycare because, Mary had a business called "Kidsmobile", where she would transport youngsters from home to preschool…dancing lessons…soccer…things like that. She had a little girl that she transported from Detweiller Drive, to an in-home daycare up at Mossville Grade School…about three days a week."

"One day, we happened to be together, and when we picked her up, the people that had the in-home daycare said, "This is what you should be doing." From a liability standpoint, I think our insurance on the van was about $500 a month. So, you have to haul a lot of kids to cover that cost. So, we kicked around the idea for a couple of weeks, and then decided…yeah, that would be rewarding and fun. It would keep us busy, active…that sort of thing. So, we took the next step and got licensed…and we been doing that for a number of years…eight years, going on nine."

"The couple that encouraged us to do that had been doing it for a number of years. We learned a lot from them and have a tremendous amount of respect for them. They both got sick and passed away within thirty or forty days of each other…cancer."

"My husband had testicular cancer when he was 35. At about the same time…he also had some friends that had cancer…and they were both dead by the end of the year. We both talked about it, and we thought the reason for his survival was that something greater was going to happen for him…in years to come. By greater, I don't mean monetarily…or being crowned…or being famous or anything…but, something significant."

"I was told that catching it when they did, saved my life...another two weeks and it could have been different...my number would have been on the wall. I couldn't figure out why I made it...and these other guys didn't. So, I was 44 when we had our son. I wonder if that was the reason why I didn't die. I suppose that is one of the things about religious belief...having a religious background."

"Our son was diagnosed as an epileptic when he was fifteen months old...and was treated for that for a number of years. Right before he was sixteen, we were told, after an EEG that there was no more seizure activity. We worried so much about him driving...and that was a relief. Just before that, there was an accident on Knoxville...and a family got killed in a fiery collision. It was basically because of a young man who had seizure activities and had not taken his medication. He hit them full blast in the rear...the car just shot over to the side of the road and blew up. That just haunted me for awhile...so when the phone call came that Rich was free of seizure activity...I just broke down. Rich went on to play...from his sophomore year on...he concentrated on baseball...played at Richwoods, played at ICC...and still plays in the Kickapoo Valley League."

"I guess if you labeled my husband and me...we would be labeled as liberals...but, we hate that word. We always feel like we have to apologize for it, because in this day and age, they've made liberals out to be that we're some sort of criminals, or something. We have a very difficult time with the Christian evangelical movement...the Jerry Falwell's...all these people that seem to be so...so judgmental. You have to follow their way of belief...so, we have a difficult time with that. We're still part of the Catholic Church, but we do our own thing...and, we just don't understand why everyone is so judgmental."

237 *Jan Stoia*

"My name is Jan Stoia, and I am 56. I am an artist with a degree in journal-ism…and I do variable color monotypes. What motivates me is color…I love color. So, form is secondary to color for me. Originally, I got into the journalism program at college because the art program was closed. So, I got my degree in journalism, graduated from that, and now I am doing art again."

"The monotypes that I do…called a transfer process…I paint on a clear acrylic plate…and then I transfer it, section by section, to art paper. I am selling my art-work at the Sugar Creek Art Festival. This is my first year here…but I do maybe six or seven shows a year. I show primarily in the Chicago area."

"I actually fell back into this in a period when I was sick. My friend and I both had chronic fatigue syndrome. She suggested we both take a class at the commu-nity college…and we did, and I loved it because I had always been interested in art. The art teacher said, "You guys oughta put on a show." That's what started things for me."

"I once worked for the Journal Star. I worked the city desk…the state desk…I was an intern there. I worked features as well, and I had something published in the New York Times…in their journal. I covered the Lincoln-Douglas Ottawa re-enactment debate. I was one of their correspondents. It was interesting, but the pay was rather low, I must add…but there is a certain honor working for the New York Times."

"I am originally from a little town west of Chicago…a little prairie town called Warrenville. When I grew up there, there were no curbs, there was one grocery store…and we were often teased because we were from Warrenville. Now, it's just a part of suburbia."

"As a kid, my mother bought me paint-by-number sets. I did a lot of drawing. I did a lot of writing. I entered my first art contest when I was in the fourth grade. It was a Girl Scout contest, and I won…I placed in it. My mother was a piano teacher for fifty years, so I also wrote music and performed in a state competition that I won…for a piece I composed. So, I had this artistic bent following me through this life. I considered getting a degree in creative writing instead of journalism, because I wanted a paycheck. Now, look at me now…I have no paycheck, but…I am an artist. Good for me."

238   *Ken Baxter*

"I moved to Louisiana in '83. I went to grad school there. It was the first time I had lived out of Arkansas. Then in '85, I went to Kansas…and I haven't lived in the South since then. I've lived here for thirteen years."

"I work at Eureka College as an assistant dean…and wear a lot of hats in a small school. I get to meet a lot of people. I met William F. Buckley. Do you remember Coach Boone from "Remember the Titans"? The guy that Denzel Washington plays? I met him. He's a lot older. I met Maureen Reagan…she was on our Board of Trustees for awhile. She's dead now. I met John Ritter…also dead. By the time I came to work here, President Reagan didn't come here any more."

"Around '99 I think…somewhere around there…we brought Morris Dees to campus, from the Southern Poverty Law Center. He's a big civil rights attorney, and represents people who are persecuted….by the Aryan Nation and all these hate groups. He's out of Alabama, or somewhere in the south. He's pretty well known."

"About the same time, we had all this stuff going on in East Peoria, with Matt Hale. We had a former Northwestern basketball coach that was killed by an extremist…and it all happened about that same time. We had booked this speaker a year in advance, and this guy…he had death threats against him…all the time."

"We had to close the CERF Center so the FBI could come in with their dogs and check for explosives. They had to black out all the windows so snipers couldn't be sitting outside shooting through the glass. Then…we actually had the event down at the Reagan Gym because it got too large for the CERF Center. And…there were probably thirty or forty police officers…had metal detectors. CSPAN was there broadcasting…and I was actually on CSPAN holding a microphone, which was kind of funny."

"Some of the people said, it wasn't quite this intense when the president came. I wasn't here then, so I didn't know. We even had an undercover cop as a protestor. He had racist stuff on signs printed…he didn't look anything like a cop. He was out front in an area they had designated for protestors. I don't know if anyone joined him or not, but he looked like the worst hoodlum you can imagine."

"I remember several big national events...not that happened here, but we watched it on campus. The largest was 911. We hooked up a TV projector in the auditorium and just had CNN on all day, for people to go in and out all day long. We cancelled classes...and had a big ceremony out at the Peace Garden. I remember when the OJ Simpson verdict was read. I was in the Burgoo watching the TV. You think...big things that are happening across the country...you watch on TV...and whatever it is...crowds gather."

"Before there was a Eureka, there was a settlement called Walnut Grove. There wasn't a college, there wasn't really a city...and every year during the spring, the settlers would gather. There was this big social occasion...roughly in the area where the CERF Center is now...around that area. It was called the Old Spring. They would gather there and there would be a sort of a potluck...except they would make this Burgoo stew. People would bring whatever leftover vegetables they had...that made it through the winter. They would kill rabbits and squirrels and stuff...and make this huge pot of stew called Burgoo that they would serve. They had games and contests...it was just this big social event. So, when we built the CERF Center...we found out about that, and decided to name the snack bar "The Burgoo". We thought that people would interact and socialize and kind of blend together...just like Burgoo stew."

239   ***Melinda Feger***

"Melinda...I'm 34. I live in Marquette Heights, but I was born in Bloomington and grew up in Danvers. Danvers is a real small quiet...kinda sleepy community just outside of Bloomington...to the east of Bloomington...no, west. There is nothing in Danvers. There used to be a little coffee shop, but not anymore. It's a little historical building now...a little library. There's an FS...the FS is the gas station."

"We used to go to Indiana...to the races. We didn't go to any of the big open-wheel...well, we went to the open-wheel, but like...midget sprint silver crown cars...they're small. My parents had done that when they were dating, and they just took us as kids. If there was an infield, my brother and I would play there...otherwise we'd have to sit in the bleachers, which was not as much fun."

"I've met guys who have become Nascar drivers. I've met Kenny Irwin, who is now deceased. I've met Tony Stewart and Ryan Newman, Ken Schrader...the open-wheel guys that come from open-wheel that are now in Nascar."

"I am a customer service manager here at Walmart, which means I am over all of the cashiers, the cart pushers, the service desk, layaway, the greeters...ummm...on a typical day I do a lot of walking. Any of the registers...anywhere there is a register, if they have any sort of issue with the register...I go and take care of it. I am frequently in electronics, or automotive, or sporting goods...wherever there is a register, I have to take care of it."

"This is my wireless handheld...it tells me, uh, what the cashiers need. They can put in requests for, like, change...or if they need any help, they just put a request in and let me know. I think sometimes it makes it too easy for the cashiers to get a hold of me. They don't try to figure out problems on their own...let's just ask Melinda."

"I have three boys...Devin, Damick, and Drew. My oldest is nine, he just turned nine on Saturday...he races quarter-midgets. They are little race cars...they are really cute...and they're really safe. They're very safe. He has a five point harness that he wears...neck restraint...arm...arm restraints, so that the arms can't come out of the cage. The five year old, he started racing, and he has his own quarter-midget, and he started racing…but he decided he didn't like going fast…so he's gonna wait for awhile. He doesn't race anymore. He's always been somebody who's been on his own timetable. My two-year old doesn't race yet, but I think he will be the racer…the best racer of the three boys. He just seems to…ummm…just pay so much more attention to what's going on…during the races, when they're working on the cars, he seems to pay much more attention than the other boys do. Devin definitely likes racing, but he doesn't have the aggression. He's content to just sit back and follow the car in front of him…he doesn't really have the desire to try and pass, I guess."

"The cars run about thirty miles and hour. We have go-carts too, which can go much faster…they can go…my brother's was clocked at, like, eighty miles an hour. I've been around racing for a long time, and we're still into racing. Devin won his first race this year…in the same night he won his heat race, and then he won a feature…and he was really excited. We were all excited for him."

240   *Juanita Kurtz*

"We went visiting nursing homes today. Our son lives here and we told him to meet us at Cracker Barrel and we would pay for his dinner. I had the chicken salad."

"I grew up out in the country...from a little town called Richview. It's close to Centralia...about three hours south of Bloomington. Now, Interstate 64 runs through that town. It is a poor little town. It used to have a seminary there...there used to be a large...large, train station, and a university and everything. Now it's down to one café...not even a store in the town. Nothing. The population is 250 now...everyone has left. I left 54 years ago and moved here. I used to be Juanita Skibinski. Been married 54 years, husband worked for forty years and retired."

"I graduated in May...got married in August, then came up here, and I hated the town. I cried every day. I had never been away from my parents. I didn't like the big city."

"I lived on a peach and apple farm, and people used to come from all over and buy peaches from my dad, because back then we had Hale peaches and Red Haven peaches. That's what everybody came to buy. I never dreamed I would live in the big city. We had cows and pigs and chickens...we walked back and forth to school...didn't have to pay to ride a bus. You know, that's why our schools are going broke...I think...because of the busses...the gas...and you hafta pay."

"We used to walk back and forth to school. It didn't hurt us at all. Our neighbor kids can walk...but they get picked up on the bus instead. I think it's ridiculous."

"All my kids went to school in public schools, until the second grade...and then they went to the Christian school. It was wonderful. They had Christian teachers there...and they didn't teach evolution...and all that other garbage."

241   *Tim Popp*

"I live in Peoria and I'm 38. I'm from Iron Mountain originally…the upper peninsula of Michigan. I'm a *UP-er*. Those are the people from the UP…Upper Peninsula. I went to the University of Michigan in the lower peninsula, then went to Chicago as a consultant…and that's how I got assigned to Caterpillar…and that's how I met Amy, who you just saw…my wife, who was my girlfriend then…fiancé, then my wife. And now, here's Miranda, age two…and Riley, age four"

"Riley went through potty training, and Miranda is starting. The tradition that we had in my family…and passed down to this family, is…when you're on the potty…when you're good enough to do it yourself…but not ready to do the wrap-up…what you do is yell across the house…"I'M ALL DONE." So, my brother…we send a lot of emails back and forth about these stories…and he remembers that my mom had to step out for a short time. I was maybe about age three or so…three or four…and my brothers were three or four years older than me. My mom had to step out for a short thing and come back…and they had to use the potty when I was done. This was a short house…maybe a forty-foot house with three inch un-insulated walls…and they pretended not to hear me. I was yelling. "I'M ALL DONE…I'M ALL DONE." After awhile I was crying it…"I'M ALL DONE…I'M ALL DONE." They pretended they didn't hear me, because they didn't want anything to do with the wrap-up. Now, these two…they're hearing that story too. This one…she'll just chirp across the room in a tiny voice, "I'm all done."

"I was just picking out a soda…and do you remember the Mountain Dew commercials where they would show somebody, you know, rafting down a river or swinging from a rope…out into the water? We had this place…and just seeing Mountain Dew reminded me…this was an iron mining community up in the upper peninsula…where you have Iron Mountain, Iron River, Iron Wood…Copper Harbor…it's all mining of some sort. But, in Iron Mountain, there's an old iron mine that caved in and filled in with water. So, you have these cliffs on one side, maybe ten feet off the water. On the other side…like a hundred feet off the water, there were these bluffs…bluffs all around…and in the middle was the water…crystal clear water. In some places, it was maybe a hundred feet deep. It was parts of mine shafts…old mine shafts, just filled in with water. We would jump off those cliffs…and my brother would just dive in. I would never dive in. I would always jump in feet first. That was on one side…but on the other side was this big rope…and you would run off the cliffs and swing out, and drop about thirty feet into the water. That's a good kind of fun you can have with an old iron mine."

"I played football in high school…never in college…but in high school, I had four touchdowns on my birthday…my sixteenth birthday. That was a big thing. I come from a football family, and that was a big thing. Within a year of that, even before I turned seventeen…my parents divorced…and I never saw it coming. There was a kind of strife going on…and my family was like, the pillars of the community. I was very proud of our family, and each person in the family. We just had this…you know, a lot of fun…very active…very present. You know, my dad was just a big personality…the one you look up to, and put on a pedestal. My life came, really crashing down after that. But, that's how I became very independent."

"My job lately was kicking my butt, and I was thrown into family life…where I was so used to being an individual before. I was part of a project team that was failing, and part of a marriage and a family that was just pulling me. I couldn't just do my own thing…my own way…at my own pace. So, I kind of saw the thing going full circle. I got through with my independent life…and now I'm kinda pulling back into an interdependent family unit…and a project team. So, I was part of a family…spun off into being an individual, found my own path, and then came back to being a part of a family…and a community too. I'm part of a church…so now it's kind of a *we* thing again. It went from *we* to *me*, and then back to *we* again."

"My dad wasn't home a lot, but that was the nature of his business. He was a hearing-aid salesman and covered most of Northern Michigan, so he was on the road more than he was home. But now, I am seeing the potential in me…in my family to be what he was in our family. He was very much an individual…cowboy…free spirit kind of guy, too…and just the pressures of being in a family, where…very little of it is about me…it is we…almost entirely. But, I saw that he…he just couldn't handle the responsibility of being a father…of just being…of having so many people dependent upon him for being the provider. So, now, I've kind of gone the other way…where I've become overly responsible…as a father, as a project leader…as a whatever."

"Where other people have left Caterpillar...and I'm very much a free-spirited, abstract, spiritual, and philosophical person...and most people like that go on to either a smaller operation, or a church, or academia...I am the idiot that stays there and tries to make it work. It's a tough call...but I try to make it all work."

242 *Joseph Khouri*

"I am 26. I don't live here any more...I now live in the Denver area. Have you heard of Lakewood? That's where I live. Do you remember the Columbine High School shootings? I live just a couple of miles from there. I come back here once or twice a year to visit my family and get a Steakburger. I also like to eat tenderloins when I come back. We don't have tenderloins in Denver."

"I went to a Catholic grade school. You know where Holy Family is? I went there. Holy Family is really...kind of a dumb name for a Catholic Church and school. Usually, it's Saint...Saint *Somebody*. When I was in eighth grade, my dad called it St. Eggroll, because there was a place right across the street called Eggroll Express. It was a place with these big signs plastered everywhere. What do you call those machines that make the text stickers...you know...you peel off the back and stick them on things...the black and red hard plastic tape, where you dial up the letters and you press the trigger to make the raised letters? You know what I'm talking about?"

"The guy that owned the place, a Chinese guy called George...he had one of those machines that made the giant labels. The letters were like, an inch tall. He had everything...everything labeled. The whole menu was scattered throughout the entire restaurant...it was carryout only...lots of labels...signs. There were also these giant Chinese proverbs on the front of the counter, top of the counter...and all the walls. The guy just went nuts with the label maker. Almost every inch of everything was covered. There was one saying that went almost all the way across the top part of the front counter...it was a continuous stream of tape about nine feet long. It said something like, "Man who lives in glass house should change clothes in basement...and call Egg Roll Express and order Kung Pao Chicken with eggroll and rice for only $4.95." It was something like that. George was a funny guy."

"So, one day at lunch...Joe Klein and I...we weren't supposed to be off the grounds...but we snuck over there to get some eggrolls. We ordered the eggrolls from George...and while we were waiting...and after he went in the back...we started to play with some of the labels...you know, running our fingers across the top to feel the raised lettering. Then I put my finger underneath the edge of the long one and started to peel it off a little. I guess I got carried away...and due to the weight of the label, and the greasy atmosphere, all of a sudden, the whole…the whole damn thing came off…fell off the counter. I got scared and started folding it up…gobbling it up into a sticky plastic tape ball. We could hear George talking to his wife and coming back to the front….so I stuck it in my front pocket. I also had, in the crotch of my pants…a pack of Salem's. That's where I hid my cigarettes. So, I had my Salem's…and I had this big ball of sticky plastic tape right there in the front of my pants."

"So…George starts doing stuff, talking on the phone and writing stuff down…and he finally looks over at me and looks right at my crotch. I look down, and it's like I have a…Peking duck or something in my pants. Joe Klein looks at George looking at me and gets up and walks out the door. I look at my crotch, and George looks at my crotch and finally says, "You eggrolls almost ready…you pay now…two dollar." So…I'm digging in my front pocket for the money…and I can hardly get my hand in because there's just…no room. He's still looking at my crotch, and I'm still trying to get the money out of my pocket…and I can't. I can't do it."

"Meanwhile…Mrs. George comes up front with a little brown bag of eggrolls, and as soon as she sees me…she starts staring at my crotch. They don't say anything to each other, but they're both staring at my crotch. I don't know if it was because I was embarrassed or that I couldn't get the money out…but I finally pulled out this plastic ball of…Chinese proverb…and handed it to George while I hear myself saying, "Ummm…this fell off.""

"He takes it from me…looks at it…looks at the counter where it wasn't…and says, "Why you have Kung Pao sticker in pants?" I said, "I don't know." He looked at his wife…he looked at the sticker ball…and then he looked at me as he was handing me the paper sack, and he said, "Two dollar." So, I found the money in my pocket and gave it to him just as the phone rang. I grabbed the bag off the counter and walked out as quickly as I could."

"Joe Klein…yellow-belly Joe Klein, was sitting on a yellow parking barrier on the other side of the parking lot. He said, "Did you get in trouble?" I said, "I don't think so." Then we walked across Sterling and went behind the Pizza Inn. We sat on a metal pallet and ate our egg rolls…and then smoked a cigarette before sneaking back onto the playground."

243 *Jim Klaus*

"In about a month, I'll be 78. I was born and raised in Eureka...worked at Klaus Radio in Peoria. I worked there for 45 years. I worked in the parts department. My father was one of the original starters of Klaus Radio...my father, my uncle, and my grandfather. They're a little different now...they don't have RCA anymore...Whirlpool, and some of them. The factories have decided to go direct to stores like Walmart and so forth. They still handle other lines, but not what they started with."

"Ronald Reagan went to school with my uncle...in Eureka...Eureka College. He used to go down to my grandmother's house...went there quite a bit. He also worked for Hecker's Restaurant when he went to college. Of course, after he graduated and moved on, we heard about...we followed his activities. After California, he came back to Eureka on two or three different occasions...library dedication...pumpkin festival...he came to town three or four times. When I was on the city council, I met him, and talked to him. Like I say...he double-dated with my uncle while they were in college."

"At our house, my dad had fixed up a basketball deal in the driveway...and we had a pretty good sized driveway with the neighbor...and we used to have basketball games there every night, 'til about midnight. The three old-maid sisters that lived next to us didn't appreciate it too much, but we had a good time...and they were good people."

"At age thirteen, I set pins in the bowling alley. We used to get four cents a line for setting pins in the bowling alley. At that time, I weighed about 85 pounds and I had a heck of a time trying to get the machine down. But, yeah...I set pins there for quite some time. Two of my uncles owned it...they built it...the Eureka Bowling Alley. Of course when any of the relatives bowled, they didn't pay anything...so we didn't get paid. The pinsetters didn't get paid for setting the pins for them."

"Then after high school, I got drafted...in '45. I ended up in Japan...in the occupation forces. We were there until Truman came over and signed the armistice deal with the Japanese. Then, when that happened, anybody that was drafted was released, unless they wanted to enlist and stay in the military. I was only in about fourteen…fifteen months. I took my infantry training in Little Rock, was sent to San Francisco, and then sent to Japan. They came around to the tents we were billeted in and said, "This tent…you're in the Signal Corps…this tent, you're in the Infantry…this tent, you're in the *whatever*." I ended up in the Signal Corps…no experience whatever. But, we were in charge of all the long-distance toll lines to Korea. That was about the time the war broke out there…and I came back just before that."

"I was mayor here for four years…and one of the founding fathers of the Lions Club…and I'm still involved. I come up here on Eureka Reagan Fest, and the Lions Club cooks pork chop sandwiches…and have a ball. We furnish eye exams and glasses for people that can't afford them…hearing aids too. We also take care of firing off the fireworks on the 4th of July."

"There are a lot of people here now, that I don't know. When I was a kid…I knew everybody. I don't know a lot of people anymore."

244   *Doug Smith*

"Do you know why the alien took a bar of soap with him in outer space? In case he ran into a meteor shower. Thank you ladies…you're from Mattoon, you're honest people."

"Where are you from? Florida? Flora? Where's Flora…close to Mattoon? South of Mattoon? I hope you guys aren't driving home, because you don't know where you live. Okay, okay…bye guys…thank you very much…good luck tomorrow."

"Hey sir, throw a couple of green George's in there and I'll take care of you…a couple of green George's. There you go…thank you very much sir."

"Now…sir, what is your name? Zach? Green and black? Sure…you want a two-toned alien? Okay, two different colors…we'll give you a green and a black. Is this your girlfriend, sir? Come on over here, Zach. Okay, you're the older brother…and that's your older sister. She's you're sister…you're her sister. Okay, that makes you her sister, and she's your brother. Yes, that's what I said…she's your mother and you're her son. Okay, let's start all over again…your name is Zachariah…and what's your girlfriend's name? Hey…you just told me that was your girlfriend…not just two seconds ago, you told me that was your girlfriend. Alright Zach…careful of that frog right there. You seem a little jumpy. You guys…you know what one frog said to the other frog? Time's sure fun when you're having flies. Did you guys hear about the frog that went to the hospital? He was very unhoppy. Did you hear about the frog that double-parked? He got toad."

"Come on over here sir…one two-toned alien. There you go sir…thank you guys…if you have any breakage…I repair…just bring me the pieces and parts, and I'll take care of you. Nothing for your girlfriend Zach…she didn't want anything? Nice little princess hat? Alright."

"Did you get any leaches? You know there are leaches in that fountain. There's one on your leg right there…and she looked. There are no leaches in that fountain, Miss. Whoo-hoo! Spiders…but no leaches."

"I've been doing this…starting my tenth year. My family got tired of me making the same thing over and over and over…so I started learning a few more. When I first started out I was making twelve basic figures…and you get tired of dogs and flowers and that kind of stuff…quick. Now I can do nearly 200 different things from memory and about another fifty that are specialty items only. I do them for private parties, or gifts, or what have you…stuff I just don't have the time to do out in public."

"My favorite is when I do a monkey in a tree. That's my favorite creation that got me where I am. I'll ask people…I'll ask them, "Would you like me to make you a monkey in a tree?" They'll go, "Sure, we'd love it." So…I'll bring them….Oh, hi guys, how are you? Here…this is better demonstrated."

"Can I use one of these young ladies for a second? Who likes monkeys in a tree? Excellent. What's your name Miss? Haley? Come on over and stand right here, Haley. Haley, turn around and look at all your friends for me. This one I do…I take somebody who likes monkeys in trees…and I say…Haley…raise your right hand up in the air for me please. I want you to wave at everybody Haley. Now go, "Hello everybody". No, wave at them while you do it. Okay, everybody wave back and go," Hi Haley." Now, Haley raise your right hand up in the air for me please. Your other right hand. No, your left hand…I'm sorry. Now wave at everybody and go, "Hi everybody." Everybody wave back and go, "Hi Fred". Now, Haley I want you to raise this up with both hands…high up in the air as you can. Now…remember what you asked me to make you right? I love making monkeys in a tree. Everybody raise your right hands up in the air for me please. Everybody got their right hands up? Ok, everybody got their hands up? You too Miss…get your right hand up…very good. Now, don't anyone spoil this for Haley. Haley, look at all your friends out there. Everybody ready to start waving? Don't tell Hal…don't tell Haley…don't spoil this for Miss Haley. Okay, everybody waving? You know why they're waving Haley? Because you are a monkey in a tree. See your tail? You're the monkey. I said I would make you a monkey in a tree. Haley, can you go, "Hoo, hoo, hoo, hoo, hoo?" Very good. Thank you…give it up for Haley."

"That's an example. I take someone with a great sense of humor and turn them into a monkey in a tree. One year I was down here, and there was a young man celebrating his birthday…and as soon as he realized what I had done to him, he started crying. The more he cried, the more his family laughed. The more they laughed the harder he cried. It was a no-win situation."

"One lady said to me, "That's so cool, where did you learn how to do that?" I looked at her and said, with a straight face, "prison.". She stepped back two steps with the kids. I said, "Miss, miss…I'm just kidding." She stepped back forward and I said, "It was really just work-release."

"Haley, what's the last letter of your first name? Y…because I want to know. What's the last letter of your first name? Y…because I want to know. Bye Haley…bye Haley"

"I am 43 and my name is Doug Smith. I picked this up as a way to entertain family and friends, and they got all…pretty bored with it. So they said to go and entertain somebody else with it. Anybody can do balloons, but you gotta have a little personality to go with them…gotta be able to tell some corny jokes…even if they're groaners for adults, the kids have never heard them, most of the time. You'd be surprised how many kids don't get jokes. Me…I go to garage sales and find dog-eared joke books. You gotta have sizzle. Anybody can do balloons, but you gotta have fun. I never thought when I started out, I would make this a semi full-time job. I would go into this full-time, you know, if it wasn't for the high cost of inflation. I have worked as a photographer for WEEK for fifteen years, and have been in the TV business for over twenty years."

"Hey lady…do you know how to cook a monkey? You gorilla them."

245   *Philip Jose Farmer*

"I was born in 1918. I've written seventy-five books. Of everything I have ever written...if I had any particular words...any particular sentence that I am the proudest of...if I had one...I've forgotten it."

"The most exciting event in my life was when I was about six years old. I was outdoors playing when I looked up and saw this...this magnificent air ship in the sky over Peoria. It was a dirigible. I ran inside and told my mom, who had to come out and see it. She looked up and said, "Oh, that's nice Philip." She wasn't impressed in the least."

"I have never forgotten this other incident. My parents gave me a football for Christmas. My brother grabbed it and took it out to the outhouse and threw it down the hole. Of course we never got it...and my parents didn't replace it. I don't think anything has ever made me that angry since. But...I really didn't play with toys as a child. I had books as soon as I could read...and had lots of exercise playing Tarzan with my friends."

"When we moved back here from Los Angeles, it was to be in a smaller town with old friends, where you could easily drive out in the country. Now the developers have expanded our town...even though there are no more people here than when we moved back...in 1950. So, the traffic increases and the "small" town feel is gone...you go out in the *country* and there's a new development going up there."

"One night, I was having trouble getting started...writing. I told my wife that it was because she always asked people to come over and visit. She said...that was just an excuse, and the argument continued for quite awhile, until she said I was using her as an excuse...and that from now on, *I* would say when we had company. I started a regular routine the next day...and that went on for...fifty years."

"My books have urged many people to read, because they have been forced to look things up...by other authors. I know many young people tell me they never would have read some things if I hadn't mentioned them in my books."

"What is important to me right now is...having my children, grandchildren, and great grandchildren visit...and just...being alive. An important philosophy for me at this point in my life is...don't fight...accept."

246   *Kris Hoak*

"I know I'm not a good parent. Like a lot of parents…I gave my kids what they wanted. If I'd done my job better, they wouldn't like me very much."

247 *John Bennington*

"I'm from Elkader, Iowa…originally. It's up by McGregor…northeastern corner"

"I grew up on a farm and went to a country school. Growing up there, where you walked everywhere, you froze your butt off in the winter. We walked a mile and a quarter to the country school…and when you got there, the fire wasn't going. It was a one room schoolhouse, and the teacher was supposed to be there early and have the fire going. She usually did everything. We had…maybe fifteen kids…and that was kindergarten up to the eighth grade."

"I opened a shop when I graduated from high school and worked on radios. I also worked for Collins Radio in Cedar Rapids for ten years…but…I was always interested in history."

"I've got stuff that was handed down from the family. I have needlepoint…a sampler that was done in 1842 by a great-great grandmother. I have a little book that's dated 1839 that was a wedding gift…things like that. I was…the one person in the family that took care of things…a lot of the old things…and so, they were given to me. Because, if somebody else doesn't care about something, it just gets broken. I have my great-grandfather's wedding vest that he was married in…in 1852."

"I do a lot with the history of our family…tracing where they came from. I am English and Irish. From the time they were born in England and Ireland, I have everybody documented, down to like…2000. The earliest weddings I have documented were in 1836."

"My grandfather was a wonderful man, but my father was a horse's ass. I grew up on the homestead farm. Some people say *homestead*, and actually they weren't even homesteading…because that was when you went out west and got the land without paying for it. In the 1850's…you paid for the land. It was a dollar and a quarter an acre, and the people that came from Ireland or England, or wherever…they went to the land office and picked out land that nobody had bought yet. My grandfather bought 39.6 acres from the government…and the same day he bought forty acres with a slab house on it from the guy next door. Over the years, he just kept buying people out."

"I haven't really been involved in much history myself. When I graduated, it was just after the Korean War...and I stayed in Iowa. Iowa was clean...safe. I felt secure there. There's no crime. If you don't lock your car, it's just...no big deal."

"I know so much family lore...and it's hard to write some of this stuff down. Some things...shouldn't be written down. It might hurt somebody, and that shouldn't be the goal...to leave something written that will make somebody feel bad. But...one thing about history...you know, when you lose some-body...that's when you have the question. You think, "Why didn't I ask him this?" You never...you never think of it until they are gone. I'm sure that when I'm gone, there will be somebody who will say, "Why didn't we ask him?"

248 *Jim Fyke*

"I'm originally from Southern Illinois…and I am 69. I was born in Marion County. My folks moved here in 1940…literally, because my father's horse died. He had a little farm, and two horses…and one of them died. He went to the bank to get a loan, and they said, "We don't loan on horses anymore." They said, "You can buy a tractor." Then he said, "I can't afford a tractor." So…he came up and got a job at R.G. LeTourneau…making tractors. He was hired there…and a couple of his brothers-in law that worked in the Centralia area, also came up. He worked there 35…37 years…something like that. We lived on North Madison for a long time. So, my family was transplanted when I was four…here."

"I went to Woodruff High School…and then went to college at Michigan State…and then worked as police chief in a couple of different areas. Then I came back. My son had contracted leukemia…and was beginning to have problems, and wanted to come back and be with his grandparents…aunts, and cousins…and so forth. So, I decided we'd come back. I resigned and came back to the Peoria area, and then I went with ICC as a professor. But, he died…my son, unfortunately, about a month after we got back. So, that's how we got back here."

"We lived up there…up on Bradley Avenue. The university started building fraternities and sororities and so forth, to add on. We lived right across the street from the Bradley library. They said, "Tell you what…we're buying all the houses down the street." And when we looked, out of six lots, they had already purchased five homes. We were the only single family home left in the whole square block. So, we sold our house there…then couldn't afford a house in the Peoria area at the time, where we could put all our kids. Older daughter said, "Gee there's a nice house down by Grandma's in Eureka." So, we ended up buying it…and came here in 1990. So, it's just kind of an unforeseen set of circumstances that got us here in Eureka."

"On Thanksgiving day, down in Southern Illinois…and my brother and I were the only ones in the family at the time…my first recollections are…the two of us were standing on the back seat, or on the floor…looking out as we drove across the pastures and fields, as we were going to my grandmother's house. We didn't use the roads for some reason or another. They…they take down a gate…and then you would drive through it…and the gate was just wire with a big stick on the end…and a big loop of wire on the top to hold the gate back in…just to keep the cows in. That was my first recollection…going across the fields, you know…to grandmother's house we go. So…that song kinda had a meaning to me after that…"Over the river and through the woods, to Grandmother's house we go."

"I now work part-time. I'm retired from the government…and so I work part-time as a minister at a little church down by Decatur. I work part-time at a print shop here…and I work part-time at a small newspaper, doing some editing and so forth. I'm also very active in historical and genealogical things. My hobby is really genealogy…and I've gotten into the computerized…and there are tremendous advantages…you still can't get the original copies of documents and so forth…but the advantage you have now is, you can blend your research with the research of other people. You can look at other people's work…and you may have some information, which challenges that."

"In one case, I was looking for my great-grandfather in Southern Illinois…and I found another man named Granville Fyke. At the time, everyone thought that it was my great-grandfather, but after I went down and did some research…I found there were two Granville Fykes. Now, that's not a common name. Born eight years apart…in the same county. One married a woman named Ida…one married a woman named Ada. So, they conflated those families…and all of a sudden they had fifteen or sixteen kids. Well, it turns out, these are two different men, living in different townships…in the same county…but related, maybe one…one step apart. But, people…for many years…thought this was the same person…rather than someone had just made a mistake in the spelling of the wife's name. Actually looking at the digitized census reports of the time…you can see neighbors…I found some of the people living next door to some of my kinfolk. But, two generations before…those two families became related by marriage. So, it's easy to make the mistake that two families were relatives…but they weren't at the time that occurred."

"The research using electronic means has dramatically increased the activity, and the number of people that are doing this. So, it really makes it worthwhile…because you can dig into things. Of course, you can come into some roadblocks. I've got one now in the 1720's, in Virginia…and at that point, we're not even in the U.S. yet…so, the records are hard to come up with. I may have a permanent roadblock…may not be able to get through that gate…I don't know yet."

249   *Mildred Snyder*

"I was born right here...down the street a little ways. The house is just a house now, but it was a combination nursing home and hospital in the early days. There was a registered nurse that kept it going. It's an intriguing house...it's down on Douglas Street. I don't remember house numbers...let me look in the phone book. Ummm...I don't know if the owner knows anything about the history of the house, but she has learned a little about it. She is restoring it...and she was tickled to death because they found the door to the laundry chute...it was hidden in one of the closets. So, they put it back the way it was. Here it is...205 West Douglas...by the Catholic Church."

"I've worked at the insurance agency for awhile...worked in the Sale Barn office for awhile. I worked at the library for awhile. I worked at Foster-Gallagher for awhile. I've been around. I've been single my whole life...don't know anybody I could get along with. I can't face anybody over the breakfast table...at all. I have an older sister I live with...and we've been together forever."

"It was my little sister that got me into arranging flowers. She was here when the boy opened the shop in 1962. He kept it for ten years, and then decided to open one in Lake of the Woods. She didn't want it to close, so she conned us into going into it with her. That's how I got into it. She was trained for it, and I'm not...I just kind of picked it up across the table here."

"The funeral home...that's our bread and butter, always. Funerals aren't what they used to be...weddings aren't either...but funerals, because of the many, many places they give donations to now, instead of buying flowers. Memorials are a good thing, but it cuts into our business."

"My 50th birthday, I suddenly realized I had lived half a century and had nothing to show for it. I'm 77 now...still don't. I know when I was younger, we had an old lady...and you couldn't get by her house. When you went to go home, she was always hanging out the door, wanting you to stop and talk. She was a sweet little old gal...very lonely. I think sometimes we're all just tiny little frogs in a big pond."

"We used to have an old bandmaster. He was so good…and every time we have a parade we talk about old Saxton, because he was so good…and boy, those kids marched. You don't see a good marching band any more…one that can stay in step. He was military-bearing, and just got a lot out of those kids. We haven't had as good of one since, really."

"We don't like to drive in to the city, because they change the streets so often…you never know what's going to be a one-way the next time you're in. I'd rather drive to the Kewanee Walmart. There is so much less traffic between here and there…and no stop signs to mess with. It's only about thirty miles north…straight shot. We have our cleaner up there…so we have to go up every week anyway."

"Eighteen years ago, we had a really nasty accident…up by Aurora. I was in Mercy Hospital for three and a half weeks. I wanted to leave so bad…I was homesick to get down here, where my family could come and visit me. The people up there kept saying there was no way that any small town had an ambulance they could send…that distance. Well, my doctor lined it up…and they came up and got me. The girls up there were astonished. I think the ambulance crew, and the people here in Princeville are the greatest."

"This is my scanner…I couldn't live without it. There was just a problem over at the medical center, somebody with a heart problem. I imagine Joe will be on his way there now. They are afraid they can't treat the problem, and they need an EMT…to send him to the hospital. Maybe the doctor is already gone for the day…and the girls are not real brave about taking on something like that. If they have any doubts, they send them on in to the hospital. Our ambulance crew is the greatest."

"We have the best bunch of guys, and they run like crazy. I can speak from experience, because my sister had a heart attack in May…early May. We didn't know it, and she didn't know it. She went to the clinic because she had such a back-ache…and they took her in…and Joe was on the crew when they took her in. He came back out and said, "Lock the door, you're coming with me." He took me to the hospital because she had a heart attack right in the Emergency Room. Because Joe is so tender-hearted…I don't know how he can do the job he's doing…not really."

250   *Taylor Johnston*

"Really, my full name is Robert William Taylor Johnston. Taylor is like, my second middle name. It's the way my parents, like…had it. They're from the South…and like, from Texas. They do that a lot there. I lived in Galveston actually. It's like, that island that was almost hit by the hurricane a couple of weeks ago. I know I was like, around second grade when we left…so that would be…I don't really know ages for grades in school. I'm nineteen now."

"I'm really into media…things like that…like, movies…music…that kind of thing. I want to be…I want to be a video editor, video producer…that kind of thing. I'm going to ICC now, but I'll transfer somewhere eventually. I want to be in some kind of video production…work for a video production studio, or just probably start out freelance video editing. Basically, someone needs a video made…whether it's a documentary…well, not really a documentary…like, a training video for their employees, or a wedding video…they need someone to put together a slide show…that kind of thing. I'm working a little bit with "Life Memory Videos" for funerals. People die, and they want to remember them…have a slide show going on in the background…and all kinds of stuff like that."

"I've done a lot of that with my school. I made a really cool Senior DVD that I gave everyone. I filmed all of our special events. I'm also interested in like…let's say a business had a retreat…and they wanted someone to like, tape it…and put it together into a collage of stuff going on with that. They could hire me out for that. So, yeah…that kind of thing. There are a lot of openings for that kind of thing. Companies hire in-house video editors…and there are production studios all over the place now."

"I'm like…I'm way into music right now. I listen to…just a ton of music. Different broad genres…like movies and stuff…I'm doing a lot of that. I listen to a lot of classic rock, and some 80's music. My favorite band is U2. Also, I'm into underground rock…stuff that's going on right now, and it's getting more popular. I have a…a music blog that I spend a lot of time on. I find a new artist and stuff…and write about them…and I send it out to the world. They get to download a couple of tracks…and stuff like that."

"We had been watching this movie called, "Napoleon Dynamite", I'm sure you've heard of that. So, I had seen it like...six times in theaters...and like...the friends around my age...we got obsessed with it...and quoted it. Everything that we said was from that movie, at that time. We wasted a lot of time and money with that...well, not wasted...it's still a good movie. So, we went out and saw the movie together...we all went out to see the movie...and it was like, my seventh time seeing it...and my girlfriend and I had just met. So, afterwards, we went out and played late-night tetherball...because of the movie...they play tetherball on this playground. They play tetherball. We went to a grocery store and took pictures of stuff...and did all these wacky, fun things. We did all this cool stuff...and it was a really great time. So, we've been together for a year and a few days now, my girlfriend and I."

"I work in the Barnes & Noble café. Me and my friends there...we're really tight. We make this *top ten* list every day...put it on a notepad and post it on the refrigerator. We've done, like...top ten favorite movies, and today we're doing top ten songs from our junior high...like Spice Girls...Blink 182...you know, Bare Naked Ladies...all the cheesy 90's pop hits and stuff like that. Every time we work together we make a list and put it up."

"I am a guy that is just fun, and random...and stuff like that. A nice guy to hang around with, and probably...oh, oh...I can juggle. Yes, I can juggle, and do that cool Tiger Woods thing on the golf club. Also, I kind of have the world record for pull-ups. I can do, like...24. It's not really a world record, but I have good upper body strength...and that kind of defines me."

"This white bracelet that I'm wearing...it's like, about the "1 Campaign". It's something that Bono from U2 started. It's about the AIDS epidemic in Africa...and how like, every three seconds a child dies...and stuff like that. The whole campaign is just getting people aware of it and everything. So, I wear it, and every time someone asks about it...I tell them. Also, they just forgave 37 countries...third world debt...through the "1 Campaign". I think Bono is really cool."

251   *Rachael Allen*

"I am a hostess at the Texas Roadhouse. I greet the people that come in the door, and seat them at their table with bread and butter, plates and silverware...and anything else that isn't at the table, that already hasn't been sat. I am thirty...just turned thirty this year."

"Christmas Eve is probably the biggest thing at our house this time of year. My grandmother, she would bring...she would bounce around from grandkid to grandkid and deliver presents...and our house was the last house she would visit. She would stay the night...her and my grandfather. My biggest thing was to open the gift from my grandmother when she got there. My dad would always make it a point to say, "No, you can't open your presents." And one year, he actually did make us wait until Christmas morning to open our Christmas presents from my grandmother. I cried all night...until I fell asleep. That next morning, the first person I woke up was my grandma, so I could go and open her Christmas present."

"They lived in Bloomington...my grandma and grandpa, and they would leave Christmas Eve morning, bright and early, and make their rounds from town to town. I have cousins that live in Bloomington and Morton...Peoria...East Peoria. She would go from house to house...and I grew up next to the BMX racetrack next to Detweiller Park...so our house was the last stop."

"We lived on 127 acres, and we were the only house...right next to the BMX racetrack. We didn't actually own the property. The gentleman who owned it...and he's now long since gone...let us be caretakers of the property. We moved in, May of 1981, and moved out in July of 1997."

"We used to go sledding on the biggest hill at the south end of Detweiller Park. If you come up to the Elk's Lodge...I think it's the one all the way in the back...there's a great big hill. That's where all the kids sled. We had our own little trails nearer to our house, and had a big hill down the backside of our house. One year we had a really big ice storm...and a big cable that was frozen into the ground. Do you remember those big orange disk sleds...the plastic ones? Those things are really slick on ice. We came sledding down that hill, and my little brother caught his foot on that cable. You could hear him screaming as he was turning around in circles…getting dizzier and dizzier. He was out of control and spun around for a long, long time."

"My husband is a carpenter. We met at a bar in Bartonville. It was the old Ron's Tap. I seen him in the bar one night and…I was shooting pool, and we got to talking. I gave him my name and number…and we been together since then."

"I have been to Vegas twice to play pool. I went to Vegas twice…and playing in the pool tournaments out there was the absolute best. The Hotel Riviera is just the coolest place. You walk into these great big ballrooms, and you have nothing but pool tables and pool balls for as…far as the eye can see. We played girls from Michigan. We played girls from Canada. We played girls from Minnesota. We played girls from all over the world. There were teams from Canada there. You name it…they were there. You see a lot of new people…meet new people…it was just one of the most indescribable experiences that there is."

"When my husband and I first met, we got into a pool tournament…a pool league. We played for The Warehouse, which is out in Hanna City. Some other girls that I played with at The Warehouse…our team that we played on…won the state championship. So, then we were able to go play out there, in Vegas."

"Out of 135 teams, we finished thirteenth. It wasn't too bad. We did really good. There was a lot of tough competition. You really have to be on your game. It takes a lot of focus…a lot of concentration. You have to block out everything and really focus on your game."

"Some of the guys out there in the Camel Light Room…there were guys there doing jump shots and trick shots…all kinds of neat stuff. There is a trick where the ball is in motion, spinning around and around, and while it is spinning, they take the shot, and it jumps over other balls, through the rack…hits two other balls, and they go in the end pockets. You would be surprised what you can do on a table with a pool ball."

252 *Sarah Foster*

"My name is Sarah…not my real name…but my stage name. I am a student at Bradley University. I was nineteen years old and I was trying to work days at a normal job and go to school…I worked at a daycare. I worked at a daycare and kept getting sick. The kids would some in with different things…and I would get sick. It started to affect my grades…so I had to quit."

"I had a friend who was a dancer for awhile…and I wanted to see what it was about…so I went to the strip club, and they didn't want to let me in because I was only nineteen, and you had to be 21 to get in. But then somebody said, "Well, somebody called to audition. Is that you?" So, I was like, "Yeah…yeah…that's me.""

"I just went there to investigate it, but after I was up there, the club owner came over and said, "You're an attractive woman, would you dance for me?" He asked me to dance at another strip club, in a strip mall…in Champaign. So, I danced there one night and came back with as much money as I made in a week at the daycare. It was going to be a one night deal…or a one week deal…but now three and a half years later, I am still doing it."

"It depends on how many days you work, and which club you work in…but sometimes you make fifty bucks a night and sometimes you make three or four hundred. Some girls make five or six hundred. It depends on who your clientele is…how many people are at the club…it's everything from what kind of clothes you wear, how you do your makeup, what perfume you wear, how you do your dance onstage. There's a lot of luck involved in it too."

"I've only had a day job before…and my mom and dad don't know what I'm doing. Nobody back home knows what I'm doing. My parents…I'm very protective of them, and they live nine hours away…and I love them a lot. It's not about me. I don't care if people know I'm a dancer…it's about them. They're very religious and stuff. The town that I grew up in…they're very concerned about appearances…and I'm not. I want to protect them, but I still want to pursue my own interests. I think I do the best that I can."

"I think I've always had a little bit of an exhibitionist streak in me. I always liked to walk around my house naked. I always liked to be naked. But, my first dance, I was still nervous. So, being out on stage the first time...and there were like thirty people out there...every one of them got up and sat in the tip row. That gave me a huge boost, because I was this small town girl. I never thought there would be anything happen like that. It's funny...after people started putting dollars in my garter...I wasn't afraid anymore."

"Most of the girls that are here...they're like me, and they just dance in the club. They don't try to make extra money by having sex with guys...on the outside. You can make as much money inside...and you don't have to worry about a lot of other stuff. It's all a fantasy anyway...both inside and out."

"For thirty dollars I give lap dances...couch dances. We go to another room where they have these long red couches...you sit down, and I take off all my clothes. You're not supposed to touch me, but there is a certain amount that happens anyway...it just happens. I like to tell my guys that they can massage my back...I like that. I lay in your lap and move around. I pull on my nipples, and kind of writhe around...turning over, and talking to you. I think a lot of guys really just want to talk...I've even had guys tell me to leave my clothes on and just talk to them."

"I keep moving and eventually get to a position where I am turned around, kind of sitting backwards on the guy's chest, with my pussy about eight inches from his head. Sometimes from that point, I do a sort of somersault and turn around so I am facing him...sitting on his chest...again with my pussy about eight inches from his head. I will move around rubbing myself against his erection...under his clothes...and then lay backwards on him...with my head next to his, both looking out...and rub against his penis with my body...my ass. I will talk to him while I move around a little, and by this time we are usually into the second song...the couch dances go on for two songs. During the last part of the second song...we talk, and I relax while I lay on him. I do this purring thing that is very relaxing."

"My boss made a comparison of prostitution and dancing. He said a guy can pick up somebody outside a club...and it's kind of like a car dealership. You can buy a Mercedes Benz...which are the fantasies we sell here...for say, fifty dollars a week. Or, you can buy a beat up Ford every week...and feel like you just bought a beat up Ford…and usually never see the same Ford again. If you do the dancing…something that is more classy…more upscale…they're going to come back time and time again. You're going to make more money from the same customers. And guys talk…once you get a good reputation…you're going to get other customers. And…of course, more customers means, more money."

"I will be graduating this year…and will go into…well, I won't say what that is…but I will go into that…and I think I will also keep dancing here at Fantasyland. It makes me feel good. The money is good…and it makes me feel good. I like the attention."

253   *Chris Caras*

"The day I became a Muslim and accepted Islam as my way of life was shortly after September 11th. I had no thoughts, about Islam, whatsoever...but...I went to the library and picked up a copy of the Koran...for the heck of it. I just decided to start reading, and I liked what I saw, and what I read...and decided that I wanted to become a Muslim. It's very simple really. One just says that there is none worthy of worship, except God...and that Muhammad is the messenger of God."

254   *Ron Davis*

"I am 34, and my name is Ron Davis. My dad's family moved down here...I'm from Janesville, Wisconsin...and when Mom and Dad got divorced, I moved with Dad. My parents are Jim and Vickie Davis."

"I think the...this city needs to concentrate on the family-oriented things, and not so much the beer crowd. They need to get a mayor that has some knowledge of family values...something that the working man is aware of...not something the rich man is aware of. Ummm...most of the things that go on here are for the upper middle-class people. There's really nothing for really lower...lower mid-class to low-income, or poverty people...to do. Take Eastside Center...it costs eight bucks to get in, and a lot of families can't afford that. I live across the river...but in the city, there's Lakeview Aquatic Center...they've got Caterpillar...and the city is spending I don't know how many millions of dollars to put in a museum downtown that does not really need to be there."

"You know, if you don't work at Caterpillar...you still pay the high dollars for your groceries, gas...your cigarettes, and whatever it may be. Even if you don't work there, you still pay the same prices as they do. There's a lot of people that don't work at Caterpillar...or now they don't work at Maytag...so you know. I think the mayor and the city council really needs to be looked over...to see what needs to be done, for families. We need to keep a family atmosphere here. We're not a big city like Chicago or New York."

"Rob Blagojevich, our governor...guaranteed all these things, and not one thing has he done. See...I have a lot of friends that are truck drivers...ummm...the state license plates went from $78 to $98, to *god-only-knows-what* you're paying now for license plates. The state is mandating now that you have to have insurance, and I agree with that. However the insurance companies are now going to start judging your premiums by your credit scores...as of August 1st. I don't think that is fair, and Rob Blagojevich has not stood up for any of it. After January 1st, there's a lot of changes that people aren't aware of with the DOT...Department of Transportation...that have taken a toll on the semi drivers, truck drivers, and independent business owners. The state is about big business, and not *mom and pop* businesses. My parents have owned...for many,

many, years...Mr. Softee. Mom and Dad owned all of them...swear to God. I swear to the Lord...Mr. Softee trucks."

"About 25 years ago, the state decided there were certain cities that we were not allowed to run in, not allowed to set trucks in...one of which was East Peoria. Another was Rockford. Chicago still has some, but they're not actual Mr. Softee trucks. Back in 1978, we sold those and bought Good Humor. You can see why I don't like the Illinois government. They're all liars, they're all thieves...it doesn't matter who they are. I think the best politician we had, out of all of 'em, was Bill Clinton. You name me one guy, who, if he could get a blow job at work, he wouldn't do it. Name me one guy who wouldn't. I'm sorry...I can't."

255   *Aldeine Witzig*

"I was born in 1918 and am 87 years old. Until I was eighteen, I lived in Minnesota...Morris, Minnesota...'bout a hundred fifty miles west of Minneapolis/Saint Paul. I grew up on a farm and we raised grain...oats...flax. They say it was a windy place, but I think Illinois' got it beat...blow your hat off your head anytime."

"There was a drought up there a couple of years and dried everybody out, and a lot of them moved away. But, my brother bought my dad's farm and raised his kids on that."

"My mother, she was baking bread when they was first married...and uh, she found it wasn't gonna be good, so she buried it...on the ground. And my dad...he was always looking round and he was noticing the ground...sorta rising up and cracking...so he kicked it and the dough flew out of it. Her dough that she thought wasn't rising was rising in the ground...so he went and teased her about that. It's a story that I like to tell."

"So, when I was eighteen, I came down with my brothers. They came down to find work, and I came down with them. I had seven, but I only had...I only got one left...all gone. I have three children...and they uh...all three married...live here in town. I've got grandkids and nine great-grandkids...gonna have another one here pretty soon."

"My husband was with the schools...was a superintendent of junior-high and grade schools and that. He was always in the school system...in Morton. I like Morton 'cuz it's a homey town...nice town...clean town...good town. I go to the Apostolic Christian Church downtown on Jefferson, right down there by the grade school. My son is an elder, and my grandson is a minister. They're good people. Morton has a lot of good people."

"I just had some breakfast at the Cracker Barrel...and now I got to go...got me a dentist appointment at 2 o'clock...if I can rise up outta this rockin' chair."

256   *James Dillon*

"Ummm…well…when I…when I was a kid, I played this game called Dungeons and Dragons. I played other games like that too. I was really a dork…I still am, but I was an even bigger dork then. I would get together with my…ummm, friends, and we would spend hours in our own little dorkdom. Sometimes we would literally spend days, performing…what we thought, were daring actions, incredible feats, and, uh…admirable deeds. It was all part of the schtick. We would all get together around my mom's crappy card table with some even crappier chairs, and we would…ummm…slay monsters, and save kingdoms. Of course, this was all imagination, which was helped along with these little pewter figures which represented our alter-egos…our heroic selves. We kept track of everything that went on, and wrote it down in these little notebooks that we got from my dad's office. He took them from his office…actually stole them, I guess. Thanks Dad."

"We would…uh, roll this twenty-sided die, and then that would determine life or death, really. My character was this ranger with super strength and intelligence. I could shoot fire from my fingertips…break through fortifications…or slash through entire legions of orcs. I always thought…why limit myself to one particular specialty…I could have several…you know. It was my fantasy."

"But, I think some of that probably carried over into the real world. I don't think that I, uh…learned to settle for any one particular thing. I consider myself a multi-faceted person…I think that is the proper term. I probably never get really good…really good, at any one thing because I have such wide interests, and I get bored with routine. I can become an expert in something, but then go onto the next thing, and lose a good part of that knowledge by not focusing on it anymore…not using it on a day to day basis."

"But…that can be a good thing and a bad thing. I think it is mostly good, though. I know that having many interests can sometimes be good, as there is a lot of cross-over…and what I mean by that is…well, let me give you an example. Right now, I work…oh, I'm in my early thirties…I forgot to tell you that. Right now, I work in the consulting business. I literally never know what I am going to be required to know until I get onsite and…determine, what the customer needs. I have to show these customers that I am an expert in whatever they need. Maybe

I am…maybe I'm not. It really doesn't matter, because…if I'm not…I soon will be. I will do all those things necessary to become an expert."

"I think that having such wide interests and having the wide experience that I have…helps me in many, many ways. For example, I was recently involved with a project that started out with imple…implementing a software solution for a trucking company. The project…as a lot of projects do, changed focus from implementation to training and documentation. For this particular customer…it required a certain level of training that was more in line with military training…military instruction. Luckily, I had that experience in the Air Force…training and documentation for, excuse the term…for dummies. I'm not saying that truckers are dummies, I'm just saying that in the military, training has to be designed for a wide variety of intellects…and backgrounds. People are so different in how they come to understand something…to get to that…"aha" moment. To train them…you know, sometimes you have to shoot fire from your fingertips."

257   *Jerry Martis*

"Jerry Martis...I'm 63. I'm from South Pekin...Green Acres."

"I'm a truck driver...an over-the-road driver. I'm actually home every night. I go to Hannibal, Missouri and back every night. I haul bread down there for Butternut Bakery. I've worked for Riesinger...Riesinger Trucking, out of Morton for fifteen years."

"My subdivision in Pekin...Green Acres it's called. Some people call it Tornado Alley. Everybody usually thinks of the television show when they hear it...the one with Eddie Albert. We've had a lot of tornadoes over the years."

"I used to work for the railroad up by Waukegan...and then after that went into trucking. I been into trucking most of my life. I've done other things...but it seems like I always get back into trucking. Trucking is a little more challenging than it used to be, with the regulations...and what you have to pass. They're harder than they used to be. Some things have improved a lot...like they have computer stuff on the trucks, like they never had before. Some of it is good...some not so good...but overall, it's been good for the trucking industry. Trucking has been very, very good to me."

258   *Joyce Mercer*

"Joyce Mercer...I am 61 years old. My husband is in the dunk tank. He is earning money for the chamber of commerce. I have no idea what they do with the money...I really don't. I think it is for community events. We have lived in this community since 1966...Chillicothe...since my husband graduated from Western. We're both from Macomb."

"Paul actually started at Western when he was four years old. They had an experimental kindergarten class...age four. He went all the way through the campus...from kindergarten through his masters. He doesn't like change. He's been in the IVC school district...well, he graduat...he retired after 35 years of teaching in the district."

"We went to rival high schools. I went to the public school, and he went to the laboratory school, at the university...and he was a big basketball star, football star...at Western...at the high school. We met through a mutual friend. I dated one of his best buddies so I could get to see him."

"When we were expecting our second child...we lived here...but I didn't think there were any doctors up here that were good enough. I had worked at a dental clinic in Macomb...so our first two children, I had in Macomb, with a physician that I knew. I was in the labor room, expecting our second child, when I had this pain...which they call a crowning pain. It's the pain where they say, "Let's go, we're going to have a baby." Well, they had brought my dinner tray in...and they said I couldn't eat it, but that my husband could. So, he's sitting there eating my dinner, and he's just getting ready to eat the cherry pie...and I said, "Paul, you'd better get the nurse...It's time to go." He looked at me and said, "Wait 'til I finish this pie." If I could have gotten up off that bed and kicked him...I would have. So, I will never let him live that one down."

"We have three children...a daughter and two sons. I am proud of all of them. All three are happily married. We have five grand children. Our daughter is director of wellness at Methodist Hospital, and just received an award that she will get in September. Our oldest son...when my husband retired...he took his job. So, they traded old Mr. Mercer for young Mr. Mercer. Our third son is in the restaurant business, doing very well. Right now he is with the Arby's Corporation."

"I have worked for a dentist for thirty years. One time we had a dentist in the chair, and he swallowed the crown that we were getting ready to cement in his mouth. He swallowed it...and he's a dentist. We had to make him a new crown. But, we also had a physician that swallowed a crown, and he went, and grossly passed it...found it...and then took it to the hospital to have it sterilized. He brought it back to us, and we put it in his mouth."

"We were both watching "Remember the Titans" this afternoon, and I cried...and he probably shed a tear, too. It's with Denzel Washington. It's a true story about a football coach...I think, out in Virginia...when they were trying to integrate the schools. He took over the football program at this high school, and all the problems of the black and white community coming together. It's a true story. One of the players ended up in an automobile accident...being paralyzed. He was a white boy...and the team pulled together...and then ten years later he was killed by a drunken driver. All the football players are at the cemetery and they're all...doing their chanting...they chanted as a team, "Na, na, na, na...na, na, na, na, hey, hey, hey.........goodbye.""

259 *Whoopi Goldberg*

"I was born Caryn Johnson in 1955...in the Chelsea Projects...New York City. I'm here in Normal, Illinois doing a show at ISU."

"Let me tell you about FEMA and Hurricane Katrina. You know...this is still America...and we know what to do in an emergency. We know. We do it for other countries all he time. We have all these fucking...what do you call them...fundraisers. After the tsunami...seconds after it hit...the waters hadn't even receded, and there were concerts going on."

"It took the government seven days to just get the president in line. We got all these people...and nobody has shit in the works. And all those FEMA people...let me tell you about the workers...it's the high...it's the folks up here...it's not the people who work at FEMA...'cuz they want to do the job. And you might say, "Well, Whoopi, how do you know that?" Because, I went down to Mississippi. I went down to see it...see what was goin' on...to see what I could do...'cuz I'm not sending money anywhere. Every time I send money, I spend days thinking, "Did they get it...what's it doing...what's happening with my money?" And, you know...you call them and they say, "We sent it where we think it's necessary.""

"So...I went down. You have never seen anything like this. You cannot...you've seen war-torn places I'm sure...you've seen insane disasters...but you've never seen anything like this. It would be like this wonderful town of Normal...it would be like, Godzilla and Rodan coming through, and scraping their claws on everything...the entire city...and then stomping on it, and making splinters. You can't imagine it...because it just goes on. There's nowhere you can look where it's over. Everywhere you look...it is. I said to myself, "What's happening?" I started to realize that people don't really know what to do for each other in a disaster...because we're depending on FEMA...and things like that."

"Mississippi...Alabama...New Orleans...it's wonderful that they had all the water and food that people provided...but people would get back to their...little space...and they couldn't cook it. You know why? No stoves. Camping gear is what people need...'cuz you can cook on those little Coleman stoves. If you're thinking of stuff to do for those folks...that's what they need. Tents...if they ain't got no house, there's nowhere to sleep…'cuz it's not like there's a house a couple blocks away…there's nothing there. Tents…and bicycles. If the building has collapsed on top of your car…you can't get the car out…you can't get to work…if work is there. Bicycles…these are the things that people need."

"What's happening in this world is almost biblical…almost biblical. You see these giant earthquakes and floods, and tornados…and you think, "Maybe there's something to that."
So…I've been thinking a lot about death of late…because I want to think there is something more…that the Hindus are right when they say reincarnation is about coming back…and coming back."

"When I was younger…I worked for the morgue, and I did hair and makeup on dead people. It was good hours…good pay. So…I go to work the first night, and the guy is showing me around…and said, "Go into my office. Wait for me in my office." In those days the doors were this thick…and there was wood on this side, and wood on this side…and steel bands around them. They were very heavy doors…like a big old refrigerator…so, when it was closed, it was closed. So, I'm sitting around…and I'm looking…and in the old days…I don't know if they still have them, but there were drawers. You have the bodies in the drawers, so you could pull them out and do whatever you need to do. And…we would be crazy in there having some fun…you'd be teasing somebody's hair and go, "Oh…Joan Crawford…let's give you some Bette Davis lips." And then you would take them off, because you don't want to freak the people out."

"But now…sitting in the guy's office…and he's gone about ten minutes…and out of the corner of my ear, I hear this scraping. I think, "What's that sound?" Then everything snapped to slow motion. So…I start to turn around 'cuz I hear this scraping…and my eyes register that one of the drawers is moving. My body says, "Well, let's get up." So…I start to go this way as the drawer is coming this way. My mind is saying, "Scream." I start to scream and nothing comes out. The drawer continues to open, and I think, "I need to run." As I turn to run, I turn my head…and a body sits up and goes, "Hello there!" Bam!…into the door. When I came to…I discovered it was my boss. He was playing a trick on me, so that I would understand that nothing worse than that…was ever going to happen there…and he was…he was right."

260   *Jesus Castillo*

"Mexicans are doing jobs that nobody here wants to do...and they do it with dignity...hard work and long hours. NAFTA has created many jobs in Mexico...but people are still poor. The wages have not increased...and people want a better life. The only way that things will change in Mexico...is...is...when small business is allowed to grow. Big business is the same all over...they're against the people that work...they want them to be poor. They want control."

261   *Charles Martin*

"I'm having a gingerbread latte…which tastes burnt…a little. I'm gonna get me another one in a minute. I just about live here at Barnes & Noble. I come here and read the paper almost every day. I was working for IDOT…upstate…but, I'm retired now. Probably my biggest job was working on the Dan Ryan Expressway."

"This afternoon I was just reading this article about *Deep Throat*…he's a guy named Mark Felt…an FBI guy. He was the guy who was feeding information to Woodward and Bernstein. He said that after the book came out…"All The President's Men"…he was shocked that he was referred to…in that way. He didn't know that was what they called him. I think they let the cat out of the bag because he's sick, and his relatives want to cash in on it before he dies. So, this guy…this professional…he'll always be known as *Deep Throat*."

"You know the woman in that film…Linda Lovelace? She died a few years ago in Denver. I was out there when she died…she hit a concrete post or something. She was always going around saying that her husband held a gun to her head to make her do things in the movies she made…but nobody really believed her. He died right around the same time she did…it was in the papers. He married Marilyn Chambers…another porn star, after he divorced her…but before he was married to either one of them, he was Jay from "Jay and the Americans". You ever hear of them? They did a song called "This Magic Moment". You remember that song, "This magic moment…so different and so new"…you ever hear that?"

"I read a lot of books here…but, don't ever buy them. It's a library to me. I'll start reading a book and before I leave…I'll put a bookmark in it and hide it. Then, when I come back, I pull it back out and read it some more. I read almost anything. You ever read a book called, "Dress Your Family in Corduroy and Denim"? That's what I'm reading now…and it's very funny. There's a story in here about him helping a ten year-old boy carry some coffee to his hotel room. The guy who wrote the book is gay…and he tells about helping a boy carry coffee to the boy's hotel room…and then looking like a pedophile. He's a very good writer…funnier than Seinfeld. I saw him on David Letterman one night…ummm…David Sedaris is his name."

"Yesterday I was reading this book and he's talking about going to a nudist colony…and describing the people there…and…I did one of them spit-takes and got coffee all over that page…but it's dry today."

262   *Jim Rainey*

"I grew up in Kewanee. I left there when I was seventeen…seventeen years old. That was in the 70's."

"After quitting high school, I hopped on a bus…went to St. Louis and caught an L-1011 to Charleston, South Carolina. I remember reading the plastic card in the seat pocket…about the L-1011. It was the first commercial airplane I had been in…although I had flown before in a private airplane…for selling magazine subscriptions when I was eleven or twelve. From there, I hopped on another bus, which took me to an island not far from Charleston….called Parris Island. I don't remember the time, but it was in the middle of the night when we…when we arrived."

"We pulled up to some old buildings where a bunch of drill instructors were yelling at everybody to get off the bus and stand in line. We stood in line, and stood in line, and stood in line, around these old wooden tables…and learned not to lock our knees."

"It was about a million degrees, and this was July 15th…with humidity so thick, there was literally no difference between standing next to the swamp…or standing in it. I was wet the whole time I was there. You would sweat just lying in your rack at night…doing nothing. It was a place where you would sweat in the shower. I think half of the people that arrived that night…at some point…passed out. Luckily, I didn't. Those people that did pass out…they got to be intimidated by five or six drill instructors, and then had the pleasure of doing "bends and motherfuckers"…until they got so hot and worn out that they passed out again."

"The next day, after a night of no sleep, a haircut that took ten seconds, and a lot of paperwork…we formed up into regular platoons and marched to a three story brick building on the other side of the parade grounds. That was where we lived for the next twelve weeks, except for the week we were at the rifle range. I don't remember the exact sequence of events after that, but we were issued uniforms, boots, shower shoes, PT clothing, had a medical examination, a dental examination…and we took several types of written tests."

"The most memorable experience I had on Parris Island…not the hardest…and there were a lot of…physically demanding, and you know…they would fuck with our heads…teach us how to cut our wrists if he wanted to be a momma's boy and wimp out. But the most memorable to me, involved our whole platoon and one of our drill instructors, Sergeant Lechnar. Sergeant Lechnar was a "Marines Marine" He lived for the Marine Corps. He was one of those Marines that lived the mythology."

"The whole platoon was on line in our barracks…we'd just formed up as a regular platoon and moved into the barracks, and it was our first "head call". In boot camp, the drill instructor says, "Port side to the head", and at that point, everybody on the port side of the barracks files into the head…and as soon as the last guy is in the head, he starts counting to ten…and when he gets to ten, everybody better be out of the head and on line. Then he says, "Starboard side to the head." It's the same deal for everyone on the starboard side. Everybody rushes in there and there are these…big long troughs that you pee in…and everybody is always in a hurry, it's like a pee free-for-all. Urine is flying everywhere…you're pissing on people…they're pissing on you…you've only got a few seconds to empty your bladder, so you do what you have to do…push people out of the way, and try to pee in whatever spot is relatively clear. That first head call, we really didn't know the rules…but it didn't take long to find out."

"After we were all back on line, Sergeant Lechnar went into the head, and was in there for a few minutes. He soon came out with something in his right hand. We were all standing at attention on line, and he came down within inches of everyone's face, one by one, and said that somebody…somebody, took a shit and did not…*did not* flush the toilet. In his hand was a big piece of shit, dripping with toilet paper. He waved it, inches in front of everyone's face, so that everyone could smell the stench, and said, "The next time this happens, ladies, we will all brush our teeth with this. We will all get out our toothbrushes and brush our teeth with this.""

"I will never forget the blood rushing to my head…and it was at that moment…and I remember exactly how I felt. I knew I was in a world that I knew…absolutely nothing about. It was a moment where I just thought, "Holy shit…how do I get out of this place this fucking place." It literally…shocked the hell out of me."

"That was my *first* day in the Marine Corps…that was just my *first* day. Strange things like that became…normal. One day I was told to do bends and thrusts over a clock that Sgt. Martinez had torn off the wall…because he caught me eye-balling it. He told me to keep going until the second hand moved…and it was unplugged. The clock was unplugged. I got to the point where there was so much sweat on the deck…and I was so exhausted…I slipped and hit my head and almost knocked myself out."

"The drill instructors would fuck with your head all the time…all the time…sadistic crap. I remember one day, we were told that we had a new president…that Nixon had resigned. By that time, we pretty much knew not to believe what they told us. It wasn't until I graduated that October…that I found out for sure, that…it was true. So, then, Ford was the president…and before I got out…Carter was president."

"In '78, I was stationed at the MCAS in Beaufort…and they were just starting to film "The Great Santini" there. Do you remember Robert Duvall from that movie…Bull Meacham? The Marine Corps is full of guys like that. I think it has to be like that…because you actually do become what you convince yourself you are. You live the mythology."

"Do you remember the scene where Bull Meacham gives the guy a "swirly"? I think he was a corporal. He stuck his head in the toilet and flushed it? That was a pretty common thing when I was in, to bring somebody in line…and…it was a lot of fun."

263-264   *Dan and Kim Philips*

"We met at Peoria Players…we were in a play together…many, many, many years ago."

"It was Cabaret…25 years ago. I was a Kit Kat girl…dancer."

"I was a drunken sailor."

"Today, we're going to work together, like we do every day of our lives. We own this business…and it owns us. We've been working together for twenty years."

"I like the history behind antiques…the…you know, it's not just a bunch of merchandise…it's everything that they meant to people before. It's the unique character that they have…kind of like each of us. I really like the fact that they represent a time before us that was…that was really different."

265   *Nancy Roggy*

"I'm Nancy Roggy…52. We're taking a walk. We like to come down to the river and walk. We try to get four miles in. A lot of times, we go all the way from, is it Roxy's? We go from Roxy's all the way down to Detweiller and back. We try and see if we can spot a woodchuck."

"I grew up on a farm outside of Washburn….kind of between Toluca, Larose, and Washburn. It was awesome…we just drove by it yesterday, and I started bawling because my mom and dad moved away from there fourteen years ago."

"I would wake up about five in the morning, hearing pheasants walking across the road. They walked by my bedroom window…and they make a certain noise…and I also listened to raccoons outside. It was totally away from the rest of the world, and I loved it. A perfect life for a kid, but I think lonely for my mom."

"A couple times a week, someone's cows got out from someone's farm…including ours. I mean, it would be like, "So and so's cows are in our yard." or "Our cows are in somebody else's yard." I got to thinking about it, and thought…there are just so many little things that we took for granted. "So and so's in the ditch and we need to pull him out." There is just so much that went on that, now it kinda makes me laugh. I thought, "How's come the cows were always out?" How come we couldn't keep our cows in our own pasture? What was the deal back then? It makes me laugh now…about things back then that just seemed normal."

"We came down to the riverfront hoping to find a woodchuck. That's why we come. This time of night, we'll probably see two to three woodchucks…really."

266   *Jim D'Orazio*

"I'm about two blocks from Greektown in Chicago. I live about two blocks from there."

"The biggest mistake I ever made was…we were at what's called the Iron Fair in Paris. This was a number of years ago. It was a gigantic metal building…and it's a wholesale thing for dealers…antique dealers. I was walking along and there on the floor…dealers just throw things on the floor…there's a gigantic silver thing laying on the floor. It's like a mountain…and it has cattle on it, and people sitting on the mountain…and it was about four and a half feet in diameter, and about two feet high. I looked at it, and it was about $300…fifteen or sixteen hundred francs."

"I said, "That's nice, but I don't think I want to get involved with it." The French dealer I was with didn't want it. Several other French dealers I was with passed it up. Finally, the only smart person in the building bought the piece. After that, it changed hands six times…and by the time I saw it again, it was $75,000. It was solid silver…not just plate…it was a solid piece, and it weighed about…about eighty pounds. Not only the weight, but because of the artistic and historical significance…it was very valuable."

"My father was born in Alfedana, in Abruzzo, Italy. It's the middle of the boot. My mother was a Neapolitan and was born in the United States. I've been to Paris thirty-some times…but never been to my own home-country, except for Rome…but, it's on our agenda to do that."

"I spent 32 years in the Air Force. I spent most of my time in Europe and Alaska…spent some time in South America…was there for the Dominican Crisis. I was active for the Cuban Missile Crisis…Grenada. I went to the Gulf for the first Gulf War. That was just before I retired. Panama…"Just Cause"…getting rid of Noriega…I was there for that."

"I lived in Topeka, Kansas…a very nice town, but there is absolutely nothing to do there after seven at night. They used to roll the streets up. I started going to auctions, for lack of anything else to do. I started buying things…and been doing it ever since. I'm in town today, trying to sell what I bought."

"I became a street-rodder...and have antique cars. I have old cars with new engines...and they're all new inside. I have a `48 Studebaker convertible that has a modern Chrysler engine in it. I've had several Rolls Royce's over the years...not new ones...old ones. I've had Packard's and Chevy's...a '34 Chevy which was also a street rod. I had a `49 Buick Convertible. I probably had about 35 cars."

"After I'm gone, my wife will be taken care of...you know, financially and psychologically...and stuff like that. There will be support for her...mostly because, you know...all because Topeka was such a boring town."

267   *Ian Zelinski*

"We're hanging out having a good time and seeing what's happening at Joe's Crab Shack…they got good pizza here. We're going out to a few bars later and see who can drink the most. I drink Jack and Coke, vodka tonic, you know, no beer…if it's more than three drinks, you know…I'll go to the bathroom every five seconds…so, not for me."

"Ian Zelinski…and I'm 28…originally from Pittsburgh, but live in South Bend. I'm in sales & marketing for the South Bend Silverhawks. I'm here for the game. I plan to stay involved in baseball, of course…but who knows. I got a twin brother who is a lawyer in L.A., you know…maybe he can get me a job or something…who knows."

"I grew up in Pittsburgh in a section called Foss Chapel…you know…big Pirates fan, Steelers fan. Penguins fan…not so much. I always got into trouble back home doing the old vandalism thing, and that kind of fun stuff…but, you know, that's all teenager kind of stuff. Everybody got into trouble doing that kind of stuff."

"Junior year in college I backpacked around Europe with my roommate. It was fun…I mean…we went everywhere from Manchester to London, to Budapest, Hungary…to Berlin, Germany…and it was just a good time seeing people…you know, the crazy Europeans…if you will. I was there for about a month…and…it was a lot of fun."

"My dad is Jewish, and I'm not real big into religion. My mom is Christian, and I'm not real big into that…so I just kinda go with the flow. I slept in on Sundays, you know, and didn't have to do anything with that."

"One time I met Barry Bonds, and have you ever seen the movie "Can't Hardly Wait"? Ethan Embry, who played the main character…I went to a party of his in L.A. one time. He was a real asshole…not Barry Bonds…Ethan Embry. He was a real asshole."

268 *William Marion*

"My name is William Marion…that's my name…but I go by Bill. I just turned eight…eighteen in November. I have been here…well…before we opened. I was hired-in to help stock the store…and I was put in "Pets". I work in the Pet Department…stock everything…make it look all nice and pretty. I stick my hands in the fish tanks about every other day and clean them out…scoop out dead fish, and make everything look really good in there."

"I had this one kid…I came in at 5 o'clock, and he came in about 5:30 or so…and he was there until six, just watching…just watching the fish. Then his mom came along, and he didn't want to…didn't want to leave. He just kept staring and watching the fish, and I watched him kick and scream…like, "Can we get a tank?" I get that all the time. Little kids coming through…looking at fish…then crying and screaming."

"I live about five minutes…that way. I've lived in Washington about three fourths of my life…then I moved out into the country…uh…yeah. We have three horses, about ten chickens, two dogs, cats…a small pond of fish…and, ummm…a horse trough full of fish. I live on a farm."

"I go to ICC right now. I'm looking at probably Midstate College after ICC. I'm looking there, but I'm not sure…just depends on timing and everything. Actually I graduated high school a semester early, because I just got enough classes and everything. I went to ICC early, in the spring semester. I'm actually studying business administration…business admin, and minoring in accounting. I want to eventually open up my own store."

"It's a gaming store…sells role-playing games and uh…comic books, video games, electronics…uh…just everything like that. None of the stores around here…there are like, two stores in the general area, and a lot of the people don't like going to them, for a number of different reasons. So…I want to take everything that they do right, and everything that they do wrong…take out everything they do wrong…and make my own store out of it."

"My favorite game is, uh, I always revert back to the old "Dungeons and Dragons", which has been around since the 70's…and there are a lot of urban myths about it, but none of them are true. One of my favorite games, called live-action role playing...the game is called "Vampire the Masquerade". You basically take on the persona of a vampire and live in the final...final nights, they call it. So we actually get up...put on stage makeup and actually act all this out. It's in a very safe, strict environment. I actually help run them. I run one here in this area...from as far away as Galesburg, the people come."

"You know, the Jubilee Ren Fair...the Renaissance Fair and everything? A lot of times, I am one of the guys walking around in the medieval garb, trading...talking, and everything else. I normally have a white tunic...brown...brown pants, and really big sword. I'm not a part of the official organization or anything...but, yes...I was. But I just realized that it wasn't as good as I thought it would be. Yeah...I sometimes go by my different name there...Wilhelm Helvig. Well, my entire family is from somewhere in Germany...and uh...before my family came over here, our name was Helvig."

"My furthest trip has been New Orleans. I loved it. It was an amazing city...it really was. I was about thirteen when we went. It was actually pretty cool. We went down over the 4th of July. So my dad, my mom, my brothers...actually my step-mom...as we were driving...and we drove from city to city...it was just an almost endless night of fireworks. You could always see fireworks off in the distance...all the way down there...just fireworks, fireworks, fireworks...everywhere."

269   *Theresa Thomason*

"I am 42…recently from Maquoketa, Iowa. I waited tables there. I've worked in restaurants for the last 25 years. We're living here now because my daughter, Amanda is going to go to college at ICC…she starts Monday. Her best friend is from Milan, Illinois, and she picked Illinois…her best friend did…for college. But, Amanda picked Peoria…'cuz she wants to go into business. She figures Peoria is big enough for her field. She's been planning her classes…her courses, for four years. She's seventeen…graduated in January…and starts college on Monday."

"I am very proud of my daughter. I'm a single parent, and have raised her the last twelve years by myself. Her graduation from high school was like…the biggest accomplishment. Getting her there…it's been a long road. I'm very proud of my daughter."

"Where I'm originally from…the town is called Monmouth, Iowa…there were like, eighty people there. About seventy of them are still there. There are maybe 25 houses. In the summers there…if you wanted to do anything…you'd have to go through the town and gather up all the kids…and there weren't that many. If you wanted to play baseball, you had to get everybody 'cuz there were only about ten kids in the whole town.
There were two bars, a grocery store, and a post office…and a gas station. I worked in a restaurant outside of town for a dollar an hour…I was fourteen. I waited tables and cooked. No matter what I did…I made a dollar an hour. I went to school with the same kids from kindergarten to my senior year…from seven towns…and my graduation class…there were 49…49 kids."

"I've lived here in "Chilli"…about a month and a half. We've lived here in the area…about three months. We moved here so that Amanda could go to school at ICC. I'm working here at the Track Inn…and I work at ITI…in the factory. They make parts for Caterpillar. I work here on the weekends. On Saturday I do dishes…and Sundays I wait tables. I make decent tips on Sundays…which surprised me. This place is packed on the weekends…Sunday is packed. It's nonstop…from the time you get here, until the time you go."

"My car got stolen since I've been here. The car got stolen April 15th...and it's now in Arizona. The cops found it six days later, because the guy who had it...there was another guy riding with him...the guy was peeing out the window. The cops didn't know at the time that it was stolen...so they put the car in storage...and 72 days later...they called me and told me that they found the car. They said there was a charge for towing and storage for 72 days. I called, and the guy said...he would only charge me for twenty days...$572. The car is still there...I sent them the title. It's just a little Plymouth Horizon...and not worth going there and getting. But, I got a new car...it's right outside...a Grand Am. I like it very much."

"My daughter's car blew up. So we started here with two cars, and then had none. We rode busses for two months...but now we both got new cars...both got good jobs. We're buying a place...so life looks good right now."

"I've been working on the house I'm buying, 'cuz, it's a real mess. I tore out one of the walls between two bedrooms for my daughter. I usually get off at 10:30, and then I work on the house. Last night I was painting...and I met one of my neighbors at two in the morning. He came over and wanted the wood that I had sittin' outside...from the wall. He ended up helping me paint my bedroom. I didn't have any curtains on the window...so he could see what I was doing...and he just came over at 2 o'clock. These people around here are very nice."

"It took me five years to get a divorce. I was in Iowa, and he was in Texas...and Iowa law says you have to serve them a paper. It took me four years to get an address on him...to serve the papers. It took him six months to sign it...and then it was a year to get the divorce. I've been married twice...and I'm done. My second husband is 31 years old...and a nightmare. We were together six months...and we've been married five years...and that's my next goal...a divorce on him. I've been married eighteen years in all...and have spent the last ten trying to get divorces. I'm never getting married again in my life. My Christmas present to me will be a divorce."

"I did go on a date a couple of weeks ago...to a comedy club. The guy that I was on the date with...he's a deacon in a church. Ummm...there was ten of them up there getting hypnotized. This guy made him do...one thing he did was, he told him that he...he lost his...dick, and he had to go out in the audience to find it. I'm going, "Oh my gosh...this guy's a deacon...and he's out in the audience try-

ing to find his dick." After that, the guy told him, "After you leave here, anytime somebody touches your forehead…you'll get instantly horney." He told him as soon as he walks out the door, it will happen. So, when he came out the door, all these people were standing there, going, "Touch him, touch him." Well, I'm not gonna do that, and embarrass him again. So, we got to the car, and the first thing I did was touch his forehead. He said, "Oooo Theresa, I'm so horney."
I just kept doing it…I did it like…thirty times."

"I haven't seen him for…that was like…two weeks ago…but, I'm going to tap his forehead the next time I see him."

270   *Nick Dykstra*

"I'm nineteen…and I'm glad I graduated high school. I have a little more freedom now. The curfews and rules have lessened up. I definitely have a lot more
freedom. My parents were always real strict about things. I had a real stiff curfew…and if I was just a little late, I would be grounded for awhile. But, once I hit
college, I, pretty much, had control of what I did. There's a lot more flexibility."

"I'm at a community college now, but I'm going to transfer to St. Ambrose in the
Quad Cities. I'm kinda leanin' on being a Chiropractor."

271   *Katherine Miller*

"I probably shouldn't tell you this…but I am in my late 40's. I am often told that I look younger than I am. I try and take care of myself…eat right and exercise. My only vice is that I smoke about a pack a day. I have tried to quit in the past…but have been consistently unsuccessful. I also drink on occasion. I'll have a few mixed drinks when I am out of town…vodka…but, I mostly drink wine."

"I actually work for the Hilton organization…in management. I make good money. One of the perks of the job is that I can travel almost anywhere and stay at a Hilton for free. Yesterday, I stayed in Chicago at the Palmer House Hilton. It's one of my favorites. I love the architecture…especially the Sistine Chapel-style ceiling in the main lobby. It is just beautiful…absolutely beautiful. I love to just sit in the lobby, and look up…and also watch the people. I love the location…it's right in the middle of the theater district."

"I'm no longer married…haven't been for about eleven years. I think I prefer not being married. I like the fact that I can just decide to go somewhere with my friends and not have to worry about a husband. Sometimes I find that it…it is definitely lonely…but, the feeling usually doesn't last for long. Some of my friends ask me, "Well, don't you miss the sex?" I guess I would have to say…sometimes. I miss the closeness…the touching…but, to be quite honest, it doesn't take much to get a man in a hotel. I can usually go have a drink at the bar, and within a few minutes, will be talking with someone…and if I feel like it…ask him…although mostly he will ask me…ask him to go back to my room."

"Friday night, I went to this event put on by the Art Institute of Chicago. It was called "Glamorama". It was this star-studded fashion show at the Chicago Theater. I went a little early and watched the celebrities show up and walk down the red carpet. There was one of those gay guys from the E! Network…I don't remember his name…and he was interviewing Ryan Seacrest. Right after him, a guy from Saturday Night Live came…what was his name…Seth something. Then, there were a couple of people from "Desperate Housewives". After that, there were several more that showed up…but I went into the theater with the friend I was with, and I didn't see them. I heard later that Sarah Jessica Parker and Jennifer Lopez were there."

"The event started with the B-52's singing a couple of their more famous songs...then there was a hi-tech split screen showing Sean "P. Diddy" Puffy Combs...and he was the emcee...and not really there at all...it was pre-recorded. I think he has a line of clothing at Marshall Field's...and they were the ones putting on the fashion show. Then, there were some songs by the East Village Opera Company...very good...sort of Queen-like...you know...Freddy Mercury-esque. Then throughout the event, they had models come down this glass runway, which was apparently too slick and too steep, as quite a few times...the models almost fell."

"The event only lasted about an hour and a half...kind of disappointing because the B-52's really only sang two songs...one of them was "Love Shack". During their second song, I dropped my sunglasses under the seat in front of me, and borrowed a flashlight from one of the ushers to find them. It was just as I was about to look for them, that they started this thing where they dropped confetti and balloons from the ceiling, and they piped dry-ice smoke down the aisles. So...I'm looking for my sunglasses through all the smoke and confetti...and meanwhile, the guy in the seat in front of me stands up...and steps on the glasses...crunch. So...I need to get a new pair of sunglasses."

"After the show, there was this thing called the *afterparty* at Marshall Field's. They closed off the entire seventh floor, and had a big dance area, and all of the food and liquor you could possibly stand. This was all for a hundred dollars...which wasn't bad, considering you have a dinner and a few drinks in Chicago, and you can easily spend more than a hundred dollars. They had pinball machines all over the place that people could play for free. There was an oxygen bar...and a photo booth, where you could go inside and have photos snapped...kind of a thing from the 60's. They probably had twenty or thirty different stations where they would have a variety of appetizers...like, shrimp...Chinese noodles...ice cream sundaes...tiny hamburgers...salmon...lots and lots of different foods. Also, they had a martini station...a Jell-O shot station...sparkling wine...beer...and a large variety of mixed drinks."

"My friend and I...she also works for the Hilton Corporation...we stayed there for a few hours...even spoke with the main B-52 guy...I don't remember his name...talked with a few people that we met...and then came back to the hotel for a Jacuzzi. But, what we found out after getting back to the hotel, is that the

Jacuzzi was broken. So, we went to the cigar bar and talked for awhile, while we sipped some drinks."

"My friend, Lisa, went back to her room after awhile, and I stayed in the bar talking to this gentleman that sat down next to me...I can't remember his name. He was recently divorced...or said he was...and we mostly talked about being single. He talked about his ex-wife and the problems of being recently divorced. After awhile...we both left the bar together...walked to the elevators...he was on the twelfth floor, and I was on the eighth...so, different elevators. The elevators are divided so that if you are on one of the first eleven floors, you take one set of elevators, and then the upper floors take another set."

"So, as we were standing there talking, waiting for the elevators, he handed me a torn piece of a Hilton notepad that had his room number on it...12-258. He said that if I wanted some company, to just come to his room. I thanked him and said, "That's very nice." He then went up his elevator, and I took my elevator to the eighth floor."

"I went back to my room and watched some old movie on TBS."

272   *Greg Wessel*

"There's not much in Yates City…but, that's the way we like it."

"I'm from Beardstown originally. The bank president in Beardstown was a paper route customer of mine. I carried papers up until I graduated from high school…the Springfield Journal. I was talking with him, and he asked me what I was doing. I told him I'd just graduated, and thought I'd end up in the Springfield area. He said, "Well, we're looking to bring somebody in." Banking had been the furthest thing from my mind…but I ended up starting with them. That was '73…and I been with banks since."

"My high school coach, his name was Ed Lewis…and you have to remember, this was back in the 60's…when some of us started growing more hair. The coach was pretty strict about our appearance. He said that our sideburns shouldn't be any longer than the bottoms of our ears…simple enough. But, like any other teenager, I tried to stretch that a little bit. I let my sideburns grow long. Well, I'd always been in the rotation for starting pitcher…and it came my turn…and I…stayed on the bench. I didn't think too much about it…and he never said anything….but, I went home and trimmed my sideburns, and the next day…I was starting pitcher."

"He was a good guy about getting his point across without beating you over the head about it."

273   *Carol Patton*

"A principle God has taught me is…if you ask him to lead you in serving him with your business, job or career…you'll be very successful…more than you can imagine. But to make this happen, you have to devote everything you have…your profits, your resources and your time to a good cause that has been given to you by God. Then watch out, because God will help beyond your wildest dreams."

"I was baptized in Israel…in the River Jordan…and I accepted Jesus Christ as my savior when I was eighteen. I asked Jesus to let me know him personally. I thanked him for dying on the cross for my sins…and asked him to open the door of my life so that I could receive him as my savior and lord. I asked him to take control of my life and make me a good person."

274 *Gabriel Johnson*

"I'm 24. I went to Metamora High School. I was home-schooled when I was little, then went to Metamora High School. I had good parents, so it turned out well. My mom taught me from third grade to eighth grade. We did a correspondence course...we would send our work in to teachers in Baltimore...it was called Calvert...and I think it's been around for about a hundred years. They would send us a big book with daily text, and all our lesson plans for the whole year. It was real regimented, but not a lot of work. I definitely want to do it with my kids, if my wife is willing. I think it's good to home-school when kids are younger. But, I'm lucky I went to high school too...a normal high school...basically for the socialization."

"We lived out in the country...my mom was a runner...did the Chicago Marathon every year...and so she'd find tons of animals, strays that had either been hit or hurt. We sort of had a halfway house...and that was sort of cool. We raised baby birds that had been kicked out of their nests...fed them with a syringe every half hour. My mom hasn't been running as much lately. I've got a little brother and sister that are twins...and she just hasn't had as much time...but she still works out a lot. My parents got married right after high school and have been together ever since. I've got great folks...a really good family."

"I have a studio down at the Murray Building. I do my own art down there. I do pen and ink on mylar...just drawings...you know, layer them...kind of a mylar transparency. I can do a lot of layering...a lot of cool effects...real small...real tight...real detailed. What I'm doing right now is kind of non-objective. The last year or so...I have kind of loosened up...and going kind of non-objective as inspired by all these diagrams that I found of parasites...different fish and fish parasites. That kind of got me going on that non-objective stuff. That, and like the Rorschach tests, where they're splattered and all symmetrical. So, I'll draw one side, fold it and trace it...and spread it out. They're a little creepy...and can be interpreted as a little sexy...a little dirty."

275   *Ken Hamm*

"I was a machine operator at Caterpillar for 32 years. My wife now…my second wife and I, started selling on Ebay…and as I got closer and closer to retirement…we decided we would open up this store in Canton. Our Ebay sales…we sell on consignment for other people…and that is a very big part of the business. I have more business than I can handle. It's a twelve hour day, every day."

"Remember Alpeter-Miller…the auctions out by where the mall is now? I think Carpetland is there now. We'd sit in there when I was a kid…and I can remember they had a fifty cent grab bag…we'd get that every time. That was a big place to go back then. We'd drive all the way in from Canton."

"I got this great big set one year…basically a space set. You could launch rockets…it was multi-level…plastic…spring loaded, little rocket launchers. I played with that for years and years. I wish I had kept that."

"I had an older gal come in and said, "I have this old painting on the wall…Grandma had it…Mom had it on her wall. I have it now and I don't even like the thing. I want to get rid of it." So, I went and looked at the thing. Now, I don't know if you know what Maxwell Parrish prints are? He was a famous early 20th century artist. She said, "I just want to get rid of it…I'd take $10 or $15 for it." I told her, "No, I think we can get you more." So…we ended up getting her $200 for it on Ebay."

"That's the good part of this business. Of course, there is a flip side to that also. Sometimes you have to disappoint people who think their stuff is worth something…and then you have to tell them…no…they're not."

276 *Perry French*

"I am 58. I am originally from the Rock Island/Moline area. I've lived in Illinois my entire life...all parts central and northern. I got transferred here about eight years ago...nine years ago. I worked for an independent adjusting company and got moved here as a promotion. I am currently working with a company called Great Central Insurance. We have a great big flag and marquee on War Memorial Drive and Sheridan...can't miss it."

"In junior high school, I had a gal that I dated for awhile...thought the world of her, and then found out...she was fourteen, and was dating a guy in the Army who was nineteen. It kinda blew me out of the water, but taught me a lesson or two. And then in high school, we were playing with a ouija board, and at the time, I was dating a girl whose initials were "SZ", and they kept asking the board who I would end up marrying, and it kept coming up "SZ". Well that one never really worked out, but I ran into my future wife, and her initials just happened to be "SZ"...strange. It will be 36 years in August that we have been together...SZ and me"

"When I was a younger kid, we built a go-cart...you know these old little push go-carts. An old wagon fell apart...so we took the wheels, and built a wooden pushcart. Well, we got tired of pushing, so we built a sail for it. We saw, I think it was Ronald Reagan's Playhouse, where they talked about the wind wagons that sailed on the plains. We did a little studying on it, and we ended up building what was similar to the old Viking single mast roll-up type sails. It worked great, but I'm sure we scared the hell out of some drivers coming down the road. But, it went like crazy."

"We finally managed to destroy it when my brother took it out and didn't know how to control it. He tried to take a corner with about a thirty mile an hour wind...it rolled over and demolished the mast and snapped the body. He walked away with just a few scrapes. We resurrected it later with a Honda 90 motor on it. We salvaged enough to have a platform and wheels, and somebody found a Honda 90 motor, and figured out how to change the gears by just reaching back and bumping it. It was kinda cool. Lucky nobody got killed."

"I always said that I wanted to be canonized when I die. There is a civil war regiment...a reactivated artillery battery, and if you can get yourself cremated, you can ship your remains to them. They will load you into a Napoleon twelve-pounder and fire you into the woods. I figure that's the only way I'm ever going to see canonization."

277   *Sonny Moore*

"I prayed for ten years and got no help. The day I stopped…the very same day…I prayed to myself…my head, my hands, my own ability. That is how you should pray. If you want something…don't look to heaven…look in a mirror. You can quote me."

278   **Bob Bishop**

"Well, I turned 71...last month, and I don't feel that old. I do find that when I get up in the morning, it hurts for awhile, but I get over it...after a walk around for awhile. I do a lot of walking. I try to walk five and a half miles a day, not because I like to, but because I know it's good for me. I listen to the radio...to make the time go faster."

"Do you know what a chivaree is? A chivaree is a custom that people practiced years ago...and I think it must be French. When people would get married...at their honeymoon, people would gather at the house...and do all kinds of things to the bed...trick them. Everyone got together and played cards...and everyone smoked, including the kids. They would pass bowls of cigarettes and bowls of cigars around the room and you almost had to chop your way through the smoke."

"I was a kid...smoking cigarettes and cigars, and nobody was paying any attention to that...and this was in Mason County...and not uncommon. I've talked to other people and this was not uncommon. Now, not everybody knows about chivarees, but we would do things such as go out to the hen house and turn chickens loose in the kitchen...and just do stuff to bug the bride and groom...upset their honeymoon. But, what it was...was a celebration of the wedding. So, I remember a few chivarees...and looking back on it...here we were smoking cigars...and that wasn't good for kids, but we all just did it. It was a celebration."

"I have written a book. My maternal grandfather had written a book, kind of chronicling his life in Missouri. He was a Lutheran minister...he did not come from Germany, however, he was so tied in...so tied in to the German culture, that I had to include him in the book I wrote. My grandfather came from an area known as Herman, Missouri. His father was a farmer and also had a machinery business. My grandfather did not go to the Lutheran Seminary in Saint Louis until later in life...however he graduated in 1900...and all of my family on that side was German. My grandfather's name was Johann Friedrich Wilhelm Horstman. He married a lady by the name of Sophia Wilhelmina Haselbrock on the other side of my family. They are all German people also."

"During World War II, when my sister and I were old enough and smart enough to learn the German language…that was something that was forbidden. Both of my parents, who were fluent in German, would not teach us the German language…because they were patriotic to this country…and we did not learn it. Later in life, my wife and I had to go to a junior college and take studies in German so that we can speak and understand a little more German."

"Now…my mother was shorter even than I am. I had met my wife in college, and we had dated for about a year…and decided to get married. But, before we got married, I said something to my wife and my mother…I said, "Well, maybe I'm getting cold feet, but this is a pretty big step in my life." And I remember my mother…little woman that she was…looked me in the eye, grabbed my by the arm and squeezed my arm and said, "Yes…but she's a good Lutheran girl, and the important thing is…she's German." That was the important thing to my mother…that she was German. Now, my momma had never been to Germany, and her father had never been to Germany…but there is something in the German people that ties them…binds them to the…"Fatherland" or "Motherland", or to each other, or whatever it is. It is difficult for me to understand."

"Let me tell you a story about Grandpa Horstman…and this explains what I just said.
During World War I, my grandfather was a pastor in Texas…and my mother told me this story…I assume it's true. Anyway…there was a newspaper, and it was wrong. This newspaper said that Germany had won the war…of course it was a false account. Well, when my grandfather had read this one morning, he came rushing out of his study…jumped on top of the kitchen table and started singing "Deutschland hat Gewonnen" "Deutschland hat Gewonnen". He then started singing the German National Anthem. This was a man that was not born in Germany. He was born in Missouri…but he had that unspoken tie with Germany. I've never forgotten that, and I always tried to think, "Why was that man so tied to Germany?" I find that so interesting. He was a man of the cloth…but there was that tie to Germany."

"The most important part of my life…and I didn't know it at the time…was when I was baptized. That had to be…the highpoint of my life. My grandfather baptized me…my grandfather confirmed me…and started me on a relationship with the Lord."

"You know…if someone is great enough to create this world…and create the people…and everything else in this world, it is not for me to question what God does or doesn't do. What really turns me on is the realization that all things work together for good to those who love the Lord. That doesn't mean things will be easy. I could be in a situation right now that is a tough situation. It might strain a person…test a person…but if one has a strong faith…and that is something given to me by God, then, I can bear up to those things. I really can. That's just the way it works…I think…I believe. Some people blame God for bad things…I don't. If you look at the Old Testament…study the Old Testament…it's the most fascinating reading there is. You have everything in the Old Testament…like murder…it's like a soap opera…all kinds of lust…all kinds of sex, and everything else that is going on in there. But, if you really study it, you can see God's hand…his patience, and everything else. It's really pretty cool."

"I was supposed to be a pastor, my grandfather wanted me to be a pastor…and my grandmother, in her wisdom said, "No, he's going to work with his hands." So…I became a shop teacher. Now, my younger son, who is out here drinking beer, he became a pastor…so I guess he substituted for me."

"I've got my funeral planned…and I don't want it to focus on me. I don't want it to focus on me. What my funeral is…and let me explain why I say that…I have a lot of friends that don't know the Lord. I know a lot of people that go to funerals, and they don't know the Lord. I know the pastors very well…and so here is an opportunity to hear the gospel message. So, my funeral is written, first and all, to give praise and glory to God, alert them to their sins, and then show them what God has done through Jesus…through his sufferings and death. However, the little plus thing that I'm going to put in there…is a Bach toccata that I'd like them to play for the recessional…because I like that. It might be corny, but I like that."

279 *Bill Henness*

"I am retired...age 72, married for over 52 years...factory worker 31 years. I am a licensed Baptist preacher, and a deacon for over 25...but, I gave it all up at the age of 58."

"I believe that there is no life after death...no spirits whether good or bad...that no one knows the future, and death must not be so bad because...everyone does it."

"I suppose when I finally turned away from belief in Christianity....virtually all my believing friends dropped me. For so many years, I did not have many unbelieving friends, but now I have two or three. My wife is still a believer...and we can't really discuss religion at all. I am happier now that I live by my own rules of conduct. I still live a very moral life, but guilt over religious things...they just don't bother me any more."

"It wasn't one thing in particular, but some of the books I have read, have helped me make the complete break from Christianity. The authors of some are...Farrell Till of the "Skeptical Review", and the "The Encyclopedia of Biblical Errancy" by C. Dennis McKinsey."

"Let me tell you about my grandfather...my maternal grandfather, who was a surgical veterinarian. He was a little crazy and had a violent temper. After doing some research on him through some old newspapers, I discovered he once choked a boy to near unconsciousness before the boy revived and then...he hit him in the head with a rock...causing deafness the rest of his life."

"He was once walking down the street and some men were sitting on a fence. One of them laughed at him, so he pulled out a knife and cut his abdomen and...chased him down the street slashing at him with his knife. Another time a man who had left his horse to be tended for the day got into an argument with him over the price...fifty cents. So Grandpa pulled out a two barreled derringer and shot him in the face, burning him badly...then he shot him in the groin. Then he ran upstairs to get his shotgun to finish the job."

"He was sued and had to sell his business to pay it. Another time he choked his wife to near unconsciousness...and she ran to the Justice of the Peace for help but he didn't want to get involved with him...Dr. Crocker. Next, his house burned to the ground and a spark from the blaze landed in my mother's eye and...she became blind in one eye as a result. He finally died a pauper cutting down a tree for fire wood...the tree fell on him."

"A few years later one of his daughters got influenza and died, and the next day my grandmother died of it also. When my mother was twelve years old she came to this town to live with a distant relative who was married to a man that would be my dad. When she was about fourteen, my dad raped her...and she was his mistress until she gave birth to me at age 22. About five years later the distant relative divorced him and Dad and Mom got married. I recall the wedding. Up to that time all four of us lived together. Talk about Peyton Place."

"Over the years...one of the several things I have learned is...you cannot tell anything about a person by looking at their face. Ted Bundy would be one example...my grandfather might be another."

"My own life hasn't been as colorful as my grandfather's. My wife and I were on vacation in the Ozarks once, and were swimming in the lake. She had on a yellow one piece swim suit and I was swimming around under water. While swimming under water with my eyes open I spotted a one piece swim suit that was yellow, so I swam over to her and grabbed her ankle. It kicked and I came up to the surface and looked into the face of a lady I had never seen before. I'm just very glad it was only her ankle I grabbed."

280   *Santa Claus*

"I'm currently under contract with a company…an out of state company, and I have signed an agreement that I won't talk with anyone in the media about my job…or about myself. But, I've done it before…and I most likely will do it again. It's really kind of hard not to talk about it…I mean…look at me, I get comments every day from people on the street…so…I do talk about it to a certain point."

"I won't give you my real name because I don't want to lose my job. I'm what you would call a *picture-perfect* Santa. During the holiday season I'm contracted to department stores or malls to be Santa Claus. I usually sit in a chair for ten…sometimes twelve hours a day, and let kids tell me what they want…and have their picture taken with me. I get breaks during the day…but I have to stay in character…always. That's…that's important."

"I still work in construction, but during the holidays…usually mid-November to December 26th, I become…Santa Claus. This is my real hair and beard. I don't dye it or bleach it…and that's one of the reasons why they call me *picture-perfect*. I've been doing this going on…six…seven years. I'll probably continue doing it as long as they'll let me…and as long as the money is good. Depending on where you are…and who you are…you can make six or seven thousand in a six week period."

"There's not supposed to be any smoking or drinking when we're contracted out…and I'm talking about after-hours too. We're not supposed to be watching any porn…or anything like that. But, I still go out for a beer every now and then…as you can see. I have to have a Killian's every once in awhile. I just have a few, really. I wasn't supposed to be here, but another one of the Santa's had a health problem…so I'm taking over for him."

"I think every other kid this year is asking for an X-Box…at least the boys are. The girls are still asking for Barbie. They've been asking for Barbie as long as I can remember. Now, that's a toy that has had some staying power. I'm not too sure I know exactly what an X-Box is…I know it's an electronic game of some sort…but I haven't seen one."

"You couldn't be in this job unless you like kids…and I do. You have to come across as a genuine person. You have to have that twinkle in your eye. Some kids come up to me and pull on my beard and say, "You really are Santa." Of course a lot of kids are intimidated by Santa…so they cry…and some parents try to make them sit with me…but I tell the parents they don't have to force the…their kids to sit on my lap. It just freaks the kids out sometimes. I know I was scared of Santa when I was a kid. A lot of kids are."

"A couple of days ago, I had this kid sit on my lap…and he said, "You don't have to bring me any toys…I just want my daddy to come home…he's in Iraq with the Army. He flies on those big green helicopters. He doesn't like the food they have there, so my mom is sending him some snacks." So…that was sort of an emotional one. I've had kids tell me that they just need some money for their parents or…their grandma. Mostly though…they ask for whatever is popular on the TV…or they say nothing at all. I can't…I can't…really say that I have had any bad experiences as a Santa…except for the occasional parent that is a little too pushy…but that's kind of expected."

"One kid asked me for a rifle last night…not a toy…he wanted a real rifle so he could go hunting with his dad. This kid wasn't old enough to tie his shoes, but he wanted to go with his dad and shoot something."

"I used to be a hunter…but I haven't done that in years. I never really hunted deer…or any other kind of big game…usually just rabbit and squirrel…and that was with a shotgun. There was this one time that I remember…I was down in Arkansas with my brother and some friends of his…and there was a period during the 80's when I tried hunting turkey with a bow. One day we all got up about five, and got settled into the blind about 6 o'clock. The weather was cold…the sky was cloudy. We were using a decoy and a caller…and we only got a few in sight…not close enough for the bow. I like it better when it's sunny, because they get more active."

"Anyway…we ate lunch…and about 1 o'clock I was getting my call answered. Pretty soon, two Tom's came walking up…and one was about fifteen yards in front of me. I placed the site pin in the middle of the body…squeezed it off…and put my arrow right through Tom's chest…going through both lungs, and his heart. That was…that was a big thrill. I'll never forget that."

"I was going to clean and freeze that turkey for Thanksgiving or Christmas…and this was in early March…but I decided to cook it up for my brother's family. We cooked it Cajun-style, which is frying it in peanut oil and then dusting it with Cajun spices…lots of cayenne pepper basically…and garlic. That was the best bird I ever ate, because, you know…I killed it."

281   *Crystal Potter*

"I never learn anything well by being a student. I only learn when I'm the teacher. It's the whole process really...getting to the point where you can stand in front of people and claim to know what you're doing. Like, some people might say, "I wish I could play the piano as well as...Elton John." In reality, they could...if they were willing to do what he did...practice for years and years, and hone your craft...have the perseverance and dedication to do all that is necessary...force yourself to practice each and every day...or, have a mother who hounds the hell out of you. That works too."

282 *K. Morris*

"I was at the Sandburg mall the other day…it's a ghost town…a ghost town. Since the Amana plant closed up, it's a ghost town. We're famous here in Galesburg for trains and Carl Sandberg and not much else. I don't…I don't really know how this town is gonna survive, you know?"

"There's a poem right over there, by Sandburg…and I thought it was, you know, kind of descriptive of what the town is going through. I might not remember this exactly, but it goes something like this—*Out of the prairie rise the faces of dead men…they speak to me, but I cannot tell you what they say. Other faces rise up…they are the unborn future. They cross and mix on the skyline and are lost in a purple haze. One forgets…and one waits.*"

283   *Duane Collins*

"I'm from Avon. I'm an alcoholic…and I quit drinking fifteen years ago. I don't drink any longer. I went to AA…and church. I'm a believer in the Lord Jesus Christ. I believe I am a saved individual…and I believe the day I die, I'm going to heaven…so I don't have to worry about having the sting of death in this life I live. Without the drink…my life has become so much better."

"I started a year ago last January…my own website business. I wouldn't have been able to do that as a sloshing drunk…you know? I'm fifty…but most people think I look thirty. I guess that's one of the advantages of being pickled the first thirty years of my life."

284 **Ken Jennings**

"I was born in 1974. I remember some stuff when my dad was in law school...which means I was like...two years old. I remember for Christmas...and this is like some nerd embryo story...I was given these letter blocks...Sesame Street blocks actually. I used them to spell messages out, instead of asking my mom and dad for something, I would like, spell something out with these Sesame Street blocks...very exciting."

"I was so excited to win that first game on Jeopardy...and it was because I had this goal my whole life. I was this little kid watching Jeopardy after school, thinking, "Wow, these guys are so cool...these guys are cool...I should do this some day." To achieve that goal, decades later...it's a good feeling. That's really what makes us all happy, achievement...not the monetary or other rewards that follow. It's achievement."

"I'm not crazy with every result of being that guy on Jeopardy. I used to be a very private...you know...kind of guy...enjoyed my privacy. Now, I just can't go anywhere without people in the airport just yelling, "Is that the Jeopardy guy?" It's like the other day, this woman says, "You're Gary Jenkins." As I'm walking away, I hear, "Gary, Gary." I know there are some people who just can't wait to get into the limelight. When they're famous, it's like...that's when their life starts. But, I never expected to be famous from a game show. No one has ever really been famous from being on a game show."

"I've also noticed that some of the stuff that you think is going to make you happy...the money, or whatever it is...doesn't really change your life at all. I'm just as happy now as before I won. That doesn't mean I'm going to volunteer to write you a check...but, it does sort of make you think, "What can I do with this money other than it sitting in my investment account?" So, one of the things I think about is, "How can I make good come out of this and not change my life at all?"

"I still live in the same house. I still drive the same 1998 Toyota Corolla...which, by the way, is a pretty sweet ride. Suddenly having all this money, and this ego boost...and temporary fame...it really didn't make me happy at all...wasn't the cause of my happiness. It really didn't affect my lifestyle at all. There is more to life than that."

"How I wrote my name differently every day…it was by accident really. It was just an accident, where different people in my family had advice for me on how I should write my name. My sister said, "You should write your name in small letters." So, after the first show, which I won very narrowly, I thought, "Well, I'll write my name in all small letters like my sister said." And then the next day, I thought, "Well, I did it differently those two days, so now I'll do it the way my parents said." So, I keep going, not knowing that I would have to come up with 75 different ways. I have three letters, it's not like my name is Bartholomew or something. It really turned into this albatross around my neck…I'd be backstage not even thinking about the questions and the answers…I'd be sketching on a cocktail napkin…trying to come up with something original."

"We all like trivia facts because first of all, they're weird…and second of all they're true. Both elements sort of have to be there. A good trivia fact, because they're both weird and true is a reminder to us that truth can be stranger than fiction…that the world is a wild and wonderful place. A lot of times we have these humdrum daily routines. I've been a college student for example, and this is a daily routine that might sound familiar…wake up…library…class…lunch…class…Starbuck's…study…class…study…bed. Repeat until graduation. In the middle of this kind of repetitive humdrum routine, a trivia fact is almost like a bolt out of the blue…it reminds you how much bigger the world really is…like the finger of God choosing you for a second, "KEN, OPOSSUMS HAVE THIRTEEN NIPPLES……THAT IS ALL.""

"Where trivia really comes in handy has to do with…relationships between people. We live in an age of specialization. There is just so much more to know today than in the past. When I think about these great Renaissance men of the past…Leonardo Da Vinci or Ben Franklin or whoever…these were people who knew a little bit, or a lot about every possible subject under the sun. That was sort of their thing. But, there's sort of a lot more to know today. These people would be totally stumped about things that are so commonplace now…because there is so much more to know. Sure, maybe Ben Franklin knew his stuff in the 18th century, but…put him on Jeopardy and see how he does with disco music."

"I was actually reading something about this...the entire sum of human knowledge is now increasing so rapidly that it doubles every eighteen months. That means, in the last eighteen months...roughly the time when I was first on Jeopardy...until today...the human race has learned as much...has produced as many bytes of knowledge...as it did, in all of human history combined, back to the cave man. The last eighteen months. That is incredible."

"There's a great bond that's created when somebody else realizes you know something in common with what they know. When I'm sitting on an airplane for example, and the person next to me tells me he is from Fargo, North Dakota...that could be a conversation killer right there, because I know nothing about Fargo, North Dakota. That's pretty much the ballgame right there. But...if I know a little, just a little...an icebreaker of trivia to get my foot in the door...if I've seen the movie Fargo, for crying out loud...or if I remember the baseball player Roger Maris is from Fargo...I could ask him if he has ever been to the Roger Maris museum...or if I remember that Fargo sits on the Red River...I can ask him if he has ever fished the Red River. There are opportunities for bonding when you share knowledge with other people."

"Some of the best moments after winning on Jeopardy...I like going to schools just talking to people...visiting the elementary schools in my area...telling kids that I like to read...or whatever their teachers want me to tell them. I once got to go on Sesame Street and hang out with Grover...on the actual Sesame Street set with Snuffleupagus...on the air with a talking pineapple. That was cool."

285   *Bill Jaynes*

"I'm in my mid 50's. I've done quite a few things in my past...mostly common man types of jobs...blue collar jobs. I've worked in the restaurant business...never really made much money, especially in the restaurant business. I'm in the restaurant business now, because it is what I know...actually opened up my own Subway, down south. I read through all the information they sent me, and even after reading through all of the lawsuits that were pending against the Subway...the parent corporation, I decided to take...take the plunge anyway. Through some dumb luck, I got some money from a friend that died about eighteen months ago. He was thoughtful enough to leave me some money when he found out he had cancer. He was a good friend...someone I could trust."

"I had a dog...a Spitz named Raleigh. I had him for almost eleven years. Every time I would let him outside...I knew he wouldn't go in the street. He always came when I called him...always. I could always count on Raleigh to stay with me when I went on walks. He was a very...obedient dog...never gave me any trouble. About six months ago, I let him out...and this is a dog...he never, ever would cross the street. I trusted him. But...there was a squirrel that ran from my yard to the house across the street. I looked out and Raleigh was running as hard as he could to get that squirrel...and BAM...run over in an instant. He died about six hours later. It just...broke my heart."

286   *Sue Troxall*

"I was born in Alton, Illinois, and I grew up in the suburbs of Chicago…Brook-field, and then I moved down here. My parents moved to Brookfield because my grandmother and grandfather lived in Maywood. My parents met in Alton in college. My dad was on the G.I. Bill…and my mom was there. After they graduated, they moved to Maywood and lived in an apartment that my great-grandmother owned. Then, after my dad got a teaching job…got some money…the four of us moved to Brookfield. Then, I came down here to visit my brother and his wife…I got a job, and have just sort of been here in the area ever since."

"I'm a school teacher at South Pekin Grade School. This year I am teaching third grade, but I have taught Title I fifth grade, Title I second, kindergarten…you name it I have taught it."

"My husband and I go to Canada every year. My parents had gone up there…well, they still go up there. For thirty years, my parents have gone there. That's why I told my husband, "I know this great place in Canada. We have to go camping up there." So, we go to Ojibwa Provincial Park. Since we have been married…sixteen years this summer…we have only missed four summers. The fishing is wonderful, and the scenery is gorgeous. The people at the campground…and we have been there many times, and they knew me from before…are really nice."

"The day I graduated from Rosemont University…the day I got my teaching degree was truly a great day. School didn't come easy for me. I had to work very hard. Some of my teachers in high school would have told me, "Don't even bother, you'll never make it." But, I graduated my senior year on the Dean's List. I really had to work hard…and that was a high point in my life. My older brother got in on an academic scholarship, and now he's a doctor. My younger brother…my parents got a student loan for him…and my youngest brother got an athletic scholarship. I had a fourth brother, but he died very young. I don't remember that the pain for me was that bad, but I remember the pain of seeing my parents so sad."

"I'm going to Bradley University, and I will have my special ed endorsement at the end of this semester…and then I will take some time off, and go back and get my masters. I don't know what…but I'll keep teaching. When I retire, I plan on writing children's books. I already have several written. I just need to get up enough gumption to send them in."

287   *Gary Sandberg*

"I have children from my first marriage. That divorce was horrific, but probably deserved…and I would not be the person I am today, had I stayed in the traditional marriage and relationship. It was probably too soft and comfortable…the Cleaver family. It was after that marriage that I got registered…and turned from a very insulated and secular existence to truly caring about other people. That experience, as painful as it was…hurtful…it was part of…I guess I would describe it as the biggest surprise, and not exactly what I had planned for. Looking at it 34 years after the fact…it was probably what needed to be done to get me where I am. I gave up a lot of things, which still mean…and certainly at the time…meant a lot to me. But, now I have grandchildren."

"I rebounded…met a young woman that had a child…fell more in love with the child than the woman…we were married for a short period of time. Very short, because it didn't take me long to realize it was the child I loved…more so…I mean…I cared a lot for Mary, but it didn't work out. A few years after that, I married Barbara…who is also on the city council. We were married for twelve years, and now I have been divorced for almost ten. I'm good friends with all my wives. We all go out for pizza…and Barbara is also on the city council now."

"My daughter and son…when they graduated, wanted to live in Chicago. That's where the action is. My daughter is a forensic criminologist…now the assistant lab director over in Morton. She loved the nightlife and the excitement of Chicago. She was married for six…seven years, and got pregnant…she decided that probably the best place to raise a child was not Chicago…so, she came back to Peoria. My son is a stilt-walking, fire-breathing juggler, who, right now is riding a motorcycle on a tightrope over a steel pier in Atlantic City. He's been all over the world."

"When both my kids turned 21, I gave them a trip to England. I'm an anglophile…I just love England. But, they had to do all the research…I was just the driver…and they had to tell me where to drive. I had been going over there for years. My daughter was older, and so we went over and did all of the castle things…and things that a 21 year old girl would like to see in England. We happened to stumble…the day Princess Eugenie was born, Andrew and Fergie's

Daughter...we stumbled into a rugby pub in Cranbrook, Kent...which was south and east of London. They adopted us...and we had a great time."

"When we got back to the United States, my son...who was a year younger than Terry, heard about the trip...but only paid attention to the rugby pub. So, when he and I went over the following year...it was a totally different experience than anything he had experienced in the United States. When we returned, he sold everything he had...everything...motorcycle...TV...VCR. He invested in some Chicago Police jackets, because he knew who was making them up in Chicago, and figured he could turn a profit over in England. He then went over to live...was going to go to school to become a chef."

"As he got hungrier...and his path moved around, he got involved with some theatrical people. He had never done anything in the theater here...but in London he was living with some young people that did some theatrical performances. They all go black...the theaters, after Christmas...and the performers than go on holiday. He went with them, and didn't have any money, so had to figure out how to...he started learning street performer juggling...and then fire-eating...and over the next ten years...he just evolved, and got better and better, and more well-known. He said, "I got hungry Dad." He had to figure out how to earn a living. He was six time zones away...totally by himself. Between '92 and '98, I'd go over, wherever he was at...which was fun, because he was always *someplace else*."

"Three years ago, he came back to the United States...lived in New York, because that is the entertainment hub of the United States. But, literally...about seven months ago...he has decided Peoria is his base. He's come back, and figures he can work anyplace by way of plane or whatever. He comes back next Tuesday. He'll be in New Zealand in October...Australia, for a three week festival there, and then...he's a production manager...it's a production called "Firedance"...based on Indian culture. He's hoping to do that in the Far East...Malaysia."

"I'm originally from Princeton. I like Peoria because of the people...and its scale. It's small enough, that individuals can still make a difference...at every level, on any issue...but yet big enough to offer diversity. Princeton had one minority family, and they lived just outside of Princeton. So, technically, they were the only minority family in school. We were all pretty vanilla...which has certain strengths about it…but also very, very limiting. A city the size of Peoria brings to the table…a diversity of society, which represents the United States. It all revolves around the people."

"In Princeton, I remember falling down a hill on Mother's Day, and then coming to Peoria…my first memory of Peoria…to meet the surgeon who would repair my arm. Princeton is such a small town. Coming to the big city of Peoria where the doors…open automatically…open automatically…that's just something that you didn't see in Princeton. I was five years old…just going into kindergar-ten…and I broke my arm, out on my grand…my grandfather's farm, where I was born."

"Most people think they know me. I'm 57…and no male Sandburg has lived this long in a couple generations. My cousins all died before they were fifty. My father died at 51. So, I have lived a life, expecting to be dead before 57…so I'm on grace time right now. I have always tried to do my best in solving other people prob-lems…whether it is architecture or the political arena. People look at me, per-haps, as a problem-maker on the city council. I just try and bring the perspective that…problems can only be solved if you take in…all the facts…instead of just the facts that you want to know."

288   *Jane Smiley*

"I remember when I was four months pregnant, and I was sitting at the table with my fourteen year old daughter that was staying home from school that day. We were sitting at the breakfast table, bickering…and the phone rang. It was a caller from the Ames Tribune. He said, "Have you heard anything from New York?" I said, "No." He said, "Well, have you heard anything from Columbia University?" I said, "No." He said, "Do you think you might have won the Pulitzer Prize?" I said, "No." He said, "Okay…if you *had* won the Pulitzer Prize, what would you say about it?" So…I gave him some quote."

"I came back down and sat at the table, and I said…and I went into a cold sweat actually, and I had never done that before…I came back and sat at the table and said, "You know, I think I just won the Pulitzer Prize." And my fourteen year old said, "Huhhh.""

"I went to my office…I was going to teach a class that afternoon…and exactly at 2 o'clock central time, the phone rang, and it was the guy from the Washington Post reading the ticker…he was reading the wire service. He read aloud to me that I had won the Pulitzer Prize. And then about two minutes later, there came someone running and screaming down the hall…screaming in anger. I opened the door, and it turned out to be the reporter for the Des Moines Register, who was holding the Ames paper in her hand…and realizing she had been scooped by the Ames newspaper. I'll never forget the site of her screaming down the hall. She was really, really, really mad."

"A long, long time ago, I was spending the weekend at a friend's apartment in New York.
I think I was 27. I fell asleep in the afternoon…and I dreamt, and this is true…I'm not just making this up for you. I dreamt that one of my creative writing professors, a man named Leonard Michaels…I dreamt that he stood up in front of the group, at the head of the table and said, "Okay now…I'm going to tell you the meaning of life." We all leaned forward…and at that very moment in my dream, when he was going to tell me the meaning of life…there came a knock on the front door. It was so loud that it woke me up…so, I didn't get to find out the meaning of life. It was just some neighbor from the apartment I was in, ask-

ing some stupid question…much less interesting than the question about the meaning of life."

"I later decided that nobody wants the meaning of life to be one thing. Everyone wants the meaning of life to be something that they find…moment by moment…as their lives progress. So, that's why…in my dream, I concocted someone to knock on the door…so I wouldn't have to listen to Leonard Michaels tell me what the meaning of life was."

289   *Simone Morgan*

"I am 35. I'm mostly a mom, but I work part-time at Kohl's. I'm a cashier and I get to meet a lot of people. I like people."

"I came from Pine Island, Minnesota. You know Rochester? You know Rochester? There's a Highway 52...and Pine Island is smack dab from the center of Rochester, and fifty miles the other way. It is one of your small, little, cow towns. You know, we had 1500 people, with a K through 12 school. I don't think I realized when I was young, how much I got as a child...you know, in school...and all the friends I had. It was so nice to grow up there. I still have a friend that I have known since the third grade...Julie. She's married and has two kids."

"My parents were not together. They originally divorced when I was three...my mother and father divorced when I was three. My father remarried when I was five, and married another woman for twelve years. My father was one of these men that...wanted to save women. My mother was being abused by her father...and then the next one was being abused by her husband. I had a wonderful father, and a very...very smart stepmother. But, I didn't spend a lot of time with her or her daughter. I stayed away from them...and I had a lot of great friends."

"My mom couldn't handle stress. She loved us dearly, but...you know, she didn't have the money. Back in the 70's...I think it was just beginning where divorce was a big thing...you know, there weren't that many people divorced. My father's parents were Catholic and judges...and had more clout than my mother had. It was a safer place for us to go...on my dad's side of the family versus my mom's. But she had custody during vacation...summer vacation...so, we saw her. But, it was sad...a very unhealthy divorce...not a good thing. My mom never remarried, and she lives in Denver. My dad is married to his childhood sweetheart, and he lives in the Black Hills of South Dakota. They're both happy...I guess."

"For twelve years, this woman and her daughter, and my brother and I...and my father...when we were together...and my father was a go-carter...he raced go-carts, so, every weekend my stepsister and my brother and my father would go to the track. That was our family thing."

"In high school, I was the mascot for the Pine Island Panthers. I had great girl-friends...and if things were rough at home, I could go and be with them. They spoiled me. There was a foursome of us girls...we would always hang out together, and anytime it got hard...we were there for each other."

"We waited until our senior year. We were always boy-crazy...we would travel to other towns...and you know how girls always sit back and giggle at the cute guys...they never actually approach them? There was this one guy who wore a brown tie. His name was Leo. He was a debate...discussion guy, who was really smart and good-looking. He was nice, and so we just sat back and giggled. We never did anything. But, my senior year in speech, there was one boy...I was reading a book, and he came over and sat down and started talking to me. We ended up exchanging addresses and then we went on one date...at the state fair."

"That was my first kiss...and it was horribly awkward. It was horrible. It was awful. People kept coming out and laughing at us, "Well, if you're going to do it, just do it...are you gonna kiss?" I was shy...and so, it was just a peck."

290   *Tony Nishimura*

"I was a history teacher six or seven years ago, but changed jobs after my divorce. I sell investments now. I think one of the greatest lessons in history is…is…people…having been fooled long enough, after a certain period of time…tend to reject any evidence that they were fooled. Once you give someone the power over you…you almost always never get it back. Once you have committed yourself to a decision or belief…you do everything you can to feed it."

291 *Darryl Simmons*

"Basically...I sell frozen food products to retail outlets."

"I'm not sure what year it was...I think it was 1973...maybe 1974. We went to the Bellevue Drive-In to see all five of the "Planet of the Apes" movies. They were having this movie marathon showing all five movies. My mom took us...I think my dad was working second shift...or third shift."

"About the third movie...which one was that? I think it was "Escape from the Planet of the Apes"...it starts raining. So, my mom and me...and my sister, we're sitting in this white Pontiac Star Chief watching this movie in the rain. This was the same Pontiac that I wrecked a couple years later after I got my license. My dad bought it used, maybe two weeks before. The windshield wipers are going and it starts raining harder and harder...the wind is blowing the rain into the crack where the speaker is hanging. Mom said it would end after awhile and we're gonna wait it out. We couldn't see anything on the screen at all, it was just a blur of color...and pretty soon the speaker starts getting static...fading in and out...and then there's nothing...no sound."

"So we sit in the car for awhile not really knowing what's going on...we can't hear the movie or see it. Then, Mom said that there was an empty spot one row up...so, she starts up the car and we move to a new spot. She rolls down the window and pulls the speaker in...and after a few minutes, the speaker starts sparking. Sparks are flying off the speaker into my mom's lap. She starts screaming...my sister starts screaming...my mom is climbing out of her seat into mine...and I've got a foot-long hot dog and soda on the glove-compartment tray."

"She smacks the tray and the hot dog flies up into my face and hits me in the eye...so now I've got an eyeful of mustard...which burns like hell. The soda spills all over the passenger side of the car...all over my legs and my mom's chest...because now my mom is in my lap. She's got mustard in her hair...and the speaker is still sparking. My sister is screaming...and the speaker gets louder...and it's still sparking. In the background, we can hear the monkeys going nuts."

"Mom reaches over and roles the window down...grabs the speaker by the cord and throws it out. So, it's hanging off the pole, with the bottom corner of it dangling in the gravel, and it's still throwing sparks. My sister's crying, "I wanna go home. I wanna go home." Mom sits there for awhile and doesn't say anything...then she starts the car and we pull out of the drive-in onto 116...just as the rain stops."

"All I can think about is that I didn't get to eat my foot-long...so I start complaining, and my mom stops by the A&W...that one in Bellevue. She buys six chili-dogs to go...and we drive over to my grandma's. After we got there, I ate three of those chili-dogs and drank some water from the bathroom faucet...which had these rusty iron stains all around it, because...it was well water. The water tasted terrible....and one time my sister told me that the water came directly from the toilet...so I had that in my mind...and the combination of that and the chili-dogs kind of grossed me out...and on the way home...I threw up in the car. I filled the ash tray...which was already full of cigarette butts. Chili-dog vomit and cigarette butts...not a pretty site."

292 *Beth Green*

"It's been quite awhile since I been there…Havana…but, that's where I'm from. It's just a small river town. It's where I grew up at, and went to high school. We had a lot of parties out in the country there. We used to outrun the cops there. We'd get a whole bunch of people and park in a line…and when we was ready to go out to our favorite spot drinkin', we'd go separate ways…all of us, and confuse the police."

"I moved to Lincoln, because my job is there. I'm a setup operator there in the factory. I set up presses at the Cutler-Hammer factory. We make electrical boxes. We do business with Ford and Chevy…companies like that. I've worked in a garment factory…restaurants…worked out in the fields when I was younger. I cut beans and corn, and sorted corn. I worked in the tomato fields, planting tomatoes…picking the tomatoes…and sorting them. I did things like that. I left the garment factory to work at Cutler-Hammer, and I've worked my way up."

"My first job, I worked in a grocery store as a cashier. I didn't like it at all. I'm kind of a people person, but I don't like somebody pushin'. The job I have now…I like being able to be by myself and being able to do my job without anybody bothering me."

"I got two sons. They're both welders. One of 'em is in the union out in Morton…he's a boilermaker. The other one lives in Kentucky with his wife and family. He's a welder for some kind of business that makes buildings alongside the railroad tracks. He welds them. They're doing pretty good. My youngest son…the boilermaker, lives in Canton. He lives there with his girlfriend…and they got two girls. My youngest son travels. He's in Danville right now…does all the boilermaker stuff there. I'm pretty proud of both of 'em."

"I think I'd like to move to Kentucky. It's a beautiful country…the people are real nice down there…and my oldest son lives down there…and, I don't know…I just always wanted to move down there. I don't like Lincoln at all. There's nothin' there. The people are very rude. I have no family there. I have to travel to see anybody. Lincoln…it's just Lincoln. I go to Springfield more than I come up here."

"I'm going to the movies here pretty soon with a guy I ain't never been out with before…from Canton. We're going over here to this new 18-show theater."

"I got my motorcycle license this year. I thought about gettin' a Harley, but for the price, I can get a Yamaha or Honda…at a better price. For what you pay on a base price for a Sportster, you can get a full-dressed Yamaha…and Yamaha's are good. They last longer…don't rattle apart like a Harley does. You pay for the name…and it's a nice bike, but the price is kinda high. I just want somethin' I can cruise around on…you know, somethin' that can get me out of Lincoln."

293   *Paul Eschelman*

"I am fifty years old…almost 51. I was born in Ethiopia, but didn't live there very long. I grew up mostly in Iowa…Ames, Iowa. My parents were there…it was called Point Fore, which was similar to the Peace Corps. Right after they got married, they went over and spent a couple years teaching. While they were there, my brother and myself were born. I was about two when we left, so I don't remember much."

"My mom's family was real close. We had other cousins the same age, and we would go to the farm they lived on in Wisconsin…and we would just go wild. We would go into the hay mound…and we had tunnels built. My cousin would hitch up the electrical fence charger to things, and then go tell us to touch it or pick it up…and we would get a big jolt."

"I was out in the field one summer, chopping thistles in about 98 degree heat, shooting pigeons and goofing around. We came back in…and we got into trouble for poking knives in a wall. We were throwing knives. My cousin bought a new knife and target, so we had to go try them out. We totally destroyed a couple of panels downstairs…and got walloped."

"I had strict parents…fairly strict…solid parents. Church was always a big part…a big part of our family…family life. It continues to be. It was Free Church…Evangelical Free, it's called. Now…now, we're going to a Lutheran Church…they're both pretty conservative. Garrison Keillor talks about the Lutheran Church a lot, although he wasn't really Lutheran. He gets a lot of mileage about that, but he was part of some smaller church…Bretheren…or something like that…some smaller, more restrictive church."

"Before we moved to Ames, my dad taught in a small college in St. Paul called Bethel…right across from the St Paul Fairgrounds where Garrison Keillor does his show, at the Minnesota State Fair. It was on Snelling back then…so I lived right across from the state fair. So, I spent…the only time I went there was when I was in third grade. My parents gave us each fifty cents and sent us across the street to the state fair. I got lost almost right away. I spent my money on…one of those games where you try to win stuff. Myself, and my best friend, Danny David spent the whole day being lost…and then finally found our way out, and walked home."

"My father was a grad student in college, in Ames…university town…small when we were there. He was in metallurgical engineering…which is kind of the route most of the people in my family have taken…the technical sciences. I am the only one that has delved into art much, at all. I was always interested in visual things, especially functional…woodworking or pottery, or those kinds of things. I have done this for, well…I guess I was about three years into a biology major, and then switched to art…pottery."

"What I do is all functional work. I started out, throwing on the wheel…pretty much what all potters do. In grad school, I changed techniques a little bit…but still worked in regular clay…plastic clay. After grad school, I developed this technique, after going to a workshop with the chief designer of Lenox China. This process is known as slipcasting, which is quite a bit different than the standard approach. It involves making a piece out of a plaster model. So, the original forming isn't done in clay…it's done in another material, usually plaster…and then making a mold. The pieces are made in molds. So, the outcome is a lot different than something I would model in a soft material. It is precise and clean…and more like something you would make in a hard material…which for me, is plaster."

"Since I have gotten into this technique, I have become more interested in industrial wares, and other sources for my ideas outside the world of clay. Architecture is a big influence…European design, especially. I have looked at a lot of Japanese and Chinese pots…and have some small teapots. Those are a big influence also. We took a trip to Italy…and looked at villas designed by an architect named Pilladio. In the 1500's, he worked around Venice. I really enjoyed looking at those…the sense of balance…the symmetry."

"My wife and I are a team, and without her, I couldn't be doing what I am doing. She handles all the business aspects…all the computer things. All the shows now, the applications are done on the computer. The images have to be submitted via email. She takes care of all that…and keeps things running smoothly as a business. We do about fifteen shows a year…spread out a little, but concentrated in the summer. We sell to half a dozen shops…and sell from our own studio."

"Dave Berry bought some of my pieces in Miami. I don't know if you have ever met him, but he was very low key, easy to talk to, and not egotistical at all. I wouldn't have known it was Dave Berry. He looked slightly familiar to me, and then his credit card said Dave Berry. I quizzed him about it, and he said he was. That was the show we did at Coconut Grove."

"Doing these shows…it was a real different experience when our kids were young…bringing them to shows…and trying to keep an eye on them. One of our kids got lost at a real big show in Ohio. He was two…no…about four…and ran off, and couldn't find his way back to the booth. There were hundreds of thousands of people in that show. It was scary. Eventually, the cops saw him crying…and brought him back. They asked him his name…and he told them his dad was an artist in the show. So, we got him back after he was lost. That was scary."

294   *Mark Hagen*

"I'm Mark Hagen…I am eighteen years of age. I'm kinda just roaming around, looking at the scenery…looking for some girls, I guess. It's kinda something to do on a Friday or Saturday night, I guess. I've had some luck picking up girls before."

"My friend's name here is Aaron Joseph. He's in the Marine Corps…hasn't been overseas yet…hasn't been to Iraq…just got out of boot camp really."

"I'm from Metamora…been living there for four years. Before that, I lived in a small town called Varna. I'm currently unemployed, but I guess you could say that I'm a struggling model. I've done some model work out in New York City. I did a couple of portfolios and a couple of photo shoots…but, that's about it."

"My cousin and me are bi-racial, and my aunt is, you know, my cousin's mom. We don't really get along with the family. So awhile back we decided to take a little trip to Mexico and decided to have some fun instead of spending family time with the relatives. That was a fun trip."

"So, today I'm just kinda chillin…hanging out…relaxing. Gonna go back to ICC and study graphic design here…in the fall. I might be a graphic designer…I might do some modeling. I might take a trip out to the west coast to see California, and settle down eventually…don't really know for sure."

"I'm also looking for some food now…looking for the cheapest meal item I can find…maybe a corn dog or something. I might go listen to a band later. Mostly, I'm just gonna kinda chill."

295 *Jane Curry*

"During the depression, my grandma took in sewing…and she had a thimble she used nonstop. She lost the thimble…and 45 years later, she found it inside a doll she had made."

296   *Chris Carr*

"I am Chris Carr...38. I'm in Peoria this weekend to race in the TT. I have won this race thirteen times in my career. I have won seventy races...thirteen of them here. I won my first race right here in Peoria...my first Grand National in 1986. I was riding a Woodrow flat-tracker. I'm now riding a KTM based motocross bike...500cc. I started racing in 1973...and been racing here since 1984. I don't know how long I'll be coming here...it could be my last year...or it could be ten years. This is my job...right now it's all I do. I am an avid golfer, but as far as a job...this is my job. You can make six figures doing what I do. This race...on Sunday...a guy can make over $12,000 with bonuses and different contingencies and what not."

"I grew up around racing...I was six years old when I started riding. My dad was a TV and VCR repairman, but he was also an amateur flat-tracker...back in the 70's. So, I kind of grew up around it. It was my destiny I guess. I grew up at the race track. I started riding at the Lodi Cycle Bowl out in Lodi, California at the age of six...and you know, we did a lot of races around northern California...growing up. I did a little motocross...never really raced motocross...I mostly raced flat track. I don't ride a street bike...I do all my riding in the dirt."

"There are only two TT race tracks...this one and the one in Springfield. The one in Springfield is a makeshift track...not an amphitheater like this one. It's in a rodeo arena and they just kind of lay out the track. It's not like the one here."

"When I come here, we don't practice until the day of the race. We'll go out tomorrow morning...and we'll get three five-lap sessions. They don't give us a whole lot of time to practice."

"I've never been in any major accidents...just scared the crap out of myself a few times. You know, any time you get in a wreck. At the Springfield mile about five years ago...five of us collected the hay bales in turn one. Two of us got up and walked away...and three went to the hospital. I was one of the two that walked away. Anything can happen."

"When I get a chance, I golf...play with the kids. I am a typical father away from the race track. I have two boys...eight and six years old. They keep us hopping…my wife and I, Pam…we're busy all the time. My kids are not into riding…they could give a flip about motorcycles. They're into video games…they're into soccer and karate. Their dad just happens to be a motorcycle racer. They don't have any desire to ride or race motorcycles…which is ok by me."

"I think if I hadn't been a motorcycle racer…I thought about being a basketball coach. I probably would have been teaching, and coaching basketball. Growing up, that was my fallback…go to college, and coach basketball. That was a passion I had when I was a kid. Instead…I'm racing motorcycles, and I never made it to college. But you know…I do what I love to do. I do it on my own terms. That's important."

297   *Louis Patterson*

"I'm looking for a job…another job. I have a job now…but, I'm looking to move up."

298   *John Simison*

"Cornfed or grassfed…it makes no difference to me, I want it hung for darn near three weeks. Now the government is telling me that I can't have our beef hung, they're tellin' me how to eat my own animal. Pretty soon, if I want to eat some good farm beef and want it hung…I'll be goin' to jail. If you're wonderin' what the big industrial packers do…to tenderize their beef…well let me just say, they don't hang it. They electrocute the hell out of it, to break down the cells and make it more tender. But it never gets the great flavor of hung beef."

"I've been struggling with this a little lately…how a person just wants to take care of family and friends and it gradually makes him a criminal as the laws change. But the only thing I can do is…keep on keeping on."

299   *B.J. Ponder*

"I drive a truck…I'm a long haul truck driver. Been doing that since the 70's."

"My buddy, Paul, had a Plymouth Valiant…I think it was made in the early 60's. He bought it from one of our buddies who was being sent to jail for possession. It was mostly rust, but you could still tell that it was a light blue…just barely. The bumpers had a little chrome showing through…but also mostly rust. The door handle on the driver's side was completely missing and the door was kept closed with safety wire. It had bald tires…it was basically a car that should have been sitting in somebody's yard with tall grass growing around it."

"This was the car that we used every weekend to drive to Savannah…which was about 45 miles away. This car had many problems, but probably the worst problem was the radiator. I was no mechanic then…and I'm still not…and Paul wasn't either. This was the kind of car that…when it quit running, you would just kind of walk away from it and pretend that it wasn't yours. It could go maybe…five miles before it overheated…and there would be no water in the radiator. So, it wasn't a bad car to take into town and go to the movies, or Lenin's…but Savannah was always a big deal."

"We had these big plastic buckets…I think they were five gallon buckets. They were the kind that you see at farms and stuff…tall white buckets, with a thin metal handle…the kind that you get berries in. When we went to Savannah we would fill a couple of these buckets and put them in the back seat. Of course the water sloshed around and the whole back of the car got wet…but we really didn't care. So…having two buckets would get us about fifteen miles before we had to refill. In that fifteen miles, we would refill the radiator a couple of times."

"The big problem was, about fifteen miles down the road…which was basically a thin patch of asphalt laid down in the swamps…there were no businesses. It was pretty much a swampy wasteland…except for the turnoff to go to Hilton Head. But, after the turnoff, Hilton Head was many more miles the wrong way. So, we filled the buckets from the swamps…and then filled the radiator from the buckets. I know we poured a lot of swampy things into the radiator…chunks of seaweed…little tiny fish…pieces of wood…I think one time I saw a tiny alligator go into the radiator. It didn't seem to affect it much...the car still ran after it cooled off a little, and we were good to go for another five miles."

"When we got close to Savannah, we had to cross this long bridge that arched up in the middle. It was one of those old-time bridges that had more steel girders than it probably needed. We were always careful to time our "overheating" so that the car wouldn't stop on the bridge. We did come very close one time. Just on the other side of the bridge was a Howard Johnson's...an old dirty Howard Johnson's...and the car overheated and quit just as we got to it. We coasted into the parking lot and went inside to get some water...and because we were there, decided to have some dinner...this was on a Friday night."

"I ordered some pancakes and Paul ordered some eggs and bacon...and then we both got milk. I'm not sure why, but I drank a lot of milk in those days. I smoked cigarettes also, two packs a day...Marlboros. While I'm thinking about it...probably the best set of tits I have ever seen, I saw at this strip club right down the road from that Howard Johnson's. Have you ever seen the picture of the honey dipper on a box of Honeycomb cereal? These tits were like that. This was before women had silicone injections...I think. They were shaped like that honey dipper with these perfectly round, big and hard, puffy nipples...they looked like one of those Helmut Newton photos. But...to get back to my story...when Paul got up to go to the restroom, I took his car keys and put them in his glass of milk."

"I thought it would be funny for him to drink his milk and then find his keys in the bottom of the glass. But then...I screwed up and accidentally got some cigarette ashes in the milk. Paul came back and saw the ashes in the milk...at about the same time the waitress came by. She quickly picked up the glass and said, "That's okay, sugar...I'll get you another glass." She walked away with the car keys in the bottom of the milk...and she disappeared into the kitchen."

"So...now I had to figure out how to get the damn car keys back. I was too embarrassed to tell the waitress what I had done...and I figured Paul would get mad at me if I told him...so I didn't. I didn't tell him...ever. I always knew the Valiant would most likely kill us sooner or later...and I figured it was a good time to let it go. When we got ready to go, he couldn't find his keys...and I told him I didn't remember that he brought them in. We looked for them outside, and we never found them. We took off on foot and spent that night and part of the next day walking around Savannah. On Saturday, we hitched a ride back home…and never did go back for that car."

"After that…and I'm not kidding about this…two weeks later, we both went to a Kawasaki dealer and we each bought a Kawasaki XL-250. They were having a sale…$550 each…both blue. We soon found out that our keys fit each other's motorcycles. A couple months after that, Paul was at a baseball game and lost the keys to his motorcycle…but he had a spare set. A couple of days after that, my motorcycle was stolen…not his…mine. Most likely because someone found his keys and tried them in my bike. I was mad at the time, but I guess everybody gets what they deserve sooner or later. At the time, I didn't see…I didn't see the irony with the keys. I got what I deserved then…and I guess I always have. Every time I've fucked around and done something bad to someone…I've paid for it."

300 *Pam Putney*

"I'm from Elmwood...and I work at a vet's office as a vet assistant. We're just a small clinic...do basic stuff."

"I'm originally from Winter, Wisconsin...a real small town. I grew up on a farm...four kids...and we're real close. Actually, my oldest brother is an astronaut...Jeff Williams. He's getting ready to go on his second launch...the end of March. They're shooting him into space from Russia. His first launch was in 2000, and he was called the "Rookie Spacewalker". For this flight, he'll be the flight engineer and science officer for Expedition 13...a six-month flight."

"We had a dog come in...a Husky...and it had a small lump above its eye. The doctor did some surgery to open it up...and there was a .22 bullet in there. The dog acted fine...and didn't act like it was shot or anything. The guy who brought him in...the first words that came out of his mouth was, "Who would shoot my dog?""

"We used to have another dog that came in regularly...we boarded him, and his name was Roger. Roger smiled. The first time he came in, I thought he was growling at me...but she said, "No...no...he's smiling." He was a good dog...and he really did smile."

301   *Stan Harris*

"Name is Stan Harris, fifty years old. I was born in Fort Wayne, Indiana. Started out…went to college in the small town of Angola, Indiana, which is north of Fort Wayne…close to the Ohio and Michigan borders. Went to school and graduated from there. Moved around different places in that area. In 1982, my then wife and I, up and moved to…well, we had visited Peoria…had some friends of ours come over here. He was kind of a traveling pastor who would kind of come over this way every weekend. So, we got to traveling and got to meet a lot of the people that were a part of the church. So we decided…well…we'll just go ahead and up and move. There were a number of circumstances that went behind that…too deep to go into. But, Peoria is a lot like my home town of Fort Wayne…ummm….so we moved over here in 86."

"I took a co-op job at CDI and did a lot of work for Komatsu…well, then it was Dresser…and Caterpillar. I moved over before she did, and lived with a family…looking for a house after work. Here I am with a map and a burger in my hand, driving around Peoria…trying to find a house to rent. I found a place over on Maplewood…across from the Bradley Fieldhouse. I went in there, looked at it and said, "Yeah, we'll take this." She hadn't even seen it…until the day we moved, and that was the first time she saw it. I was hoping she would like it."

"Later on, ended up buying a house, and had two kids there. Since then, I've gone through a divorce, and now I'm living in East Peoria…just across the river…so, not too far away from Morton. Getting ready to get married again in October. Two kids, and a divorce and two more kids later, I'm getting married again. I've got a two-year old, and a six-week old baby."

"First time my dad…he took us to Texas, and told us we were going to visit his sister. I had no idea…never been in Texas…didn't know what it was gonna be like…knew it was gonna be hot, but I had no reference. We drove down in an air-conditioned car, and we passed through Texarkana…part of Arkansas and Texas there. I remember, we went through a small town and it kinda struck me, 'cause I looked off to the side and I saw these signs on a lavatory…a bathroom, downtown that said *Black* and *White* on the doors. I had never seen anything like that before. I'd heard about it in grade school, but never actually seen it. That was kind of a pivotal…well not pivotal, but it stuck in my mind…significant."

"We get down to my aunt's house, and here we been in this air-conditioned car. We stop and get out of the car, and it was liked somebody slapped me in the face. The heat was that intense. So, we're there for awhile, and I'm not used to backwards type living and all that. I'm walking around the house and ask my dad, "Where's the bathroom?" He brings me to the door, points across the gravel driveway at a little building...like, put together with plywood and boards, and said, "That's where you go." I said, "You do?" He said, "Yeah." He walks me over, opens this door, and shows me this board with a hole in the middle, with a role of toilet paper sitting in the middle. I said, "Okay, but where do we take a bath?" My aunt brings out this big tub, sits it on the floor and starts to boil water on the wood stove...pours it in there and says, "There's where you take your bath."

"Pittsburgh, Texas...that was a number of years ago, early 60's. It was a good experience for me...coming from city living to go backwards to what my dad grew up with."

302   **Bob Hutchens**

"I looked in the mirror one day and found acceptance for myself as a person. I was up in the Superstition Mountains in Arizona...way, way...away from home...sitting there in the quiet...the silence, and nature...and that whole feeling of calming down and getting away from the rat race...and I finally felt myself and my own voices. The Superstition Mountains is where the Lost Dutchman Mine is...and home of the Apache Thunder Gods...it's like a sacred spot outside of Phoenix."

"I walked outside my motel last night, and then went back in and told my buddy, "There are just so many...cars." I said, "There are so many people." He said, "This is just...little old Peoria." But...it's different for me. I go places where you don't see a house for...fifty miles. It's awe-inspiring for me...to see this many people...it's neat."

303   *Edward Bailey*

"My name is Edward Bailey. I'm 36. Well originally I grew up…up and down the west coast…uh, in California…and then settled in Seattle. My dad was in the military so we moved around a lot, so…but mostly…mostly Seattle, I'd have to say. My dad was in the Navy. My dad switched into the, uh…the reserves. He was active duty while I was young, so we lived in San Diego and Los Angeles and Seattle. We kind of did a rotation up and down between those places and then he switched into the reserves when I was about eleven…so we stayed in Seattle then at that point. But, before that, my dad would take us wherever he went."

"My friend Michael…a woman named Michael…learned how to make a style of book in Venice, Italy. She was an architecture student and after she graduated with her degree in architecture from ASU she went off on a European vacation. While she was in Rome she had her backpack stolen. She lost, most importantly, her journal that she was keeping on the road. She lost all of her passports and her plane tickets and all of that other stuff too…but those were all replaceable. Her journal was not replaceable because it had all her writings and a bunch of people's addresses that she was going to visit…so she was pretty heartbroken."

"A couple days later after she lost it, she was in Venice, and she met a street artist there. He asked her how she liked Italy and how her trip was going. She told him that she was sad she lost her journal and…and needed a new book, and so he was quite fond of her, being a nice blonde American girl…and said, "Oh no problemo, my friend he is bookmaker…you know, we will go and see my friend…we'll get you a new book." So, she ended up going to the bookmaker's shop and discovering this style of book…which is really the oldest style of…of bookmaking that's probably still active today and…and definitely in Italy. It's a real traditional style."

"So…uh…she gravitated toward this kind of book and stayed a day or two there at the bookmaker shop, and learned about the books, and ended up making one for herself, after she got home from her trip. Then everyone wanted one because no one had seen them before, even though they're traditional in Europe. They are unique here in the United States. Everyone wanted one, so she started making them for friends and then started selling them at a little sidewalk sale…and then I came into the picture. We were quite fond of each other and I started helping her make books...and that was about ten years ago. So we've been working together ever since and...uh, and we stopped dating about five years ago...six years ago now...but we're great work partners. So we...that's where I got on board. I started tearing paper and making the books...and uh, I started having some flashbacks to some past lives or something...I think I did it before. I think I did it before at least a couple times...but there's no way to prove that...it's just a feeling that I have. So ever since I first started making the books, the very first paper that I tore...it just felt natural and I kept looking...I kept thinking that if I looked up I was going to see this particular window looking out over a particular landscape...of course it wasn't there, it was just in my mind. So that was the beginning."

"We use a couple different kinds of handmade papers that we really like...they're made out of recycled fabrics...we have the paper made for us in India. They're made out of scraps from the garment and textile industry there, and...of course India has a long history of making paper and textiles...fabrics. So we haven't been able to find any papers here to match the papers that we use. We get it in large sheets and I tear it by hand down into smaller pieces, and fold it and collate it into what's called signatures...which is, groupings of paper. My partner Michael, she is the one who mostly selects the leathers. We use real supple, but thick durable leathers that are surplus leathers, which are produced for shoes and bags and saddles and western tack and things like that. We cut these down with hand tools into book covers and sew the paper into the cover with a hemp twine that we wax with a beeswax. This is a real traditional construction and it's a real durable construction...it's not...there's no glue in the binding and it's not stitched with a fine thread as most books are and most books are more fragile than these. These are the kinds of books...actually in Latin the term for this book is "vademekum" which means to go with me or to take with me...it's a style of book even referred to in Canterbury Tales, for example, "..as the travelers were gathering their vademekum." It's something...something you can take with you."

"In medieval Italy, when the only people who were reading and writing were basically monks and scribes, they would make themselves a book like this so that they could go into the library and access a manuscript there, uh...and of course the libraries of those days were much different than the libraries we know of now...those libraries contained the original manuscripts. They were handwritten and often very ornate and painted with gold, and of course you couldn't just check those out of the library. Often they were chained down or locked up in a...triple locked even...in a cabinet and you'd have to go to great effort to have access to these manuscripts...and so the monks and scribes would make themselves a book in this style, so that they could go into the library, access those manuscripts, copy down the information that they wanted and then they could...take it with them. So...yeah...nowadays it's a lot easier...you can just go check those books out and take the take the copy out of the library."

"I met my wife about two years ago now...saw her from across the street...and we had love at first sight. We just knew...and we were about fifty yards away from each other. We caught each other's eye and we both just knew at that...at that very minute, that we were destined for each other. It sure enough still seems to be true...for sure."

"I'm here in Peoria as a bookmaker, trying to sell my books. I didn't bring my wife with me on this trip...but will bring her with me if I come back again. Today is nice, but tomorrow...I think it might rain. I hope not...rain isn't good for my books."

304   *Barb Leslie*

"Name is Barb Leslie...49. I am a nurse, a medical intensive care nurse at a local hospital. My aunt was a nurse, and that's all I ever wanted to be...well that or a nun...or a teacher. I guess I varied a lot."

"I think that one of the best things is when you see someone who is very, very critical...and they leave the ICU, and they come back to visit you. It's like...you've worked and worked and worked to cure them, and they're appreciative and they...they thank you. There was one that I worked with...and I got fairly close to the wife...he came back and he didn't remember me at all. He looked at me...and didn't know me. He was so totally sedated in the hospital...then all of a sudden because he, he heard my voice...he remembered my voice...he heard my voice, and he remembered me. You know, every time I took care of him, I would say, "You're going to be okay...we're going to work this out." So, yeah, that was okay, that he remembered. That's one of the better perks of life."

I'm from Massillon, Ohio originally. My dad was transferred when I was in high school, and what I remember most...it was a big football town...Paul Brown was from there. Everybody was into football. Massillon and Canton were still mad at each other, because Canton got the hall of fame. They had Republic Steel...they had all these...steel industries...and so...last year, I went back. My aunt died, so I went back...actually it was this year. Massillon lost all the steel industry corporations, and as far as the town...it was very bubbly when I was younger, but now is depressed...dingy looking. You know how you go to different areas, and they have new subdivisions being built? There's none. It's really sad. All these businesses that were downtown are closed. It's very sad."

"What was bittersweet is that my mother had brain cancer, and you know, it was very tragic. She was only 59...but we were kinda laughing tonight about this...as the cancer got worse...and my mom was very German...very stoic, and some of the things she said when she had cancer was funny as all get out. I mean, she was confused, and it was very tragic, but funny. My mother who was this very prim and proper person, all of a sudden determined that she was Tallulah Bankhead..."Heelllooooo, how is everybody?" She would make a total personality change. You would sit there crying...going, "This is not my mother." But, she was so funny."

"I'm going through menopause right now. I cry a lot. The thing of it is…what do I cry about? Not a clue. In the middle of the night, the blankets go off…and then you're cold. I take Evista. It is a little embarrassing, because I was at the grocery store the other day…I had my sunglasses on, and I was going to buy some wine…and they were going to "card" me. All of a sudden it was like, "Ohhhh…Ohhhhh". The cashier said, "What's wrong?" I said, "I'm having a hot flash." She said, "I don't need to see your ID…just go.""

"I have a new puppy. My dog of sixteen years, died in November. I was going, "Okay, I don't want to get a dog…I don't want to get a dog." Well, I got this call at work that they had this half Scottie, half Westie. I had a Scottie for sixteen years…pure bred. This dog was at Pets for Seniors. I called to take a look at him, and they said, "You know, seniors want older dogs…they don't want puppies.""

"So then the joke was…"Ha ha, you're old enough now that you can get a pet for seniors." Yes…I'm old enough now to get a senior…*puppy*. So anyway, I said, "I'll come take a look at him…but I don't know." But then, I walked in and it's like, "There's Jack." Now, trying to raise a puppy after sixteen years…it's like, you know, you get out of the shower, your robe is gone…the dog has drug it off. I have the toilet paper holder…and there's toilet paper everywhere. So, I walk into the bedroom, and there's Jack with toilet paper in his mouth going, "Ehhhh?""

"I really like dogs. My very first job, I worked at a vet's office. I was fifteen when I took that job. I worked as a receptionist at the vet's, one day a week…on a Saturday. I would always get into trouble because we had the kennels in the back, and I would go and play with the dogs. They would bark, and then I'd hear, "Quit playing with the dogs." But the worst thing about being there was, we had the cats upstairs, and I never really liked cats…and they had this big old cat that somehow got out of his cage. So, I go walking to check on him, and all of a sudden he jumped out and clawed up my entire back. It was like, "Ahhhhhh". The customers were downstairs, and I was like "Ahhhhh". I definitely like dogs better than cats."

305   *Ray Williams*

"Williams...Ray Williams...I'm 86."

"I was with the Navy. I sailed with the merchant ships that delivered the cargo to all of the other guys that needed it. I had nineteen months of sea duty...and I was in 21 countries. I was in French Haven, New Guinea, when the Japs surrendered. New Guinea had nothin'...except what we took in there. But they...they had a big black sergeant...and somewhere along the line, we lost out refrigeration in the ship. We had nothin' but dehydrated cabbage...and we had some bread. It had weevils in it. You'd look at a piece of bread...a slice of bread...and you'd see a black spot in it. That was a weevil. We knew...we knew what that was...but you didn't throw it away because...you didn't have any other."

"We sailed into New Guinea, and they marched us to shore there...and that big sergeant...big Army sergeant on that base...he said, "Bring 'em on in. I'll give ya anything they want." So, we ordered steak and eggs for breakfast. He said, "Well, I'll fix you up like you've never been fixed up before." Great guy...great guy."

"I'm originally from Portsmouth, Ohio. I'm a visitor here. Our school system has decided that our...this generation coming up should know something about the world wars. I told 'em I had nothing to tell 'em about the first one. I also told 'em I missed the Civil War...but my knees didn't. I got bad knees. I was just joking...I'm too young for the Civil War."

"I was born in 1919. I'm old as the American Legion. The American Legion was formed in France...in March...March, 1919. I was born May the 22nd, 1919. So, when they throw a big party for our legion post...for the age of the legion...well, I said, "That's for me. I have to be special when they do that." They all laugh of course."

"I grew up on a farm in South Webster, Ohio. It's a little village of 500 people. We had a 280 acre farm and a big team of mules. That's what we used. We had no tractors. I spent most winter-times with my grandfather. He was a taskmaster. He could teach you to do a lot of things...and you didn't even realize you was workin'. He was smooth. My daddy...he'd try to teach you something right away, and if you didn't get it...he'd knock half your head off with his fist. He was the meanest. I didn't like to work with him. My granddad...I worked real well with him. He was a country blacksmith. Truck after truck would come in with teams of horses and mules that needed new shoes. He'd make shoes and put 'em on. One truckload come in and the man said, "Frank, I got one that'll kick your head off." Granddad said, "He won't bother me." He just hauled his legs together and put him on his side...and put his shoes on him. That's how you do it."

"My first job was with the Shelby Shoe Company. I worked, carrying what they called "deadheads". If you went and bought your wife a set of arch-preserver shoes, and she wore 'em out and brought 'em back to the factory to get fixed...for free...that's what I did. The only thing she'd get back was the upper. I did all kinds of lifts...and pockets for bunions...crippled feet. I look at everybody's feet anymore. Of course, that was my job. I made the shoes...I didn't sell 'em. They were returned to the customers...their owners. Shelby Shoe Company...arch preservers...that was an expensive shoe in those days. But...lots of women bought 'em."

"They had three show factories in Portsmouth. Shelby Shoes was the main one. One of the others made summer shoes and spring sandals. The other one...they didn't build the shoe really, they just put them together."

"Me and my first wife...we wasn't getting along too good. I was getting ready to go to work...I worked at Alcoa...in Cleveland. She said, "I'm going to Mom's, and I'll be gone when you get home." I said, "Well, that'll be a problem. Take everything that you own because...you're not coming back." She said, "Yeah...I'll come back when I'm ready." So she went...and I reported to the Navy that next Monday. I called into work and reported gone. I enlisted in the Navy and the Navy guy told me, "Well, the Navy quota is full right now...you'll have to wait a month, or go into the Army." I said, "I don't want to go in the Army." He said, "Well, I'll tell you what I can do. I'll sign you up in the ten year reserves." He said, "I can sign you up, and even if you're in or out, you don't have to go to the meetings...it's inactive reserves." I said, "Do that." He said, "It'll be a month before you get a call." So, I went back to work on that Tuesday...and Wednesday I got a telegram to report to Huntington, West Virginia for my examination. So...I was in."

"My brother was in the Marine Corps...the 3rd Amphibious...3rd Marines. His station was New Caledonia. Was you ever there...in those waters? There was a thing out there in the ocean that you could see for miles. When you're looking for the horizon, it's nineteen miles away, normally. You could see that structure for nineteen miles. It was a structure to lift boats out of the water...right there in the ocean...hydraulic-committed. It could pick up the Queen Mary and one liberty ship at one time. That's how big it was. It was made in the United States and floated there in sections...and then put together. I suppose the Seabees handled it."

"I wasn't over in Europe...but I heard that when the Russian soldiers killed prisoners, they didn't shoot 'em...they knocked 'em in the head...with a hammer. There would be a whole row of 'em. They did that to save bullets...they needed the money. Also...a German doctor would take the skin right off you if you had a tattoo...and make a lampshade. Now, that was pretty gruesome. They'd take the teeth right out of your mouth if you had a gold filling. I know a lot of stuff that the normal public doesn't even know about. I saw me a picture of piles and piles of shoes over there in them concentration camps. Them Germans killed those people and piled up their shoes. They had piles of other stuff, too...but I remember them shoes."

306-307 Barbara McGee Pryor and Sharon Wilson Pryor

"This is Richard Pryor's hometown….this is what made him. He was born and raised here. I think everyone wants to remember him as the comedian…the funny man from Peoria."

"I'm 63. I worked in nursing before, but right now…I'm retired. I worked for Spoon River Home Health. I grew up on Green Street, back in the 40's…early 50's. Richard and I had different mothers, but the same father…our father's name was Leroy. He died in '68…he was 53 years old. I have three girls and two boys myself…my oldest is 44…well, she'll be 44 in March…and my youngest is 27. I have fifteen grandchildren…and seven great. I had to think about that. Sharon likes to talk…so I let her do all the talking."

"I'm Sharon…51. When I was born, we lived on Fourth Street. I live on Peoria Street now…and I work at Manor Care. I been raising kids and grandkids all my life. I have three grown…and five grandchildren."

"I came home from work and my mother called and told me Richard had passed away. We couldn't make it out to California because of the sudden death and everything…arrangements of trying to get there and stuff. But…we have our memories in our heads."

"As a young girl growing up…at the age of seven…Richard would take us to the Rialto Theater. Do you remember Rollie Keith's "Bids for the Kids"…Producers Points? People around here would buy Producer's milk…and then cut the points off the carton. You saved the points up, and you could get prizes. But…we never had enough points…so, we couldn't get nothing off the stage. Then the screen would come down, and we had to sit there through all them cartoons while Richard was…laughing…laughing at everything. We had to walk all the way from Fourth Street to the Rialto…and we'd be cold…but Richard…he just be laughing at everything."

"Richard Jr. was supposed to come to town tonight, but he had car trouble. He's not gonna make it. His car broke down on his way down here last night, and he needs a part…and can't get it until Monday. He was driving here from Iowa…from Altoona."

"When Richard came home from the service, he used to sit around and tell jokes and keep us laughing…my dad and stepmother…my stepsister. He was playing down at Harold's Club…but he used to practice his routine on us. Harold's was down on…ummm…down on Washington…back then. But when we were younger, he used to run off and leave me…disappear. He liked the girls…so, he would go find his girlfriend and leave me hanging."

"Richard had a lot of tricks up his sleeves. I used to like it when he would make pennies come out of your ears. He also would take a glass of water and a pack of Camel cigarettes…and when he set the glass of water down, the camel would be facing the other way. He had a lot of tricks. Richard always had a lot of tricks."

"He couldn't dance. He was a singer…just like our father…but, he couldn't dance. I can't remember which one of his movies that he was singing in…but he done pretty good. His father's favorite song was, "If I Didn't Care". That's an old song…I think Red Foxx used to sing that…"If I Didn't Care"…on his TV show. You know that song? *"If I didn't care, more than words can say…If I didn't care, would I feel this way?"*

308   ***Carla Mellins***

"I'm this…biological thing. Even though I don't believe in killing animals so that people can eat them…I eat them. Even though I find it disgusting when people take advantage of others…I find myself manipulating events, you know…to satisfy my own needs. Even though I can't stand people who lie…I know that I do. I've tried to figure all of this out…but, I can't. I blame it on biology."

309 *Mike Fitzgerald*

"The religious people in the country...mostly Christians, look at the Muslims who were responsible for 911, and see their belief system as totally ridiculous. They can see the absurdity of other religions, but can't see the absurdity of their own. If they could just step back and look at their own religion...objectively...they would see the absurd ideas involved. If they could look back over the last few thousand years, they would know that their own religion is responsible for more death and destruction than any other."

"They make fun of the virgins waiting in heaven for the Muslim martyrs, yet they can't see the ridiculous idea of their own savior being born *from* a virgin. They can't see the whole concept of their entire faith being this...this closed-loop system where their supposed god...this all-powerful god, caused certain events to take place, and then...and then made it a crime. He then created himself in human form to be killed, so that he could forgive his children. It's this big stage play. It's this closed-loop system that...makes no sense. In the Christian world, mankind is just this little mouse caught between two celestial paws."

310 *Monica Poncinie*

"I'm 24, and I am a teacher at Limestone High School. I am selling Mardi-Gras beads for the Leukemia-Lymphoma Society Team-in-Training. In October I am going to be running 26.2 miles in the Chicago Marathon…and I'm trying to raise $300 dollars to help patients and their families."

"I'm going to run Chicago because it's close…and my family is from Chicago. It's flat…no hills. I've always been a runner and…my mom had Non-Hodgkin's lymphoma, and my dad currently has leukemia. I have never run a marathon. I've run two half-marathons…but never a full. I've run Indianapolis…and I loved it. I have done one in Indy and one in St. Louis. Indy was better because St. Louis had a full marathon going on at the same time…so there were a lot more people "cheering on" the marathon people than us…we kinda got second billing. But, in Indianapolis, you feel like a star. So, the furthest I have run is 13.1 miles."

"I started running when I was a…a sophomore in high school. I was playing shortstop…for softball, and I caught the softball with my face and broke my nose, and after that I was kind of…I never got back onto the horse. I didn't want to do anymore contact sports. So, the next year, to stay in shape I joined track…and I've liked running ever since."

"I would like to go to Australia and New Zealand some day. It seems different from other places I've seen, and the Travel Channel makes New Zealand seem very appealing. If I go there, I will probably run."

311   *Riley Robinson*

"I was born in 1970 in Roswell, New Mexico. My wife tells me that, that explains a lot. I try not to listen to her too much. From time to time I can't help but wonder, though."

"From Roswell, we moved to Norton, Kansas. It's a small town, not too far from Nebraska, in the northwestern corner of the state. I have to tell you...I developed a strong taste for small town life. It's something that seems to be hard to shake out of me as I get older. Norton was a town that you never had to lock your doors in. There was crime, of course, but it didn't happen often...at least not in people's houses. All summer long, the only thing across either of our doors was a flimsy screen."

"In January 1985, just a couple days after my 15th birthday, my mom married a gentleman from ranch country, back in New Mexico, and we moved down there. We went from small to even smaller. Gladstone didn't even have city limits. It was really just a place for people to send mail to. I rode a bus for fifty miles one way to high school every morning. This was even less of "locking country" than where we had come from. Here they went one step further...instead of simply not locking your doors...you left the keys hanging in the ignition of your truck, 'cuz you never knew if they might need to come borrow it."

"My folks had been out one day in the car, leaving me at home with the truck. For exercise I used to walk down to the mailbox, which was not quite a mile from the house. I got back from my walk, went upstairs to read...like I normally did. About half an hour later my folks came home and my mom asked me, "Where's the truck?" "What do you mean where's the truck?" "Where's the truck...it's not out front." Sure enough, the neighbors had driven over the back way and had taken the truck to use...to do something or other, I can't remember now what it was."

"I was in Phoenix with this singing ensemble I was a part of...in my church. I've always read...always been one of those people who have to be deep into a book, or the world is somehow...not right. The problem with this...on that trip to Phoenix...was that, I had finished the book while we were waiting for our rental van. This is bad juju for a person who has to be reading. Luckily one of our first stops was a mall, and one of my first quests at that mall was to find a bookstore. Otherwise I was looking at two days in a strange town with nothing to read, which is bad."

"I find a Borders...head right to the geeky science fiction/fantasy section. One of the books catches my eye, something called "The Eye of the World," by Robert Jordan. I pick it up, and about a month later...I'm shaking my fist at the sky and cursing this "Robert Jordan" fellow for sucking me into this...world of his. It is a very involved series of books, and it just sucks one in completely."

"So I have this monkey on my back, right? A monkey called "The Wheel of Time" series. It's big and large, 'cuz he's got out four of these books out already, but there's many more that have to be written, that he hasn't written yet. So I'm waiting. After my second three year period of torture, waiting on the next book of this series so I can find out what happens next, for christsakes...a friend of mine tells me about this website that she's a part of, called TarValon.net. I take a look at it, I guess it was only six months old or so at the time, and it looks like just the ticket I've been looking for. There's already threads on the message boards for people waiting for the next fix...ummm...installment of the series to come along."

"In these books, which are fantasy...the magicians are all women, but they enlist men to be a combination of partner and body guard. For nothing other than fun, the web community I had just joined...mirrors those partnerships."

"I met my partner, my Aes Sedai, about five years ago...something like six months after I joined the community. At the time she was a sixteen year old girl living in Seattle, Washington. Her parents were abusive, and while I couldn't do anything to help her, I could support her as best I could, and do my best to keep her from shooting her entire family, and winding up on the national news. She quickly became a part of my family, and I lined her up in my heart, right along with my own two daughters."

"After she turned eighteen she realized she couldn't take it anymore from her parents, and got the hell out. Through our web community, which now stretched across the world and had close to three hundred active members, we found her a family in the Chicago area that would take her in. Again, I couldn't do much but send her a little bit of cash now and again...and just be there to listen to her. She was calling me on an almost daily basis with the ups and downs of her new free-dom. Sometimes it would be just to giggle about something, sometimes she would just need someone to listen to her while she had a good cry. Soon after-wards she moved to Peoria to go to ICC."

"I guess it was an outgrowth of the weird second father/big brother relationship we had sprouted, but we both decided we'd be each other's "partners". I would become her "Warder", the term they use in the books. So, when she became engaged about a year ago, I knew I would I would be there, to again lift her up and support her, like I had been doing for the last four years."

"In fact, all of us who knew her from our web community decided we were going to show up and be there for her. So…I got on a plane to St Louis…rented a car, and drove to Peoria to watch her get married. This is now the morning after the wedding, and we decided to invade the Barnes and Noble after our traditional IHOP breakfast. We always have one when we get together, us Tar Valon geeks. She and her groom are now waiting for their train to Chicago…to go on their honeymoon…and I'm standing in the doorway talking to a complete stranger."

312   *Brian Sagko*

"My last name is pronounced "psycho".

"I was emptying these boxes of books, and I found a book called "The Falcon and the Snowman". Inside of it was…or on the front cover was a yellow post-it that said, "To Eureka College—look on pages 13 and 14-RR." Here he is…President, in his private residence, reading this book…and he sees a reference to Eureka College. He finishes reading it and makes a note on the front…and puts it in a box of books. I thought…I don't know…it just seemed very powerful."

"I was lucky enough to go out to Los Angeles in '98 and meet him. He was pretty ill then. I had never really known anyone personally that had Alzheimer's…and when I saw President Reagan…there's always this image that…here's this icon. It was a little weird. Somebody who I felt I knew very well, because I had gone through his attic and basement…I felt that I needed to be careful what I said. I met him, and he leaned forward and shook my hand…and it was really strong. In his eyes, it was like he was there in…there were no conjunctions between his thoughts…it was like I was there for the first time…every time. Every second, there was no connection with the previous seconds…that was the feeling I had. It was like, he knew who I was…but not in a connected way."

"I felt a little weird because he stood up next to me…and I felt like…if he would have been okay, he probably would have put his arm around me or something. It was sort of the culmination of putting the Reagan Museum together and being connected to him for so long. But…he didn't. I wasn't about to put my arm around him…and I felt a little weird…like it was sort of a cardboard cutout."

"I presented him an afghan…an afghan that has places of the college on it. It said "Eureka College" in the middle. I opened it up…and he said, "Eureka College!" Everybody in the room just stopped, like he hadn't spoken in awhile. He remembered Eureka College. I about lost it then…it was too much. There was this point where I realized…why I was there…what I represented…and how important it was to him."

"I never knew anyone who was so intensely connected to his school. This was like…his family…big time."

313   *Angela Britmeyer*

"I'm Angela Britmeyer and I am 26. I'm moving to Phoenix to pursue my doctorate in clinical psychology. It's actually a school of professional psychology. The program I got into, it's called a PsyD, it's not a PhD…a PsyD is a doctor in psychology, as opposed to a PhD, which is a doctor in philosophy. It's more clinically oriented, rather than research-based. So, I'll be getting that there…and actually the program has an emphasis in sports and medicine psychology…so…ummm…so, when I am done with the program, I will be able to get licensed as a clinical psychologist and a sports psychologist."

"With the sports psychology…what you would do is contract out with teams. Actually, when I go out to Phoenix, I'm kinda hoping…the department head…he's from the Chicago area…so, I'm hoping he has some connections with the Cubs spring training camp. I think it would be neat to…neat to…like, job shadow the sports psychologist for the Cubs. I doubt that will happen, but it's a nice little dream. They typically do, like, performance enhancement for each individual athlete…if they're having some troubles achieving their goals. Ummm…they might work with athletes that have injuries…and try to get them, more back, in a place where they…you know, it's a big adjustment, where your whole livelihood is your sport…and you cannot do it."

"I went to the University of Illinois…and I just got these fun little talking bottle openers…they were on sale, so I had to buy these…aren't they cool? I went to the U of I, and graduated there in 2000, and then I got my masters. I actually already have my masters in clinical psychology…and I got that at the University of Dayton, out in Ohio. I have been all over…been here for three years. Since September of 2002, I moved back home. So now, I'll be leaving again to go to Phoenix."

"Last weekend I had my big going-away party. A lot of my closest friends…from undergraduate college, graduate school, and friends that I have made since then…all of them were there and we went to Old Chicago…and we had fun. My friend Paula got me a really nice going-away present, and I got teary-eyed."

"I actually worked at a bagel shop, as well as working at Owens Center, and in the summers, I typically like to do camp counseling, working with kids. My dad is actually a psychologist, over at the Antioch Group…and so I intern there…Dr.

Britmeyer...Rudy Britmeyer. He's a psychologist. The Journal Star has actually done a couple of articles on him...that would be my dad. I call him Rudo...good old Rudo. The Antioch Group is Christian-based, and I'm into that too. I am involved with TAC...Teens Encounter Christ. It's a local...it's actually through the Catholic Diocese. So, I do that on the side, as well. But, I intern at the Antioch Group."

"When I went off to graduate school...my internship...they like, threw me in head first, in terms of one of the hardest populations I have had to work with. It was...dually diagnosed inpatients in a drug and alcohol treatment facility. So, we're talking about individuals that have schizophrenia, and crack addictions. I also worked at a children's treatment facility with pre-schoolers that had emotional and behavioral disturbances. So, they would act out...and I worked there for a year as well. I was kinda just like a staff person...and do group notes and charting and everything."

"Since I've moved home, the past two years I have worked at children's homes, and I am a clinician, which is basically a therapist for the supervised independent living program. We work with sixteen to twenty year olds, who are pretty much on the last legs of the system, and so any intervention we do, is preparing them for the adult real world. This will be an interesting week for me, because it will be my last week at home since I have moved back...and it's a really transitional point in my life right now. I am going out to Phoenix, and I have family out there...cousins and my aunt...but it's going to be rough because I'm leaving my whole support system...everything."

"My grandma told me a story when she was a kid. They, like, picked dandelions...and they squeezed dandelions, and put dandelion juice in their eyes so they could stay home from school. I would never picture this, because, this is my Polish grandma...but I shouldn't get started on my family. I have a whole lot of...my aunt calls it the Springer side of the family, where...I have a cousin that was a Chippendale...ummm...oh yeah, oh yeah...my uncle, he passed away, so I'm going to be moving in with his wife...he had a cactus that fell on his head. He had to get it removed from his head. He was like, a traveling cowboy burger-flipper...that was one of his jobs. Oh yeah, when my grandfather...no, no...when my grandmother passed away...there was a bar in Cave Creek called "The Horney Toad". To her visitation, he wore a shirt that said "The Horney

Toad"...to a funeral. I don't think the word "horney" is appropriate for a funeral...not on a T-shirt that you wear to a solemn, blessed event."

"It's my mom's side of the family that is more colorful and animated...although my dad...my dad imigrated here from Germany, when he was fifteen. So, he's like the first generation here. They actually have an old world mentality. And then my mom...oh...I actually thought of a good story. I was raised very Catholic...like strict Catholic...Holy Family Grade School. I remember this dinner once. My parents wedding anniversary is April 8th...and my birthday is October 2nd of 1978...so I did the math at a family gathering, and I go, "Well Mom, your twelfth anniversary is already here...and my twelfth birthday is this year." I go..."May, June, July, August, September...October?" I looked up at my mom with complete innocence, "You never told me I was three months premature." I remember she said, "Angela let's leave and go to the mall." That's where she explained to me that there was a little bun in the oven...and all this stuff."

"I think my parents might not appreciate me telling that story."

314   ***Thomas Bolger***

"I'm not gay. If I was, I would dress better…and I wouldn't be using a cardboard box as a desk…and I wouldn't find women attractive. But…I get razzed all the time because I have so many shoes. I have over thirty pair…mostly Adidas and Nike. I'm attracted to new shoes. That doesn't make me gay…does it?"

315   *Rocky Simpson*

"My real name is Dave. I am retired Navy...from Hanna City. I now live in Kokomo, Indiana...and I come back to cook for that guy right over there. You know where that big two-story house is, in Hanna City? You go through, and it has that little jog to the left...as you go...that way. The only corner on 116? That's where I used to live."

"I was on the U.S.S. Joseph Strauss, U.S.S. Davidson, and U.S.S. Nimitz...three ships, four years each. I did Instructor duty up at Great Lakes. I remember going into the Persian Gulf and saying to the guys, "This is not a drill. We're going to war." We went to General Quarters as soon as we got in the gulf. I had a repair party that was on the island of the carrier. I had 56 guys that did hose teams, and stuff like that. I got them all together and told them that."

"I was in charge of all the main propulsion engines onboard...270,000 shaft horse-power. I had 150 guys in the Reactor Propulsion Division. Now...now I'm a man-ager in a hospital...food service, supplies, boiler operation, and housekeeping."

"In Hanna City, when I was in eighth grade, we won a basketball tournament...my coach was Larry Whitmore...you know Larry? We were down 24-12 at the half. We didn't have a chance in hell of winning the ballgame, but we won it by two in the end. We played against...we played against the Logan Patriots at the time...so, not only did we beat the team for a title, but we beat our friends. That was pretty...pretty neat."

"Any time I am within three hundred miles, when they have the Spoon River Drive, I call him up...Richard...he owns the Ribeye Barn. I let him know...and he lets me cook. You see these pork chops here? You pick 'em up, and you put a line through them right there and you look...and if there's no red at all...it's a done deal."

316   *Venkatesh Anandasayanam*

"My father…he is a technician in a plant…he used to be a technician. He used to work for a government company that produced thermal power. They used lignite for thermal power. My father was working in that plant…on instrumentation. He was an instrumentation technician."

"Life in India is much different than life here. My parents are from a village…it is a small village in Tamil Nadu…and my father and mother, they are from the same village. For work…my father had to leave the village and work in the town. For myself, I grew up in a town…from kindergarten to after I graduated. Then, I went to college…to a different town."

"We lived in an independent house. This town where my father worked…it was a government company, so it was built by the company…and nobody else could live in that town. People that worked for the company…they could live there. Most of the houses are independent houses…and they are surrounded by a big garden. The garden had mango trees, coconut trees…banana…banana plants…all kinds of things. If you want, you can have a vegetable garden there. We used to eat vegetables…only vegetarian…we don' eat meat. My mother's side…I think they used to eat some chicken or some fish…but not my father's family…so, we don't eat meat in our house."

"Here…I usually don't eat outside. I eat in the house. Sometimes I go out for lunch…at the office, if I don't have lunch that I made. Pretty much, I prefer eating at home, rather than outside."

"Life in India was more entertaining…more fun…even though I didn't have a lot of money, or my parents did not have a lot of money. I didn't have much…just a few clothes…but in spite of that, I had a good time. I had a lot of friends…we used to hang around and play…you know, all those things that children do."

"I moved to the U.S., and I've been here for seven years now. Here, it is a different life. I do have fun here, but it is a different kind of fun. After I came to the U.S., I started researching…basically to understand the meaning of life. Once I started the research…that is pretty much…that is fun for me. That's what I have been studying the last several years…and then, what I discover in my research…I train...teach others. My research has enabled me to transform my life...and look at my life differently than I used to before. I now teach several classes in meditation and yoga. That's what I do for fun."

"Meditation is how to master the mind...not only to master the mind, but go beyond the mind, to connect with your spirit. Yoga...is for the body...but also for everything...body, mind, and spirit...emotions...all those things. I also teach a workshop called "Creating Health Workshop"."

"In the Hindu Temple, there are two aspects. There is a religious aspect and a spiritual aspect...although they are hard to separate. Hinduism is not really a religion...it is a way of life. It existed for thousands of years, even before Buddha was born. It is a way of life...and actually, Hinduism was a name given later. The real name for the culture is called "Sanatana Dharma"...and it means "a universal way of life". So, it was a way of life, and not really a religion. The way of life...it is not something that you go to temple or church...and do. Like...when I am coming...meeting you, I look at your eyes...and I see the god in you. I see the divinity in you. Everything...when I drink...I see the divinity in the drink. When I put on my clothes, I see the divinity in the clothes."

"Everything...everything in life is divine. So...that is a way of life...looking at the divine. That's what life is about...to see the divinity in everything at every moment.
Once it did become a religion...because the way of life did become a religion...they incorporated a spiritual way of life in the form of a temple. They have different deities...well, not called deities, it's called archetypes. The English translation is called archetypes. What each archetype represents is a unique representation of a higher human potential."

"If you go to the temple here, off of Farmington Road...you will see the different statues. They are not statues...they are living archetypes. Energy is in them...and so it is as good as a living being. Even though they do not breathe, they are energized. So...the moment you go there...the energy gets transferred. The person who goes to the temple will find the human potential in themselves. I go to an archetype that strikes my ego. I want to remove my ego so that I can find more love. I go to that archetype and invoke that archetype's potential in me...so I can destroy my ego and destroy my ignorance. I can invoke another archetype if I want to remove pain and suffering. Animals are also archetypes. They also express a unique potential…monkey…elephant…rat…snakes…tiger."

"There is a wholeness in nature…in everything. Wholeness is…looking at everything as if it is divine…as complete. We are all *one*."

317   ***Michael Isenberg***

"I am 52. I grew up and stayed in Pekin...to a certain point...until the music thing started taking off for me. I found out very early on that I am a different type of person. In all my travels all over the United States in the last forty years...I have never met anyone like me. I know I'm different...I've always been singled out as being different. I knew I was going to get picked on in school. My dad said, "Look, don't worry about a thing. Everybody in town knows me. You'll be alright. Let me tell you something...all anybody is going to expect of you is to do the best you can. As long as you do that...nobody is going to expect anything more from you."

"I found out that was absolutely the furthest thing from the truth...and it has remained that way throughout my life. I don't know whether talent is a blessing or a curse...because, when I was in kindergarten...no, it was actually the first or second grade...I know this sounds crazy, but I have an incredible facility for everything. I am a better artist than anyone I have known. I was doing college level artwork in first grade. What happened was...a teacher came up and handed each one of us some construction paper, and crayons. She goes, "Look, I want each of you to sit down and draw a picture of something that interests you."

"So, all the kids started drawing their little stick figures and stuff...and at that point in time, Liberace was a big star...he had his own TV show. I use to watch him all the time because...it was like, him and Perry Como and Arthur Godfrey had shows...and that was about the only way you could get music. Steve Allen's show too, I guess. I used to love watching Liberace play the piano...and he always had the candelabra on his piano. So I drew a picture of this piano with a candelabra on it, in great detail. The teacher came around and said, "Okay Mike, where's your picture?" I said, "Here it is." She said, "No, the picture you drew." I said, "This is it...this is what I drew." She goes, "Mike, look...you didn't draw it. I know it and you know it. If you don't tell me the truth, I'm taking you to the principal's office."

"They took me out in the hall and called all the other teachers and they ridiculed me. They went. "Look, we have another Leonardo DaVinci here. He claims he drew this. A first-grader drew this in detail...isn't that lovely? I guess we should give you straight A's." All the teachers are laughing and ridiculing the hell out of me. I said, "I drew this, I'm not lying, and my dad knows I drew this." I said, "I'll prove to you I drew this…I'll draw another…it only takes a minute." Then…I did it. Instead of going back to the classroom and apologizing to me, the principal just said, "Okay young man, get back to class." I went back to class and the teacher was so pissed off that I embarrassed her. I got no apology from anyone. That's basically how my talent ran until eighth grade or so…and due to the Beatles and the fact that I had been playing guitar since I was nine years old…and we soon became the biggest band in town…the same kids that had ridiculed me and picked on me in school, and beat me up, were paying to come hear me play."

"Back in those days I only knew two guys that had a guitar. Today, it's weird if you walk up to someone and they don't have a guitar. But, back then it was just a cool scene. The music was all positive…the vibe was positive. The songs were all about love and happiness. Today, and especially in Hollywood where I live now…people just write these…dirges. It's terrible."

"But, back then…things got bigger and bigger and bigger, and I ended up in a band called "The Jets". We first got together at a big 4-H fair in Pekin, and Flores Music had a display there…and I started playing around his booth…and people gathered around. Then some friends of mine showed up and we started singing in harmony. So, we started this band…to instant success. We played this "dip and dance" at the Pekin Pool…and thousands showed up. It was like we were the Beatles. We went, "What is this? What's going on?" The next thing we knew, we were hooked up with an agency…WIRL took a liking to us…and we became the biggest thing in the Midwest. It was ridiculous."

"We changed the entire music scene in the Midwest for years. Finally, after we called it quits, each one of us went on to bigger and better things. Peoria and Pekin was a wonderland of entertainment at that time. I'd walk into Warner Brothers Circus on Adams Street…I'd walk in and they'd put a spotlight on us. They'd say, "Look everybody, we have a celebrity in the audience…Mike Isenberg from The Jets." I'd sit down and people would wave and ask for autographs. It was very cool thing."

"I was in Peoria when they started the "Walk of Fame"…down by the Madison Theater. Mike Sullivan was the guy who I think instituted it. He called me up and said, "Look, we're going to start this Walk of Fame thing…and I know you and Sam Kinison were big buddies, because you did shows at the Madison. He said, Why don't you come down and we'll have you introduce the Kinisons? They're very good friends of yours. Bill will be here, and Marie Kinison...Bill has his new book out, about Sam's life. You are the only real connection to Sam, besides them...so why don't you introduce them when they come down?"

"I went down that night, before the ceremony, and helped Mike put the actual stone in the ground...in the sidewalk. Immediately, Peoria just raised holy hell...and I still have the articles to prove it. They threw a fit. And then when someone suggested...when Richard Pryor was still alive...to do something for Richard...they threw another fit. They've continued to do that over the years. "Why should we glorify a foul-mouthed drug addict?" It's just ridiculous how stupid the Peoria leaders are. If Springfield thought like Peoria, Lincoln's house would be a strip mall or a parking lot."

"I grew up with Dan Fogelberg. His dad, Larry, was our high school orchestra teacher. I remember when Dan used to...there's a place on Galena Road...a big barn. In the 80's, Jay Goldberg turned it into a huge concert hall. Everybody played there, from Alice Cooper to the Allman Brothers...Canned Heat...all these iconic bands played there. I remember Dan, just to get a start, would play a short fifteen minute set...and that's how he got his start. There is so much musical history that is just completely ignored in this area...and I was the biggest unsigned act to ever come out of Peoria. Richard Pryor became huge as a comedian and movie star...but didn't make that much of a difference in Central Illinois. Dan Fogelberg...same thing...he went away."

"The guy who was most glorified in Pekin was Everett Dirkson. He was the fucking town drunk. They built buildings and statues after the town drunk...but people who started from nothing and had no support from the town...and became the biggest thing the town ever knew...there's no mention whatsoever...not at all. There's no mention in that town's history of me and my friends. Almost all of us in The Jets had major label deals. We had records that went all over the planet."

"I had a friend who explained it this way...He said, "The Midwest hates anything but mediocrity. If you are an innovator, if you rise above the crowd...you are beaten down...until you fall into the mundane. They kill their kings...they eat their kids."

"The two best songs The Jets ever did was "Lover Boy"…and the flip side was called "Paper Girl". I wrote both those songs. There is a label in Minneapolis called Twin Tones Records…they were courting us…and we had five of the biggest labels in Los Angeles having a bidding war over us…but now I would say to others…don't sign with a major label, you're just shooting yourself in the head. They're going to take all your money. We were starved out with the management label we were with…and we just quit…we broke up."

"Paper Girl" was huge in England and parts of Europe. Another song that I wrote, "This Is For You", was a hit in some markets. Another Jets song that I wrote was "Be For Me" and got up to number thirteen of the Top Twenty. Have you ever heard of Golden Voice? You can still see the building in South Pekin, I think. Golden Voice was a huge, unsung recording studio…state of the art…and the guy who built it is a legend. Dan Fogelberg did all his albums there…early ones anyway. Grand Funk Railroad recorded there. Flash Cadillac and the Continental Kids recorded all their sound tracks for American Graffiti there. We did all our sessions, except for two, at Golden Voice."

"Then one day…after being the biggest thing in Peoria and Pekin…I was living in a house on McClure…and my wife had gotten hurt in a nursing home…damaged, and unable to work…we got ripped off by two law firms…they cleaned our clock. We were homeless two different times…and the last time, we knew the next day the sheriff was going to come and kick us out. We were lying in bed that night…both of us crying…and I just couldn't believe what had happened. I was respected, came from a respected family…and here I am, about to become homeless for the second time. Everybody…had turned their backs on us. We had nothing. I remember laying there with my wife, and I said, "Look, you mean more to me than anything in the world." She still does. I said, "You don't have to be out in the street, you've got relatives…you've got somewhere to go." I said, "We don't have…anything. We have no money. We have no place to go." She put her arms around me and said, "If we're out in the street tomorrow…we'll both be standing there together because…I'm not going…fucking…anywhere.""

"She has stuck with me through thick and thin. She's been through some shit. But…now she's the most *looked at* woman in Hollywood, if you can imagine that. People like Jennifer Lopez and Paris Hilton…Nicole Richie…have stolen her clothing designs verbatim. She's a trendsetter. She now works for Disney, and is one of the most loved people in Hollywood. We've been happily married for seventeen years…and we're madly in love. That night…the night that she said that to me…that meant more to me than anything that was ever said to me in my entire life. That was the biggest moment in my entire life."

318

Carol Miller

"I am a lesbian. You know…I really don't care where people put their genitals. I don't think others should be concerned either."

319   ***Chris Waters***

"My name is Chris Waters, and I'm 27. I work for Regent Broadcasting, 95.5 GLO. I am on the air part-time, as well as the creative services director. Basically, I have control over all non-music content that goes out over the air...commercials...promos, and the like. I went to Eastern...and one day in the auditorium, I was reading a student newspaper, and it said a new radio station was going on...over in Mattoon. I was bored...I didn't play sports in college...I wasn't on the debate team, or whatever, and just thought that it was something to do, and it would get me out of my dorm room. So, I called and asked them if they needed interns or whatever, and they said, "Yeah, come on over." So, I went over, and they talked with me for awhile. I ended up doing that for a year, then I was hired on part-time, slash full-time. Well, it was part-time, but doing full-time hours while taking eighteen hours of classes. That...ummm...fluctuated for a year...I would do about thirty hours one week, and then maybe twelve the next."

"My junior year I got hired full-time to do six to midnight. I did that for a year, graduated, moved...came back home...this job opened up, and I been here ever since. Actually, I'll be on the air in about five minutes. I'm doing a remote."

"My family is pretty down to earth. One side of the family is fairly religious...they are faith-based, very spiritual. I am not that way, so I kinda disagree with them, but in the interest of family harmony, I keep my mouth shut. You know, I'll debate them, but I won't let it get really heated...or make them mad, because it is family. My honest answer is, I don't know what I am. I think it is naive of me to think that I'm just...I'm just here. I think it's pretty...well, when I think of Christianity, I think that man has been around for millions of years...and suddenly in the last two thousand years, Christianity has it all figured out? It's hard for me to fathom...how someone can think that way. It scares me to death to think of what is next, but I don't think it is what Christianity...Christians think is next. I just don't believe in their interpretation of what the afterlife is."

"I'll be on the air in thirty seconds...so, like most of us...I'll have to put the afterlife on hold."

320-321   *Cara Bale and Brandon Green*

"I'm 21. I write in a journal every day…everything that I do. Every day. I'm not going to say where I keep it, but I write down all my experiences…all the good times, all the bad times. I can read it someday, or other people can read it and see all the stuff I've done. It's not like I want to be a writer or anything. I'm actually going to school to be a drug and alcohol counselor. I hope I can be successful in that, and get lots of money. I never want to have to depend on a man for anything…anything. I want to be independent."

"I'm 23. We…both of us…live across the river. She used to work for me a few years ago. We randomly ran into each other in a bar, I don't know…a month or so ago. We've known each other a few years. She used to work for me…was a telemarketer for me. I was the manager for a telemarketing firm and I had, I don't know…250 people."

"I went on a cruise after that job, and went to Jamaica and a few other countries. One day, we spent the entire day on the ocean. That one day…after I paid the bar tab that night, cost several hundred dollars. The cruise itself cost a couple thousand. I spent most of the day on the ocean, scuba diving, seeing Mako sharks…seeing all kinds of stuff. If you're a nature guy, or an ocean guy…any time you do something like that, it's great. I had a slight accident…cut my hand on a piece of metal…but not too bad."

"I was in my first car accident when I was twelve years old. Pretty much…I was out with a friend, and she asked me to drive her dad's 4x4 vehicle. I did…and we ended up flipping the truck on its side after skidding across the road. My hand got crushed between the pavement and the truck. I had to have eight hours of reconstructive surgery on my fingers…but it's okay now."

"One Christmas…and I was like thirteen years old…I was peeling an orange with a butter knife, and almost cut my finger off. I was like twelve or thirteen, and I almost cut it off with a butter knife…Christmas morning. I know…it's retarded…but that's what happened. It was like…I saw my finger falling down…and then they took me to the hospital to get it fixed. I had to have a lot more than stitches because I cut tendons and everything. I don't have any feeling in this finger anymore. But, when I was in the hospital, no matter what they give you, you steel feel the thread going through your finger when they sew you up."

"Both of us…we have this is common…we both bite our nails. I don't even know why I do it…and I don't think he does either. My mom used to buy this stuff that she would put on my fingernails…and it had this real bitter taste. I think it was called "Control-It", or something like that. It had this bitter taste that was supposed to make it where I wouldn't bite my nails…but it didn't work. I think I just got used to the taste. So then, she glued these fake nails on…and I bit them also. Mostly though…I bite the skin around my fingers. I know it's kinda gross, but it's a habit."

"I actually bite my nails more than she does. It's embarrassing to show anybody. I made a few attempts to quit doin' it, but I think it relieves stress. Some people smoke…I bite my nails. Sometimes I caught myself doing it in meetings, you know…when people are talking to you. I even had a few people say something. I always do it when I drive…don't know why."

"My mom used to have a bowl of nuts on the table all the time…mixed nuts in the shell. She would tell me to crack open a few nuts when I got the urge to bite my nails. But, for the most part, I didn't realize that I was biting my nails until I was already doing it. I did try cracking open a few nuts, but it wasn't the same. I did learn to like Brazil nuts from doing that…they're good. I don't care for the walnuts…but the walnuts are fun to crack open and pick through."

"My mom is a counselor for people with mental problems. She works for the state, and does assessments and stuff like that for people who have problems. She doesn't make much money…for someone with a masters…but she's independent. Yesterday, I was going through the bowl of nuts and saw that she had thrown a couple of her business cards in there, with the names of some of her patients on the back. She didn't see the humor when I pointed out that her clients were in there with the rest of the nuts. She was opening a can of dog food, and I'm not even sure she heard me."

322   *Jessica Christianson*

"I hate Valentine's Day. I hate it forever...there's nothing good about it. You never get anything you want...and everyone's expectations...it's like, you know that commercial that you see? That old couple that you see walking in the park...and they're thinking, "Oh, remember how we used to be?" You know, that jewelry commercial? It makes everybody else feel that their life sucks...because, you know...my guy doesn't give me diamonds and rubies."

323   *Graham England*

"I am Graham England, and I am 49 years old. Originally I was born up in Canada, but I grew up in New Jersey. Toronto…back then it was a small city, but now it is a very large city. I am here working in Mapleton at a chemical plant. I live in Cleveland, Ohio and I work for an engineering/consulting firm…and I came down to look at one of their applications."

"As a kid, I would always spend my summers in a small town up in Newfoundland, Canada. Newfoundland is a very interesting place. It's about the size of Ireland…and it still only has one main road. Very small population…and everybody knows everybody. So, when I would go up there…people used to hitch-hike to go into the woods to go camping, or hitch-hike to go up the road. It was more like just flagging down somebody you knew. Since everybody knew you…and even though I was from New Jersey…people would know who I was…would know the whole story of why I was up there for the summer…visiting my aunt. A very interesting place…a very poor area, but not too many people thought of themselves as being poor."

"Down the street lived an old woman, Miss Lilly…lived in a little one bedroom house, and had three kids and a husband. She never owned a car…I don't think she ever left town…but if you asked her, you know, where the poor people lived, she wouldn't say she was poor…because she donated money to the church….donated money to other things too. She's still alive…she's in her 80's."

"My brother and I…when I was about fifteen…he was a little bit older…seventeen, we decide to go wilderness camping and only eat what we could catch and all. On the first day we caught 57 trout…and it kind of blew the whole concept away…and we caught them right close to the highway, the closest stream to my uncle's cabin."

"One thing I have noticed about my father and father-in-law. My father who was in D-Day and was torpedoed twice, and sunk on a ship that had ammunition on it…and luckily it didn't blow…and my father-in-law, who was one of the Chosin Few…The Frozen Chosin, up in the Chosin Reservoir when the Chinese attacked, and a huge percentage of them were killed…both of them…both of them…because such bad things happened to them when they were like, nineteen years old…neither one of them have a temper. They don't ever get upset when things…you know…I could just see it never happen, with either one of them…if I came home at some time and totaled the car, they would say, "Oh well, those things happen.". Rather than getting upset about things…they would just never get upset about material things or problems in life."

"I have been a sailor all my life, and my wife…reluctantly, is saying yes…to getting a larger sailboat. I sail in Lake Erie which is fifty miles across, so you can go out far enough and pretend you're in an ocean, even though it's a lake. It's about 200 miles long…so it's a pretty big lake."

"That's my dream…to cruise around and pretend I'm a beatnik or something."

324   *Johnathon Frericks*

"I talked to a man the other day who was 76. While I'm talking to him, I play this scene in my head, "This is what I will be like in 36 years. There isn't much time." I think about age...about death...a lot. I see these people that are in their 90's...and I wonder what they're thinking. I wonder if they see someone that's like, 102 and think, "This is what I will be like in a few years. There isn't much time."...or, do they just think...nothing. Does it even bother them? It bothers me now, and I'm only forty. I've seen people die, and it's just...not a pleasant experience. If I die of old age, I don't think I want to be there when it happens."

325   *Andy Driscoll*

"I remember going to see "The King and I" with my grandma at Corn Stock Theatre. I saw a number of guys on stage...performing. I thought, "I can do that. I would enjoy that.""

"The point where I realized that this is what I wanted to do with my life...beyond just a hobby, or the enjoyment of it, was when I was cast as Joseph for the very first time at Eastlight Theater...by Eddie Urish. It was really his tutelage...he was my mentor in theater...and he really helped me realize that this...this is not a choice I have. I'm not choosing whether I'm going to be a performer or an accountant or whatever...this is what I have to do. I was seventeen...and I feel blessed knowing at that time that...this is what I had to do."

"My parents said, "No, you're not going to do that." They wanted me to do something with more "stability". I don't disagree now, having been in the profession for ten years. I understand what they were trying to keep me from. But...the bottom line is...when you've got that thing that you have to do...it doesn't matter what you have to do in life to get to it. You'll go through any struggle that you have to...to get to that end result...if it is what your heart tells you to do. That's what my heart told me...it was my calling to be a performer. Being in front of an audience and entertaining...that is what I have been called to do."

"I wanted to be in New York. That is the mecca, and that is where you have the most opportunities. That's also where you're competing against the most people...but I didn't look at it that way. I, like everybody else, had my struggles. During that first year...that was really tough. I was working at what I called a civilian job more than I was performing. In the business, they say you can't really call yourself a professional unless you've gone to a hundred auditions...and those first hundred are the hardest. In this business, you get rejected a ton more times than you get accepted. A couple years ago, I went through and added up...because I kept a log of all the auditions I went to...what I got callbacks for, what I got offers for, what I accepted and didn't accept...and I had been to over 800 auditions. I had been offered less than forty jobs out of those 800. As a baseball player...I wouldn't have been successful...but in this business, that's actually pretty good."

"I did "Miss Saigon" on Broadway for gosh...almost three years. Other ones were...a movie where I worked a day. One of the hardest days for me...my dream show was "Les Miserables"...and I had been trying and trying, and this was before "Miss Saigon". I was still struggling to try and get a foothold on where my place in the business was. This audition came up, and they were looking for an immediate replacement. They did a "type out", which meant they stood you in a line and asked you a question. You answer it and then they tell you to stay or go. They were looking for a specific role...they had a specific body type...a voice type they were looking for. And...although I wasn't right for that role, they felt I was right for another role...and called me in for *that* three months later."

"I went into the audition...and I fancy myself as a nice person...an outgoing friendly person. I like to shake people's hands. I find that to be an appropriate greeting. So, I go into the audition and the monitor introduces me to the casting agent, which was a guy named Ron LaRosa...who now is the...the guy who casts all of Disney's live entertainment. Then...the associate director was a guy named Richard J. Alexander. So, he introduces me...and I go up to the desk like I always do and shook Ron LaRosa's hand...handed him my picture resume...and I stuck out my hand to Richard J. Alexander. He looked me right in the eye and...put his head down. He wasn't going to shake my hand."

"It was one of those moments...and in this business you see rejection and receive rejection so often...and you get to the point where you find out where actors have a difficult time with confidence. They are constantly being rejected because they're not tall enough, they don't have the right hair color...or in somebody's view, they're not good enough. And...I was so incredibly offended, but at the same time...I felt like I had two choices...suck it up and make a joke out of it...or stand up for myself. That time...I stood up for myself. I took a step back and took a breath, then looked him in the eye and said, "There's nothing more that I would like to do as audition for the role of Marius in "Les Miserables". It's been one of my dreams to play this role...but I don't think today is my day. Thank you so much for the opportunity, and have a great day." Then...I walked out."

"The minute I got onto the street...I just cried...because I was nineteen years old...actually twenty at that point. I had this dream...and I started thinking, "What is this business that I'm trying to get myself involved in...where people are going to disrespect another person in such a way...that they can't even give a common human courtesy of a greeting?"

"A couple weeks later, I went in to audition for "Miss Saigon". The casting director was...Ron LaRosa. I came in and he goes, "That's the guy." He said to all these people at the table, "That's the guy. That's the guy. That's the guy that walked out on Richard J. Alexander." I found out that I made a huge impression on him because he felt that this was an asinine thing...that this guy had done...and here is this young, green actor standing up for himself...and not doing it in a disrespectful manner. So, I sang...and because of that, they gave me more attention than they would give to a normal auditioner. They called me back for the lead role. I didn't get that, but they cast me as an understudy."

"At 21 I was in New York...I had a few offers...I had done a few shows...but I was ignorant to what I was getting into. I really did not understand how difficult this business really is. Every audition I would go to...I would be competing against 200 or 300 people that looked just like me. I was in a residential hotel on the upper west side of Manhattan...great location...but, it was a slum. People living in my building were on some sort of public aid. I worked for Tower Records making six dollars an hour...putting in sixty hours a week, usually working the night shift. I would wake up at seven and go to auditions. I was getting rejected, getting burnt out and thinking, "I don't know if this is really worth it." I thought, "Maybe I should do this some place else...maybe New York is not the place." I gave myself a cutoff date of October 1st."

"I didn't get the "West Side Story" job in July...and if I hadn't secured work in my profession, and I was getting to the point where I was asking myself, "How can I call myself an actor? While I am pursuing a job in acting...I am working at Tower Records...and while I am auditioning six to ten times a week, I'm not getting anything." So, I gave myself that date, to go to Chicago...come closer to home...smaller market...fewer opportunities, but also less people to compete against. I hadn't had a single offer for a show in six months. Then...within a three day period I had four good offers...and on October 15th, I opened on Broadway."

"I came back to Peoria in 2002 to fulfill a dream I had, of starting and running an equity theater. My first ten shows here at the Apollo Theater...I brought in 27 people with Broadway credits. When I came back and started the theater...I

knew that financially, it may not succeed. We were coming up less that five percent short each year, which for a startup company...isn't bad. It's just that, this
was all on my shoulders with limited resources. I got to the point where I was
going to have to make a decision on how I was going to start making some dollars, to start resolving some of the debt that I incurred."

"I feel fortunate that I kind of backed into the business that I'm in right
now...The Waterhouse. It is a banquet and reception facility. People are getting
married all the time. Companies are having parties...class reunions. I fortunately
backed myself into a winning business. In the near future...I'm going to stay
right here and utilize some of the skills I have learned in business and marketing...and we're booked every Saturday night for the year...our marquee night.
It's not four walls with chandeliers...it is a refurbished warehouse with exposed
brick, wood floors...and just has this really cool feeling. The atmosphere is what's
going to sell people on The Waterhouse. Good food and good service...as well as
word of mouth will also sell people."

"I will go back to New York. I will continue my career as an actor. Music theater
is where my heart is...to sing and act. Having the experience now as a producer
and a director in an equity theater...having sat on the decision-making side of
the casting table...I have a whole different perspective on what they need to see.
When I go to an audition, my approach will be completely different. My respect
for the producer and director will be completely different. My goal is to work on
Broadway again. I am 31 years old...and if everything works well with this
endeavor...The Waterhouse, I will have a little bit of a financial subsidy that will
allow me to be a little more choosy...to give myself more opportunities for a
show in New York."

326   *Rashonda Hunt*

"I'm working at this vendor...selling fresh lemonade and pretzels. I'm twenty. I don't normally do anything. I just sit at home in the summer, but I'm doing this today."

"Just a few years ago, I was a tomboy. I used to jump out of windows, and climb trees...a very adventurous person. I was with my mom...she was staying in this apartment complex, and it was on the second floor. We would climb out of the bathroom window, and then jump to the bottom, climb up the building...and then go back in before she found out we were outside. We thought it was fun."

"What I do every day is...I shop, go bowling...to the movies with friends...out to eat...skating...stay at home and watch TV."

"I got my boyfriend back this year. He just called up and we got back together. We met about two years ago when I was at a school dance at his school. We broke up and got back together this year...although this morning I cried because he called and we broke up again. But, I think we're back together now...this afternoon. It's a big soap opera."

"I'm a free spirit. I just like having fun. When you get to know me, you'll find I'm a good person to be around. I am a great friend to have."

"I want to teach history in high-school, and then college. I'm going to Southern Illinois University in Edwardsville. I like it there...I've met some new people. It's always fun meeting new people."

327   *Wade Brown*

"I work for, what used to be…well, it was originally R.G. Letourneau. It's been Komatsu Mining Corporation in one form or another for several years. I basically help build giant mining trucks…the types of trucks that are much too large to ship in one piece. I'm over six feet tall, and barely go halfway up one tire. Like it or not…I'm in the mining industry…which basically goes up and down with the price of copper. Most of our trucks are at copper mines."

"I grew up across the road from a coal mine not far from Hanna City. It belonged to Joe Zaborac. I don't know if it ever had a name…we just called it Joe's Mine. The coal mine entrance was directly across the road from my house…but the main part of the mine, where the entrance to the shaft, and the scale-house were…was down this long steep coal-covered hill. The road snaked around a little and was as steep as…steeper than Farmington Road Hill…down by Kickapoo Creek, but not quite as long. I'd say from my house to the shaft was about…oh…maybe half a mile away."

"There was an old guy who lived down at the bottom of the hill, lived at the coal mine…and his name was…well, we called him Toomey. I don't think Toomey drove…because he walked everywhere. When my family would go into town…about seven miles away…we would sometimes see him walking alongside the road. He always had a bag of something with him…it wasn't liquor…I think maybe it was just a sandwich or something. I don't remember Dad, or anyone else offering him a ride. I don't remember anyone ever really talking to him. Really, the only thing I knew about him was he was old…skinny…and he lived and worked in the mine."

"Toomey worked with the guy who owned the mine, Joe…who provided coal to people who still had coal furnaces…and my Grandpa still had a coal furnace. This was in the mid to late 60's…so not that many coal furnaces. Grandpa would drive down the hill to get his own coal. The problem was, when my grandpa's truck was full of coal…he couldn't quite make it up the hill…so he had to make several trips."

"One time my grandpa and Joe were down at the mine drinking, and Grandpa started his run, to get up the hill…but never made it to the top. When my uncle, who was just a few years older than me, came down the hill, he found Grandpa's truck…with the door open and Grandpa passed out on the hill. It looked like he had tried to make it up…and got to a point where the wheels just spun around and dug a hole. Then I guess he was just too tired and drunk to come back down and make another run. The truck was still running, the door was open, and Grandpa was laying in the road…snoring."

"Joe and Toomey did other things to bring in money. They had piles and piles of old electric motors that they would burn. What they were doing was trying to get the copper from the motors…and then resell the copper. Another thing Joe did was go down to Liverpool and catch snapping turtles…and sell the meat to restaurants. I never went with him, but he would bring back these turtles…and they were still alive…and they would be in this old train coal car that was filled with water….right behind the scale-house. Joe would chop off their heads…and then my friend Joey and I…Joe's grandson…we would each take a side of a turtle…and these were big and heavy turtles…and carry them to the back of the scale-house, where Joe would cut them up and clean them."

"At the mine, there were several walnut trees close to the mine shaft…and one of the things that we did was throw walnuts up into the air and try and shoot them. At that time, I had a single shot twenty-gauge that I got for my birthday…I think I was eleven or twelve, but maybe younger. My dad would throw a walnut up in the air and tell me to shoot it…but I was never any good…I really don't remember hitting very many. I wasn't much of a hunter, either. I felt sorry for the animals…so, my heart wasn't really in it."

"Mostly it was my Dad and Joe throwing walnuts up for each other. Joe was missing several fingers…and I don't know if it was from the mine or from snapping turtles…but, it didn't seem to affect him…he was a pretty good shot. He had enough fingers to squeeze off a shotgun shell and hit a walnut. My dad was pretty good, too."

"One Saturday, I went into my mom and dad's room…got the rifle off the gun rack…there was a 12-gauge, an old double-barrel shotgun, my shotgun, and a .22 rifle. I got it down and walked down the hill towards the coal mine…and then veered off down a path to go sit by the creek and watch for squirrels. I was by myself. I wasn't supposed to have the rifle by myself. Dad told me that a rifle shell can travel up to a mile away…and you had to be real careful with the rifle. I sat on a fallen tree next to the creek and after a little while, I saw two squirrels play-ing up in the trees. They were just chasing each other…jumping from branch to branch and chattering."

"It was almost a straight-up shot. I got one of the squirrels in my site and squeezed the trigger. Click. I didn't have a bullet in the chamber. The squirrels heard the click and it scared them off. So…I sat there for a little while more and played this scenario in my head. I fantasized that I shot at the squir-rel…missed…and the bullet hit Toomey as he was walking up the road. Then I pictured the bullet hitting the sandwich that was probably in the bag he was car-rying…splattering mustard and chunks of baloney or something all over his pant leg. I probably played a dozen more fantasies in my head…threw a few rocks in the creek and then went home and cleaned the rifle…and put it back on the gun rack."

328   *Nate Butler*

"I think most intelligent people can't really be very happy…I don't think it's possible."

329-330   *Walter and Empress Freeman*

"Empress is from Peru, South America. We met in Alabama…it was 1969 when we met…and got out of the Army. We were both in the Army. She joined to go to Vietnam, and then they wouldn't send her there because she wasn't a citizen at that time. We got married in the Army and came back to South Pekin to live. We been back to South America…once a year for the past 37 years."

"It's just been me and her against the world…by ourselves. We both had some rough times."

"My dad was a cripple. They used to work in the fields…and about every three feet, or five feet, there was a pile of hot ashes. His mother and dad went into town and left the little ones in charge…left his sister in charge. He was just old enough to stand up and walk for a little bit…and then fall down. He was a baby, and crawled mostly. His older brother was jumping over the ashes. Well…he took off and fell right in. His sister was so far away…she had a boyfriend with her…she screamed at the little ones to pull him out of the ashes. Well…when they got him home, they took his gloves off…and his fingers come off. They took his shoes off…and his toes came off with his shoes. Well…he was just a baby…and there was no doctors around there that close. So…she took a pan, and filled it with linseed oil…and laid him in it so just his mouth and face was sticking out. When the doctor come…when he got there…he told her the only thing keeping him alive was her love. He said she should have let him die."

"He had a nub for a hand…had a claw hand…burnt over 90% of his body…had a six inch difference in leg growth. But…he was never on welfare or state aid. He had four kids…and never relied on anyone to help him. He couldn't work in a factory, but always found other work. He managed to hunt…and with us four boys, hunting out of season…he managed to put food on the table. Well…all us boys turned out pretty good. None of us ended up being thieves, or taking from nobody…or hurting nobody. We had to learn at a young age. We had paper routes…and he taught us to fend for ourselves. We had to buy our own school clothes…and sodie…and candy. Not one of us boys has been on the welfare line…ever."

"I came to America because I heard about the work...and we were very poor...and Peru...not many opportunities. It was a peaceful country...not like Vietnam...but no opportunities. I was a bookkeeper...and I saw an opportunity to come to the United States and work in the Army. I couldn't come right away...so I worked as a babysitter for a doctor and his wife. I was with them for a year, and then I joined the Army. I was there for two years...and we met and moved to South Pekin. He already had a house in South Pekin."

"I figured I need a roof over my house...so I thought if I buy a house first, instead of having new cars and stuff...that would be good....and I bought a house. Then I switched jobs and got drafted...but I figured I needed a house and didn't want to pay rent when I come back. So...my uncle lived in it while I was gone. We've since bought five other houses...all from that first house...and we rent those. Somebody up there is looking out for us."

"When he was laid off from Caterpillar...we both mowed lawns...and it was the first time he had drawn unemployment. They were on strike for a long time...then, Caterpillar, they lay a lot of people off. The Pekin and Peoria area was dead at that time. It was hard for us...for a long time."

"When I was in Peru...when I was nine years old, my father died...and we were very poor...and we were very religious. We were Protestants...Pentecostal. Everything was God...our lives were run by whatever God wanted us to do. I had seen my mother suffering so much because sometimes we didn't have enough to eat...and I used to think, "What happened to this god?" We were so poor. How could he take my father and make it worse for us? So...for many years I went without believing...until I was eighteen or twenty or so."

"So many things happen in your life, you know, and you don't believe in miracles. You don't believe in a higher power...you lose your faith. But...just because you don't believe...that doesn't make you a bad person. If you don't believe in somebody up there...that doesn't make you bad. We all have our own beliefs. But...there is something...somewhere. It doesn't have to be God. The name doesn't have to be God...but somewhere, there has to be some kind of force. Don't you think?"

"Sometimes you see so much suffering in this world...and you can't believe. If there is a god, and he is a god of love...and he let all these little children die of AIDS...and starve to death...things like that...it makes you wonder."

331   *Barbra Espey*

"I'm from Quincy…61, from Quincy."

"When I was a kid in Quincy, and we were in our first house…people…there were still people that had iceboxes…real iceboxes. The ice truck would come by and chip off a chunk of ice, and put it in their icebox…and the man would chip off a sliver of ice for us to suck on. I think the ice was frozen in an offshoot of the Mississippi River, because I have seen pictures…this was in the 1950's. It was a big old truck with a rubber flap…and then the ice was inside there. You don't see that anymore…do you?"

"I have worked overseas. I was a special education teacher in Africa…in Cotonou Benin. Then, after that I went to Rio De Janeiro for three years…then New Zealand. Then I went to California for five years…which is almost a foreign country."

"Where I lived in Africa, was about five degrees off the equator. We had to learn to think slowly…because, it was so hot. It was the first time that I realized that when you ate, you actually generated heat….because I would sit at my breakfast table doing nothing but eating my breakfast…and I would be sweating. In January they have what they call "harmaton", which is French for "the dusty season". It is when all of the sand comes from the Sahara…this was a sub-Saharan country. It is the time of the year when the sun would be clouded…so that you couldn't look right at it. At that time the natives would wear what we would call winter coats…heavy winter coats. Remember, this is right off the equator. They…the natives, would be so cold…and I would be very comfortable. It's interesting how you acclimate to a particular weather pattern…and then…when someone else comes along that is used to something different…their response is quite different."

"I taught in the American School in Rio De Janeiro. I danced in the Samba…with one of the samba schools at one of the carnivals. Anybody can join, as long as you're willing to pay the money for a costume. I had a friend, and her husband was in the band…I think it's called the "batteria". It's a Portuguese group…the band. They have this mile long promenade…it's like, a long boulevard with stands on either side. When your school comes on, they send up all these fireworks…and then your band starts…your batteria starts, and leads you into an alcove…and then you stand there…and the rest of your school…all the different classes, and all the different costumes come by…and you're singing your song. The surprising thing was…everybody in the stadium is singing your song…because they have it in the program. It was such a…I would call it a "kundalini" experience…you know what I mean by that? The fireworks going off…and just sending all that energy up…and it just went with you the whole way you marched down the promenade. It was a wonderful, wonderful experience. My life has been wonderful."

"In my life, and in everyone's life…you know, there are never any accidents…we are always led. Whether we pay attention to the signs that are in front of us…we are always led. I think learning that we don't have to be in control…that's really freed me up quite a bit. I believe that…everything begins with a thought. We manifest our lives by our thoughts…and everyone should take that seriously…be mindful of our thoughts."

332   *Willie York*

"I wake up every day and create this world. How you likin' it so far?"

333   *Suzette Boulais*

"I was allowed…I didn't ask for it, it came my way…I was allowed to host a radio show, which was a half hour women's issues program. It was a Saturday show, then moved to Mondays, called "At Heart"…on NPR. The show asked, "What is at the heart of your joy? What is at the heart of your dreams?" This was a program about women who, in the midst of their lives, changed their paths to follow their hearts. In essence, it was about talking to people heart-to-heart…about following their heart. This program made a plea for following one's heart by finding one's own personal truths, despite race, color, creed, or background."

"I was raised in the Catholic faith, and have been a Christian all my life. I've tried to follow…Christian truths. I had an epiphany as I was watching a program one night that spoke about taking personal ownership in one's life, and the absurdity of blaming bad behavior on such things as a devil. I had this epiphany when watching this program, because I knew…I knew it was speaking the truth to me."

"It was a big lesson in non-judgment when the credits rolled at the end of the program and I saw that the program had been produced by an Atheist organization. I had grown up to judge Atheism as blasphemous. Yet…when I watched this program about taking ownership of your life, treating your fellow man in civil ways, doing no harm to anyone, blaming no devil for your own misdeeds…and when I bought everything the show was saying…hook, line and sinker…it was a shocking eye-opener. If anything, it reinforced in me that I am attracted to any and all belief systems and philosophies that are focused on finding what I call, "Truth with a capital T". These are universal truths about honorable ways in which to live…involving principles of personal harmony, as well as a peaceful existence with humanity."

"I was raised with a belief system that was completely opposed to Atheism, because it did not believe in a god. But my epiphany came when I understood one element of Atheism for the first time. While Atheism may not claim to believe in God, and while I do believe in God, what I appreciated hearing is that…it believes *completely* in humanity and in doing whatever good we can today…right in the here and now. While it's not focused on what will happen to us in any afterlife, I concluded that it actually seemed more "Christian" to be an

Atheist by name, yet believe in humanity in the here and now...than claim to be Christian in the here and now, or any religion for that matter, yet kill thousands in the name of it."

"Not long ago I saw a television special on Bruce Lee. I'd been hearing about Bruce Lee and his movies for many years, but knew little about him. In the course of the program it talked about a philosophy he had, and that he even wore a medallion around his neck extolling his own personal philosophy..."No way as way". What that said to me was that no *one* official way was his way to his personal truth. Rather...Bruce Lee's belief was that, as seekers...*conventional ways* are not the way. Rather, we all need to find our *own* way. I believe that, too. The inner way...that's my way."

"My father thought the Catholic faith was the only way...the right way. So what happens when I go off to college? I read the Tao, the Buddha...Kahlil Gibran. I realize all these writings have Jesus-like statements. Even when I read the Bible, I hear Jesus saying, "I'm God's son. If you think I can do all these miraculous things, so can you...because you're God's son, too." He kept deflecting his own ego and self importance and spoke to the power of personal faith. Where I had to take my own leap of faith was...believing that we human beings are all empowered to become Christs, too."

"About ten years ago I was introduced to "Course in Miracles", a class I attend on Monday nights when my schedule allows. The miracle of this philosophy is that...we can all change our attitude to create a happier life. While we may not change outside reality, we all have the power to change our perception of reality. Why I'm fascinated by Course in Miracles is because I'm intrigued by the fact that it's possible for us all to live happy lives. Because our minds are so powerful...it's within our mind-power to choose to be happy."

"When I saw that television show, produced by an Atheist group, it completely opened up my mind. Without a doubt, it dispelled my strong inbuilt prejudice, "How can anyone not believe in God?" I then read a beautiful statement by Agnostic, Robert Ingersoll, whose statue is in Glen Oak Park...right here in Peoria. It further reinforced my new belief that the Agnostic and Atheist live by a strong moral code."

"This is what he says…and I quote…*"For while I am opposed to all orthodox creeds, I have a creed and my creed is this: Happiness is the only good. The time to be happy is now. The place to be happy is here. The way to be happy is to make others so. This creed is somewhat short, but it is long enough for this life, long enough for this world. If there is another world, when we get there, we can make another creed. But this creed certainly will do for this life.*"

"So I say…forget words like Catholic, Jew, Muslim, Atheist. There is some beautiful poetry and beautiful writing that speak to capital "T's" in life…beyond the Bible. Ultimate truths that speak about peace, harmony, civility, love…and personal fulfillment, can be found everywhere, in all types of books and philosophies, religious or otherwise. Ultimately, what I'm seeking to find is my own personal truth. What is the capital "T" for Suzette Boulais? I believe it's up to me to find my own path to personal joy and happiness…and be as humane as possible while doing so."

"What I have to do in my life is find these truths wherever I can, and extract from life…whatever feeds, elevates, and advances my soul. My happiness depends on choosing consciously to evolve. I hope that tomorrow I'm a little more evolved than I am today."

"So then, I wonder…what exactly are you doing? I wonder if what you're doing when you talk to all these people for this book…you may think or say it's about 333 people, but is it ultimately your book…about your soul? Are you ultimately putting all these pieces together…and using all these different people to find out more about yourself? In the end, it may be about this puzzle called *life* that you are trying to piece together…just like the rest of us."

Conclusion

I sat at a table drinking coffee, when a woman I had never seen before started talking to me about her recent experience. Seventeen minutes later, she left my table and left me with a story of *forgiveness*. I went into a diner for breakfast, picked up the fallen cigarette package of a complete stranger, who then told me a story of being mangled in a corn picker. A man who I had seen many, many times before, but had never spoken to, described being shoeless in Greece during World War II.

In the entryway of a bookstore, a young girl stared out into space and talked about a fishing trip she took with her father when she was nine. With teary eyes, I sat by a fireplace at a funeral home in Princeville, as a mortician described the death of a friend. I found the nicest, friendliest, and most caring person in a porn star. A man who didn't need to give me the time of day, told me about interviewing Johnny Cash. A woman whom I admire very much, told me of sending a letter to Madalyn Murray O'Hair.

I jumped a fence and sat at the table of a war hero while he described his battles, having to repeat himself several times over, while fighting the jet aircraft noises in the background. A lady told me about getting her car stolen while she washed dishes at the Track Inn. A man from India talked to me about seeing the divinity in everything, and that we are all *one*.

A homeless man told me that he creates this world we live in…every day…just like the rest of us.

These are the people from my prior year.

978-0-595-39157-8
0-595-39157-5

Printed in the United States
53018LVS00003B/4